The U.S. Empire, the Media, and Twenty Years
of Coup Attempts in Venezuela

Extraordinary Threat

Joe Emersberger and Justin Podur

MONTHLY REVIEW PRESS
New York

Copyright © 2021 by Joe Emersberger and Justin Podur
All Rights Reserved

Library of Congress Cataloging-in-Publication Data
available from the publisher

ISBN 978-1-58367-916-6 paper
ISBN 978-1-58367-917-3 cloth

Typeset in Minion Pro and Brown

MONTHLY REVIEW PRESS, NEW YORK
monthlyreview.org

5 4 3 2 1

PRAISE FOR *EXTRAORDINARY THREAT*

"In this insightful and highly-readable book, Joe Emersberger and Justin Podur tell the story of how Washington—aided by powerful media interests—responded with a relentless and brutal campaign to destroy Venezuela's model of independence and bring the country back under U.S. control. It's a sad and infuriating tale."
—LINDA MCQUAIG, author of *The Sport & Prey of Capitalists*

"It is an essential corrective to the highly misleading accounts of the mainstream media, the U.S. government, and from human rights NGOs, which regularly demonize the Maduro government while falsely presenting the opposition as noble freedom fighters."
—GREG WILPERT, Co-Founder of VenezualAnlaysis.com and author of *Changing Venezuela by Taking Power*"

"The book, with abundant detail on every page, will be an invaluable tool for solidarity groups."—STEVE ELLNER, Associate Managing Editor of *Latin American Perspectives*, retired professor at Venezuela's Universidad de Oriente

"Seldom has a book expressed so clearly the outrages that the U.S. has visited upon the Venezuelan people."—MARIA PÁEZ VICTOR, Venezuelan-Canadian political activist and sociologist

"Beyond their detailed analysis of six coup attempts since 2002 . . . reveals the deceptions beneath the concept of democracy for industrialized capitalist societies."—JESÚS RODRÍGUEZ-ESPINOZA, editor, *Orinoco Tribune*

"Demonstrates that Obama's 2015 declaration that Venezuela poses an 'extraordinary threat' to the national security of the US was precisely an inversion of reality. This compelling account illuminates the hope that Venezuela holds for the peoples of the world–and the lethal costs of resisting the U.S. empire."—ROGER HARRIS, Task Force on the Americas

"*Extraordinary Threat* shows that without a doubt it is not Venezuela that represents a "national security threat" to the United States, as former U.S. President Obama would have you believe. Rather, it is the United States and its allies that represent an existential threat to Venezuela, as they deploy the weapons of "liberal (capitalist) democracy" against millions among their own citizens who find it increasingly hard to receive basic healthcare, put food on the table, or even secure a roof over their heads. A must read for anyone who cares about democracy, human rights, and just plain human decency."—CLAUDIA CHAUFAN, MD, PhD, Associate Professor of Health Policy, York University, Canada

"If the Biden administration is serious about ending the Venezuela policy that senator Chris Murphy rightfully dubbed an "unmitigated disaster," it should look no further than Emersberger and Pudor's fact-packed, well-organized and updated guide to twenty years of U.S. coup attempts in oil rich Venezuela."
—EIRIK VOLD, author of *Hugo Chavez: the Bolivarian Revolution Up Close*

"This is a carefully documented book. It challenges mainstream media journalists and political analysts, among others, to read it with an open mind."—NINO PAGLICCIA, editor of *Cuba Solidarity*

"From media-styled to overt mercenary incursions and everything in between, Emersberger and Podur deconstruct the history of U.S. interventionism against Chavismo."—TERI MATTSON, CODEPINK Latin American Campaign Coordinator

"A detailed run-through of recent Venezuelan history and a thorough debunking of its terrible media coverage: *Extraordinary Threat* is an extraordinary book."—ALAN MACLEOD, author of *Bad News from Venezuela: Twenty years of Fake News and Misreporting*

Contents

PART I: EXTRAORDINARY MYTHS (ADVANCED VERSIONS) | 7
   1   The Extraordinary Threat to Venezuela | 9
   2   Yes, Maduro Is a Duly Elected Leader | 24
   3   The Guaidó Era as a Sixth, Very Long
       Coup Attempt | 36
   4   How Could Chavismo Flourish in "Once Prosperous"
       and Democratic Venezuela? | 58

**PART II: EXTRAORDINARY SEDITION (AND CHAVISMO'S
       TOLERANCE OF IT) | 71**
   5   First Coup Attempt: April 2002 | 73
   6   Second Coup Attempt: Oil Strike,
       December 2002–February 2003 | 95
   7   Third Coup Attempt: Fatalities over Frivolous
       Claims, April 2013 | 111
   8   Fourth Coup Attempt: February–April 2014 | 124
   9   Buildup to the Fifth Coup Attempt | 141
  10 Fifth Coup Attempt: April 4–July 31, 2017 | 160

PART III: EXTRAORDINARY DECEIT (AN ANALYSIS) | 181
  11. Read Carroll and You've Read Them All (2006–2012) | 183
  12. The Human Rights Fraud | 206
  13. Colombia's U.S.–Approved Horror Show
       Could Come to Venezuela | 224

Acknowledgments | 235
Chronology: Six Coup Attempts | 237
Notes | 239
Index | 317

for Monica

PART I

Extraordinary Myths (Advanced Versions)

1

The Extraordinary Threat to Venezuela

For over a century, the United States has used terror tactics—including everything from direct military invasion to economic strangulation—to assert its self-appointed right to rule over all countries in the Americas. It has smashed small countries such as Haiti, Nicaragua, El Salvador, and Guatemala that could only have posed the "threat of a good example" by developing in defiance of U.S. orders. But Venezuela, at the start of the twenty-first century, "threatened" to do much more than that. For many years, it provided a promising example of democratic and social reform under a government described by itself and its adversaries as socialist. Venezuela also began to finance the liberation of other countries in the Americas. It helped Argentina pay off debt owed to the International Monetary Fund (IMF) and launched an initiative called PetroCaribe that helped many countries in the region buy oil. Venezuela also spearheaded regional integration initiatives that sidelined Washington—weakening the imperial grip of the United States.[1]

For two decades, despite winning elections, Venezuela's "Chavista" governments (under the presidencies of the late Hugo Chávez, who died in 2013, and then his protégé and elected successor, Nicolás Maduro) have been smeared as dictatorships. No one in the Western media is ever held accountable for telling outright lies about the country. And these lies have deadly consequences: as a result, the Western public has accepted sanctions that have killed tens of thousands of Venezuelans since 2017.[2] If a military attack on Venezuela occurs at some point by the United States or its allies, the way will have been prepared by the stories that have been told about Venezuela over the past twenty years.

The most audacious lie told about Venezuela's government occurred when President Barack Obama imposed economic sanctions on Venezuela in March 2015. He issued an executive order that formally declared a "national emergency" based on the claim that Venezuela was "an extraordinary threat to the national security of the United States."[3] Every year since, the U.S. government has repeated this outlandish claim, to keep its increasingly murderous sanctions in place. The sanctions are designed to starve the Venezuelan government of the hard currency it needs to import food, medicine, and the parts required to maintain basic infrastructure such as its electrical grid.

A *New York Times* analysis in 2015, without being explicit, conceded that Obama's "extraordinary threat" claim was absurd, but focused instead on concerns that it may have "backfired." And the article also downplayed the importance of Obama's lie by uncritically quoting U.S. officials saying it was "a formality required by law in order to carry out sanctions."[4] In fact, the article completely reverses the truth. It's the U.S. government that poses an extraordinary threat to Venezuela.

Why is it so easy to lie about Venezuela? Why is it so difficult to clarify the reality? The answer has to do with the structure of capitalist democracy—a structure that facilitates aggression by the world's most powerful states. The limitations that capitalist democracy places on voters at home also constrict what voters can do to restrain their governments' behavior abroad.

What Makes a Democracy?

Democracy means rule by the people. Under capitalism, our global economic system, power accrues to those with wealth. When you refer to any real-world government as a "democracy" you are, by necessity, using the term loosely. A "capitalist democracy" is one where crucial decisions about investment, employment, and how one spends most of one's day are all decided by an ownership elite or the managers they appoint—not decided through democratic means. Basic economic questions—what gets produced, how, and for whom—are dominated by private business owners and wealthy investors, even though such questions are essential to everyone's well-being. Keeping these economic questions "insulated from political pressures" (that is, voters), as *The Economist* magazine once suggested should be done to an even greater extent, guarantees the political dominance of the wealthy.[5] It's an aspect of any capitalist democracy that is obscured because people can vote in elections even as they are disenfranchised when it comes to major economic decisions.

In practice, similar comments apply to the liberal values that capitalist democracies claim to champion. People who actually threaten the dominant political class—not through violence but through effective journalism—may face brutal consequences.

In 2019, Julian Assange and Chelsea Manning were both in jail. Assange's organization, Wikileaks, published documents leaked by Manning, an intelligence analyst who had been based in Iraq, that exposed war crimes perpetrated by the U.S. military. According to the UN Working Group on Arbitrary Detention, Assange has been arbitrarily detained since 2012, and yet the UK and Sweden, two of the countries responsible for his plight, simply dismissed the Working Group's decision.[6] The Lenín Moreno government in Ecuador (which took office in 2017) reversed the previous government's policy of protecting Assange in its embassy in London. After failing to hound Assange out of its embassy, Moreno's government stripped him of Ecuadorian citizenship rights and withdrew his political asylum. That has opened the door to his possible extradition to the United States. If the UK allows that extradition, Assange is to be tried in the States for conspiracy with Manning to hack computers and commit espionage—but in reality doing journalism that revealed war crimes.[7]

During the COVID-19 pandemic, many prisoners have been released from UK prisons for public health reasons. Assange has not. Manning, who was released in 2020, had spent seven years in jail, double the time spent by William Calley, who perpetrated the My Lai Massacre.[8] But Amnesty International still refused to call her a Prisoner of Conscience, and in 2019 merely said it hoped Manning's latest arrest (for refusing to testify against Assange before a grand jury) would not last "any longer than necessary."[9]

The Western media's relentless vilification of Assange, which has been extensively documented by media critics Media Lens in the UK, makes this open assault on supposed liberal values possible.[10] Another aspect of how capitalist democracy selectively applies liberal values at home is that the line for acceptable dissent, or for simply being left alone as you go about your life, is drawn very differently for ethnic or racial minorities: African Americans in the United States are subjected to mass incarceration and other police violence; Indigenous people in Canada are subjected to various types of institutional lawlessness.[11]

Still, the maintenance of elite dominance does not always require outright dictatorship and can accommodate periodic elections. Candidates who seriously threaten elite rule can be marginalized. Their electoral bases can be discouraged or disqualified from voting. Freedom of association can be guaranteed even if some forms of nonviolent protest and political activity are criminalized. The "free press," which is not free at all but accountable to billionaire owners and corporate advertisers, is key to obscuring and justifying the limitations of capitalist democracy to the general public. This does not always require deliberate dishonesty provided that a compatible worldview is internalized by editors and journalists. Which facts and sources matter and which can be ignored? Which stories run on the front page and which get buried in short articles deep inside, if they are covered at all? In answering these questions, there is ample room for one-sided and error-riddled coverage that is driven by the sincerely held political views and unconscious bias of journalists. But there is often negligible accountability for the most egregious falsehoods and lies of omission. To see how these falsehoods and omissions work to facilitate the aims of imperialist policy, there is probably no better case study than the media's coverage of Venezuela.

Traditional media outlets are not alone in whitewashing the worst actions of the powerful at home and abroad. Today there are other tools for ensuring the consent of the public: social media platforms that are also ad-dependent, owned by billionaires, and increasingly pressured to become as closed off to dissenting views as traditional media; and human rights organizations that present a face of neutrality but serve the world's most powerful governments through selective emphasis, omission, and falsehoods. Together, these organizations pressure the public to believe in a series of themes and tropes—all of which serve the powerful at the expense of the powerless.

There are many such tropes in domestic politics: black-on-black violence, looters, greedy unions, welfare queens, super-predators, out-of-control deficits. The media frame stories in these terms so that the public will accept these elite premises as common sense. Getting the public to accept deep cuts to social spending at home so that elites can get an even bigger share of the country's national income is bad enough. But when U.S. propaganda is turned on a poor country, it represents an extraordinary threat to the targeted government and its people. At least in domestic politics, the lived experience of voters offers a reality check, however inadequate, on the myths they are sold. Distorting the reality about faraway places like Venezuela is easier since few have the incentive to research beyond the most readily available sources for news and analysis.

The Empire and Democracy Do Not Mix

Voters in poor and middle-income countries must contend with an additional limitation to capitalist democracy: threats from the U.S.-led empire.

The word *empire* evokes ancient Rome crushing smaller kingdoms on the road to dominating much of Europe and Asia. There is an extensive literature about empires and their history, and even a debate about whether the United States is an empire. The evidence overwhelmingly suggests that it is with military bases in most countries, its navy in every corner of the high seas, its dollar as the reserve currency of the globe, and its undisguised efforts to overthrow or punish other governments for defying its orders (Venezuela, Iran, Nicaragua, Syria, China, Russia). The United States fits all the basic criteria for being an empire. There shouldn't be much cause for debate. But being ruled by an empire is not a desirable state of affairs for the people of the world.[12] The empire rewards obedient governments for brutality at home and even aggression abroad, provided they follow orders. On the other hand, the empire severely punishes independent governments even if they function within the rules of capitalist democracy. Democratic legitimacy does little to restrain the empire when it decides a government must be targeted for "regime change."[13]

Sometimes dictatorships are targeted, such as Iraq in 2003, Libya in 2011, and Syria in 2011. But six times in this century (so far) the United States has decided that a democratically elected head of state in the Western Hemisphere had to go: Venezuela's Hugo Chávez in 2002, Haiti's Jean-Bertrand Aristide in 2004, Honduras's Manuel Zelaya in 2009, Bolivia's Evo Morales in 2019, Nicaragua's Daniel Ortega and Venezuela's Nicolás Maduro in 2019.[14]

Venezuela is not a threat to the national security of the United States as outlandishly claimed. But it *does threaten* the U.S. capacity to bribe and bully governments throughout the Americas. Like any emperor, the United States casts itself as a victim to defend an indefensible right to rule, but it relies more on the use of propaganda at home than a dictatorship would. At home, brutality against welfare recipients, undocumented immigrants, union members, and racial minorities is justified through truth reversal: depicting the victims of cruel policies as threats. Abroad, reversing the truth has allowed the United States to pose an extraordinary threat to Venezuelans. This escalating campaign against Venezuela has many features that are worth discussing in detail.

The same propaganda emanates from seemingly ideologically

diverse sources. The entire public, not just the Fox News–watching segment of it, must be targeted. The public must be made to support, or at least be largely uninterested in opposing, the crushing of a foreign government. For maximum effect, propaganda must emanate from high-profile NGOs and academics, not just from state and corporate media. Liberal participation in this campaign is also crucial.

For instance, Bernie Sanders was the great hope of the U.S. left for his programs of universal health care and free education. But his 2016 presidential campaign, through a fundraising email, spread the lie that Hugo Chávez is a "dead communist dictator." Sanders has said several times that he opposes intervention in Venezuela, even while using this disparaging language.[15] But saying that one opposes "regime change" or is "against broad sanctions" does very little to impose moral and legal constraints on U.S. criminality when lies are transformed into truths that everyone across the political spectrum seems to accept.[16]

Another example of liberal participation: in February 2018, Amnesty International was asked for its position on Trump's financial sanctions on Venezuela that he imposed in August of 2017, a dramatic and lethal escalation of Obama-era sanctions.[17] Amnesty replied that it "does not take a position on the current application of these sanctions but rather emphasizes the urgent need to address the serious crisis of the right to health and food which Venezuela is facing. In terms of human rights, it is the Venezuelan state's responsibility to resolve this."

An illegal and devastating attack on Venezuela's "right to health and food" by the United States was not something Amnesty International felt it needed to denounce. When liberal NGOs such as Amnesty take reprehensible positions, then liberal politicians and media can do the same without appearing to shed their liberal credibility. For instance, on February 3, 2019, Sky News asked Shami Chakrabarti, the British Labour Party's shadow attorney general, if Labour leader (at the time) Jeremy Corbyn had been "tough enough" on Maduro. She replied, "When I'm not an expert in a particular region like South America, I go to my trusted sources for the picture and for me as a human rights campaigner my trusted sources have always been Amnesty International and Human Rights Watch." Predictably, given that neither of her "trusted sources" denounced Trump's financial sanctions, she failed to say a word about them herself. Instead, she said only that Amnesty and Human Rights Watch reports on Venezuela had been "pretty damning" and that "as a member of the left" she had to decry abuses in Venezuela.

On the right, the Mafioso-like tweets of U.S. Senator Marco Rubio and former Trump National Security Advisor John Bolton threatening Venezuela are incomparably worse. Rubio even went so far as to relish the destructive impact of U.S. sanctions on Venezuela's electrical grid. Politicians like Bernie Sanders or Shami Chakrabarti ought not to be equated to bloodthirsty maniacs like those on the right. But when liberals join a campaign to demonize a foreign government, it makes the campaign more effective, and that must be countered without partisan exception.

U.S. propaganda about targeted governments is also reliably spread by liberal media around the world. A particularly revealing example is the way the supposedly left-leaning *Guardian* in the UK covered Venezuela from 2006 to 2012. This was a period when the government of Hugo Chávez was at its most popular and rapidly improving living standards, reducing inequality, and increasing political participation—all things one might expect a progressive outlet to welcome. And yet, the *Guardian* was overwhelmingly hostile in its coverage of the Chávez government during those years through the prolific anti-Chávez output of its Caracas-based correspondent, Rory Carroll. The Venezuelan government was attacked by private media around the world long before an economic depression gave its assailants, especially Trump, even more leverage.

Unquestioned assumptions and double standards are crucial to imperial propaganda against Venezuela. One such assumption is that it is fair to test a government's democratic legitimacy by the extent to which it tolerates a violent U.S.-funded opposition. For the United States or its allies to tolerate a violent foreign-funded opposition would be considered ludicrous. Something as comparatively trivial as Russia's alleged hacking of Democratic Party emails generates outrage in the United States, a special investigation, and obsessive media coverage.

In Venezuela's case, the U.S.-backed opposition has made six attempts since 2002 to oust the Venezuelan government by force. For all the nonsense written about Venezuela being or becoming a dictatorship, the only time in recent years that Venezuela was a dictatorship was from April 11 to 14, 2002, when Hugo Chávez was ousted in a military coup and Pedro Carmona, the head of the largest business federation, was appointed president. The U.S. State Department's Office of the Inspector General admitted that the United States provided funds and other support for the perpetrators.

There is no reason to doubt what would happen to anybody in the United States involved in a coup that kidnapped a U.S. president. There would be no second attempt by the same domestic and international actors. Moreover, there is no legitimate reason why an elected government should be expected to tolerate a violent opposition, especially one backed by foreign muscle. Indeed, this impossible expectation seems to apply only to U.S. enemies.

International allies are useful for providing cover for U.S. violence and making its propaganda at home more effective. The Canadian and British governments, like those of other rich countries, are very popular with the U.S. public.[18] So when these governments support U.S. assertions about other foreign countries, it helps make the claims look credible.

In 2003, the United States did not need military allies for the narrow purpose of overthrowing Saddam Hussein. Iraq had been thoroughly disarmed of weapons of mass destruction (the most important of the fraudulent pretexts for the invasion), and its economy had been broken by a decade of sanctions. Still, the United States managed to get over forty countries to join its Coalition of the Willing—including two with quite progressive reputations, Denmark and Norway.[19] Canada and France provided invaluable political and propaganda cover for the Bush administration (discredited internationally by then due to the Iraq War) when it overthrew Haiti's elected government on February 29, 2004. U.S. troops kidnapped Haitian President Jean-Bertrand Aristide while Canadian troops secured the airport in the Haitian capital. In 2017, Canada helped establish the Lima Group, a collection of right-wing governments in Latin America that, along with Canada, helped wage Trump's vilification campaign against Venezuela.

International allies helped the United States justify its economic sabotage of Venezuela—a form of indiscriminate violence against many countries that has been normalized to a horrifying extent as a supposedly non-lethal alternative to military force. *The Economist* has referred to it approvingly as "Financial Carpet Bombing."[20] In 2015, Obama imposed sanctions that were indefensible under the UN Charter, OAS charter, and even U.S. law—the utterly fraudulent "national emergency" caused to the United States by Venezuela. Trump drastically intensified the Obama sanctions in August 2017. Trump's sanctions cost Venezuela at least $6 billion in lost oil revenue in their first 12 months. This meant that the government lost hard currency needed for essential imports. To best understand the devastating impact of a $6 billion loss, consider that, according to Torino Capital, an anti-Maduro investment firm, Venezuela imported only $10 billion in goods in 2018.

In April 2019, a paper by U.S. economists Mark Weisbrot and Jeffrey Sachs estimated that Trump's sanctions may have killed about 40,000 Venezuelans in the 2017–2018 period alone.[21] In 2019, the United States effectively imposed an oil embargo, and then a blanket ban on all dealings with Venezuelan state entities. In 2020, it imposed "secondary sanctions" on a Russian firm that was helping Venezuela to sell its oil. The United States even announced that it would harass a Mexico-based company that had entered into an "oil-for-food" deal with Venezuela's government.[22]

In 2018, Venezuela could only import $140 million worth of medicines, down from about $2 billion in 2013–14, when the economy was still growing.[23] The food import figures are also stunning: $2.46 billion in 2018 compared to $11.2 billion in 2013. Despite these shocking numbers, Reuters didn't mention the study by Weisbrot and Sachs until a month after it came out. When it did finally acknowledge the study, it nonetheless continued to produce articles that reported the impact of U.S. sanctions as a mere allegation made by Maduro.[24]

Economic sabotage creates a "humanitarian" pretext for overthrowing the targeted government. In 2002, pro-war pundit Nick Cohen mocked opponents of the looming Iraq War for opposing a war that would "end the sanctions."[25] Ignoring the impact of sanctions on Venezuela, or presenting their impact as an allegation rather than a fact, is a way to sell the idea, even when not stated explicitly, that if only Maduro were ousted his people would be much better off.

Under Trump, U.S. officials have been extremely open and emphatic in encouraging the Venezuelan military to oust Maduro. For instance, the Twitter accounts of four key U.S. officials—Senator Marco Rubio, National Security advisor John Bolton, Secretary of State Mike Pompeo, and Vice President Mike Pence—were intensely focused on Venezuela in early 2019. By the week of February 18–24, 2019, when the United States was attempting to stir rebellion in Venezuela through an aid delivery stunt at the Colombian border, these accounts tweeted a combined 153 times about Venezuela, which represented a whopping 77.2 percent of their collective Twitter activity.[26] Bolton and Rubio even tweeted directly to Venezuelan military officials suggesting that a coup would save their own skins and their families as well.[27]

Just as important as prominent Republicans attempting to incite a coup on Twitter was the negligible opposition from Democrats. Bernie Sanders's only tweet during this crucial period reinforced the lie that Maduro was refusing humanitarian aid. Maduro had in fact requested and received humanitarian aid from allies and internal aid organizations working in Venezuela.[28] Collectively, Bernie Sanders and five other progressive Democrats—Elizabeth Warren, Tulsi Gabbard, Alexandria Ocasio-Cortes, Ro Khanna, and Ilhan Omar—tweeted only a combined twenty times about Venezuela during this period, a drop in the bucket compared to the 648 tweets by four Republicans between February 4 and March 24, 2019. This disparity was not only about quantity: at best, these Democrats tweeted timid objections to military intervention. Only Tulsi Gabbard tweeted something that seemed to oppose the incitement of a coup. She tweeted that the United States should "stop intervening in Venezuela's military."[29] None rejected the false premise that Venezuela was a dictatorship.

Military Invasion, the Last Stage of U.S. Aggression to Come?

For the past two decades the U.S. campaign to overthrow the Venezuelan government has escalated from flagrant involvement in coup attempts, to lethal economic sanctions, to threats of military attack. Could it escalate even more, to direct U.S. invasion?

U.S. planners face a durable problem: the default stance of the public is antiwar. The targeted country must be thoroughly demonized before overt military threats are feasible. Trump first made them against Venezuela's government in 2017 after the country had already been relentlessly vilified in the Western media for sixteen years.[30] The threats also came after Venezuela had been mired in an economic depression since 2014 that allowed the threats to be spun from a "humanitarian" angle. Panama was invaded in 1990 by the United States under George H. W. Bush, but the country effectively came pre-invaded through a U.S. military base. In 2004, Haiti's democratically elected president was kidnapped by U.S. troops and flown off to the Central African Republic; the neighboring Dominican Republic served conveniently as a forward base for the proxy forces that helped overthrow Haiti's president. In 1980s Nicaragua, the U.S.-backed Contra terrorists, based in Honduras, were used to attack the Sandinista government. In 1990 this eventually produced an "electoral victory" for U.S. allies in Nicaragua that everyone in the world should have ridiculed. Nicaraguan voters were asked to choose between the Sandinistas and continued war and economic strangulation.

In Venezuela, it appears that the Trump government really believed the military would be quickly frightened into overthrowing Maduro after the United States recognized Juan Guaidó as interim president in January 2019. The public nature of the U.S. threats and their often juvenile nature points to a lack of serious planning to actually follow through. John Bolton pretending to accidentally reveal plans to send troops to Colombia by holding up a notepad is an indication of how confident Trump's team was that threats alone would work.[31]

Despite an array of difficulties and disincentives, it's obvious that a U.S. invasion is now a very real possibility. One disturbing consideration is always the United States' concern about its credibility—not wanting to be seen as making empty threats. But even without entering that final state of aggression, the United States can, as in the case of Cuba, keep up its economic warfare, even when it stands nearly without allies in doing so.

Motive for the Crime?

In the case of Venezuela, with its massive oil reserves, U.S. motives against Chavista governments may seem too trivially obvious to discuss. John Bolton brazenly told Fox News in January 2019 that he wanted U.S. corporations to have unfettered access to Venezuela's oil reserves because "it'll make a big difference to the United States economically."[32] But upon closer inspection a *direct* economic incentive is insufficient to explain the sustained and increasingly barbaric U.S. assault on Chavismo.

The Venezuelan government never denied the United States access to its country's oil. According to the U.S. Energy Information Administration, as of 2017 Venezuela remained the U.S. economy's third-largest foreign supplier of energy.[33] Because of Trump's sanctions, Venezuelan oil exports to the United States dropped by over 90 percent in 2019. But that was by choice of the United States, not Venezuela—and it has not made "a big difference to the United States economically."[34] In October 2019, Chevron was given a special exemption from U.S. sanctions to continue operating in Venezuela.[35] Despite two decades of Chavista governance, U.S. corporations still found that it was profitable to operate in Venezuela, although not always as profitably as they would have liked. Kimberly-Clark, the paper products manufacturer, did not withdraw from Venezuela until 2016, well into the economic collapse. In April 2018, Reuters reported that some multinationals were "keeping a foot in the door, hoping for improvements."[36]

The true preoccupation of empire—and the real explanation for U.S. animus toward Chavismo—is the fear that a poor country may develop along an independent path and succeed, thereby posing a "threat of a good example" that could inspire others.[37] Haiti, the poorest country in the Western Hemisphere, is the ultimate example of a country that's too small to ever be a U.S. rival and yet has been repeatedly crushed by U.S. intervention—right into the twenty-first century.[38] An oil-rich country such as Venezuela could potentially do more than provide a "good example." A secret cable published by Wikileaks revealed that in 2007 U.S. officials were demanding "more (and more flexible) resources and tools to counter Chávez's effort to assume greater dominion over Latin America at the expense of U.S. leadership and interests." Ominously, the cable stated: "We should continue to strengthen ties to those military leaders in the region who share our concern over Chávez."[39]

By the end of 2019, military leaders and police willing to serve "U.S. leadership and interests" had not emerged in Venezuela but had done so in Bolivia: the elected government of Evo Morales was overthrown and replaced with a pro-U.S. dictatorship. The Trump administration and the Venezuelan opposition were overjoyed and didn't care to hide it. Trump made a statement that not only called the coup a victory for democracy in Bolivia but said that it would "send a strong signal to the illegitimate regimes in Venezuela and Nicaragua."[40] Liberal media and NGOs gave Trump and Venezuelan opposition leaders no incentive to be discreet. The *New York Times* editorial board applauded the coup in Bolivia.[41] Human Rights Watch described it as an "uprising" for which Morales was to blame.[42] Bernie Sanders, to his credit, did find the courage to oppose the coup, and even lauded Morales's key accomplishments while in office.[43]

The pushback from Sanders shows that, compared to Venezuela, the story used to sell the coup in Bolivia was slapped together quickly and clumsily. Nevertheless, U.S.-led propaganda against Evo Morales was deployed effectively enough to provide cover to the Jeanine Áñez dictatorship as it went on to massacre dozens of protesters to consolidate its power.[44] Much worse awaits Venezuela if the U.S. succeeds there.

2

Yes, Maduro Is a Duly Elected Leader

On January 23, 2019, the opposition leader Juan Guaidó declared himself Venezuela's interim president and was immediately recognized by U.S. President Donald Trump.[1] Had he not received that recognition, Guaidó's self-declaration would have been a joke, another in a long list of opposition blunders since 2002. By late February, about fifty governments followed Trump by recognizing Guaidó, including Canada, Latin America's right-wing governments, and most European countries. But Russia, China, India—indeed, about two-thirds of the world's governments—did not follow along.

Guaidó had just been elected president of the opposition-controlled National Assembly, thanks to an agreement the anti-Maduro parties reached to rotate the job among themselves after winning control of the Assembly in 2015.[2] Guaidó's party, Voluntad Popular, saw its turn come up and he got the post. Guaidó's case for declaring himself president was based on two closely related lies. One was that Nicolás Maduro's election victory on May 20, 2018, was illegitimate. The other was that Maduro had abandoned his post. Based on these two lies, Guaidó invoked Article 233 of Venezuela's constitution which specifies the conditions under which the president of the National Assembly can take over as "interim president."

It's very easy to disprove the lie that Maduro abandoned his post. The Caracas-based journalist Lucas Koerner, writing for the website VenezuelAnalysis.com, explained Article 233:

> Article 233 of the Constitution of the Bolivarian Republic of Venezuela specifies that an "absolute vacuum of power" occurs in the following circumstances: the president's death, resignation, impeachment by the Supreme Court, "permanent physical or mental incapacity" certified by a medical expert designated by the Supreme Court and approved by the National Assembly, "abandonment of post" declared by the National Assembly, or recall by popular referendum.
>
> Guaidó's claim to the presidency rests on the second to last of these conditions, namely the argument that Nicolas Maduro has failed to fulfill his constitutional responsibilities, thereby abandoning his post. Article 236 outlines in detail the duties of the president, which include everything from conducting international relations and leading the armed forces to granting pardons and convoking referenda.
>
> The opposition may not like Maduro for a variety of reasons, but a cursory glance at the head of state's Twitter feed will reveal that he has hardly abandoned his presidential functions.[3]

A hardline opposition blogger acknowledged this fact only a week before Guiadó declared himself president:

> Nicolás [Maduro] is usurping the Executive Power and imposed a de facto government, which means our current political and judicial thread doesn't fit the options of vacancy of the legitimately elected President established in Article 233 of the Constitution. There's no way to strictly apply the Constitution to our situation.[4]

The much more important lie, however, was that the 2018 presidential election was illegitimate.

Maduro Won the 2018 Election

When the opposition made its third U.S.-backed effort to oust the government by force, it insisted that the 2013 presidential election had been "stolen" from opposition candidate Henrique Capriles.[5] Jump ahead to 2018 and nobody was claiming that Henri Falcón, Maduro's opponent in the 2018 presidential election, actually won. By all accounts, Falcón was the second-place finisher behind Maduro. Guaidó, who was not well known in Venezuela at that time, was not even a candidate. One pro-government pollster claimed that as of January 16, 2019, over 80 percent of Venezuelans had never heard of Juan Guaidó.[6] Guaidó was not even a figure who had any significant base of popular support at the time of the election.

Falcón's economic advisor, Francisco Rodriguez, gave an interview months after the 2018 presidential election in which he accused Maduro's side of inflating his vote tally through vote buying.[7] This allegation doesn't hold water but, even if true, does not begin to account for Falcón's massive defeat. Rodriguez did not claim that Falcón received more votes than Maduro (that is, that the election was stolen).[8] With a turnout of 46 percent, Maduro received 6.2 million votes (67.7 percent) to Falcón's 1.9 million (21 percent). The rest went to a few lesser-known candidates.[9] Maduro's vote tally was in line with his popular support even according to opposition sources at the time.

Datanalisis is an anti-government polling firm. Its work has been frequently commissioned by Torino Capital, in which Francisco Rodriguez, Falcón's advisor, was the chief economist. Datanalisis has been described by Reuters as the "respected" and "most closely watched" polling firm in Venezuela—implying that Datanalisis is both reliable and politically neutral.[10] A Lexis Nexis search of English-language newspapers over the past decade shows how often Datanalisis was cited compared to other Venezuelan polling firms. Clearly, Datanalisis has been the polling firm most heavily relied on by Western media to assess Venezuelan public opinion.

Luis Vicente León, one of the directors of Datanalisis, writes opinion pieces every few weeks for *El Universal*, one of Venezuela's leading newspapers. He has done so for years, it's important to add, given how frequently Venezuela's media is described as "caged."¹¹ In the Venezuelan context, León could be called a "moderate" government opponent, but his hostility to the Maduro government, which he once likened to a kidnapper, is very strong indeed.¹² For example,

TABLE 2.1: Pollsters Cited by "English Language News" on Venezuela (1 January 2009– 5 April 2019)

POLLSTER	HITS
Datanalisis	1,986
Consultores 21	149
Hinterlaces	253
Venebarometro	148
Delphos	131

Source: Lexis Nexis.

in November 2018, León wrote a piece in *El Universal* saying: "We face the impact of generalized sanctions, which it should be clear is the absolute responsibility of the [Maduro] government for being authoritarian and hostile."¹³ In a TV interview that was broadcast in October 2018 on Venevision, one of Venezuela's largest networks, León defined the moderate opposition as those who are "not fools" and who "know" that "democracy doesn't work" in Venezuela, that "tricks" are used against them, but believe they must participate in elections anyway.¹⁴ The opposition "radicals" he defined as those who want a foreign power to remove Maduro. The other director of Datanalisis, José Antonio Gil Yepes, also writes regularly in *El Universal* and takes a similar line.¹⁵ It's almost certain that Gil Yepes signed the infamous Carmona Decree in April 2002, which abolished Venezuela's democratic institutions when Hugo Chávez was briefly ousted by a military coup.¹⁶ So Datanalisis is not a polling firm one would expect to exaggerate Maduro's level of popular support—quite the contrary.

According to Datanalisis, Maduro had 20 percent support at the time of the May 2018 election.¹⁷ Given Venezuela's twenty million eligible voters, this is equivalent to about four million votes. That's twice the number Falcón received. But there's reason to think that Maduro's support was actually greater than what the anti-Maduro polling firm claimed. Considering Venezuela's dire economic conditions at the time of the election, those would be four million hardcore supporters of the Chavista political movement that has dominated Venezuelan politics since Hugo Chávez was first elected in 1998. Months before his death in 2013, Chávez urged his supporters to vote for Maduro, an endorsement that, several years later, still meant a great deal to millions of Venezuelans.

The appeal of Chavismo is inseparable from the revulsion millions feel toward the U.S.-backed opposition—and fear of what they would do in power. By the time of the 2018 presidential election, the opposition had made five major U.S.-backed efforts to oust the government by force. Collectively, those five attempts took approximately three hundred lives. About half of those deaths were government supporters, security personnel, or bystanders. These numbers do not include hundreds of Chavistas murdered in the countryside since 2001, who were most likely killed by wealthy landowners opposed to land reform.[18] If Maduro had four million hardcore supporters on Election Day, according to an anti-government pollster, then that's reason enough to view the 6.2 million votes Maduro received without too much suspicion.

But the regional elections of October 2017, which took place only seven months before the presidential election, provide strong evidence that Maduro's hardcore support was about six million voters (30 percent of the electorate), not the four million suggested by Datanalisis polls.

Lessons from the 2017 Regional Elections

Francisco Rodriguez's analysis of the opposition's defeat in the regional elections of October 2017 was very different than his analysis of the 2018 presidential defeat.[19] In the 2017 regionals, the opposition lost seventeen of the twenty-three governorships that were up for grabs. This was an almost complete reversal of the results Rodriguez predicted.[20] When Rodriguez analyzed the election results, he did not even attempt to blame vote buying for the strong Chavista support:

> As others have noted, government mobilization efforts likely

played a role in the differential change in turnout. In surveys taken before the election, 71% of respondents reported receiving food through the CLAPs, and the share of respondents who viewed the food supply situation as positive rose from 5.0% in July of last year to 23% in September. This might help explain the impressive turnout for oficialista candidates, even without direct vote-buying last Sunday.[21]

The CLAPs that Rodriguez believed helped Chavista candidates win so decisively are "Local Supply and Production Committees" that were set up by the Maduro government in 2016 to distribute food and other basic products directly to households at discounted prices.[22] The program has become crucial to abating the impact of the economic crisis, and no doubt drove support for government candidates from voters who recognized this. Rodriguez and Kronick noted another factor that helped Maduro to mobilize his base—Trump's belligerence and the opposition leaders who welcomed it:

After the Trump administration imposed financial sanctions on Venezuela, Maduro came out swinging, blaming opposition leaders for lobbying for sanctions and saying that "those who are happy because of sanctions are digging their own political grave."

He may have been right.[23]

They added that opposition leaders nevertheless "quixotically refused" to condemn U.S. sanctions.

In 2017, the idea of economic war resonated with voters and drove support for the government. That wasn't the case in 2015, when the opposition won the National Assembly elections, its greatest electoral triumph of the Chavista era. At that time, Maduro's talk of "economic war" waged by treasonous U.S.-backed opponents fell flat. Yes, he was saddled with an insurrectionary opposition backed by a superpower. But Maduro also refused to make policy adjustments that would have ended the economic crisis.[24] And oil prices didn't collapse until he had been in office for about a year and a half. But two years later, the economic war was undeniable. Trump had drastically intensified the economic sanctions that Obama first imposed in March 2015. Additionally, the opposition had used its control of the National Assembly to undermine their own country's economy.[25] The first two presidents of the opposition-controlled National Assembly openly lobbied investors to stay away from Venezuela.

Opposition leader Henry Ramos, who had been president of the opposition-controlled National Assembly for a year, said in an interview in March 2017 that every time Maduro tried to make any kind of economic deal involving foreign investors, he would immediately contact the government abroad to undermine it. He effectively boasted about hurting Venezuela's economy while it was in crisis. By 2017, not only was an economic war on Venezuela impossible to dismiss, but Trump also began making overt military threats against Venezuela, which must also have fueled support for the government.[26]

After losing the 2017 regional elections, the faction of the opposition that participated (to the disgust of hardliners who advocated abstention) had a long list of complaints: last-minute changes to voting center locations, confusing ballots, food handed out near polling stations, and strong evidence that 4,568 votes were fraudulently tallied in the state of Bolivar, one of the seventeen states won by Maduro's allies. Nevertheless, Rodriguez and Kronick concluded that all these factors combined "explain only about one percentage point of the government's eight-point lead."

Venezuela's highly automated system for counting votes was called the "best in the world" by Jimmy Carter in 2012.[27] Despite this, during any contested election in Venezuela, a tiny amount of fraud in the actual vote count is detectable. And yet in the 2017 election fraud could not begin to explain the opposition's defeat.[28] Nationwide, the government's candidates received 700,000 more votes than the opposition. The allegedly stolen votes in Bolivar were only about 0.08 percent of the government's total votes nationwide. The government won by such a large margin that fraud was simply not a remotely credible explanation for its victory.

Datanalisis had predicted that the opposition would receive double the government's vote. There are two reasons why Datanalisis made such an inaccurate prediction. First, it underestimated the government's level of support. As it would seven months later in the presidential election, Datanalisis polling suggested that Maduro's allies could get four million votes nationwide in the regional elections. They actually received 5.8 million. Second, it overestimated the willingness of opposition voters to participate in the elections, and predicted an overall turnout that was off by eighteen percentage points. Datanalisis polls suggested that the opposition candidates could get about eight million votes nationwide. They actually received five million.

While turnout was not nearly as high as Datanalisis predicted (79.2 percent), it was still high (61 percent) for regional elections—seven points higher than in the 2012 regional elections.[29] Indeed, 61 percent would be considered high turnout for a U.S. presidential election. The 2017 regional elections showed that while Chavismo was certainly beatable at the polls, it was no pushover.[30] Maduro could still count on a hardcore base representing about 30 percent of the electorate, which won him reelection in 2018. A Pew Research poll conducted several months after the presidential election found that 33 percent of Venezuelans "trust the national government to do what is right for Venezuela."[31] In most of the Western democracies whose governments dismissed Maduro's victory, 30 percent support from eligible voters wins the election. So, putting aside appeals to Western establishment groupthink—"widely dismissed as fraudulent" in a standard Reuters formulation—if you look at the hard data, including polls from an anti-Maduro source such as Datanalisis, the case for a stolen election in 2018 falls apart.

Maduro's Share of the Vote Was Not Low by International Standards

In recent U.S. presidential elections, Barack Obama received 31 percent in 2008 and 28 percent in 2012. Donald Trump received 26 percent in 2016, and didn't even win the popular vote.[32] In the UK, Theresa May's Conservative Party formed a minority government after receiving the votes of 29 percent of the electorate.³³ David Cameron led the Conservatives to a majority government in 2015 by winning the votes of only 24.4 percent of the electorate.³⁴ In Canada, Justin Trudeau's Liberals won a majority government in 2015 by receiving the votes of 27 percent of the electorate.³⁵

Some dismissed Venezuela's presidential election mainly by pointing to the scale of the economic crisis under Maduro: an almost 50 percent drop in real GDP by the end of 2018. How could any government win a clean election under those conditions? That was essentially the approach of a *New York Times* analysis published in January 2019.³⁶

This facile analysis fails to account for the unpopularity of an opposition openly working to make the crisis worse, and openly collaborating with Trump—who had been threatening Venezuela militarily for nine months before the presidential election.³⁷ Maduro's vote tally in 2018 actually did show the impact of the crisis. In 2006, Chávez received the votes of 47 percent; in 2012, 44 percent. Turnout in those elections was 75 percent and 80 percent, respectively.³⁸ In the 2018 election, turnout was only 46 percent. This shows that support for the government did falter because of the crisis. However, as Venezuela-based journalist Ricardo Vaz noted, "In the most recent presidential elections in Chile and Colombia, to name just two examples, participation was respectively of 49 and 48%, and nobody even floated the possibility of questioning their legitimacy."³⁹

There are democratic shortcomings in all the countries mentioned above, most of all Colombia. Winning with only 30 percent or less of the eligible votes is not a healthy sign. However, the Venezuelan government's democratic shortcomings stem primarily from facing an extraordinary foreign threat. And, again, tolerance of a violent foreign-backed opposition is not a fair test of a government's democratic legitimacy. It is not a test that countries such as the United States, United Kingdom, and Canada would ever pass.

What About Disqualified Opposition Candidates?

The international media made much about two opposition leaders,

Henrique Capriles and Leopoldo López, who were disqualified from running in the 2018 presidential election. Lucas Koerner dealt with this objection succinctly in an op-ed for *Mint Press News*:

> Capriles was indeed disqualified from running over Odebrecht corruption allegations that were likely politically motivated. Nevertheless, in any other country he would probably still be in jail, or legally barred from holding office, given his high-profile role in the 2002 coup, in which he led the siege of the Cuban Embassy and participated in the kidnapping of Interior Minister Ramón Rodriguez Chacín together with former Chacao Mayor Leopoldo López. Capriles and López, along with other prominent opposition leaders, including Julio Borges, Antonio Ledezma, and María Corina Machado, would go on to spearhead five more brazenly unconstitutional attempts to oust the Chavista government: the 2002/3 oil lockout, the 2013 post-election opposition violence, the 2014 and 2017 *guarimbas*, as well as the current Trump-led coup.[40]

While Capriles (belatedly) served a few months in jail for his participation in a briefly successful coup, López avoided any jail time thanks to a wide-ranging amnesty Hugo Chávez granted many of the coup perpetrators at the end of 2007.[41] In 2014, after being involved with four different attempts to oust a democratically elected government by force, López finally went to jail. But the Western establishment demands nothing short of total impunity for U.S.-backed insurrectionists: no limits to the number of times they can try to overthrow the government.

Puntos Rojos: The Perfect Blackmail?

Kiosks set up by the government close to voting centers on Election Day, known as *Puntos Rojos* or "Red Points," were depicted by Reuters as "voting bribery."[42] U.S. sanctions, however, were not depicted as an attempt to coerce voters, even though they clearly were. Puntos Rojos are used for exit polling, and have also been used by the opposition, except in a different color, in numerous elections over the past twenty years.[43] By law, they are required to be 200 meters away from voting centers. On May 3, Maduro said that people who came to a Punto Rojo after voting could "probably" win a prize. This is hardly an exemplary practice, but it could only indirectly incentivize people to vote. Moreover, voting is secret, so nothing would prevent people from voting for the opposition and then showing up for a chance at a prize. An opposition blog referred to the Puntos Rojos as "The Perfect Blackmail," but even this account concedes that the government can't know how people voted.[44]

Opposition leaders have often accused the government of undermining public confidence in the secrecy of the vote. Ignoring that their repeated allegations of fraud (when they lose) could have undermined confidence in the secrecy of the vote, opposition leaders have sometimes publicly reassured their supporters that their votes are secret. One example is an emphatic statement put out by an opposition politician, Pablo Perez, a month before the 2015 National Assembly elections. It was published in the notoriously anti-government newspaper *El Nacional*.[45]

But turnout in the October 2017 regional elections was 61 percent, despite the most hardline segments of the opposition urging abstention.[46] Most opposition supporters therefore seemed to be quite confident in the secrecy of their votes. Four different groups of international observers concluded that Maduro's electoral victory was clean.[47] One of those groups, the Council of Electoral Experts of Latin America (CEELA), denounced electoral fraud in the November 2017 general election in Honduras before the OAS did.[48] In February 2018, the Maduro government had formally invited UN observers to monitor the election.[49] Revealingly, a new opposition coalition, *El Frente Amplio Venezuela Libre* (FAVL), lobbied the UN not to send the observers.[50] VenezuelAnalysis reported that, in March, opposition supporters marched in front of the United Nations headquarters in Caracas demanding that the UN not send observers. This amounted to pressuring the UN to declare the elections fraudulent in advance.

An objection to UN observers can be reasonable if an election really is stolen in advance—in other words, if no viable candidates against the government were allowed to run, or if they were barely allowed to campaign.[51] But that just wasn't the case. Neither Datanalisis polling nor a cursory glance at losing candidate Henri Falcón's media access and rallies during the campaign supports that claim.[52] Protesting UN observers in this case was a tacit admission that the votes would be counted properly—an idea that the opposition and its foreign backers accept when it comes to elections their side wins, notably the 2015 National Assembly elections. In any event, the UN refused Maduro's request for observers.

To repeat: objections to Maduro's electoral legitimacy in May 2018 do not hold up, regardless of how often they have been repeated.[53] An outlet such as Reuters, for example, would simply report ad nauseam that the election was "widely dismissed as fraudulent" or words to that effect.[54] Support for Chavismo, in both the 2017 regional and 2018 presidential elections, was obviously far stronger than the Western media cared to admit. Closely related to these facts, there was never any reasonable grounds for taking seriously Juan Guaidó's claim to be interim president of Venezuela. Constantly reporting the claims of Western officialdom—as if there were no reasonable case against them—is lying by omission.[55]

3

The Guaidó Era as a Sixth, Very Long Coup Attempt

U.S. sanctions killed tens of thousands of Venezuelans before the recognition of Juan Guaidó as interim president led to even more murderous sanctions. In August 2017, President Donald Trump imposed financial sanctions on Venezuela that caused the government to lose at least $6 billion in oil revenues over the following twelve months. That's about 6 percent of Venezuela's GDP, in a region where most countries spend about 7 percent of GDP annually on health care.[1] Western journalists decried the Puntos Rojos exit polling stations but were too indoctrinated to see that U.S. sanctions are a gun to the head of the Venezuelan electorate. The message is that tremendous economic pain will be inflicted on the country until Maduro is gone.

Francisco Rodriguez, an anti-Maduro Venezuelan economist, acknowledged the dramatic correlation between Trump's financial sanctions and a greatly accelerated fall in Venezuela's oil production in a piece he wrote for the Washington Office on Latin America (WOLA).[2] His key findings are provided in Table 3.1 (page 37).

Rodriguez found that oil production in Venezuela followed the same general pattern as in Colombia until Trump's financial sanctions

TABLE 3.1: Oil Production in Venezuela and Colombia (2013–2019)

TIME PERIOD	MONTHLY PERCENTAGE GROWTH	
	VENEZUELA	COLOMBIA
January 2013 – December 2015	0.0	0.0
December 2015 – August 2017	−1.0	−0.8
August 2017 – January 2019	−3.0	0.3

Source: Compiled by the authors.

were imposed. Production levels in both countries basically tracked international oil prices. But after Trump's sanctions were imposed, production levels in both countries diverged drastically: Venezuela's plummeted while Colombia's stabilized. Had Venezuela's production continued to follow the same pattern as before the financial sanctions, then its oil revenues would have been drastically higher.

How exactly did Trump's financial sanctions hurt Venezuela?

One of the Venezuelan government's major assets, the state-owned CITGO corporation, is based in Texas. CITGO's parent company was PDVSA, Venezuela's state oil company.[3] The sanctions blocked CITGO from sending profits and dividends back to Venezuela, an amount averaging about $1 billion per year since 2015.[4] Rodriguez explained that Trump's sanctions also made it impossible for PDVSA to continue paying suppliers through the issuance of New York law promissory notes. The United States has tremendous leverage because all the Venezuelan government's outstanding foreign currency bonds are governed under New York State law.[5] Sanctions similarly ended PDVSA's very effective practice of getting loans for joint ventures that it subsequently paid back through oil production.

Table 3.2 (page 38) shows Venezuela's estimated oil revenues for the first twelve months after Trump's financial sanctions. The price of Venezuela's oil has increased linearly since August 2017, from $50 to about $70 per barrel. The oil production volumes are taken from the estimates Rodriguez provided in his WOLA article.

In the "No Trump Sanctions" case shown above, it is assumed that Venezuela's oil production would have continued to fall at the same rate as in the twelve months before Trump's financial sanctions. This

TABLE 3.2: Venezuela Oil Reserves for the First 12 Months after Trump's Financial Sanctions

	Sep '17	Oct '17	Nov '17	Dec '17	Jan '18	Feb '18	Mar '18	Apr '18	May '18	Jun '18	Jul '18	Aug '18
NO SANCTIONS												
Prod. MBD	1.9	1.88	1.86	1.85	1.83	1.81	1.79	1.77	1.75	1.74	1.72	1.70
Price WTI Oil	50.00	51.82	53.64	55.45	57.27	59.09	60.91	62.73	64.55	66.36	68.18	70.00
Revenue $bn	2.89	2.97	3.04	3.11	3.18	3.25	3.32	3.38	3.44	3.50	3.56	3.62
TOTAL FOR YEAR AUG '17–AUG '18: US$39.3bn												
SANCTIONS IN PLACE												
Prod. MBD	1.90	1.84	1.77	1.71	1.65	1.58	1.52	1.45	1.39	1.33	1.26	1.20
Price WTI Oil	50.00	51.82	53.64	55.45	57.27	59.09	60.91	62.73	64.55	66.36	68.18	70.00
Revenue $bn	2.89	2.89	2.89	2.88	2.87	2.84	2.81	2.78	2.73	2.68	2.62	2.56
TOTAL FOR YEAR AUG '17–AUG '18: US$33.4bn												

Source: Compiled by the authors.

means a decline of 11 percent, which is very close to the worst-case projections that were made before financial sanctions were imposed.[6] With the sanctions in place, however, production fell by 37 percent. The difference in total revenue between the two cases over the twelve-month period is about $6 billion. That estimate is larger if it is assumed that Venezuela's production would have done better (declined by less than the "worst case" of about 11 percent) in the absence of Trump's sanctions. And no additional impact of that $6 billion loss beyond the oil industry is assumed, which also contributes to making it a conservative estimate of the impact of Trump's sanctions.

These $6 billion in losses from oil exports were in U.S. dollars, which means that Venezuela lost the hard currency needed to pay for imports.[7] This is a crucial point. In 2018, Venezuela was only able to import $11.7 billion in goods, according to Torino Capital. The impact on medicine imports was especially destructive. According to U.S. economist Mark Weisbrot, while its economy was still growing in 2013, Venezuela was importing about $2 billion per year in medicine.[8] By 2018, that amount had fallen to an astonishing low of $140 million—an especially horrifying development because medicines are much more difficult to substitute with local production than food.[9] It is impossible to deny that a collapse in medicine imports has killed thousands of people in the 2017–2018 period, as Weisbrot and U.S. economist Jeffrey Sachs argued in a paper published in April 2019. Weisbrot and Sachs cite a 31 percent increase in general mortality in the 2017–2018 period, according to a survey by anti-Maduro Venezuelan academics. That increase works out to an extra 40,000 deaths. As noted in chapter 2 regarding Datanalisis, caution should be used when citing opposition sources. But there is no denying that thousands were being killed. Even Rodriguez estimated that about a third of the increased mortality in 2018 could be due to sanctions.[10] In a civilized world, these sanctions would put numerous high-ranking U.S. officials in jail for murder.

U.S. sanctions against Venezuela are clearly crimes against humanity, and not only for their impact on medicines. The Venezuelan government's Local Supply and Production Committees (CLAP) program has also been crippled by U.S. sanctions. CLAPs distribute subsidized food and other basic products directly to households throughout Venezuela.[11] About 60 percent of Venezuelan households have received supplies from the CLAP program, according to Datanalisis.[12] Another anti-Maduro source, the annual ENCOVI surveys, reported that almost 90 percent of households were receiving products through the CLAP program by December 2018.[13] Slashing the Maduro government's revenues through sanctions inevitably devastates its capacity to maintain a program on which Venezuelans have come to depend. This could not possibly be justified even if Maduro were a dictator. In the short term, U.S. belligerence entrenched Maduro's electoral base behind him. But in the long term, the U.S. may coerce the kind of electoral result in Venezuela that, in 1990, Ronald Reagan and George H. W. Bush produced in Nicaragua through a decade of terrorism and sanctions.

When Trump recognized Guaidó as Venezuela's interim president, it signaled a new, deadlier phase of sanctions. Two days after Guaidó declared himself president, Trump appointed Elliott Abrams, experienced in running genocidal U.S. proxy wars in Central America in the 1980s, as special envoy to Venezuela.[14] It was impossible to miss the significance, the flaunting of U.S. imperial impunity.

Trump's recognition of Guaidó was a legal pretext to make U.S. sanctions more devastating. Venezuelan government assets in the United States were seized and officially transferred to Guaidó's self-declared "interim government." Oil shipments from Venezuela to the United States would also now be invoiced by only the government recognized by Washington. In other words, Maduro's government would simply be throwing money away if it continued oil shipments to the United States because it would not be paid for them. This amounted to an embargo on Venezuela's oil. Torino Capital immediately revised its projections for Venezuela's economy in the coming year. It had predicted an 11 percent contraction in real GDP for 2019. Shortly after Guaidó's recognition, it revised that to a 26 percent contraction—a projection that proved extremely accurate.[15]

Recall that Barack Obama first imposed economic sanctions on Venezuela in March 2015 through an executive order that formally declared a national emergency (in the United States) based on the preposterous claim that "the situation in Venezuela" was "an extraordinary threat to the national security of the United States."[16] Both he, and later Trump, would renew the fraudulent national emergency every year. A bogus national emergency was also Ronald Reagan's legal pretext to strangle Nicaragua's economy during the 1980s and back Contra terrorists who opposed the government.

Not every national emergency is created equal. For instance, in February 2019, when Trump declared a national emergency to bypass Congress over building his infamous wall on the U.S.–Mexican border, legal challenges were quickly initiated.[17] One of the arguments used to oppose Trump was, as one law professor said, that "the president can't just say any old thing is a national emergency."[18] And yet, this has been precisely the case in Venezuela.

U.S. sanctions are also a flagrant violation of the Organization of American States Charter, which the U.S. government has signed. In Chapter IV, Article 19, it states:

> No State or group of States has the right to intervene, directly or indirectly, for any reason whatever, in the internal or external affairs of any other State. The foregoing principle prohibits not only armed force but also any other form of interference or attempted threat against the personality of the State or against its political, economic, and cultural elements.[19]

And Article 2 of the UN Charter states: "All Members shall refrain in their international relations from the threat or use of force against the territorial integrity or political independence of any state."[20]

What If Venezuela Behaved Like the United States?

Imagine Venezuelan President Nicolás Maduro saying, as Trump did, that he refused to rule out a "military option" against the United States; or saying that the U.S. military could "topple" Trump's government "very quickly." Imagine if a high-ranking Maduro government official said, as Secretary of State Rex Tillerson did, that the U.S. military might step in as an "agent of change" and send Trump off to a nice "hacienda" somewhere; or if another top Maduro official said, as Tillerson's successor Mike Pompeo did, that Venezuela was "very hopeful that there can be a transition" in the United States and that Venezuela's intelligence services were discussing with regional allies how to achieve that "better outcome."[21] All of these examples were threats made long before the United States recognized Juan Guaidó. Trump's first statement about a possible "military option" for Venezuela was made in August 2017. The recognition of Guaidó made such threats more frequent and severe.

Consider, for example, the wild remarks made by John Bolton, Trump's former National Security Advisor. After January 23 (the date of Guaidó's self-declaration) Bolton used Twitter to constantly implore the Venezuelan military to turn on Maduro. On March 12, Bolton tweeted:

> The U.S. fully supports Interim President Juan Guaidó and the National Assembly. We will continue to intensify our efforts to end Maduro's usurpation of Venezuela's Presidency and will hold the military and security forces responsible for protecting the Venezuelan people.

Bolton, a key U.S. official responsible for the Iraq War that cost at least half a million Iraqi lives, was, like his superiors, never held accountable for his crimes. The spectacle of Bolton not only out of jail but issuing threats and presuming to hold anyone "responsible" was disgusting.[22]

In a radio interview on February 1, Bolton joked about having Maduro sent to a U.S.-run torture camp in Cuba.[23] Reuters seemed to chuckle along with Bolton's thug humor: "Move over ayatollahs: Bolton turns tweets and talons on Maduro."[24] The Reuters article included a cartoon that showed Maduro behind bars and wearing an orange jumpsuit while Bolton danced outside the cell. It even claimed that the cartoon, by Venezuelan cartoonist Fernando Pinilla, hung on Bolton's office wall.

Weeks passed without the coup that Bolton clearly expected to occur immediately after Guaidó's announcement. The United States issued grave warnings to Maduro not to arrest Guaidó, but for almost two decades Venezuela had, to an amazing degree, been tolerant of an openly insurrectionary U.S.-backed opposition.[25] That crucial fact seemed to have escaped the empire's notice. Guaidó led large rallies. The government also rallied its supporters to the streets. Another U.S. provocation would have to be arranged.

The Failed Aid Stunt

On February 12, 2019, at a large rally in eastern Caracas where upper- and middle-class opposition supporters tend to live, Juan Guaidó ordered the Venezuelan military to allow humanitarian aid into the country through the border with Colombia on February 23—even though he lacked any legal authority to do so.[26] The stunt failed to incite a coup, as the military simply obeyed Maduro's orders not to let in the shipment. Frenzied propaganda aside, it was a non-event.

This was the shipment of U.S.-government-supplied items that was to be sent into Venezuela without passing through official UN channels and international aid groups already working in the country.[27] Recall that the U.S. government has objected to aid being delivered to Gaza in defiance of Israel's criminal blockade.[28] If Israel pretended to force "aid" into Gaza, as the United States attempted to do in Venezuela, it would rival the cynicism of the stunt at the Colombia–Venezuela border. The Trump administration should have been forced to answer at least two questions by the Western media.

Instead of sending aid, why not end the economic sanctions? The loss of $6 billion per year from Trump's sanctions dwarfs the $20 million in aid his administration intended to force through the border.[29] And why not simply increase donations to the UN and the International Committee of the Red Cross, two organizations that were already working in Venezuela?

Predictably, no such questioning of the Trump administration took place. Instead, Western readers were bombarded with deceptive articles, such as one by Jim Wyss for the *Miami Herald*. Its headline was: "Venezuela aid organizers imagine a 'river of people' overwhelming Maduro's blockade."[30] Wyss wrote that "Venezuelan leader Nicolás Maduro continues to reject international aid—going so far as to blockade a road that might have been used for its delivery."

Wyss's article contained two big lies. First, in November 2018, Maduro publicly requested aid and the UN then authorized it for Venezuela shortly afterward.[31] This was even reported by Reuters.[32] But that didn't stop Reuters from writing numerous articles a few months later with headlines such as "U.S. looking for ways to get aid into Venezuela: Envoy," ignoring the option of simply donating money to aid workers who were already in the country.[33]

Second, the "blockaded" road widely mentioned at the time was the Tienditas Bridge linking Venezuela to Colombia. It had been blocked since 2016, when it was completed but never opened. U.S. Secretary of State Mike Pompeo was responsible for the allegation, made in a tweet, that the bridge had been blocked by Maduro to stop aid. A CBC article from February 15, 2019, admitted to having been misled, like other news media, by Pompeo.[34] But in the same article, the CBC also claimed that the Tienditas Bridge had been "featured in stories describing how the president of Venezuela, Nicolás Maduro, is keeping international food aid from his desperate citizens." The CBC debunked one lie but spread an even more serious one: that Maduro was keeping aid from his citizens. There was also a huge lie of omission in the CBC article: no mention of U.S. economic sanctions.

An earlier CBC article from February 8 ran with a subheading that falsely claimed: "Maduro says aid not needed in Venezuela, Guaidó wants to allow it."[35] The CBC later revised the article, adding the clause "although Venezuela has accepted foreign aid in the past, and Maduro has not always been consistent in his statements on the subject." But referring to international aid received in "the past" was deceptive. The CBC should have said that Venezuela "is receiving" (present tense) international aid from the UN and the Red Cross.[36] And the dishonest subheading remained in the revised CBC article.

Numerous articles also ignored the historical precedent. When

Elliott Abrams, Trump's special representative for Venezuela, was an Assistant Secretary of State for Inter-American affairs in the 1980s, he used humanitarian aid as cover to arm the Contra terrorists in Nicaragua.[37] In the *Miami Herald* article by Jim Wyss, the use of U.S. aid for military purposes is presented as something only Maduro suspected. Independent U.S. foreign policy critics would have mentioned the historical precedent, but no effort was made to cite them. The journalistic approach used by Wyss and many others resembles the run-up to the Iraq invasion of 2003, when completely factual statements that Iraq had no weapons of mass destruction were often attributed solely to the discredited Iraqi government—and not to critical, independent observers.[38]

The aid stunt was aimed at giving the Venezuelan military a humanitarian pretext for turning on Maduro. As usual, John Bolton made U.S. intentions impossible for anyone to miss. One of his many tweets before the aid stunt warned:

> Any actions by the Venezuelan military to condone or instigate violence against peaceful civilians at the Colombian and Brazilian borders will not be forgotten. Leaders still have time to make the right choice.[39]

U.S. Senator Marco Rubio tweeted directly to Venezuela's Director of Military Counter-Intelligence:

> .@Ivanr_HD you should think very carefully about the actions you take over the next few days in #Venezuela. Because your actions will determine how you spend the rest of your life.
>
> Do you really want to be more loyal to #Maduro than to your own family?[40]

The day after the failed aid stunt, Rubio tweeted, without comment, a picture showing former Libyan dictator Muammar Gaddafi bloodied and in the clutches of the U.S.-backed rebels who raped and murdered him.[41]

This was open mafioso-style behavior intended to push a transparently fraudulent aid mission and incite a coup. The stunt was further discredited to any informed observer when the Grayzone News, and, weeks later, even the *New York Times*, debunked claims that Maduro supporters had set some of the trucks carrying aid ablaze. Guaidó supporters had actually set the trucks on fire.[42]

But while the outcome of the stunt was still in doubt, the self-identified democratic socialist Bernie Sanders backed up the stunt in his own way.

The Bernie Front of the Propaganda War

Within only one week, February 18 to 24, there were a total of 153 Venezuela-related tweets from Marco Rubio, John Bolton, Mike Pompeo, and Mike Pence. These tweets represented 77 percent of their collective tweets as they frantically pushed the aid stunt.[43]

On the day of the aid stunt, February 23, Sanders issued his only Venezuela-related tweet in the entire month:

> The people of Venezuela are enduring a serious humanitarian crisis. The Maduro government must put the needs of its people first, allow humanitarian aid into the country, and refrain from violence against protesters.[44]

Did Sanders not know that Venezuela was already receiving foreign aid? Didn't Sanders notice the Trump administration openly trying to incite a military coup in Venezuela since 2017 through sanctions? Was Sanders ignorant of the consequences of U.S.-backed military coups in Latin America?[45] Was he not familiar with Elliott Abrams's track record, or John Bolton's?

The liberal journalist Norman Solomon defended Sanders's Venezuela position by noting that Sanders was "savagely trashed" for refusing to call Maduro a "dictator" during an exchange with Wolf Blitzer on February 25, 2019.[46] But Sanders was trashed, in part, because his remarks to Blitzer were weak and incoherent. Sanders had said that it's "fair to say that the last election [in Venezuela] was undemocratic," so it did look odd when Sanders stopped short of labelling Maduro a "dictator"—as the Sanders campaign labeled Hugo Chávez in 2015.[47] Sanders clearly didn't have the stomach (and perhaps the knowledge) to hit back at Blitzer explaining why elections in Venezuela compare extremely well with those in his own country. He told Blitzer that Venezuela was not as undemocratic as Saudi Arabia. But the relevant comparison should be between Venezuela and the United States, which would never tolerate a violent foreign-backed opposition the way Venezuela has. Several months later, Sanders fell in line even more conspicuously. Sanders referred to Maduro as "a vicious tyrant."[48] In January 2020, pressed during an interview by the *New York Times* editorial board, Sanders called Maduro (along with Nicaraguan President Daniel Ortega) a dictator.[49]

On March 8, the Real News Network reported that "16 progressive members of Congress" had demanded "an end to economic sanctions and to military threats against Venezuela." It interviewed Ro Khanna, a Democratic Representative from California, who led the initiative.[50] Khanna told RNN's Sharmine Peres:

> Well, we sent a letter calling for a repeal of the broad-based sanctions precisely for your point. They're hurting the poorest folks in Venezuela. They're giving Maduro an excuse to blame the United States, as opposed to taking responsibility for his own failed economic policies and his own cronyism. So I don't think that they are productive.

It was actually very clear that U.S. sanctions were killing—not simply "hurting"—Venezuelans.[51] Khanna also spoke as if a crime against humanity could be acceptable if it were "productive" to U.S. objectives. At one point in the interview, Khanna said: "I don't understand how Bolton is still allowed to be near foreign policy. I mean, here's someone who is the architect of the biggest blunder in American foreign policy, the Iraq war."

An unprovoked war of aggression based on a pack of lies is not a "blunder" that should have merely kept Bolton away from a job involving foreign policy. Downgrading mass murder to a "blunder" exposes an inability to see Iraqis as human beings.

Khanna also claimed that Venezuela's 2018 election was "tainted" through a lack of (presumably U.S.-approved) "supervision."[52] The following year, U.S.-approved supervision of Bolivia's election produced a bogus election audit that led directly to a coup and a U.S.-approved dictatorship. As the most far-left elected politicians in the United States, figures such as Khanna and Sanders should understand the stakes and be keenly aware that they are the only ones who might hold the U.S. government accountable for its crimes. They are the only official figures who stand between millions of innocent people abroad and the horrors that the United States would inflict on them.

As the Guaidó era began, prominent NGOs also ensured that pressure was applied to Venezuela's government while U.S. criminality went virtually unopposed.

Amnesty International Adds Reinforcement

Three days before the aid stunt (and shortly after meeting with Juan Guaidó), Amnesty International issued a report that was ostensibly about denouncing an allegedly brutal response by Venezuelan security forces to recent anti-government protests in poor neighborhoods.[53] Amnesty's Americas director, Erika Guevara Rosa, wrote, "International justice is the only hope for victims of human rights violations in Venezuela. It is time to activate all available mechanisms to prevent further atrocities." Given the circumstances, the report read like a barely disguised attempt to bolster Trump's threats against Venezuela from a human rights angle. Venezuela was days away from what may easily have resulted in a U.S.-backed coup or even invasion. What were the human rights implications of a U.S.-backed military coup or invasion? Anyone with knowledge of Latin American history knows the very disturbing answer. But Amnesty was completely unconcerned.

The Amnesty report was titled "Venezuela: Hunger, Punishment and Fear, the Formula for Repression Used by Authorities Under

Nicolás Maduro." The insinuation was that "hunger" was a weapon Maduro used against the public, even though the text only referred to food distribution in the following sentence: "There is a strong presence of pro-Nicolás Maduro armed groups (commonly known as 'colectivos') in these areas, where residents depend to a large extent on the currently limited state programs to distribute staple foods."

The "limited state programs" referred to CLAP—the program Trump viciously attacked through sanctions beginning in August 2017. Amnesty not only ignored Trump's attack on the CLAP program, it also cast as thugs the organized poor people distributing food to millions of people. When using the term "colectivo," the report referred only to poor people who are armed and therefore vilified them as criminal gangs. This is a very partisan use of the term and is often deployed by the opposition.

According to George Ciccariello-Maher, a U.S. scholar who has done extensive research on the grassroots Chavista organizations in the poorest neighborhoods, "colectivo" is used by these groups to refer to themselves, and the vast majority of them are not armed. The term means armed, pro-government criminals only in the U.S.-backed opposition's definition. [54]

So while Amnesty criticized Venezuela's government for "stigmatizing" protesters in poor neighborhoods, Amnesty itself stigmatized Chavistas in poor areas by using the term "colectivos" as the opposition does. And this despite the fact that colectivos (armed or not) would be targets for savage repression by the opposition, if it ever seized power. All six U.S.-backed coup attempts since 2002 have demonstrated their total disregard for the lives of the poor and for Chavistas in particular. The opposition's applause for the brutal coup-installed dictatorship in Bolivia, which took power in 2019 and governed for almost a year before democracy was restored, dramatically underscores this point.

When questioned directly about the financial sanctions Trump imposed on Venezuela in August 2017, Amnesty replied that it took no position on U.S. sanctions. As for its position regarding statements by U.S. officials and politicians encouraging the Venezuelan military to perpetrate a coup, Amnesty replied that "responsible discussion on the current state of human rights in Venezuela should not be focused on statements made by parties outside the country."[55]

This was shocking. U.S. sanctions are attacks on Venezuelans' rights to health and food—indeed, on their very lives. U.S. threats against Venezuela and its open encouragement of a military coup are similarly indefensible acts—and also grave threats to human rights. But Amnesty claimed that staying silent about those facts was the responsible thing to do.

On January 25, 2019, Amnesty received a petition asking it to change its position and oppose U.S. economic sanctions and the deliberate incitement of a military coup in Venezuela. It was signed by filmmaker and political activist John Pilger, former UN special Rapporteur to Venezuela Alfred de Zayas, and Canadian author Linda McQuaig, among others.[56] On February 7, Amnesty updated its position on U.S. sanctions and threats—by asking the U.S. government to be careful in imposing economic sanctions and to "monitor" their impact on the "most vulnerable groups."[57] This was absurd. The deadly impact of sanctions had been well established for over a year *before* Trump made them even worse in January 2019. Regarding U.S. threats and incitement of a military coup, Amnesty now vaguely requested that the "international community" follow the law. It did not single out Trump, even though his government was driving the attacks on Venezuela. Moreover, Amnesty's timid request to follow the law was contradicted by its position that the U.S. should merely "monitor" its illegal economic sanctions.

It was infuriating to see Amnesty, a major human rights group, completely incapable of denouncing grave human rights abuses by the most transparently racist and cynical U.S. president in recent memory.

Another Eminent Fraud: The UN Rights Chief

On March 20, 2019, UN High Commissioner for Human Rights Michelle Bachelet made a statement about Venezuela:

> Although this pervasive and devastating economic and social

crisis began before the imposition of the first economic sanctions in 2017, I am concerned that the recent sanctions on financial transfers related to the sale of Venezuelan oil within the United States may contribute to aggravating the economic crisis, with possible repercussions on people's basic rights and well-being.[58]

In a literal reading of her words, even if the sanctions made a preexisting crisis worse, they would only have a "possible" negative impact on "people's basic rights and well-being"—a total absurdity. Bachelet's cowardly nonsense contrasted sharply with the candor of Alfred De Zayas, a UN-appointed special investigator who visited Venezuela in 2017.[59] He said that U.S. sanctions amounted to "economic warfare."

Bachelet said that Maduro's government did not "fully acknowledge" the scale of the economic crisis, but she failed to acknowledge the U.S. economic strangulation of Venezuela. She also said nothing about repeated U.S. military threats. And while Bachelet failed to dissent against U.S. crimes, she hypocritically expressed concern about dissent within Venezuela—where Juan Guaidó was free to lead a U.S.-backed insurrection against Maduro's government.

In July, Bachelet released another report in which she less timidly stated the obvious about crippling U.S. sanctions, but was still unable or unwilling to demand that they be lifted. Her report said that "the economy of Venezuela, particularly its oil industry and food production systems, were already in crisis before any sectoral sanctions were imposed."[60] That's precisely what makes U.S. sanctions so depraved. Imagine a defense attorney saying, "Your Honor, I will show that the victim was already in intensive care when my client began to assault him."[61] Attacking somebody who is vulnerable is much worse than attacking somebody who is not. This was especially true after Trump escalated U.S. sanctions in August 2017. But rather than make that obvious point, Bachelet's report stated the following:

> Nevertheless, the latest economic sanctions are exacerbating further the effects of the economic crisis, and thus the

humanitarian situation, given that most of the foreign exchange earnings derive from oil exports, many of which are linked to the U.S. market. The Government has agreed to gradually authorize humanitarian assistance from the United Nations and other actors. However, the level of assistance is minimal vis-à-vis the scale of the crisis and there is an urgent need to adopt structural economic reforms.

After admitting that U.S. policy was deliberately worsening "the humanitarian situation," the report demanded that Maduro's government offset the damage through "economic reforms"—*but not that U.S. sanctions be lifted*, even though their very objective is to make any economic recovery impossible.

Only two months earlier, on May 16, Marco Rubio approvingly tweeted that Maduro "can't access funds to rebuild electric grid or PDVSA."[62] In March and April, Venezuela had been hit with unusually severe electrical blackouts. Maduro claimed (plausibly) that the blackouts were caused by opposition sabotage, using snipers and cyber-attacks. But even if that claim turned out to be false, the much larger point Rubio acknowledged—and celebrated—was the obvious link between U.S. sanctions and the reduced capacity of Maduro's government to provide essential services to all Venezuelans.[63] Could Bachelet possibly have missed how utterly vile U.S. objectives were—especially after a high-profile figure like Rubio had made them explicit?

In August 2019, Trump escalated the sanctions yet again by imposing a blanket ban on dealing with Maduro's government. This basically meant a full trade embargo.[64]

In a December interview with Anya Parampil of the investigative website the *Grayzone*, Francisco Rodriguez, the prominent anti-Maduro economist, described how opposition legislators blocked a law that would have authorized the UN Development program to procure parts to repair Venezuela's electrical grid—parts Maduro's government would not be able to get on its own, due to sanctions. "The more hardline groups, in particular Voluntad Popular [Guaidó's party at the time] and Primero Justicia, decided to block the law," Rodriguez said.

"Publicly they haven't made their argument clear but everybody knows the rationale is that they believe that anything that makes Venezuelans' lives better is giving oxygen to the Maduro regime."[65] Indeed—and a conclusion like this should have been stated by Bachelet if even an anti-Maduro Venezuelan like Rodriguez could do it.

Problems Emerge as Coup Attempt Drags On

By the end of 2019, four U.S.-backed governments in the Western Hemisphere—Chile, Ecuador, Haiti, and Colombia—were shaken by massive protests against neoliberal economic policies. The unrest was met with deadly responses by security forces. The regional "good guys" in the U.S. government's story were exposing themselves as "bad guys" in a conspicuous way. The U.S. government, the OAS Secretary General Luis Almagro, and Juan Guaidó and other Venezuelan opposition leaders all responded by accusing Cuba and Venezuela of stirring up the unrest.[66] It was alleged that Maduro, cash-strapped and supposedly on the brink of collapse, was successfully destabilizing several U.S.-backed governments. Maduro mocked the allegations.[67] The protests undermined the idea that surrendering to Washington paved the way to peace and prosperity: Chavistas could now point to massive unrest under several U.S.-backed governments in the region.

Corporate media diverted public attention toward pro-United States protesters in Hong Kong. Alan MacLeod, writing for FAIR.org, showed that the Hong Kong protests received about ten times more coverage from the *New York Times* and CNN than the protests in Ecuador, Chile, and Haiti combined. This was especially striking considering that seventy-six protesters had been killed in Ecuador, Chile, and Haiti, while only two protest-related deaths had occurred in Hong Kong.[68]

The U.S.-backed military coup in Bolivia in November 2019 also exposed the hypocrisy of the Venezuelan opposition and its cheerleaders. By the end of 2019, Guaidó, who applauded the coup, was strutting around Caracas pretending to defy a "dictatorship" while Evo Morales, who won Bolivia's presidential election in October, was threatened by a real dictatorship if he dared to return from exile.[69] But, despite Guaidó's remarkable freedom to operate in Venezuela, the Guaidó insurrection became increasingly undermined by corruption scandals, internal disputes, and embarrassing failures.

On April 30, Guaidó announced a military uprising while standing outside an air force base in wealthy eastern Caracas. The uprising was exposed as farcical within hours. Trump was reduced to publicly whining that Cuba had foiled it.[70] Five weeks later, on June 6, the *Washington Post* said it acquired a recording in which Mike Pompeo, perhaps trying to shift blame for the U.S. failure to oust Maduro, aired frustrations over how difficult it was to keep the opposition united.[71] Then, on June 14, a hardline opposition outlet, *Panampost*, reported that Guaidó's representatives had stolen funds that were supposed to help recent defectors from the Venezuelan military living in Colombia.[72] The tone of the article was unabashedly angry and sarcastic. It mocked Guaidó's promises to treat military defectors like heroes, saying, "Surprise, heroes don't starve." But it also said many defectors spent money on alcohol and prostitutes and "didn't leave a good impression" in Colombia. Reuters conveyed the basics of the story the next day in far less detail and using an objective tone.[73]

In September, photographs (and later, video) emerged of Guaidó smiling with armed members of the Colombian drug-trafficking paramilitaries known as Los Rastrojos during the time of the aid stunt. Reuters reported that Guaidó denied knowing who the men were, but didn't mention that one Rastrojos member who posed with Guaidó was wearing a gun. Wouldn't Guaidó's security team have to know and trust an armed man to let him get that close? Was the man actually part of Guaidó's security team during the aid stunt?

In early December, another pro-opposition outlet, Armando.info, published new allegations that were damaging to Guaidó.[74] Nine opposition legislators were accused of receiving kickbacks in exchange for helping a Colombian businessman evade U.S. sanctions. Guaidó said he would not tolerate corruption. But one of the accused lawmakers, José Brito, fired back, saying Guaidó was corrupt, and that people close to Guaidó bought a nightclub in Madrid with illegally acquired funds. This public dispute with Brito came at the same moment when Humberto Calderón Berti, who'd been recently fired by Guaidó as his representative to Colombia, gave a lengthy interview to *Panampost* in which he portrayed Guaidó as being surrounded by "toxic" people. Calderon singled out Leopoldo López as a bad influence.[75]

Remarkably, strong attacks on Guaidó began to appear in some U.S. corporate media. Opposition figures in the United States, who had soured on Guaidó as the coup attempt dragged on, appeared to have mobilized to make him the scapegoat, and perhaps position themselves to replace him. For example, a *Miami Herald* article from December 4, 2019, ran with the headline, "Poll Shows Venezuela's Guaidó Is Losing Popularity and Has Sunk to Maduro Level." A day earlier, a Reuters headline stated "'Missed his moment': Opposition corruption scandal undermines Venezuela's Guaidó."[76]

As 2019 ended, it looked as if Guaidó may not be reelected as the National Assembly president for 2020.[77] Indeed, on January 5, pro-government assembly members voted with opposition legislators to elect Luis Parra as the new president of the National Assembly.[78] Guaidó's allies disputed the vote and held their own in the headquarters of *El Nacional*, an anti-Maduro newspaper.[79] Needless to say, they claimed Guaidó was reelected. Much more importantly, the United States continued to back Guaidó and to escalate its sanctions even further.

2020: U.S. Crimes Against Humanity Get More Brazen

As the world reeled from the COVID-19 pandemic, Maduro solicited emergency loans that the IMF was making available to member countries. The IMF quickly rejected Maduro's request, claiming that it was unclear if his government was recognized by UN member states. This was an absurd excuse: in 2002, the IMF, which is traditionally dominated by the U.S. Treasury Department, had immediately offered loans to the Carmona dictatorship after it ousted Hugo Chávez in a coup. That dictatorship, in power for only two days, was recognized by almost no government but the United States. The IMF's excuse to reject Maduro's 2020 request was also ridiculous because, in October 2019, the majority of UN member states voted Venezuela onto the UN Human Rights Council—despite intense U.S. lobbying against it.[80] And yet the *Washington Post* editorial board lashed out at Maduro over his request, whining that Maduro "must have known" the loan "would be turned down." That was indeed predictable—thanks to the same U.S. government that made a spectacle of demanding that Maduro accept "aid."[81]

In March, the U.S. began imposing sanctions on foreign firms that trade with Venezuela.[82] It also announced a Wild West–style bounty on the head of Maduro and other officials, based on drug trafficking allegations that were transparently political in nature—and in some instances, totally preposterous. For example, it was alleged that Maduro's government intended to "flood" the United States with cocaine.[83] This claim, no matter how unhinged, *was* consistent with the officially declared U.S. "national emergency" that said that Venezuela was an "extraordinary threat" to the United States: a clear example of the aggressor demanding victim status.

Michelle Bachelet said in March that, due to the COVID-19 pandemic, "sectoral sanctions" should be "eased or suspended." She added benevolently that the people in countries targeted by U.S. sanctions—though she never explicitly singled out the United States—"are in no way responsible for the policies being targeted by sanctions," as if stated U.S. concerns about democracy, human rights, and U.S. "national security" were the reason countries like Venezuela were targeted.[84]

Recall that anti-Maduro Venezuelan economist Francisco Rodriguez had projected a return to growth for Venezuela in 2020. Additional U.S. sanctions and threats therefore had a clear and savage logic to them, which was to ensure that no economic recovery would take place after years of crisis. Fuel shortages began to plague the country in May as key refineries stopped producing. That month, a raid by U.S. mercenaries who had been hired by Guaidó and his allies was easily snuffed out by the Venezuelan military (with help from armed fishermen). Secretary of State Pompeo denied "direct" U.S. involvement.[85] Indeed, "indirect" U.S. involvement was obvious to anyone who closely followed U.S. policy toward Venezuela for the past twenty years, especially during Trump's presidency, but it was still remarkable that Pompeo would issue only a qualified denial over the raid.

Iranian tankers began to arrive in Venezuela on May 23 with desperately needed gasoline. Iran has formally complained to the UN about U.S. threats against the tankers.[86] Bernie Sanders, supposedly the leading progressive Democrat, tweeted nothing about it. Only a year earlier, he had tweeted a demand for Maduro to accept aid. Now he was silent as Trump openly sought to block fuel from reaching Venezuela. Democrats in Congress were useless as an opposition—a point that came through clearly in the Venezuela-related chapter of *The Room Where It Happened*, a memoir that John Bolton had published in June. The person Bolton described as his most serious concern, in terms of stifling him on Venezuela, was Trump's Secretary of the Treasury, Steven Mnuchin. Appropriately enough, Bolton barely mentioned the Democrats.[87] In fact, Joe Biden, once he secured the Democratic Party's presidential nomination, made it clear that his aggression toward Venezuela would match Trump's.[88]

As 2020 came to a close, the United States seemed unwilling to declare an end to the Guaidó era any time soon—the very long attempt to oust Maduro through threats, appeals to the Venezuelan military to perpetrate a coup, and, worst of all, constantly escalating economic warfare. The lack of opposition to this prolonged coup attempt where it would be most effective—in Western governments, media, and prominent NGOs—has proven lethal. The empire centered in Washington is an extraordinary threat to the world.

4

How Could Chavismo Flourish in "Once Prosperous" and Democratic Venezuela?

In his State of the Union address on February 6, 2019, Donald Trump said, "We stand with the Venezuelan people in their noble quest for freedom—and we condemn the brutality of the Maduro regime, whose socialist policies have turned that nation from being the wealthiest in South America into a state of abject poverty and despair."[1] Trump's ridiculous comment was not considered controversial because the Western media, including the anti-Trump liberal outlets like the *New York Times*, have spent many years conveying a lie: that Venezuela had been very prosperous and democratic until Hugo Chávez, and then his successor Nicolás Maduro, came along and ruined everything. If readers believe that, then they may indeed wonder, "Why shouldn't the U.S. government help Venezuelans return to that prosperous state?" But this attitude is the result of common deceptions about Venezuela's economic history, and it ignores how the rise of Chávez actually brought democratic reform, not regression, to Venezuela. The story the Western media tells should instead make people wonder how Chavismo could have become the dominant political force if everything had once been wonderful in Venezuela.

For example, on March 19, 2019, a *New York Times* article by Michael Schwirtz ran with the headline, "U.N. Appeals to Maduro and Guaidó to End Battle Over Humanitarian Aid."[2] It emphasized a dubious report about poverty in Venezuela, stating that:

> As much as 94 percent of the population lives in poverty, according to the report, and up to seven million people, or a quarter of Venezuela's population, are now in need of humanitarian assistance in a country that was *once one of the world's wealthiest* [our emphasis].

The 94 percent poverty figure comes from Venezuelan antigovernment academics who put out the annual university-based ENCOVI surveys of living conditions in Venezuela. It's crucial to note that this is an estimate of income poverty, which doesn't account for government-subsided food, education, and healthcare—meaning that it gives a distorted picture of actual living conditions. In 2015, the ENCOVI income poverty estimate was shown to be anywhere from 25 to 34 percentage points too high. Its 2019 estimate was probably not as badly exaggerated, but it was still misleading.[3]

Stating that a once-wealthy Venezuela has plunged into a 94 percent poverty rate is also deceptive because it ignores the gains made under Chávez, when Venezuela's poverty rate fell by half. Even so, there is no question that poverty did increase dramatically after 2014, for three reasons: Maduro's policy errors, a steep fall in oil prices, and years of U.S. support for an insurrectionist opposition. After 2017, the increase in poverty was overwhelmingly due to U.S. sanctions. But in addition to downplaying this context and uncritically citing ENCOVI figures, the *New York Times* tells the more damning lie that Venezuela was "once one of the world's wealthiest" countries.

This vague claim about Venezuela's economic history, in various forms—"once prosperous," "once the richest"—has become ubiquitous in the Western media. A Lexis Nexis search of English language newspapers for "Venezuela" and "once prosperous" turned up 563 hits between 2015 and 2019.[4] The "once prosperous" claim cannot refer to Venezuela's *natural* wealth: the huge oil and gold reserves are still there. The clear intent of describing Venezuela as "once prosperous" is to suggest that *living conditions* were "once" those of a rich country. So, by what measure was Venezuela "once" wealthy? When exactly was that? What is the ranking criteria being used to say it was one of the wealthiest? Was it once in the top 10 percent (by whatever measure)? The top 50 percent?

It's always implied that Venezuela's economic glory days were in the pre-Chávez era, but the financial journalist Jason Mitchell has made this claim explicitly. Writing for the UK *Spectator* in 2017, he said, "Twenty years ago Venezuela was one of the richest countries in the world." So Venezuela had supposedly enjoyed its wealthy status in 1997, the year before Hugo Chávez was first elected.[5] That's utter nonsense.

In reality, when Chávez was first elected in 1998, Venezuela had a 50 percent poverty rate despite having been a major oil exporter for several decades. It started exporting oil in the 1920s, and it was only in the early 1970s that the biggest Middle Eastern oil producers, Saudi Arabia and Iran, surpassed Venezuela in production.[6] In 1992, the *New York Times* reported that "only 57 percent of Venezuelans are able to afford more than one meal a day." Does that sound like "one of the richest countries in the world"?[7] Obviously not, but it is worth saying more about the statistics that can be used to mislead people about Venezuela's economic history.

Economists typically use GDP per capita to assess how rich a country is. It is basically a measure of the average income per person.[8] If journalists cared to be at all precise when they say that Venezuela had once been "rich," then that's a statistic they'd cite.

Figure 4.1 (page 61) shows World Bank data for Venezuela's real (inflation-adjusted) GDP per capita since 1960, and it contradicts the Western media's relentlessly insinuated story that a transition from prosperity to poverty took place because of Chavismo.[9] Real GDP per capita peaked in 1977, near the end of an oil boom, then went into a long-term decline. When Chávez0 took office in 1999, it was at one of its lowest points in decades. Then it was driven even lower by the first

Figure 4.1: GDP per Capita (constant local currency)

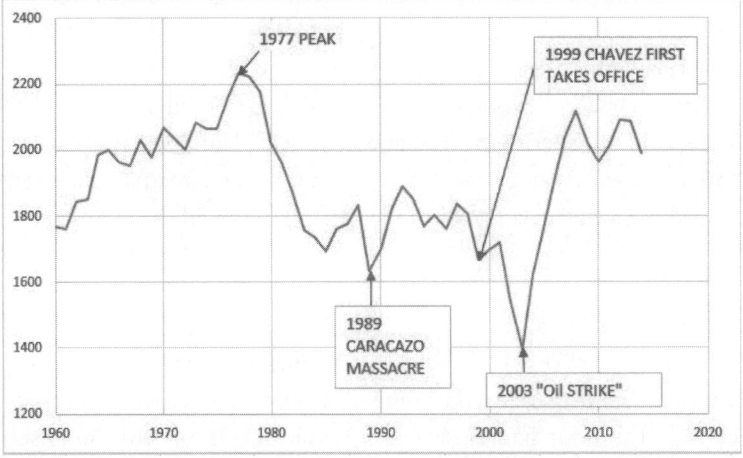

[Chart showing GDP per capita from 1960 to 2020, with annotations: "1977 PEAK", "1989 CARACAZO MASSACRE", "1999 CHAVEZ FIRST TAKES OFFICE", "2003 'Oil STRIKE'"]

Source: Compiled by the authors.

two attempts to oust Chávez: the April 2002 coup and, several months later, a shutdown of the state oil company—the "oil strike." By 2013, real GDP per capita recovered dramatically, nearly reaching its 1977 peak. Under Chávez, the poverty rate was cut in half, so there certainly is a correlation between GDP per capita and living conditions in Venezuela. But a country's GDP per capita, by itself, says nothing about how income is distributed. And that can also make international comparisons very misleading.

For example, 1980 was very close to Venezuela's historic peak in real GDP per capita, which ranked 32nd in the world that year when adjusted for purchasing power parity, as economists recommend for international comparisons. But its infant mortality rate ranked 58th in the world, far below Cuba, whose infant mortality rate was 28th that year.[10] Infant mortality is a basic health indicator that helps reveal the extent to which a country's wealth is actually being used to benefit its people. In fact, Venezuela's infant mortality rate in 1980 was more than twice as high as that in Cuba.[11] Another revealing year is 1989, when the massacre of poor demonstrators later known as the *Caracazo* took place. In terms of GDP per capita (adjusted for purchasing power parity), Venezuela ranked highest in Central and South America—while its government perpetrated the most infamous slaughter of poor people in its modern history.[12]

The massacre exposed the essentially fraudulent nature of Venezuela's prosperity and its democracy. It explains the rise of Chávez and also reveals how the U.S. government and media reflexively helped the Venezuelan government that perpetrated the massacre.

From Caracazo to Chavismo

It began on February 27, 1989.[13] Venezuelan security forces killed hundreds, and possibly thousands, of poor people over a five-day period. The poor had risen up in revolt against an IMF-imposed "structural adjustment" program that involved stiff hikes to fuel prices and bus fares. The program was imposed by President Carlos Andres Pérez, a man who had campaigned saying that IMF programs were like a "neutron bomb that killed people but left buildings standing."[14]

U.S. President George H. W. Bush called Pérez on March 3, 1989, while the *Caracazo* massacre was still taking place, to commiserate with Pérez and offer Venezuela loans. The U.S. media's Venezuela narrative suited Bush's foreign policy. On November 11, 1990, a *New York Times* article about Venezuela by Clifford Krause described Pérez as "a charismatic Social Democrat." Not a word was written about the *Caracazo* massacre. The article focused on Bush's gratitude toward Pérez for, among other things, boosting Venezuela's oil output to help protect the United States from negative economic consequences after the Iraqi invasion of Kuwait.[15]

On February 5, 1992, Lieutenant Colonel Hugo Chávez first became widely known to Venezuelans by attempting a military coup. The day Chávez's coup failed, a news article in the *New York Times* referred to Venezuela as "one of Latin America's relatively stable democratic governments" and to Pérez himself as "a leading democrat," despite the *Caracazo* massacre only three years earlier, which is never mentioned. The *Times* also quoted then-President Bush calling Pérez "one of the great democratic leaders of our hemisphere."[16]

Hugo Chávez had been secretly building a leftist movement within the military throughout the 1980s. It gained recruits and intensity after the *Caracazo* massacre. His 1992 coup attempt was initiated very close to midnight on February 4. By about 7:00 a.m. on February 5, it had completely failed, but the government allowed Chávez to briefly address the nation on TV, provided that he call on his troops to surrender.

In a seventy-two-second speech, Chávez appealed to his comrades to lay down their arms, and told Venezuelans that "for now" his objectives were not achieved. Twenty people were killed in the coup attempt. There appears to be widespread agreement that most of them were killed by Chávez's co-conspirators.[17] In November 1992, while Chávez was in jail, a second coup attempt was made by some of his supporters in the military. It was a much bloodier affair that left 171 people dead.[18]

Considering Chávez's electoral success several years later, the journalist Bart Jones's analysis of Chávez's brief 1992 speech seems right on target:

> Chávez's appearance was a bombshell . . . he did something almost inconceivable in a country where seemingly everybody dodged accountability: He took responsibility for a failure. "I accept responsibility for this Bolivarian military movement."
>
> He also indicated the rebellion wasn't over yet. Two words—*por ahora*, for now—sounded to many people like a pledge that the rebels would be back someday.[19]

Chávez served two years in prison which, considering he had attempted a coup, was a very light sentence. He was released by the government of Rafael Caldera, who was elected in 1994. The political system was by then so discredited that when Chávez attempted the coup Caldera had made statements that were sympathetic to it. But Chávez signaled his contempt for the entire establishment, which he blamed for the *Caracazo* massacre, by refusing to thank or meet with Caldera after receiving a pardon.[20]

Unfortunately, after he was elected in 1998, Chávez realized the coup attempt that catapulted his political career also handed his U.S.-backed opponents a handy rationalization for their own efforts to seize power by force: "Chávez once led a coup, so we can, too." Never mind that Chávez led *one* coup attempt, not several. He also went to jail for it immediately and did not receive the backing of the world's most powerful government (quite the contrary). More important, six years after his coup attempt, Chávez and his political allies went on to consistently triumph in elections. That alone speaks volumes about the crushing poverty and injustice under the political system he rebelled against—circumstances that are today written out of the story the U.S. government and Western media tell about Venezuela.

The Recruitment of Chávez, the Undoing of Punto Fijo

In 1958, a broad-based movement that included communists, liberals, and elements of the military overthrew the U.S.-backed dictatorship of Marcos Pérez Jiménez.[21] The capitalist democracy that governed Venezuela from that time until the Chavista era began was dominated by an agreement known as the "Pact of Punto Fijo." The pact was an arrangement by the dominant political parties to work together to marginalize their competitors. The pact was named after the "Quinta Punto Fijo," an estate in Caracas. Appropriately enough, "Punto Fijo" translated to English means "fixed point."[22]

Many Venezuelans, especially poor people, were left very unsatisfied with the "fixed" democracy. Some leftist groups resorted to armed struggle during the 1960s and '70s.[23] The 1959 Cuban Revolution was fresh and inspiring in young minds. Aspiring Venezuelan rebels took to the mountains—the same way that Che and Fidel started off in Cuba. The Venezuelan rebels didn't get involved in the battles the peasants were already fighting to seize land from the rural elite. Instead, small groups of rebels tried to initiate their own battles, assuming that these would develop their own following. It didn't happen. To make matters worse, Venezuela was rapidly urbanizing, which exacerbated the isolation of the rebels in the mountains by limiting their peasant base of support.

In the 1970s, armed rebels moved their operations to the expanding cities. The kidnapping of U.S. business executive William Niehous in 1976 was their most noteworthy (or infamous) act. The government responded fiercely and indiscriminately by assassinating, jailing, or disappearing people who were not involved.[24] The rebels therefore repulsed some poor people in the cities who had been trying to organize legally.

Douglas Bravo, a rebel leader, decided that an important lesson of their failures was that they needed to develop secret allies within the military. That led him to recruit Hugo Chávez, through Chávez's brother Adan. Venezuela's armed forces offered openings for that kind of activity, which most Latin American militaries did not. They provided much better advancement opportunities for people like Chávez who were dark-skinned and from humble backgrounds. And in 1971, when Chávez arrived at the military academy in Caracas, a revised curriculum gave cadets a much more well-rounded education which could even include a serious study of Marx. Cadets in that period were also less likely than their predecessors to study at U.S.-run military schools.[25] So, despite many rebel failures, that particular success—recruiting Chávez and others within the military—proved fateful when combined with other developments among poor people in Venezuelan cities.

The Overlooked Foundations of Chavismo

In *We Created Chávez*, the scholar and activist George Ciccariello-Maher explains that poor people in Venezuela's cities began organizing for self-help, but also for armed self-defense, throughout the 1970s. These organizations were independent of the former mountain-based rebels who aspired to lead them. As living conditions worsened during the 1980s, these popular militia became more influential. They often battled the drug trade in their neighborhoods, and that brought them into conflict with drug dealers and police. These militia and other (unarmed) political groups were the foundation of the vilified "colectivos" that would eventually bolster the Chávez government. As Ciccariello-Maher described:

> These were not petty bourgeois students headed to the hills, half-inspired by a sense of romantic adventure, but rather revolutionized poor fighting for their lives. . . .
> By 1991, the Barrio Assembly of Caracas had emerged as a sort of general assembly representing local groupings . . . long before Chávez's election, long before the communal councils, and long before even the Bolivarian Circles and the Patriotic Circles that had preceded them, there were barrio assemblies, the fruit of a long history of revolutionary failures and experimentation and the motor force of a new Venezuela.[26]

So the poor did not take things lying down as they were written out of the fairy tale of prosperous and democratic Venezuela before Chávez arrived on the scene. They organized, and even armed themselves, against an establishment that had proven it would massacre them to keep them hidden.

Chávez Was Not Another Pérez

When Chávez first took office in 1999, the U.S. government did not go immediately on the attack. When you consider the flashy anti-IMF campaign rhetoric of Carlos Andres Pérez—the president who then massacred people to implement an IMF austerity plan—it's unsurprising that the U.S. would feel Chávez out for a while. Maybe Chávez would be similarly phony—and therefore worthy of U.S. support.

By 2001, the U.S. government realized that Chávez was not going to be like Pérez, who made a sick joke of his anti-IMF rhetoric once he was in office. Chávez was actually going to try to follow through on his promises to change the system and assert his country's sovereignty. Chávez aggressively opposed the U.S. invasion of Afghanistan, and even said that the U.S. ambassador came calling and disrespectfully asked him to reverse his position. That provoked Chávez to order the ambassador out of the room.[27] This was a key event in the souring of Venezuela-U.S. relations.

Domestically, Chávez also had a short honeymoon period with Venezuela's old elite and the middle class. As Gregory Wilpert put it in *Changing Venezuela by Taking Power*:

> When Chávez first took office, he enjoyed approval ratings of 90%, which would suggest that racism and classism for eventual middle-class opposition to Chávez could not be an important factor.[28]
>
> Venezuela's middle class had been sliding into poverty for two decades and supported Chávez in 1998 because they were desperate for change.[29]

But soon enough the old political elite, like the U.S. ambassador, deeply resented Chávez asserting his authority. They had expected Chávez's deference. His African and Indigenous roots and his working-class origin could be overlooked, until he shunned the usual power brokers when making his cabinet appointments. The conflict intensified when a constituent assembly, elected by voters, drafted a new constitution which was then approved in a referendum. Transitional authorities were appointed under the new democratic order. As Wilpert described it: "The old elite then used its control of the country's mass media to turn the middle class against Chávez, creating a campaign that took advantage of the latent racism and classism in Venezuelan culture."[30]

By 2004, predictably, Chávez relied much more heavily on the support of poor people to win elections.[31]

A New Constitution, a New Era

In the first year he took office, Chávez initiated a three-step process to give Venezuela a new constitution.[32] In April 1999, he went to voters asking if they wanted to initiate the process by electing a constitutional assembly, and if they approved of the rules specifying how the assembly would be elected. His side won that referendum with 92 percent of the vote on the first question and with 86 percent on the second (which specified basic electoral rules).

Elections were then held in July to choose the members of the assembly. Chávez supporters won 125 of the assembly's 131 seats. The assembly then drafted a constitution and, four months later, it was approved by 72 percent of voters in another referendum.

The assembly also appointed a transitional body, known as a *Congressillo* (small congress), that appointed a new Attorney General, Human Rights Defender, Comptroller General, National Electoral Council, and Supreme Court.

In July 2000, Chávez went to voters again for a fresh presidential mandate under the new constitution and prevailed easily with 59.8 percent of the vote. But these were "mega-elections," as Wilpert put it, ones that "eliminated the country's old political elite almost entirely from the upper reaches of Venezuela's public institutions."

> Thirty-three thousand candidates ran for over 6,000 offices that day. In the end, Chávez was reconfirmed in office with 59.8% of the vote. Chávez's supporters won 104 out of 165 National Assembly seats and 17 out of 23 state governorships. On the local level Chávez candidates were less successful, winning only about half of the municipal mayors' posts.

Ominously, a *New York Times* editorial in August of 1999 already presumed to lecture Venezuelans and distort a very democratic reform process as a power grab:

> They should be very wary of the methods Mr. Chávez is using. He is drawing power into his own hands, and misusing a special Constitutional Assembly meeting now in Caracas that is composed almost entirely of his supporters.
>
> Mr. Chávez, a former paratroop commander who staged

an unsuccessful military coup in 1992, has so far shown little respect for the compromises necessary in a democracy, which Venezuela has had for 40 years.

Clearly, any genuine reform process in Latin America was going to be vilified by liberal outlets like the *New York Times*.

The lies peddled about Venezuela's past make U.S. aggression against it possible in the present. It is worth summing up some of these key lies:

Venezuela was "once prosperous" and ruined by socialism. In fact, Venezuela was an unequal country in which most people were poor despite the country's oil wealth, which had generated huge export revenues since the 1920s.

Venezuela was a democracy before Chavismo. In fact, Venezuela's democracy was a gravely flawed system in which politicians alternated holding power according to an undemocratic agreement and rammed austerity down the throats of Venezuela's poor by committing massacres, such as the *Caracazo*.

Chavismo ruined Venezuela's democracy. Chávez indeed attempted to carry out a coup in 1992, but he came to power through an election in 1998 and afterward made changes through extensive democratic processes.

PART II

Extraordinary Sedition (And Chavismo's Tolerance of It)

5

First Coup Attempt: April 2002

The first coup attempt against Hugo Chávez—one that was briefly successful—began on April 11, 2002. Chávez was deposed for two days, kidnapped by members of the military. Pedro Carmona, the head of Venezuela's largest business federation, Fedecameras, declared himself president.

Carmona issued a decree while he was in power. This was the infamous "Carmona Decree," a statement so wild that it alienated some of his allies who wanted the coup to have a veneer of legality. The decree dissolved the National Assembly and fired all Supreme Court judges as well as the Attorney General, the Comptroller General, the Human Rights Defender (*Defensor del Pueblo*), and the National Electoral Council. It even changed the name of the country. The word "Bolivarian" was taken out.[1]

The scholar and journalist Gregory Wilpert, who witnessed key events of the coup, summed up one ignored aspect of its significance:

> The coup showed just how popular Chávez really was and how determined his supporters were to prevent his overthrow. They went onto the streets, at great personal risk (over 60 people were

killed and hundreds were wounded by the police in the demonstrations that inspired the military to bring Chávez back to power), to demand their president's return to office.

The sixty victims Wilpert mentions do not include the nineteen people killed on the day of the coup, who were evenly split among Chávez supporters and opposition protesters. Five bystanders were also killed.[2]

Had the coup not temporarily succeeded, Chavistas might have struggled to convince anyone except their supporters that there had even been a coup attempt.[3] But the coup succeeded long enough to completely unmask numerous people and organizations in Venezuela and around the world as fraudulent democrats by the time Chávez was restored to power on April 14.

Separation of Oligarchy and State—Not Without a Fight

Months before it happened, a coup attempt began to look increasingly likely as Chávez, emboldened by numerous electoral victories within only three years, pushed through forty-nine decrees in November 2001. He was able to issue these decrees because the National Assembly granted him permission to do so through what is called an "enabling law," which was not new to Venezuela's government. Under the previous constitution, from 1961 to 1998, 172 decrees were passed through six different enabling laws.[4] There are constitutional ways to overturn these decrees in Venezuela, as there are in the United States in the case of presidential executive orders.[5] So why the outrage at the Chávez decrees? Among other things, the decrees in 2001 introduced redistributive measures such as land reform and established much greater presidential control over the state oil company, Petróleos de Venezuela, S.A. (PDVSA), to ensure that Chávez could pay for social programs.[6]

In the months before the coup, one rallying cry of the opposition was to "protect the meritocracy" at PDVSA. But any "meritocracy" within PDVSA had not benefited most Venezuelans in decades. There are also no compelling reasons for the state oil company to be independent of other democratically elected branches of government. This was really a demand that PDVSA managers who were loyal to Venezuela's traditional power brokers would deny Chávez the capacity to fund popular polices. This opposition tactic would be made even more obvious during the "oil strike" carried out months after the first coup attempt: attack Chávez by starving him of the funds to alleviate poverty. It was the same approach the United States would take against Maduro.

The fierce reaction to the Chávez decrees highlighted that the old power brokers still had undisputed control over Venezuela's private media. They also had support in Washington and, by extension, the Western media and big NGOs. Along with a hostile mass media, Chávez was confronted with strikes, protests, and, most ominously, mutinous acts by members of the military. In February 2002, for instance, Colonel Pedro Soto declared himself "in rebellion" and "in disobedience," alluding to Article 350 of Venezuela's new constitution, which legalized civil disobedience in response to unconstitutional acts by the government.[7] This obviously foreshadowed the coup attempt only two months later.

Chávez also faced the defection of some high-profile supporters who accused him of undermining democracy. Luis Miquilena, an advisor who won Chávez's trust back when Chávez was in jail for the 1992 coup attempt, resigned in January 2002 and began working with the opposition. In February, Chávez fired a general, Guaicaipuro Lameda, whom he had appointed to run PDVSA in 2000. On April 11, 2002, Lameda led a fateful protest march to the presidential palace, Miraflores, that provided the pretext for the coup. The mayor of Caracas at the time, Alfredo Peña, was also a onetime ally who turned bitter enemy several months before the coup.[8] Such defections were encouraged and amplified by Venezuela's private media which, as noted by Wilpert, was "largely taking the place of the discredited centrist and conservative parties."[9]

Chávez fought back against the private media through his weekly TV show *Alo Presidente*, which he broadcasted on state TV. He had launched the show in 1999.[10] But as the private media became more openly insurrectionary, he increasingly resorted to using *cadenas*, official government broadcasts that interrupted regular programming on all networks. That led the opposition, and the foreign governments, media, and NGOs that back them, to allege that "press freedom" was imperiled. They've been saying that ever since, in complete defiance of reality. For instance, sixteen years later, in 2018, Henri Falcón initiated his presidential campaign with a 35-minute tirade against Maduro that he delivered on state TV. Falcón also had ample access to Venezuela's private media throughout his campaign. As of 2019, somewhere between 60 and 90 percent of households had access to private TV media.[11] Second to the ludicrous claim that Venezuela is an "extraordinary threat" to the United States, the most inexcusable lie about Venezuela is the claim that the U.S.-backed opposition is voiceless in the mass media.

The True Story of the Coup that Was Only Conceded After the Fact

On April 11, 2002, opposition leaders diverted a protest march toward Miraflores, where they did not have a permit to demonstrate. That put opposition protesters in direct confrontation with Chavista counter-protesters who were stationed in front of Miraflores, after being tipped off that this might happen.

Police controlled by the anti-Chávez mayor of Caracas, who were probably joined by other opposition-aligned gunmen, exchanged fire with armed Chavistas. Nineteen people were killed, and this became the pretext for some military officers to rebel. It was not until after the coup was defeated that it was widely accepted that those nineteen deaths were evenly split between supporters and opponents of the government. Sixty people killed by Carmona's efforts to suppress the uprising that restored Chávez to power have been even more effectively written out of history.[12]

During the coup, Venezuela's private media blamed the April 11 deaths on Chávez ordering his supporters to fire on unarmed protesters. Some military men demanded his resignation. Chávez turned himself over to the mutinous generals so that they would not bomb

Miraflores, as they had threatened to do. He also agreed to resign provided that four conditions were met, the most important being that he would follow the constitution: he would resign in an address before the National Assembly, and the vice president would take over his job until new elections could be held.

The generals accepted his conditions, so Chávez authorized General Lucas Rincón Romero to announce that he would resign. But Chávez's captors reneged on their agreement and therefore Chávez never formally stepped down. In fact, while he was being held captive and cut off from the news that the coup was quickly unraveling, his captors attempted to trick him into signing a resignation letter.[13]

Events spiraled after Chávez was seized. Government officials were driven into hiding or arrested, and the state media was shut down. Carmona and his accomplices then used the absence of Chavista officials in public, or any access to the mass media for their supporters, to declare that there was a "power vacuum" they had to fill.[14] But Carmona's decree on April 12 was such a grotesque power grab, and his illegal appointments so partial to his own conservative faction of the opposition, that some of the coup perpetrators balked at supporting it. One notable example was the head of the army, General Vasquez Velasco. The journalist Bart Jones observed that Carmona had not appointed General Vasquez to any position—the general was "appointed to nothing," as Jones derisively put it.[15] Because of these internal rifts, the mobilization of Chavistas on the streets, and resistance by a loyalist sector of the military (in particular troops led by General Raúl Baduel), Chávez was officially restored to office by about 4:00 a.m. on April 14.

A very long list of people and institutions who peddled the story that Chávez had undermined democracy were exposed as frauds when the coup was defeated. If not for that defeat, the U.S.-backed opposition's story about the coup, one in which they cast themselves as democratic heroes, would have remained the dominant one. Instead, the truth about how various people and institutions supported the coup was revealed, in a process that might be called the Great Unmasking.

Venezuela's Private Media

On the day of the coup, Gregory Wilpert described the scene as he joined a crowd of pro-government supporters near an overpass, Puente Llaguno, that would become infamous thanks to footage manipulated by Venezuela's private TV media:

> Everyone seemed to be trying to hide behind the buildings that kept them protected from shots coming from the street below. At the two ends of the bridge I saw several men returning fire toward the street below, just as was later shown on television . . .
>
> Once home, we turned on the TV and I saw the scene that I had witnessed of the Chavistas shooting from the bridge. To my amazement, though, the announcer was claiming that the Chavistas were firing at the unarmed opposition demonstration. I could not believe my ears because I had seen—with my own eyes, from the bridge—that no opposition demonstrators were visible on the street below.[16]

Unfortunately for Venezuela's private media, the Irish filmmakers Kim Bartley and Donnacha O'Brian happened to be in Caracas to interview Chávez when the coup took place. They produced a documentary, *The Revolution Will Not Be Televised*, that confirmed everything Wilpert had said about the Venezuelan private media's stunning dishonesty regarding the gunfight on the Llaguno Bridge—and much else.[17]

The documentary's power is derived largely from its ability to expose the hubris of the opposition and, as the title suggests, the pivotal role in the coup played by Venezuela's private media. Chávez opponents in the National Palace are shown rapturously cheering every sentence of the Carmona decree as it was read out. The film also vividly captures what journalist Eirik Vold described as "fierce competition" to "fill the key positions in Pedro Carmona's government."[18] Getting in front of TV cameras to pose as the heroes who brought down Chávez was an essential part of that competition, and the competitors were also keen to thank the media for its help. But as the coup unraveled in the streets and in pro-Chávez military barracks, the celebratory interviews on TV screens were largely replaced by silence.[19] The documentary shows Chavista officials struggling to overcome the private media's blackout even after they had regained control of the National Palace and detained some of Carmona's accomplices there. An excerpt is shown of a CNN interview with Carmona who (by telephone) told the network he had "total" control over the country.

For years afterward, on the anniversary of the coup, Chavistas would remind people of the front-page headlines and articles that appeared in the aftermath of the coup in opposition newspapers like *El Nacional, El Universal, Tal Cual*, and many others.[20] On April 12, the day after Chávez was overthrown, an editorial in *El Universal*, one of Venezuela's largest newspapers, stated: "Repugnant images were seen of sinister characters linked to the regime shooting at defenseless citizens." It ended breathlessly: "Freedom is the most precious value of the individual. What happened yesterday shows it. Let's strive for it!" The next day, after Carmona's Decree, a huge headline in *El Universal* declared "One Step Forward!" On April 12, an editorial in *El Nacional* titled "Hugo's deaths" began "We already knew about his mental problems. . . ." *Tal Cual*'s editorial that day was titled "Chao Hugo." It said that "those responsible for yesterday's killings must be found and brought to justice, starting with Chávez himself."

Other newspapers were similarly supportive of the coup and would soon have their words thrown back at them with contempt. "The Assassin Fell," blared a headline in *Asi es La Noticia*.[21] They had unmasked themselves as hypocrites and would not be allowed to forget it when they resumed publishing articles invoking democracy, human rights, or press freedom to attack the government.

The Western Media

The *New York Times* editorial board was delighted by the coup. An April 13 editorial said that Chávez's "resignation" meant that "Venezuelan democracy is no longer threatened by a would-be dictator." The *Times* claimed that Chávez "stepped down after the military intervened and handed power to a respected business leader."[22]

But as the media watchdog group Fairness and Accuracy in Reporting (FAIR) put it, "Three days later, Chávez had returned to power, and the *Times* ran a second editorial (4/16/02) half-apologizing for having gotten carried away." The *Times*'s half-apology stated:

> In his three years in office, Mr. Chávez has been such a divisive and demagogic leader that his forced departure last week drew applause at home and in Washington. That reaction, which we shared, overlooked the undemocratic manner in which he was removed. Forcibly unseating a democratically elected leader, no matter how badly he has performed, is never something to cheer.

The *Chicago Tribune*'s editorial board wrote on April 14, "It's not every day that a democracy benefits from the military's intervention to force out an elected president." This statement was contemptuous of democracy, of course, but it was also embarrassing to applaud a military coup on the same day that democracy was restored. In fairness, events moved quickly, but the Venezuelan private media's blackout of the anti-coup uprising must also have helped U.S. newspapers make fools of themselves. If they had seen reports that the coup might be defeated, they would probably not have been so quick to welcome it.

A *Washington Post* editorial published on April 14, titled "Venezuela's Breakdown," started off strongly and seemed to set the *Post* admirably apart from the rest of the U.S. media: "Any interruption of democracy in Latin America is wrong, the more so when it involves the military." But the *Post* then portrayed the military men who ousted Chávez as the lesser evil—and depicted the coup as problematic but necessary. The *Post* editors noted that the Carmona Decree resulted in "abolishing Congress and the Supreme Court," and they conceded that the decree posed "dangers," so they advised Carmona's dictatorship to somehow "shape a transition that eases rather than accentuates the country's political polarization."

The *Post* editorial expressed some discomfort with the coup, unlike the *New York Times* or *Chicago Tribune* editorial boards, but was still supportive. The *Post* also claimed that Chávez had "exploited" poverty and inequality when he was first elected to successfully rally "much of the country" against the "political and economic elite." Of course, the *Post* did not say that capitalism had saddled oil-rich Venezuela with poverty and inequality. By 2017, major media outlets routinely suggested that Venezuela was prosperous when Chávez first took office, but then became poor due to the socialist policies of Chávez and Maduro.

To write his book *Bad News from Venezuela*, the journalist and scholar Alan MacLeod examined 501 articles (both news and opinion) in the U.S. and UK media from 1998 to 2013. He gathered his sample of articles from periods during which newsworthy events took place—one of which was obviously the April 2002 coup.[23]

Only 10 percent of the U.S. media articles from the coup period of MacLeod's sample mentioned potential U.S. involvement. Some of them even denied it. For instance, the *Washington Post* editorial mentioned above assured its readers that "there's been no suggestion that the United States had anything to do with this Latin American coup" despite "Mr. Chávez's frequent provocations."

Scott Wilson, reporting for the *Post* on April 21, offered a rare exception to the practice of denying U.S. involvement. Wilson wrote that one of the perpetrators, Rear Admiral Carlos Molina, told him, while under house arrest: "We felt we were acting with U.S. support. We agree that we can't permit a communist government here. The U.S. has not let us down yet. This fight is still going on because the government is illegal."

Wilson's article also mentioned meetings between Molina and members of the International Republican Institute, a foreign policy think tank informally affiliated with the Republican Party whose top officials were well connected with the Bush administration.[24] But this was an all too rare exception to the U.S. media's practice of reinforcing the U.S. government's perspective on the coup.

Meanwhile, across the pond, the UK media offered some contrast with the United States. On the basic matter of reporting that a coup had taken place, MacLeod found that UK newspapers got that much right. They reported the coup as a coup. The U.S. media, on the other hand, gave approximately equal weight to some kind of "alternative explanation." The *New York Times* stood out from the pack in its efforts to depict the coup as some kind of popular uprising. Table 5.1 (page 83) draws on MacLeod's data.[25]

Both U.S. and UK newspapers almost completely buried the central role of the Venezuelan private media in the coup as well. MacLeod wrote: "Of the 139 articles in the 2002 sample, seven mentioned possible media involvement." Duncan Campbell of the *Guardian* was the only journalist to make a strong case about the media's involvement in the coup, noting that the media "certainly played a major part" by collaborating with the coup plotters, then imposing an information blackout once Chávez supporters rallied to take back the palace. According to MacLeod, thirty-nine percent of newspaper articles in UK media mentioned possible U.S. involvement in the coup, but "only the *Guardian* presented U.S. involvement as a strong possibility."

The *Guardian*, by reputation, is one of the most left-leaning outlets among major Western newspapers. Considering the horrendous coverage of the coup published elsewhere, it deserves a bit of credit, as MacLeod noted. But the *Guardian* also produced some appalling coverage.

Consider an article by Alex Bellos, the *Guardian*'s South America correspondent, during a very crucial time, just after Chávez was restored to office, when readers would be paying much closer attention than usual to news coverage of Venezuela.[26] Apparently, Bellos was only able to find witnesses who backed the pretext for the defeated coup: "When the [opposition] march drew close to the Miraflores palace witnesses reported seeing Chávez snipers fire at the crowds, killing more than 16 people."

Now consider how Bellos, in the same article, goes on to describe the roughly sixty deaths that occurred during the uprisings against Carmona's dictatorship:

TABLE 5.1: U.S./UK Newspaper Reporting of April 2002 Coup

Newspaper	Coup	Alternative Explanation
The Independent	2	2
The Times	8	3
The Guardian	37	3
The Daily Telegraph	7	4
TOTAL (UK)	**54**	**12**
New York Times	22	84
Washington Post	30	24
Miami Herald	58	46
TOTAL (U.S.)	**110**	**154**

Source: Compiled by the authors.

Meanwhile, in the streets of Caracas, thousands of demonstrators supporting Mr. Chávez—or opposed to the way he was ousted—took over state TV to demand his return. Police fired water cannon and teargas. Agency reports claimed that dozens died in the violence.

Bellos switched to the passive voice to report deaths that totally implicated Carmona's dictatorship: "dozens died." Who killed them? Corporate journalists regularly use the passive voice to describe crimes perpetrated by the United States or its allies. There are no "Carmona shooters" in Bellos's article, as there were "Chávez snipers."

Bellos also accepted the opposition story so completely that, even as tens of thousands risked their lives to restore Chávez to power, Bellos speculated that they might not have supported Chávez but only objected to "the way" Chávez was overthrown. Did he see placards saying "Not this kind of coup!" or "Oust Chávez the right way!"? Do protesters risk their lives to bring back a government they dislike?

In the same article, Bellos falsely claimed that "Hugo Chávez led two failed military coups before he took power via the ballot box, in 1998." This falsehood was stated twice in the article. Chávez led a single coup *attempt* in 1992. Chávez was imprisoned for two years for making that attempt. There was another coup attempt in 1992 but Chávez, who was in prison, did not lead it.

Bellos's article claimed that Venezuela had an 85 percent poverty rate at the time of the coup, a huge exaggeration—though it was true that income poverty spiked to a high of 62 percent early in 2003, after an oil strike that was part of the opposition's efforts to overthrow Chávez. Bellos also said that Chávez had only 30 percent support at the time he was briefly ousted. The 30 percent figure almost certainly came from Datanalisis, the anti-government polling firm. The *Guardian*. despite its progressive reputation at the time, and some differences with outlets that were even more supportive of the coup, did not offer much of an alternative to the anti-Chávez consensus in the rest of the UK media. It's a consensus that would endure and solidify for years.

While MacLeod analyzed print media, British researchers Lee Salter and Dave Weltman examined ten years' worth of BBC coverage of Hugo Chávez's government. Regarding the coup, Salter described their findings:

> BBC News published nine articles on the coup on 12th April 2002, all of which were based on the coup leaders' version of events, who were, alongside the "opposition," championed as saviours of "the nation." Although BBC News did report the coup, the only time it mentioned the word "coup" was as an allegation of government officials and of Chávez's daughter.[27]

In the internet age, when people can much more easily access media from around the world, it's especially significant that the UK media in general offered no significant alternative to the U.S. media when the coup took place. Additionally, the more foreign coverage resembles U.S. coverage the easier it is for Western governments to parrot much of what Washington claims about Venezuela.

The U.S. Government

On April 12, the George W. Bush administration's press secretary Ari Fleischer, told reporters the following about the coup:

> We know that the action encouraged by the Chávez government provoked this crisis. According to the best information available, the Chávez government suppressed peaceful demonstrations. Government supporters, on orders from the Chávez government, fired on unarmed, peaceful protesters, resulting in 10 killed and 100 wounded. The Venezuelan military and the police refused to fire on the peaceful demonstrators and refused to support the government's role in such human rights violations. The government also tried to prevent independent news media from reporting on these events.
>
> The results of these events are now that President Chávez has resigned the presidency. Before resigning, he dismissed the vice president and the cabinet, and a transitional civilian government has been installed. This government has promised early elections.
>
> The United States will continue to monitor events. That is what took place, and the Venezuelan people expressed their right to peaceful protest. It was a very large protest that turned out. And the protest was met with violence.[28]

It's remarkable that, while completely endorsing all the opposition's lies and recognizing the legitimacy of the "transitional civilian government," Fleischer was restrained in expressing his support for the coup when compared with the *New York Times* editorial board.

A typical way that U.S. officials deny their involvement in any coup is to raise the standard for what counts as "involvement" to such a high level that the United States would have to micromanage every aspect of the coup, or even carry it out directly, for this to count as "involvement." The U.S. State Department's Office of the Inspector General took that approach in a report from July 2002 titled "A Review of US

Policy Toward Venezuela November 2001–April 2002."²⁹ The report, despite attempting a whitewash, is nonetheless extremely damning of the United States and shows, to any reasonable person, that the U.S. government did not just support the coup from afar—that is, through public remarks made by people like Ari Fleischer—but provided material support to the perpetrators. The report stated:

> While it is clear that NED, Department of Defense (DOD), and other U.S. assistance programs provided training, institution building, and other support to individuals and organizations understood to be actively involved in the brief ouster of the Chávez government, we found no evidence that this support directly contributed, or was intended to contribute, to that event.

Imagine Russia also confirming that it had provided "training, institution building, and other support" to people who had been involved in a military coup in the United States. We'd end up with World War III, not a debate about whether this was sufficient evidence to say that Russia was involved. Any U.S. citizen who denied Putin's involvement would be called an imbecile (at best), and more likely a traitor or a spy.

The State Department's Inspector General also reported: "Both the Department and the Embassy worked behind the scenes to persuade the interim government to hold early elections and to legitimize its provisional rule by obtaining the sanction of the National Assembly and the Supreme Court." Would Russia be absolved if it admitted to working "behind the scenes" with coup perpetrators in the United States and encouraging them to legalize their crimes after the fact?

Also in the report: U.S. Embassy staff "urged opponents of the Chávez government to act within the limits of the constitution." But as the U.S. economist Mark Weisbrot remarked, "all the admonishments from the U.S. Embassy about not supporting a coup—while Washington was funneling millions of dollars to pro-coup organizations—were a mere formality. The real message was a big green light."³⁰ Moreover, the United States and the opposition simply defined "the limits of the constitution" in such a way that allowed a coup, and the U.S. message that mattered most to the perpetrators was supported by a continuous flow of U.S. funds, as Weisbrot argued.

By 2004, using the Freedom of Information Act, the investigative journalists Jeremy Bigwood and Eva Golinger uncovered more specifics about who exactly the U.S. government was funding. Among the more prominent Venezuelan opposition leaders whose organizations received U.S. funds were Leopoldo López, years later designated by Amnesty International as a "Prisoner of Conscience," and María Corina Machado, often portrayed flatteringly in Western media as a brave dissenting voice in Venezuela. Others, such as Leopoldo Martínez and Leonardo Carvajal, were appointed as ministers by Carmona.[31] In 2010, Scott Wilson of the *Washington Post* committed a rare feat of intellectual honesty for a corporate journalist:

> The United States was hosting people involved in the coup before it happened. There was involvement of U.S.-sponsored NGOs in training people that were involved in the coup. And in the immediate aftermath of the coup the United States government said that it was a resignation, not a coup, effectively recognizing the government that took office very briefly until President Chávez returned. I think there was U.S. involvement, yes.[32]

That's quite a contrast with what the *Guardian* would say in a 2018 article by Joe Parkin Daniels:

> It later emerged that the administration of George W Bush had known about the coup plot, although distanced itself publicly from involvement. That did not stop Chávez from describing the episode as yet another example of US imperialistic intervention.

Facts did not stop the *Guardian* from describing U.S. involvement in the coup as a dubious allegation made by Chávez. This passage was even worse before one of the authors of this book complained to the

Guardian. The earlier version claimed that the Bush administration "did not support" the coup, despite the unmasking of the U.S. role that was provided by the U.S. government's own report in 2002 and an abundance of other publicly available information.[33]

The IMF, which has always been dominated by the U.S. Treasury Department, immediately offered loans to the Carmona dictatorship. IMF spokesperson Thomas Dawson, a former U.S. State Department and Treasury official, stated that the Fund was "ready to assist the new administration [of Pedro Carmona] in whatever manner they find suitable."[34]

HRW's "As Soon As Possible" Scam[35]

Human Rights Watch (HRW) published a press release on April 11 titled "Restore Rule of Law, Protect Rights in Venezuela."[36] It said in part:

> We call upon the transitional authorities in Venezuela to restore the country's democratic institutions as soon as possible and to guarantee that the human rights of Venezuelans will not be violated, regardless of their political beliefs or affiliations. . . . Human Rights Watch is deeply concerned that President Chávez may not have left office voluntarily, but rather that he may have been forced to leave by military commanders, outside of a democratic, participatory process. . . .
>
> According to press reports, President Hugo Chávez Frías left office under pressure by the Venezuelan armed forces early Friday morning. He is currently held by the military on an army base in Caracas. Pedro Carmona Estanga, head of Venezuela's largest business association, Fedecámaras, announced that he would head a transitional government. . . .
>
> We call on the authorities to ensure that any searches or possible detentions of Chávez supporters be conducted in full compliance with the law and with the basic standards of due process.

HRW basically played dumb. It tried to cover itself by saying it was "deeply concerned that President Chávez may not have left office voluntarily." But the very next paragraph acknowledges that Chávez was being "held by the military" according to "press reports," and that it was "announced" that an unelected businessman was running a "transitional government." Surely that was enough for a credible human rights group to demand that Chávez be restored.

Where does Venezuela's democratically ratified constitution stipulate that unelected businessmen get to "announce" that they will run the country when the president has been kidnapped (or even if the president had been legally arrested)?[37] Nowhere, obviously. HRW should have demanded that the so-called authorities, the coup perpetrators, immediately renounce their illegitimate authority, as they were soon forced to do. There was no other way to "restore the rule of law and protect rights" in Venezuela.

If Chávez had truly wanted to resign, there was a constitutional way to do it. That obviously hadn't happened. If it were true that Chávez had crimes to answer for, the constitution specified how such crimes should be addressed. Elected officials and the legally appointed Supreme Court were supposed to govern that process—not an unelected businessman and whichever military men he had behind him. But instead of defending the rule of law in Venezuela, HRW merely asked that the "transitional authorities" not be too rough as they carried out illegal "detentions of Chávez supporters," and that they give their coup some democratic cover "as soon as possible."

HRW's press release also said nothing about the OAS Democratic Charter, another important omission. Two years later, when HRW said that the Democratic Charter should be invoked against the Chávez government over an alleged "court-packing law," the group disingenuously claimed that the Charter had been crucial to mobilizing a "chorus of condemnation" that restored Chávez to office in 2002.[38] But at that time HRW was certainly not part of any "chorus of condemnation" that helped overturn the coup. It never even called for Chávez to be restored.

Four months after the coup, on August 14, a Venezuelan Supreme

Court ruling acquitted key perpetrators of the coup.[39] What was Chávez supposed to do about that ruling? Nothing? As Gregory Wilpert later argued, the "question thus became one of which precedent is more dangerous, that of allowing a coup to go unpunished or that of fixing a dysfunctional court by 'packing' it."[40] Two years later, HRW dismissed this huge countervailing concern and absurdly equated the "court-packing law" to the coup itself.

HRW did not call for invoking the OAS Democratic Charter when Jean-Bertrand Aristide, Haiti's democratically elected president, was overthrown by U.S. troops in February 2004. The subsequent dictatorship under Gérard Latortue would later fire half of Haiti's Supreme Court. HRW did not call for the OAS Charter to be invoked over that, either. HRW also did not object in 2018—and, in fact, applauded—when Ecuadorian president Lenín Moreno trampled all over judicial independence by having a body he handpicked stack the judiciary.[41] In November 2019, HRW responded just as disgracefully when a U.S.-backed military coup ousted Bolivian President Evo Morales. HRW America's Director, José Miguel Vivanco, explicitly called the coup-installed dictatorship of Jeanine Áñez a "democracy," and, as Morales fled Bolivia for his life, HRW's executive director, Ken Roth, accused Morales of "lawlessness" for "packing the Constitutional Court with his followers."[42]

HRW's conception of "judicial independence," aside from being selectively invoked when its serves Washington's interests, is also shallow. A judiciary may act independently of an elected branch of government while, in reality, serving unelected power brokers. The judiciary in a democratic society should ultimately be accountable to voters, like any other branch of government. In the United States during the Great Depression, President Franklin Roosevelt threatened to pass a "court-packing law" in order to protect New Deal programs, a law somewhat like the one passed by Chávez.[43] Had Roosevelt followed through on his threat (which is actually what U.S. lawmaker Alexandria Ocasio-Cortez said Joe Biden should do as president) would that have been equivalent to a military coup, as HRW essentially alleged about Chávez's judicial reforms by invoking the OAS Democratic Charter against them?[44] One can make good arguments for and against various types of "court packing," but it's clearly not something on which HRW is remotely consistent or principled. Equating the coup that ousted Chávez to his efforts to reform a pro-coup Supreme Court was preposterous.

Significantly, HRW made no call for an immediate and independent investigation into the U.S. role during the 2002 coup in Venezuela, nor did it demand any such investigation two years later, when U.S. troops kidnapped the president of Haiti. And yet, in 2008, HRW's Americas director José Miguel Vivanco publicly demanded that the Chávez government "provide a full accounting of its relationship" with the Armed Revolutionary Forces of Colombia (FARC) and that the OAS undertake a "rigorous and impartial" investigation of links between FARC and Venezuela.[45]

Amnesty International's Credibility Takes a Beating

A Factiva search of major English language newspapers turns up no statement by Amnesty International regarding the coup during the crucial days April 11 to 13. A search of the March 1 to April 30 period of 2002, using "Amnesty International" and "Venezuela," did not turn up any articles that quoted Amnesty about Venezuela. This mirrors a pattern on Amnesty's own website, where a statement specifically about the coup attempts against Chávez did not appear until December 19, 2002—a statement that equated the government with the opposition and said absolutely nothing to denounce U.S. involvement in, by then, two major coup attempts. Amnesty expanded on that approach a few weeks later, saying: "The government, the opposition and the media have appropriated, manipulated and distorted the issue of human rights, converting it into one more weapon for polarization and confrontation."[46]

Equating Chávez with the people trying to oust him would have been bad enough, but, in this statement, Amnesty also said that Chávez "has the main responsibility" for implementing Amnesty's recommendations for "restoring full respect for Human Rights" as part of a "long-term human rights agenda." Amnesty's real agenda appeared to be absolving the world's only superpower from all responsibility for trying to overthrow Chávez, and shifting as much blame as possible away from U.S. allies in Venezuela. As another incident would show, Amnesty was not above resorting to censorship to further that agenda.

A November 22, 2003, article in the *Guardian* ran with the headline "Chávez film puts staff at risk, says Amnesty."[47] Did Chávez make a film that threatened Amnesty's staff? No. A clear and accurate headline would have said "Pro-Chávez film rejected by Amnesty." The "Chávez film"—which Amnesty rejected from a film festival in Canada, insinuating it might provoke *opposition supporters* to attack its staff in Venezuela—was *The Revolution Will Not Be Televised*, the documentary that exposed the Venezuelan private media's manipulative coverage during the coup. Apparently, Fernando M. Fernandez, who has written reports for Amnesty about Venezuela throughout the Chavista era, was the key person in Venezuela who convinced Amnesty to reject the film.[48]

But jump ahead to May 11, 2019, and Fernando M. Fernandez was retweeting calls by opposition leaders to protest in the streets against Nicolás Maduro. In fact, Fernandez's Twitter timeline has consistently directed a steady stream of vitriol at Maduro's government. On April 1, Fernandez said "dictatorship" was too weak a word to describe Maduro's government and that it was now a "tyranny."[49] By this time, the opposition's sixth major coup attempt was underway; yet Fernandez had no apparent concern that his vehement attacks on Maduro's government would endanger Amnesty's staff or the staff of any other NGOs in Venezuela with which it collaborates.[50]

Amnesty's excuse for not screening *The Revolution Will Not Be Televised* in 2003 was clearly bogus. Amnesty's Venezuela-based staff, especially Fernando Fernandez, obviously calculated that the opposition would be best served by having Amnesty pull the film and, even if its excuse tacitly blamed opposition supporters, it would be widely interpreted as Amnesty rejecting the content of the film, and thereby limiting its audience and credibility abroad.[51]

Another indication of Amnesty's bias was that it designated the opposition politician Leopoldo López, despite his proud participation in the 2002 coup, a "Prisoner of Conscience" when he finally went to jail in 2014. Nelson Mandela never qualified for that designation in Amnesty's opinion, nor did Chelsea Manning or Julian Assange. How in the world could somebody with López's track record get it?

During the coup, a Chávez minister, Ramón Rodríguez Chacín, was repeatedly punched in the head while Leopoldo López and Henrique Capriles, another prominent opposition politician, led him through a hostile mob. Leopoldo López told reporters that the abduction of the minister had been "well done" and that "President Carmona"—an illegitimate title for a dictator—was aware of it.[52] López would go on to support three more coup attempts before he was finally arrested.

Ernesto Villegas Poljak, a journalist who went on to become a Venezuelan government minister in 2012 (and is presently the Culture Minister) wrote a book about the April 2002 coup titled "Inside the April Coup." He wrote that he met Fernando M. Fernandez, then president of Amnesty International's Venezuela division, in the offices of the newspaper *El Universal* on April 12. Villegas said he asked Fernandez about the abduction of Ramón Rodríguez Chacín. According to Villegas, Fernandez dismissed the incident and said of the minister's injuries, "It was just a few bumps."[53] Given Amnesty's bias in support of the opposition, Villegas's account seems highly credible.[54] With a person like Fernandez as Amnesty's key source, it is clear that López was absurdly granted Prisoner of Conscience status to bolster U.S. propaganda and impunity for its allies.

Et Tu, *Carter Center*?

In 2002, four days after the coup failed, an op-ed by Jennifer McCoy, then the Carter Center's director for the Americas, appeared in the *New York Times*.[55] She wrote that the "Chávez regime" had been "threatening the country's democratic system of checks and balances and freedom of expression of its citizens." She also said that Pedro Carmona, the dictator who had just been ousted in an uprising that left scores of Chavistas dead, "seemed to demonstrate autocratic instincts as strong as those driving Mr. Chávez." She equated a dictator who seized power at the point of a gun with a president who, by 2002, had prevailed in multiple democratic contests: two presidential election victories (1998 and 2000), along with the related victories in referenda, Constituent Assembly elections, National Assembly elections, and local elections. She accused the United States of sending "mixed signals" and said it was "not sufficiently firm about defending basic democratic values." There was nothing "mixed" about the U.S. response. It solidly backed Carmona's dictatorship. McCoy continued, criticizing Chávez (and by extension, his base among the poor) for "inflammatory rhetoric, which encouraged class polarization." So while denouncing alleged threats to "freedom of expression," she called for restricting the freedom of expression of the poor and their elected representatives—so as not to provoke Venezuela's oligarchs.

In 2004, the Carter Center would push back effectively against opposition lies that a recall referendum, which Chávez won by almost 20 percentage points, had been stolen. The Center would do other valuable work in 2013: a report on the first election won by Nicolás Maduro that contained important data on Venezuela's media, showing it was not dominated by the government. That honesty would set it apart from other big NGOs, such as Human Rights Watch and Amnesty International. And yet, the Carter Center is nonetheless deeply embedded in the U.S. establishment and shares its assumptions, as McCoy's hostile op-ed demonstrated.

The U.S. establishment is one that is never held accountable even after being completely unmasked by events such as the 2002 coup. Hence, more U.S. attempts to overthrow Venezuela's democratically elected government would follow.

6

Second Coup Attempt: Oil Strike, December 2002–February 2003

On October 21, 2002, six months after the defeated coup, the opposition organized a one-day national strike aimed at forcing Chávez's resignation. The following day, they began a symbolic takeover—or "liberation," as the opposition called it—of a plaza in Altamira, part of the wealthy Chacao district in East Caracas. The opposition leader Leopoldo López was mayor of this district—despite his participation in the April coup he was still in public office.[1]

Emboldened by an August 14 Supreme Court ruling that cleared four high-ranking military men who participated in the coup that ousted Chávez, about a hundred officers joined the Altamira Plaza protest by October 25.[2] Vice Admiral Daniel Comisso Urdaneta, one of the four officers cleared by the Supreme Court, told the press that the plaza "liberation" was "the most entertaining coup in the world."[3] Fedecameras, the business federation once led by Pedro Carmona, openly backed the officers, as did Carlos Ortega, leader of the Confederación de Trabajadores de Venezuela (CTV) union federation and a perpetrator of the April coup. Once again, Article 350 of the constitution, which permits civil disobedience in response to unconstitutional acts by the government, was invoked. The protest was quite a spectacle of elite impunity and delusion: supporters of Carmona's dictatorship claimed to be fighting for democracy.

In addition to the Supreme Court's ruling on the military officers, there is no doubt the protesters were emboldened by ongoing U.S. funding and related support. Chávez ignored the plaza "liberation" and the protest, though it continued, failed to get much attention.[4]

On December 2, the opposition escalated its tactics by beginning to target the oil industry. Officially, they kicked off a general strike, but outside of opposition strongholds like eastern Caracas, businesses overwhelmingly stayed open. Focusing on the state oil company, PDVSA, which at that time provided about 80 percent of Venezuela's foreign exchange, was far more threatening to the government. On December 3, employees and management at PDVSA who supported the opposition began to walk off the job. That same day, as the National Guard used tear gas to disperse protests outside the PDVSA offices, the National Electoral Council (CNE) voted 4 to 1 to hold a non-binding referendum in February on whether Chávez should continue as president—a proposal that Chávez opposed. But the opposition, unwilling to risk leaving things to voters who had repeatedly handed Chávez victories, ignored the CNE's decision and continued sabotaging PDVSA.[5]

Venezuela's 1999 constitution allows for a binding recall referendum halfway through a president's six-year term, if those seeking the referendum collect enough signatures in support of the measure. In fact, a year and a half later, Chávez would win such a recall referendum, in August 2004. What the opposition was pushing for at this point, in 2002, was another forced resignation, as they had during the April coup—but this time by using economic sabotage. Their strategy was to legitimize their tactics with a call for early elections exactly as they and their foreign apologists had done in the immediate aftermath of the Carmona Decree.

On December 3, the *New York Times* reported that the Bush government, totally disregarding the democratic legitimacy of Venezuela's government, called for early elections, which meant that the United

States was winking at this second coup attempt. Ignoring overwhelming evidence (including the State Department's Inspector General report, released only five months earlier) the *New York Times* stated: "In April, the United States *appeared* to support a coup against Mr. Chávez."[6] Appearance indeed; the article then added, "In the past year or more, the United States has also channeled hundreds of thousands of dollars in grants to American and Venezuelan groups opposed to Mr. Chávez." Even with a second U.S.-backed coup attempt underway, the evidence could never be strong enough or fresh enough for the *Times* to state the obvious: U.S. policy sought the overthrow of the Chávez government.

Everyone Wants Chávez Out—Even His Family

On December 4, 2002, Daniel Alfaro, the captain of a PDVSA oil tanker, the *Pilin León*, dropped anchor in Lake Maracaibo. The lake is actually a bay, and a major shipping route to the Caribbean. (Like many ships at that time, the *Pilin León* was named after a Venezuelan beauty contest winner, a practice that would soon end.) The captain said that he was acting in protest of Chávez "pushing us into a situation like Cuba." Dozens of oil tankers soon joined his protest, which magnified the impact of a walkout that had already been initiated by PDVSA's upper management and some workers. The journalist Bart Jones wrote:

> Alfaro and the other captains became the latest instant heroes to the opposition. Hundreds of supporters gathered on the shoreline of Lake Maracaibo with the *Pilin León* in sight. Others circled the vessel with yachts, motorboats, canoes, and even kayaks to "protect" it if soldiers tried to board. León herself, a Miss World 1981 who was now in her forties, eventually made her way out to Lake Maracaibo to support the strikers.[7]

On December 6, the ongoing Altamira Plaza "liberation" protests, which had limped along ineffectually for weeks, became a center of attention again when a deranged gunman, who did not even flee the scene of the crime, opened fire on the crowd assembled there. He killed three people. The opposition blamed Chávez, reinvigorating the protests and hardening their insistence that he had to resign.[8]

In an article about the shooting published on December 7, the *New York Times* quoted Julio Borges, an opposition legislator (also a founder, with Leopoldo López and Henrique Capriles, of the Primero Justicia Party) who would become president of the National Assembly fourteen years later. Borges said, "The president should resign to open the path to 24 million Venezuelans who want their liberty." With tweaks to the population figure, that would sum up his stance toward the Chavista government for the next two decades.[9] Borges, Leopoldo López, the military men leading the Altamira protests—the article mentioned all of them but never identified them as supporters of the coup that ousted Chávez and imposed a U.S.-backed dictatorship only eight months earlier. The article also uncritically quoted the U.S. government expressing its concern. Toward the end of the article, readers were vaguely informed, in a passive voice, that "the shooting came eight months after a huge anti-government protest ended in gunfire, leaving at least 19 people dead. Mr. Chávez was temporarily removed from power in the chaos afterward." Who exactly removed Chávez? During every U.S.-backed coup attempt against the Venezuelan government since 2002, the slate is always wiped clean, as the same perpetrators attempt another one.

On December 10, Chávez's ex-wife, Marisabel, appeared on TV with their daughter sitting next to her and implored Chávez to "listen to the people" and resign. She had left Chávez shortly after the coup in April and would be an outspoken opposition supporter for years.[10] Presenting a former supporter turned opponent (in this case, a close family member) insinuated that there was overwhelming opposition to the president, and therefore suggested that the president's refusal to resign could only lead to catastrophe. But journalists often accomplished this suggestion simply by stacking articles with anti-Chávez sources, and presenting fierce Chávez opponents as unbiased observers.

For example, the same day that Chávez's ex-wife urged him to resign, the journalist Juan Forero wrote in the *New York Times* that "Mr. Chávez faces what political analysts have called a nearly impossible situation."[11] Forero did not quote a single Chávez voter, but he did quote four different business people who supported the strike. Forero also quoted Ricardo Hausmann and made him come across as a neutral analyst. In fact, Hausmann is a vehemently anti-Chávez economist whom Juan Guiadó would name as his representative to the Inter-American Development Bank in 2019.[12] In 1992, Hausmann had been appointed planning minister with the government of Carlos Andres Perez, the one that perpetrated the Caracazo Massacre in 1989.[13] Forero referred to Hausmann only as a "former planning minister in Venezuela"—a description so vague that readers might even have assumed that Hausmann had been a minister under Chávez. Even Ari Fleischer, the White House press secretary who had regurgitated every opposition talking point when Chávez was briefly deposed earlier that year, was uncritically quoted by Forero—a subtle way to present the U.S. government as a benevolent and neutral party: "We call on all sides to act responsibly, continue to support the dialogue process and reject violence."

As in the months prior to the coup in April, the media pretended that the majority of Venezuelans who had voted for Chávez repeatedly since 1998 did not exist. They were written out of the story, with help from anti-government polling firms such as Datanalisis, except when they could be depicted as thugs.[14]

The Norwegian journalist Eirik Vold arrived in Caracas two months before the oil strike. Like most foreign journalists, he took up residence in wealthy East Caracas, an opposition stronghold where Venezuela's private media has always had the most influence. He initially came to accept the story that Venezuelan and Western media coverage was telling. In his book about the years he lived in Venezuela, he wrote:

> At the time I believed the best thing Chávez could do for the country as a whole was step down voluntarily and end the crisis

before further tragedies unfolded and he ended up in front of the international criminal court or being overthrown by his own people.[15]

Vold's perspective would change completely once he was able to venture out of East Caracas and actually meet Chávez supporters in poor neighborhoods. In a poor country with a lot of violent crime, this involved risk and discomfort on Vold's part, and it would hardly open doors for him in the corporate media hostile to the perspective of Chavistas. But it allowed him to understand the majority of voters who told a different story than the one he had initially accepted as true.[16]

There were, however, some differences at this time with the story the Western media would tell in later years. For instance, in a December 11 article for the *New York Times*, Juan Forero reported that "pro-Chávez demonstrators protested outside private television stations, *all of which are ferociously anti-Chávez*, ransacking the newsroom of one of them." His article also said that eight of the twenty Supreme Court judges had joined the strike.[17] In later years, the opposition was constantly presented as voiceless in the mass media. Another key difference: on December 17, Forero acknowledged a fact about Venezuela that would be written out of history many years later, when Maduro was in office: "To the government and its supporters, Mr. Chávez is simply trying to manage Petróleos de Venezuela for the good of a country that, *despite its vast oil wealth, has been mired in poverty*."[18]

With Chávez in office for only a few years, it did not yet make sense to rely on the trope of a "once prosperous" country ruined by Chavismo. Instead, the story was that a bumbling would-be authoritarian was not up to the task of reforming Venezuela, and it would be best if he resigned.

Pilin León *becomes the* Negra Matea

On December 21, the Chávez government won an important victory against the opposition's oil industry sabotage. Troops took over

SECOND COUP ATTEMPT: OIL STRIKE

the *Pilin León*, and a retired seaman named Carlos López, along with others recruited by the government, navigated the tanker and its twelve million gallons of desperately needed imported gasoline to port. The private media derided the crew as unqualified and also claimed its members were Cuban.

What if the *Pilin León* had gone up in flames? The protesting former crew had allegedly set hidden traps that could have caused a catastrophe. True or not, it was clear that the risks were higher than under normal circumstances. Another worry was the ship smashing into Maracaibo Bridge if it went off course before passing underneath it.

Bart Jones explained, "If something went wrong, Chávez could be blamed for irresponsibly sending an unprepared crew on a suicide mission to serve his political needs." Jones described the key events that most of the country was watching live on TV:

> Suddenly a puff of smoke came out of the ship's chimney. The monster was running again. [Carlos] López ordered the ship to move ahead, but as it did the engines started overheating dangerously. He sent the ship in a circle to avoid heading to the bridge while the engineers tried to bring the temperature under control. They did, and the tanker headed for Maracaibo. When it was three hundred yards from the bridge, the crew let out a cheer. Even if something went wrong, the ship had too much momentum now to change course before passing under the bridge safely. It was going to make it. Soldiers guarding the bridge pumped their fists into their palms while holding their arms over their heads in a gesture made famous by Chávez. In Miraflores the elated president shouted with joy. "There goes the *Pilin León*!" he said, and, in a soccer reference, added "Gooooal!"[19]

The ship would soon be renamed the *Negra Matea*, after the Afro-Venezuelan governess who helped raise Simón Bolívar. In the years ahead, many other oil tankers had their beauty queen names replaced by those of female historical figures.[20]

Reporting the Perspective of the Imaginary Majority

On December 22, Juan Forero reported in the *New York Times*:

> Editors and owners of the largest media outlets acknowledge involvement with the opposition and the strike, which over the last three weeks has crippled oil production and paralyzed the economy.
>
> "We are united with the strike," Víctor Ferreres, president of the Venevisión television station, told foreign reporters at a recent news conference.
>
> The owners, though, say they have little choice, citing Mr. Chávez's own attacks on the press and the conduct of the government-owned station, Venezolana de Televisión. The station broadcasts a continuous string of talk shows with government ministers and pro-Chávez analysts, who play down the strike and trumpet the government's achievements.[21]

At this point, well into a second media-led effort to overthrow the government within a year, Forero also quoted the Committee to Protect Journalists and other anti-Chávez sources expressing concern that Venezuela's private media were going too far in trying to oust the government. But despite this rare bit of honesty about the Venezuelan media, Forero attempted no real exploration of how the media-led attack on the economy looked to the Venezuelans who had repeatedly voted in support of Chávez since 1998. In fact, Forero didn't quote a single Chávez voter in his article.

Chávez had to contend with the opposition sabotaging PDVSA's computer systems. Because of this, oil-rich Venezuela resorted to importing gasoline. Middle and lower-level employees, who tended to support Chávez, were promoted to do the work of the upper-level staff who had walked off the job. The promoted workers performed far better than the private media said they would, but there was also a significant loss of institutional knowledge and expertise. A cost-free victory would have been impossible, but the fact remains that low-level workers prevailed over a strike led mainly by their superiors[22]

By February 2, the opposition conceded that the strike had been defeated. In the *New York Times*, Forero wrote an article saying that the opposition's key problems were its internal divisions and a failure to anticipate Chávez's willingness to fight back. His article clearly suggested that the opposition would prevail against Chávez in elections if only they could unify. Forero's main sources were, as usual, anti-Chavistas: Datanalisis director Luis Vicente León and Michael Shifter of the Inter-American Dialog think tank.[23] Much as during the 2019 Trump-led coup attempt, the idea that millions of voters might be deeply repulsed by politicians who were trying to starve them into rebellion was not raised. About two months later, on April 12, Forero nonchalantly wrote: "For some opposition leaders the strategy now is to lie low and watch the economy worsen, hoping that the president will be dragged down with it."

Elsewhere in this article, regarding the opposition coalition of "big businessmen, labor leaders, politicians and private media owners" that spearheaded the coup and oil strike, Forero conceded: "The coalition's tactics are so reviled and its failures so pronounced—their strike cost the economy an estimated $7 billion and led to a rash of bankruptcies—that some prominent Chávez opponents are distancing themselves from the group."[24]

Nevertheless, Forero still cited a poll by the firm Consultores 21 claiming that, if an election were held immediately, "Chávez would receive only 34 percent of the vote." In hindsight, we know that the opposition would be repeatedly defeated by Chavistas in national elections for the next decade. But even in 2003, common sense should have provided Forero with a hefty amount of skepticism toward such polls. Chávez had already won many elections and now the opposition had twice tried to overthrow him in ways that revealed total contempt for most Venezuelans and for democracy. Forero quoted five Chávez opponents and, at the very end of the article, only one supporter. If this honestly reflects who he talked to, then he appears to have hindered his own capacity to conduct a competent analysis of the situation, as well as the capacity of his readers. To put it another way, he didn't follow Eirik Vold's example of breaking out of the East Caracas bubble.

Massive Toll on the Poor

In the aftermath of the strike, Chávez fired eighteen thousand PDVSA employees, about half the company's workforce. The dismissed employees came mainly from the managerial, professional, and technical staff.[25] That may seem harsh at first glance, but not when the combined economic impact of the first two coup attempts is considered. They increased Venezuela's poverty rate to 62 percent, a jump of 14 percentage points.[26]

By the end of the first quarter of 2003, Venezuela's real GDP contracted by nearly 30 percent from the combined impact of the coup and oil strike that followed (see chart below).[27] It was the worst quarter Venezuela had experienced in decades, one inflicted deliberately by the U.S.-backed opposition.

Figure 6.1: Poverty and Extreme Poverty Rate

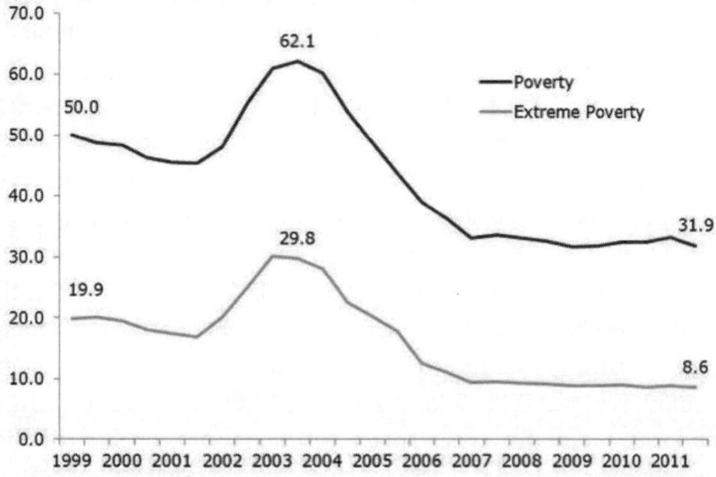

Source: Center for Economic and Policy Research.

SECOND COUP ATTEMPT: OIL STRIKE

To repeat: Any foreign government linked to a political movement that inflicted this much economic damage on the United States would suffer horrific retaliation. U.S. politicians and media outlets that supported the sabotage would be declared treasonous and never be heard from again.

Opposition Impunity, Yet Again

Initially, Chávez was far less conciliatory after the oil strike than he was after the April coup. Carlos Ortega, arguably the most important leader behind the second coup attempt, went into hiding. He was soon granted political asylum in Costa Rica, but the offer was withdrawn in 2004 and he went into hiding again. In March 2005, he was captured and that December given a sixteen-year prison term for treason. He escaped prison in August 2006. His family suggested that he may have been disappeared by the government, but he turned up in Peru, where he was given political asylum. From exile in 2019,

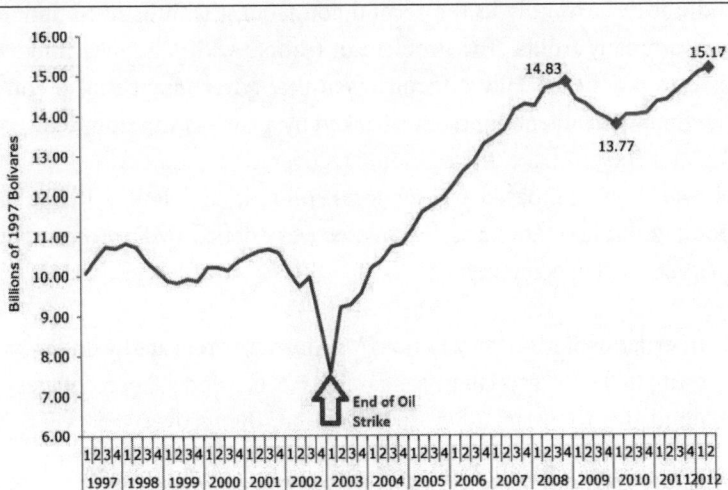

Figure 6.2: Venezuela: Real GDF (seasonally adjusted)

Source: Center for Economic and Policy Research.

Ortega has made videos, reported on by Venezuela's private media, in support of Juan Guaidó and calling for protests in Venezuela so it can "retake the path of democracy."[28]

At the end of 2007, Chávez granted a wide-ranging amnesty for participants in the April coup, including amnesty for violence committed on board oil tankers. About forty military officers involved in the Altamira Plaza protest also benefited. The amnesty excluded people such as Ortega who fled the country to escape legal consequences or were accused of crimes against humanity or "grave" human rights abuses.[29]

But Ortega's escape and many other examples of opposition impunity suggest that people within the Chávez government were assisting those who wanted to overthrow him. By granting the amnesty, Chávez was, in part, choosing to hold back on addressing corruption within his own ranks—among prosecutors and judges in particular. One prosecutor who seemed willing to aggressively pursue perpetrators of the coup was Danilo Anderson. In a crime widely assumed to have been perpetrated by opposition supporters, he was assassinated in November 2004 with a bomb that was planted in his car. To this day, Anderson is hailed as a heroic martyr by Chavistas.[30] Overall, Chávez did not react timidly to the second coup, but it is difficult to fight a war on many fronts. The problem of traitors within a government's own ranks is especially difficult when that government is also contending with violent opponents backed by a lawless superpower.

After the oil strike, the economy recovered very quickly (see chart above). The U.S.-based Center for Economic and Policy Research pointed out how dramatically this recovery defied IMF forecasts for the Venezuelan economy:

> International Monetary Fund (IMF) forecasts repeatedly underestimated GDP growth by a gigantic 10.6, 6.8, and 5.8 percentage points for the years 2004–2006. Instead, the recovery was very rapid and the economy grew at a record pace over the next five years, with real GDP nearly doubling from the end of the oil strike (first quarter 2003) through the fourth quarter of 2008.[31]

SECOND COUP ATTEMPT: OIL STRIKE

Given that the U.S.-dominated IMF rushed to offer the Carmona dictatorship loans while it was very briefly in power (and later denied emergency loans to Maduro's government during the COVID-19 pandemic), it's very safe to assume that ideological bias and dishonesty were mainly responsible for these atrocious predictions.[32]

The Forgotten Currency Float

Notwithstanding the recovery, the oil strike prompted the Chávez government to give the economy an Achilles heel through the exchange rate system it implemented to prevent capital flight during the strike.

In February 2002, only two months before he was briefly overthrown, Chávez implemented a "floating" exchange rate system. In that type of system, the exchange rate "floats" to wherever supply and demand take it as people and firms freely trade local currency (bolivars, in Venezuela's case) for foreign currency. For obvious reasons, the rate at which the bolivar trades for the U.S. dollar, given its importance in international trade, is crucial to determining how expensive or cheap imports are in Venezuela. The less the bolivar is worth relative to the U.S. dollar, the more expensive imports will be, and vice versa.

While it was briefly in place, Venezuela's floating exchange rate worked well. The government's dollar reserves grew despite tremendous political instability—until the oil strike. Reserves fell by $2 billion during the strike and the bolivar lost 30 percent of its value. On February 6, 2003, days after the strike collapsed, Chávez announced that exchange controls would be reimposed as a way to stem capital flight and prop up the bolivar, officially ending the floating exchange rate.[33]

With this change in policy, the bolivar could be legally exchanged for U.S. dollars only at a fixed rate set by the government. This created a black market for U.S. dollars, which did not cause major problems while Chávez was alive. Mind you, when Chávez introduced the system, the difference between the fixed rate and the floating rate was only about 15 percent.

But near the end of 2012, while Chávez was in Cuba unsuccessfully fighting off cancer, the difference between the black market rate and the official exchange rate increased alarmingly. For reasons that are not clear, the government had begun cutting back on the U.S. dollars it issued to the private sector, causing the rates to diverge.[34] Once Nicolás Maduro was in office, the black market exchange rate skyrocketed, especially after oil prices collapsed in late 2014. As U.S. dollars supplied by the government at the fixed exchange rate became more scarce (because the government had much less oil revenue, which it received in U.S. dollars), dollars became even more valuable on the black market. Market theory tells us that importers with the highest costs who can still stay in business end up setting prices. In Venezuela's case, that meant importers who turned to the black market in dollars. The skyrocketing black market rate drove up the cost of imports, and therefore inflation, by effectively devaluing the bolivar.[35] As the black market rate increased, the government lost money, because the dollars it would have given to private industry (for industry to provide goods and services) were diverted into various forms of illegal speculation. The government printed bolivars to cover the losses, which also drove up inflation, leaving Venezuela plagued by a devaluation-inflation spiral. Figure 6.3 (page 109) shows how both trends reinforced each other: inflation alongside the black market exchange rate, that is, the number of bolivars required to get a U.S. dollar on the black market.[36]

For several years after the oil strike, and with the fixed exchange rate that Chávez imposed in response, the Venezuelan economy performed remarkably well. Opposition analysts, and their backers at the IMF and in the business press, were left looking very foolish as they predicted an economic collapse while the economy not only grew but delivered massive poverty reduction and decreased inequality. Unfortunately, Chavista commentators and officials widely saw the fixed exchange rate system as a crucial part of that success.[37] Bolivia's example should have disabused them of that idea.

Many governments buy or sell their own currency to stabilize the exchange rate. In other words, they maintain a "managed" or "dirty float" of the currency. The U.S. economist Mark Weisbrot recommended this type of system for Venezuela in 2010.[38]

Figure 6.3: Inflation and Black Market Rate

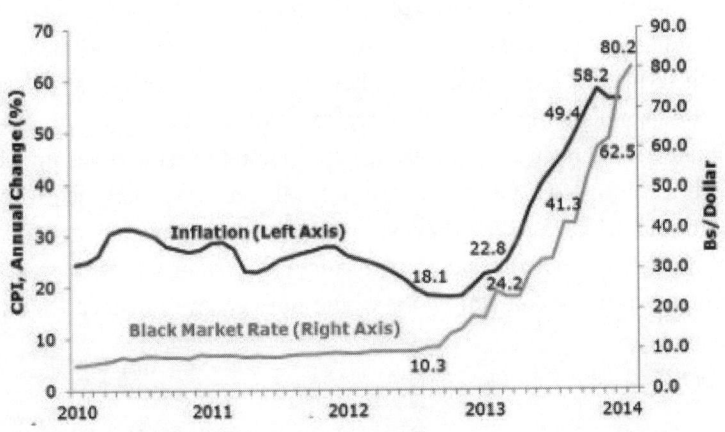

Source: Center for Economic and Policy Research.

Under President Evo Morales, Bolivia was another left-wing government in the region, one facing very similar challenges as Venezuela (including hostile U.S.-backed oligarchs who would gladly overthrow Morales by force, and tried to do so in 2009). Bolivia sustained rapid growth and poverty reduction using a "managed float" exchange rate system—basically what Chávez had abandoned after the oil strike. Tragically, Bolivia's important example was ignored by both the Chávez and Maduro governments.[39] In 2014, a Venezuelan economist, Hernán Luis Torres Núñez, wrote a piece for the left-wing website Apporea in which he claimed Bolivia's example showed that Maduro needed to cooperate more with business owners.[40] That was an erroneous and a counterproductive way to try to convince Chavistas to fix the exchange rate system.[41] (Despite his economic success, on November 10, 2019, Morales was overthrown in a U.S.-backed military coup.)

Under Maduro, extremely lucrative profiteering opportunities arose because of the skyrocketing black market exchange rate. This led to corruption within the Chavista ranks that must have been a factor blocking reform of the exchange rate policy—but how big a factor it is not easy to say.[42]

What is undeniable, however, is that the second U.S.-backed coup attempt against Chávez was so destructive that it had pernicious long-term effects on economic policy. Nevertheless, the defeat of the second coup attempt brought several years of stability, as the opposition refrained from any significant attempt to remove the government by force until 2013. Control of the state oil company, combined with rising oil prices, allowed the government to deliver huge benefits to the majority. Problems with the exchange rate system, and with granting impunity for coup attempts, would not become conspicuous for many years.

7

Third Coup Attempt: Fatalities over Frivolous Claims, April 2013

On April 14, 2013, about a month after Hugo Chávez died, Nicolás Maduro won the snap presidential election that Venezuela's constitution calls for in the event of a president's death. Maduro won by only 1.8 percentage points, a far smaller margin than pollsters across the political spectrum had predicted.[1] The Western media's favorite anti-government polling firm, Datanalisis, predicted a 9.7-point win for Maduro.[2] Henrique Capriles, the loser, used the tiny margin of victory to cry fraud and call his supporters into the streets—with fatal consequences for several government supporters. The Obama government fanned the flames by standing behind Capriles's preposterous claim to have been robbed.

Ignoring Math, Opposition Victories, and CNE Independence

After the election, Maduro immediately said that he welcomed a full recount but the head of the National Electoral Council (CNE), Tibisay Lucena, reacted frostily to the idea.[3] It was the CNE's place to say if a recount would take place, not Maduro's. She argued that the "hot audit" of 54 percent of voting machines, which was carried out in front of opposition witnesses and international observers, was more than statistically adequate to confirm the results—53 percent were audited on the day of the election and an additional 1 percent the next day, as explained in an open letter to the Western media signed by fourteen economists, most of them based in the United States.[4] The audit ensured that electronically tallied votes in the randomly sampled machines matched the printed receipts that each voter examined before leaving a voting center. A study released by the U.S. economists David Rosnick and Mark Weisbrot showed that Lucena had mathematics on her side.[5] The odds that a 100 percent audit would confirm a win for Capriles were, as they put it, "far less than one in 25 thousand trillion." A year earlier, Jimmy Carter, referring specifically to the technical aspects of Venezuela's electoral system, called it the "best in the world."[6]

Lucena also had past practice on her side. When the opposition won the 2007 constitutional referendum by almost the exact same margin, two percentage points, there was no 100 percent audit of the results.[7] However, Lucena did *not* reject a 100 percent audit. She said that Capriles should follow the proper legal procedures to request one, and that "harassment, threats or intimidation are not the way to appeal to the Electoral Power." Lucena's house had been attacked, but serious violence had not yet erupted at that point.[8] She also rebuked the Organization of American States (OAS) president José Miguel Insulza for publicly supporting a 100 percent audit. Arguably, her remarks were also an implicit rebuke of Maduro's initial comments on the matter. This is significant given that, for years, the opposition and its foreign allies had strongly impugned the CNE's independence. Many prominent people, including the OAS president, seemed to think that electoral procedures should be simply made up on the fly, and the independence of the CNE disregarded, when it suited them.

On April 17, Capriles formally submitted paperwork to the CNE asking for a 100 percent audit. By that time, several Chavistas had been killed in attacks perpetrated by his supporters.[9]

On April 18, the CNE announced that it would audit the remaining

46 percent of machines—in other words, bring the audit to 100 percent. Capriles celebrated the decision in a TV address, calling it a great victory for the protests he had instigated. Referring to the remaining 46 percent of machines that would be audited, he claimed:

> We know where the problems are—in those 12,000. That's where they are. There we will be able to perfectly prove the truth to all of you. . . . So we accept what the CNE has announced to the country. We will be there during the audit—important to remember—there are technical details. I am not going to tire the country at this late hour with technical details. But it is important to remember the fingerprints records that the CNE must disclose.[10]

Note that Capriles immediately shifted his demands. The audit now had to include an audit of the entire fingerprint registry to satisfy him, not simply a 100 percent audit of the voting machines. He also denied that any of his supporters had killed anyone or attacked a single Cuban-staffed medical center, a denial that a Reuters report would soon refute. He said that any fatalities that occurred after his call for protests were the result of common crime, and that the government was trying to pass these deaths off as politically motivated. On April 25, Capriles announced that his people would not supply witnesses for the audit of the voting machines because a review of the fingerprint registry was not included.[11] Capriles also traveled to Belgium, France, Germany, and Spain to plead his case.[12]

On May 9, Capriles told the Spanish newspaper *El Pais* that he had actually won the election by 400,000 votes. As Dan Beeton of the Center for Economic and Policy Research observed:

> Capriles is still alleging the vote count was stolen in a way that would have been detectable in the first audit, and hence the statistical analysis still applies. If tens of thousands of voters voted multiple times, it would be very difficult to stuff the receipt boxes to match the multiple voting, without having some discrepancies

between the machine and the paper count. The receipt boxes are in plain sight of all observers and it would be impossible for a voter to stuff multiple pieces of paper through the thin slot without anyone seeing. It would also be impossible to vote more than once without not only the collaboration of observers to fix the machines to allow this, but a conspiracy involving tens of thousands of people, with no subsequent leaks.[13]

Predictably, math and logic bounced off the Western media and it was Maduro, not Capriles, who was described as behaving shiftily. On June 5, Reuters reported that "Maduro originally accepted a proposal for a full audit of the close April election which he won, but then backtracked and has since hardened his stance."[14]

In a way, Reuters was correct that Maduro had backtracked. He had initially overstepped and basically disrespected the CNE with his emphatic endorsement of a full audit. He then shifted to letting the CNE take the lead, as he should have from the beginning.[15] By the time Reuters claimed that Maduro had "hardened his stance," the CNE was only days away from completing the utterly unnecessary 100 percent audit Capriles had demanded. On June 11, the CNE announced that no discrepancies were found.[16]

Media Malevolence

The Western media's failure to scrutinize Capriles's allegations clearly involved something worse than incompetence. Dan Beeton claimed that "one reporter writing for a major U.S. newspaper has told us that his editors refuse to publish anything related to our statistical analysis or regarding the audit and its significance more generally."[17]

The analysis Beeton referred to was done by his colleagues at the Center for Economic and Policy Research (CEPR), Mark Weisbrot and David Rosnick. It showed that the sample size of 53 percent that was used to randomly audit the voting machines on the day of the election was decisive. (The audit looked for discrepancies between printed receipts that all voters checked and the touch screen votes recorded by the machines. An additional 1 percent of the machines were audited the next day.) The odds that a 100 percent audit would find enough discrepancies to change the results in favor of Capriles were infinitesimally small.

A Factiva search for "Weisbrot," co-founder of CEPR, between May 9, the study's release date, and July 9 turned up twenty-seven articles, but none of them mentioned the statistical analysis. This included a May 17 *Christian Science Monitor* article that ran with the headline "Venezuela's Maduro Still Waiting on Washington's Recognition" and actually quoted Weisbrot:

> "A lot of Venezuelans seem to think that a close election is not a valid election, so this leaves room for Maduro's critics to question it," says Mark Weisbrot of the Center for Economic and Policy Research, an independent think-tank in Washington. Mr. Weisbrot says he thinks the US is trying to take advantage of this situation.[18]

Was this newspaper that quoted Weisbrot not allowed to mention that he had published a study explaining why Capriles's fraud claims were ridiculous? The article also misleadingly referred to a "partial recount" being underway. That was the "partial recount" that took a 54 percent audit up to 100 percent—in other words, a complete recount.

In a later piece, Beeton observed that while "Capriles' call for the fingerprint audit has gained traction in the English language media, the CNE officials' announcements that they plan to conduct such an audit have not." Beeton highlighted one appalling example: a June 9 report by the AP's Christopher Toothaker that mentioned Capriles's demand for a fingerprint audit but not the fact that weeks earlier, on May 17, the CNE had announced that it would do one.[19]

In September, the CNE completed this audit as well and explained its methodology to officials from UNASUR and the Carter Center.[20] A year later, a Carter Center report on the election acknowledged the validity of the CNE's approach to the fingerprint audit but said that the opposition's boycott of the process and "lack of information" led to a "loss of an important opportunity" to reassure people about the results.[21]

In other words, the U.S.-backed opposition had instigated protests that resulted in several deaths over an election that proved to be completely fair.

Contrast this with Mexico's 2006 presidential election. Then, the right-wing Felipe Calderón defeated left-of-center Andrés Manuel López Obrador by six-tenths of a percentage point, a much smaller margin than Maduro's win over Capriles in 2013. Mexico's electoral authorities did a recount of nine percent of the ballots and refused to release the results.[22] The Western media's reaction could not have been more different in this case. As Dan Beeton explained:

> "An Anti-Democracy Campaign; Mexico's presidential loser takes a lesson from Joseph Stalin," ran a *Washington Post* editorial headline. The *Times of London* declared him "Mexico's bad loser: A demagogue prepared to hold the nation to ransom." ... So far at least, no major U.S., British or Canadian paper has labeled Capriles a "sore loser" and the *Washington Post* has yet to compare him to Stalin.[23]

Another contrast was that polls in Mexico had widely predicted a win for López Obrador in 2006, an additional reason why claims of fraud in that case were plausible. Mexico's right-wing establishment had reason to fear a López Obrador victory before the election, and therefore prepared to steal it from him. But polling firms in Venezuela, including the pro-opposition Datanalisis, widely predicted a heavy loss for Capriles in 2013. In the fraud story that Capriles wanted to sell, Maduro was caught off guard as the votes came in but still managed to rig the vote count without leaving evidence, despite Venezuela's far more advanced and transparent voting process—and the scrutiny of a hostile Western media.

Of course, when it comes to Venezuela, and indeed any state that is considered a U.S. enemy, the Western media's message is largely in sync with the U.S. government and large NGOs.

The U.S. government called for a 100 percent audit the day after Maduro's election victory, and again on April 16.[24] A month later, the International Crisis Group (ICG), which was receiving about half its funding from the United States and other Western governments, echoed that call: "The validity of the election result [in Venezuela] needs to be clarified."[25] Even more imperiously, the ICG singled out Brazil as a "regional power" that should "not tolerate further destruction of the rule of law and democratic values" elsewhere in Latin America.[26]

Human Rights Watch (HRW) said on April 17: "Capriles challenged the results and asked the electoral authorities to conduct a full recount, a request echoed by the secretary general of the Organization of American States and initially supported by Maduro. However, the National Electoral Council [CNE] summarily rejected the request and proclaimed Maduro president on April 15."[27] Of course, the CNE did *not* reject a full audit. The HRW statement also said that Maduro would be "installed as President" on April 19, as if he had perpetrated a coup. It also scolded Maduro, saying he "shouldn't threaten to use an 'iron fist' to restrict and intimidate those who try to voice their opinions." But should Capriles have denied that his supporters had killed people and attacked medical centers, incited by his claims that he'd been robbed of the election? What was the message sent by his denial? Should Capriles have been asked to denounce high-profile supporters who made wild claims that put Cuban-staffed medical centers in the line of fire? HRW ignored those questions, ignored the track record of the U.S.-backed opposition, and failed to distinguish between formally requesting a recount and trying to spark a coup. As usual, HRW pretended that only Maduro's words could incite or intimidate.

Reuters Belatedly Investigates a Few Chavista Deaths

On May 8, more than three weeks after the fact, Reuters published an article about three post-election deaths in the La Limonera neighborhood in Caracas. It conceded that two of the three deaths it investigated (out of nine then alleged by the government) seemed strongly to indicate the responsibility of Capriles supporters.[28] All three victims were murdered as they headed home after protecting a medical center from attack by opposition supporters:

> When official results showed him narrowly losing, Capriles on the night of Sunday, April 14 called on supporters to demand a full recount by marching in the streets.
> A day later, opposition protesters near La Limonera went to a state-run clinic staffed by doctors from Cuba who were hired through a Chávez-era oil-for-services deal.
> Witnesses interviewed by Reuters said about 100 protesters surrounded the clinic for around two hours shouting slogans such as "Get out Cubans, we don't want you here," banging pots and pans in a rowdy *"cacerolazo"* (from the Spanish word for casserole, a loud banging of pots and pans) protest.
> Maduro sympathizers including hairdresser Rosiris Reyes and carpenter Jose Luis Ponce arrived to protect the clinic from harm, witnesses and relatives said. As the protest died down they began returning home, but never made it.
> "From a Toyota, someone started shooting and shouting opposition slogans. One of the bullets hit my mother in the back," said fifteen-year-old Yonylexis Reyes, who lives with two brothers in a small apartment decorated with the posters with the faces of Maduro and Chávez.
> "She fell off the motorcycle and we took her to the hospital." Her mother died two days later.
> Ponce was also shot while returning from the clinic, according to witnesses. A family member said one person was later wounded at his funeral by a shot fired from a neighborhood near La Limonera.

It would have been truly miraculous if attacks on Cuban-staffed medical centers, like the one described by Reuters, had not occurred. And that was not only because the opposition had been hysterically vilifying all things Cuban and Cuba-related in the private media for years.²⁹ The Reuters article didn't mention that, the day after the election, Nelson Bocaranda, a high-profile pundit who then had a regular column in *El Universal*, one of Venezuela's largest newspapers, tweeted to one million followers that he had been "informed" that Cubans in Maracaibo were hiding ballots inside a medical center and refusing to release them.³⁰

It is hard to imagine a tweet more clearly intended to incite violence against Cubans working in medical centers.³¹ The medical centers, known as Integral Diagnostic Centers (CDIs in the Spanish acronym) had expanded in Venezuela since 2003. They brought basic health care services to the poorest areas by deploying tens of thousands of Cuban doctors to defeat a boycott of the program by Venezuela's right-wing medical establishment.³² Reuters, in the article quoted above, mentioned that Provea, a local human rights group, "later released a report saying it had found no evidence that any of the CDIs had been attacked—drawing furious criticism from government leaders including Villegas."³³ Ernesto Villegas is a journalist who went on to become Maduro's Communication Minister in 2012.³⁴

Had Bocarcada's incendiary tweet been mentioned by Reuters, then Villegas's criticism of Provea would have been easy to understand. Also unmentioned was that, in 2010, Provea received funds and other support from the Canadian government, which had been openly hostile to the Venezuelan government for years. In 2009, for instance, Canadian prime minister Stephen Harper referred to Venezuela as a "rogue state."³⁵

But putting aside the limitations of the Reuters article, the bias of human rights groups such as Provea and HRW is extreme indeed when even Reuters reports facts that expose the shoddiness of their work.

Below are people whom Ernesto Villegas described in a report as victims of opposition violence in the wake of the election:

- **José Luis Ponce Ordóñez**, 45, shot after defending medical center.
- **Rosiris Reyes**, 44, shot shortly after defending medical center.
- **Keler Guevara**, 23, police officer shot while on duty.

- **Johnny Pacheco**, 37, shot after defending medical center. (One of the three cases Reuters belatedly investigated, and disputed by Reuters after speaking with his relatives.)
- **Gerardo Rico**, 39, died after spending weeks in a coma, allegedly after being beaten by group of Capriles supporters.
- **Rey David Chacín González**, 11; **Johan Hernández**, 22; **María Victoria Báez**, 12—all killed when a truck smashed into them as they were on the streets celebrating Maduro's win.
- **Luis Eduardo García**, 24, shot while next to CNE building demonstrating in support of Maduro.
- **Hender Bastardo**, 21, shot. A *motorizado* (motorcycle rider) often associated with pro-government *colectivos* that are vilified by the opposition.
- **Henry Rangel**, 32, shot while on the street celebrating Maduro's win.[36]

Capriles Shifts Again, Alleges Unfair Election

By May, Capriles had shifted away from claiming that the vote count had been rigged. His focus switched to claiming that the election should be annulled by the Supreme Court because it was unfair. Reuters described his appeal:

> "This appeal seeks to annul the elections and request new presidential elections in Venezuela," said Gerardo Fernandez, a lawyer representing the opposition, who are intent on at least discrediting Maduro even if they cannot overrule the result.
> "We've come to defend the citizens who voted in April 14."
> Fernandez said the appeal includes complaints relating to incidents prior to the election. The opposition accuses Maduro of using state resources and government media for his campaign.
> Capriles also alleges there were thousands of irregularities on voting day, ranging from intimidation of poll station volunteers to illegal campaigning by government supporters.[37]

The Supreme Court quashed the challenge in August.[38]

Elections around the world would be declared illegitimate if fair media access was taken into account. That is certainly the case in the United States, in the wake of the infamous Citizens United ruling of 2010.[39] That ruling banned legal restrictions on corporate funding of political campaigns. In Venezuela, concentrated wealth also gives some candidates conspicuously unfair advantages. Capriles is related to the founding owners of Cadena Capriles which, as of 2013, was Venezuela's largest print media conglomerate.[40] As is invariably the case with U.S.-backed political movements in Latin America, the opposition in Venezuela is solidly based among the wealthiest people in the country. That alone would make marginalizing them in the media next to impossible without a much deeper democratization of media and society than was achieved under Chávez.

In fact, in July, the Carter Center quietly published data that obliterated the opposition's complaint about media access.

The Carter Center Quietly Drops a Bomb

As part of a preliminary report on Venezuela's 2013 presidential election, the Carter Center analyzed TV news coverage during the campaign.[41] As the name of the Center suggests, it is part of the U.S. establishment, founded by a former president, making its data difficult for U.S. apologists to dismiss.[42] The data showed no significant advantage in coverage for Nicolás Maduro during the campaign. The Carter Center therefore demolished the ubiquitous lie that the opposition was silenced in Venezuela's media, without actually intending to (the Center's executive summary still called for more equitable media access) and without criticizing the Western media or other NGOs. The data was devastating and spoke for itself.

The data showed that the largest audience share for news went to a private broadcaster, Venevisión, whose quantity of pro-Maduro and pro-Capriles coverage was roughly equal during the campaign. The same kind of balance was provided by Televen, another private broadcaster that was third in audience share. Globovisión, a private broadcaster that was fourth in audience share, was lopsidedly pro-Capriles. The government network, VTV, which was second in audience share, was very pro-Maduro.

Looking only at total minutes of electoral coverage on all four networks named above, the Carter Center's data showed a 57 percent to 34 percent advantage for Maduro. But the audience share of the private media's TV news coverage was nearly three times as large as the state media's (72 percent to 25 percent). Accounting for audience share eliminated any real advantage for Maduro over Capriles on TV during the presidential campaign.

A false representation of Venezuela's media has been ubiquitous for many years. For example, the journalist and scholar Alan MacLeod has sampled hundreds of articles about Venezuela that appeared in U.S. and UK newspapers during the period 1998 to 2013. He found that 100 percent of the articles that mentioned Venezuela's media described it as being under the thumb of the government.[43] The deception was so widespread that in 2010 Amnesty International, either from ignorance or because it feared no rebuttal, made the outlandish remark that Globovisión was the "only TV station whose license has not been revoked in recent years because of its editorial line."[44] In reality, a foreign-backed insurrectionist opposition in Venezuela has media access that third-party candidates in the United States, such as Jill Stein of the Green Party (outlandishly accused of being a "Russian asset" by Hillary Clinton), can only fantasize about.[45]

Leopoldo López Laments the Aborted Coup Attempt

Eight months after the election, on December 8, the opposition leader Leopoldo López said in an interview that Capriles would "be president right now" if Capriles had kept his supporters on the streets.[46]

A few years later, Julio "Coco" Jimenez, then a member of Voluntad Popular (the political party of both López and Juan Guaidó), was much more emphatic. Jimenez, a young activist who had been on CNN a few times, went on a homophobic rant at Capriles, whom he accused of squandering a golden opportunity to oust Maduro through street protests.[47]

The United States ultimately failed to get other governments to reject Maduro's 2013 victory. At that time, there were too many left-of-center governments still in office in Latin America for such frivolous claims to be endorsed. And in 2008, those governments had spearheaded the formation of the Union of South American Nations (UNASUR), with headquarters based in Ecuador, which reduced U.S. influence in the region. In 2019, by comparison, Evo Morales in Bolivia was not as fortunate, when he faced a coup incited by bogus claims of electoral fraud and backed by Washington and its regional allies, including Juan Guaidó.[48] By 2019, UNASUR had practically been disbanded thanks to the efforts of right-wing governments in Ecuador, Brazil, and Argentina. But during the attempt against Maduro in 2013, even though other Latin American governments did not go along, the United States still had plenty of support from the Western media and high-profile NGOs—the propaganda apparatus that targets states the U.S. government wants overthrown.

8

Fourth Coup Attempt: February–April 2014

When Hugo Chávez was close to death at the end of 2012, the Venezuelan economy began to struggle. A devaluation-inflation spiral began, rooted in the exchange rate system and the country's failure to adopt a "managed float" policy, as Bolivia under Evo Morales had done. The system put in place to prevent capital flight during the second coup attempt (the oil strike of 2002) was now wreaking havoc. In 2013, economic growth slowed, shortages of goods became a serious irritant, and inflation spiked. Thanks to high oil prices, however, economic growth persisted (see Table 8.1, page 125). Real GDP in each quarter of 2013 was higher than in the corresponding quarter of 2012. Although that trend would not continue into 2014, the continued growth in 2013 helped Chavismo defeat the opposition in municipal elections on December 8, 2013.

Five days after the elections, Reuters reported:

> Venezuela's ruling Socialist Party and allies took 10 percentage points more votes [nationwide] than opposition rivals in Sunday's election for mayors that was a test of strength for President Nicolas Maduro, final results showed on Friday. . . .

Capriles, the governor of Miranda state who narrowly lost the April presidential vote, may come under pressure from within the opposition for his failure to deliver better results at Sunday's vote, which he had cast as a plebiscite.

Several other opposition leaders have advocated more confrontational tactics, such as street protests, against Maduro whom they cast as an autocrat taking instructions from Cuba and leading Venezuela's economy to ruin.[2]

Two months later, in February 2014, Leopoldo López and María Corina Machado launched the more "confrontational tactics" Reuters had anticipated: violent protests explicitly aimed at toppling Maduro.

The day before the protests began, Leopoldo López placed an op-ed in one of Venezuela's largest newspapers, *El Universal*, urging people to attend.[3] Of course, he inserted weasel words. López wrote, "We will see each other on the street, which is our terrain, in a nonviolent way, which is our strategy and for one objective: the best Venezuela." But he immediately added, "We are facing a national threat, represented by a rotten and corrupt leadership that has kidnapped the Venezuelan State, turning it into a criminal." Coming from a man who had already backed three other attempts to oust the government (and, in fact, personally led the kidnapping of government officials during the first one), the meaning was obvious. The timing of this attempt, so soon after a major electoral defeat at the end of 2013, led to public bickering with his fellow insurrectionist Henrique Capriles, who did not think protests were wise so soon after the opposition's defeat

TABLE 8.1: Venezuela's Quarterly Real GDP, Percent Change Compared to Corresponding Quarter in the Previous Year[1]

2013/2012			
1st Qtr.	2nd Qtr.	3rd Qtr.	4th Qtr.
0.75	2.57	1.07	0.99
2014/2013			
1st Qtr.	2nd Qtr.	3rd Qtr.	4th Qtr.
−5.17	−5.40	−2.67	−2.60

Source: Compiled by the authors.

in municipal elections.⁴ But López charged ahead with his attempt to oust Maduro in what was also a factional battle for control of the opposition.⁵

It should be noted that, like López, U.S. president Donald Trump also used weasel words on January 6, 2021, when he incited rioters to overrun the Capitol Building for a few hours—which led immediately to Trump's second impeachment, his banning from all major social media, calls to bar him from ever holding federal office again, a massive and prolonged military presence in the capital, and President Joe Biden's new government declaring the need for "a radical rethinking of law enforcement" to confront "domestic terrorism."⁶ López was not of course the equivalent of a lame duck U.S. president, as he launched a vastly more destructive attempt to seize power by inciting violence.

Don't Even Plan This in New York or London

Predictably, more attacks on Cuban-staffed medical centers ended up taking place.⁷ In the United States or United Kingdom, both López and Machado would have been jailed in December 2013 when it was obvious (even to Reuters) that they intended to lead another attempt to overthrow Maduro. By comparison, the Puerto Rican activist Oscar López Rivera spent decades in prison, twelve of them in solitary confinement, for allegedly conspiring to perpetrate violent attacks that scarcely threatened U.S. colonial rule over Puerto Rico.⁸ He was not involved with briefly overthrowing the U.S. government itself.⁹

In 2010, President Barack Obama ordered the assassination of a U.S. citizen, Anwar al-Awlaki, in Yemen based on allegations that he was conspiring to perpetrate terrorist attacks on the United States. Awlaki had never been charged with or convicted of a crime. In 2012, a separate CIA drone strike killed Awlaki's sixteen-year-old U.S.-born son as well. Obama's press secretary shrugged off the teenager's killing by saying he should have "had a more responsible father."¹⁰

In the United Kingdom, young men have received prison sentences for attempting to organize riots using Facebook.¹¹ Writing in the *Guardian*, a former political editor of the newspaper, Michael White, joked about the possibility that the men might be sexually assaulted in prison: "It could be like this for the next 18 months, lads. And what if that big bloke on the next floor takes a shine to you?"[12]

In the United States, the Occupy Wall Street camps were forcibly dismantled for being "a public health hazard" and for allegedly "attracting vagrants and crime." Police denied Occupy protesters the use of amplifiers to make speeches, hence the "human microphone" that protesters used to communicate, and also to mock the draconian restrictions with which the protest camps were expected to comply. And still the camps were dismantled by force. A march that slowed traffic on the Brooklyn Bridge led to seven hundred arrests.[13]

Writing for FAIR.org, Josmar Trujillo described the "moral panic" in the U.S. media in July 2019 when a few New York police officers "were doused with water during a record heatwave."[14] The dousing came shortly after the family of Eric Garner, a Black New Yorker who was choked to death, was told that the police officer who killed him would not be charged. In fact, the officer had not yet been fired.[15]

Protest tactics that could not possibly be called violent or destructive are also stigmatized in U.S. political culture. Barack Obama urged Colin Kaepernick to "listen to the pain" he may cause by kneeling during the national anthem in protest of police killings. On July 24, 2019, the U.S. House of Representatives overwhelmingly passed a non-binding resolution that opposed U.S. citizens supporting Palestinians by engaging in boycotts that target the state of Israel and U.S. companies doing business with Israel.[16]

The United States and its allies also mercilessly punish journalists who too effectively expose war crimes, as the imprisonment of Julian Assange and Chelsea Manning makes clear.[17]

It's also striking how baselessly a protest movement in the United States, no matter how peaceful and firmly rooted in harsh domestic realities, is linked to foreign interference. Senator Kamala Harris, when she was running for the Democratic Party's presidential nomination, said in July 2019 that Colin Kaepernick's protests against police violence and racism received a great deal of attention only because of "Russian bots" on social media.[18] But months before a fourth

U.S.-backed coup attempt in Venezuela, allegations of U.S.-backed sabotage were reflectively dismissed as cynical and absurd. For example, in September 2013, a news article by William Neuman in the *New York Times* stated that "accusing unseen conspirators of subjecting the nation to a variety of ills is an art form in Venezuela, honed during the 14-year presidency of Hugo Chávez, who died in March."[19]

We aren't saying that Venezuela's government is entitled to be as violent and oppressive as the U.S. government and its closest allies—just that the practical consequences of accepting an imperial double standard is obvious, when you consider the case of Venezuela and other targeted countries.[20] No democracy is obliged to let itself be violently overthrown. But if you accept or ignore the double standard, then a government targeted by the United States is easily labeled as "authoritarian" or a dictatorship if it takes *any* steps to defend itself. A U.S.-backed opposition is emboldened to use and incite violence, knowing that any response will be labeled repression and gain them even more support from the Western propaganda apparatus.

Corporate Media and Others Mislead About Who Was Killing People

By mid-March 2014, a month into this fourth coup attempt, two facts were being systematically buried by the corporate media. One was that more people had died due to the actions of protesters than as a result of police brutality or from attacks by government supporters.[21] The other fact was that the United States had been remarkably unsuccessful in its efforts to get other Latin American governments to denounce Maduro.

Table 8.2 (page 129) summarizes the facts regarding the forty protest-related deaths. The list is taken from one compiled by VenezuelAnalysis, a reader-supported website that is often critical of Chavismo from the left, based on Venezuelan news reports and official sources.[22] By March 14, the opposition's side had caused seventeen deaths, either directly or through lethal hazards they had created in the streets. The government's side was either clearly or most likely responsible for eleven deaths.

Table 8.2: Protest-Related Deaths

Date	Victim	Responsible or	Strongly Implicated
12-Feb	José Roberto Redman		1. Government
	Bassil DaCosta		2. Government
	Juan Montoya		3. Government
18-Feb	José Ernesto Méndez		4. Government
18-Feb	Génesis Carmona		
19-Feb	Asdrúbal Jose Rodríguez	1. Opposition	
19-Feb	Julio Eduardo González	2. Opposition	
19-Feb	Luzmila Petit de Colina	3. Opposition	
20-Feb	Arturo Alexis Martinez	4. Opposition	
20-Feb	Delia Elena Lobo	5. Opposition	
21-Feb	Elvis Rafael Durán	6. Opposition	
22-Feb	Geraldine Moreno		5. Government
22-Feb	Danny Joel Melgarejo Vargas		6. Government
23-Feb	José Alejandro Márquez		7. Government
24-Feb	Jimmy Vargas		
24-Feb	Wilmer Jhonny Carballo		8. Government
24-Feb	Antonio José Valbuena	7. Opposition	
24-Feb	Carmen Roldán	8. Opposition	
25-Feb	Eduardo Anzola	9. Opposition	
28-Feb	Giovanni Pantoja	10. Opposition	
3-Mar	Luis Gutiérrez Camargo	11. Opposition	
3-Mar	Deivis José Duran Useche	12. Opposition	
6-Mar	Acner Isaac López León	13. Opposition	
6-Mar	José Gregorio Amaris	14. Opposition	
7-Mar	Johan Alfonso Pineda Morales	15. Opposition	
8-Mar	Gisela Rubilar Figueroa	16. Opposition	
10-Mar	Daniel Tinoco		9. Government
12-Mar	Jesús Enrique Acosta		10. Government
12-Mar	Guillermo Sánchez		11. Government
12-Mar	Ramso Ernesto Bracho Bravo	17. Opposition	
17-Mar	José Guillén Araque	18. Opposition	
18-Mar	Francisco Rosendo Marín	19. Opposition	
19-Mar	Jhon Castillo	20. Opposition	
21-Mar	Wilfredo Rey		12. Government
22-Mar	Argenis Hernández		13. Government
22-Mar	Juan Orlando Labrador Castiblanco		
23-Mar	Adriana Urquiola		
24-Mar	Miguel Antonio Parra	21. Opposition	
29-Mar	Franklin Alberto Romero		
29-Mar	Roberto Annese		14. Government

Source: Compiled by the authors.

By the time the protests fizzled out in early April, there had been a total of forty deaths. The opposition's side was most likely responsible for twenty-one of them; the government's side was mostly likely responsible for fourteen.

There were three additional deaths—the cases of Genesis Carmona, Juan Orlando Labrador Castiblanco, and Adriana Urquiola—for which the facts are unclear regarding who was responsible. There were also two accidental deaths. Franklin Alberto Romero, a businessman, died from an electric shock in San Cristobal when he and several others tried to mount a billboard on a barricade. In the case of protester Jimmy Vargas, video footage confirmed that he accidentally fell from a rooftop. Vargas's passionately anti-government family members blamed the government anyway, which led Reuters and others to spread false claims that he had been shot or otherwise made to fall from the roof. In a subsequent report, Reuters admitted that "a cellphone video of the incident shows him appear to stumble and then plunge backward while climbing down from a ledge."[23]

Reuters, to its credit, even dared make the important point in one article that "in a country with at least 15,000 homicides last year, there is ample scope for confusion and propaganda." However, it more often stuck to a pattern of vague reporting that suggested government responsibility for all the deaths.[24]

The *New York Times* commonly used that approach, too, but media activists successfully pressured it into making the following correction to an article on March 26:

> An earlier version of this article incorrectly stated that the more than 30 people killed in the political demonstrations in Venezuela since February 4 were protesters. That number includes security forces and civilians, not only protesters.[25]

Peter Hart made the crucial point about this correction in an article for FAIR.org:

If you have been relying on US media to follow the Venezuela story, or relying on Venezuelan opposition sources, you'd probably have the mistaken idea that the violence was basically all happening on one side—which might explain how this error got into the *Times*.

A month earlier, the *Times* had issued another correction regarding Venezuela's TV media. A news article had stated: "The only television station that regularly broadcast voices critical of the government was sold last year and the new owners have softened its news coverage." The correction read as follows:

> An earlier version of this article referred imprecisely to *Globovision*. Before its sale last year, it broadcast more voices critical of the Venezuelan government than any other TV station, but it was not the only one to regularly feature government critics.[26]

Unfortunately, these corrections do not have much impact on a headline-scanning, article-skimming readership.

The Western government–funded International Crisis Group (ICG) sunk especially low in its report about the protests. It claimed that there was only "weak evidence" that any opposition people had ever used firearms:

> In contrast to the abundant evidence linking security forces and pro-government civilians to deaths and injuries, it is unclear whether some in the opposition used firearms. In any case, the evidence on this is weak. The only deaths that appear clearly linked to the protesters are those involving accidents caused by barricades, including the use of barbed wire or other obstacles.[27]

So as far as the ICG is concerned, the bodies of several people (police and civilians) who were shot to death while attempting to clear barricades in opposition strongholds are "weak evidence" of firearm use by the opposition.[28] The report was so extreme in its bias that it even tried to impugn the results of the 2004 recall referendum, which Chávez won by 18 percentage points.[29]

When the United States Is Isolated, Pretend It Isn't

The members of the Organization of American States (OAS) took a completely different stance toward the protests than did the United States, but U.S. apologists did their best to ignore it.

An OAS resolution from March 7 expressed "solidarity with the victims and their family members, the people, and the Government of the Bolivarian Republic of Venezuela."[30] One should distinguish the OAS member states from the OAS bureaucracy, which is funded primarily by the United States and based in Washington, DC. In 2014, that distinction was important due to the large number of left-of-center governments in the region.

The United States and Panama alone expressed strongly dissenting views in the footnotes to the resolution. As journalist Nate Singham pointed out, the U.S. defeat at the OAS was remarkable given that "historically, the OAS has acted consistently with US foreign policy objectives."[31]

Consider how the *New York Times* and Reuters reported this. A *Times* article published on March 14 ignored the OAS resolution and grossly misled readers about the response of regional governments to the protest: "Mr. Maduro's kinder face is likely intended only to deflect international criticism, which has come most strongly from the United States."[32]

If the words "most strongly" in the sentence above were replaced with "almost exclusively," then it would have been accurate. Not only was the United States isolated in the Western Hemisphere, but ten days after this *Times* article came out, the European Union endorsed UNASUR's efforts to ease tensions in Venezuela. UNASUR, a body created in 2008 by the left-of-center governments in South America, was obviously even more independent of Washington than the OAS.[33] Also note how the reporter, William Neuman, was not hesitant to speculate about Maduro's motives. Imagine a reporter similarly speculating about what motivated John Kerry's allegation that the Maduro government had unleashed a "terror campaign" against protesters.³⁴ The following sentence is perfectly reasonable but would never be allowed in a New York Times article: *"Kerry's allegation is likely intended to boost the morale of violent protesters who have been almost entirely shunned by governments in the hemisphere."* (Italics added.)

Reuters was less ridiculous than the New York Times but still very misleading when it reported on March 16 that "Maduro has come under pressure from some foreign governments and rights groups over excessive use of force from his security forces." ³⁵

Readers must become researchers to discover that protesters, at that point, were responsible for more deaths than government security forces, and that the United States had failed almost completely to convince other governments to support the protesters.

CBC *Reporter Admits, "I Was Not Aware of Ultimas Noticias"*

During the 2014 coup attempt, the Western media ignored the content of Venezuela's news media and constantly made or implied claims of draconian censorship—exactly as Alan MacLeod found in his extensive research of U.S. and UK media coverage during the period 1998 to 2013.³⁶

For example, on March 27, the *CBC* reported:

> For Canadians with friends and family in Venezuela the extent of the violence sweeping that country is hard to watch, but many are also working to overcome government crackdowns on local news to ensure the world knows exactly what's happening.³⁷

We sent the author of this article, Mark Cadiz, the following email:

> Were you aware that *Ultimas Noticas*, Venezuela's largest circulating newspaper, regularly features vehemently anti-government op-eds? A headline from an op-ed in today's edition

reads "Solution to the crisis: As we can see we are living at the margins of the Constitution under a military dictatorship in which a military–civic clique perpetuates itself by force."

Another op-ed from 3/24/2014 says, "Not One More Death: The deaths have been occurring daily, the most noteworthy caused by armed groups operating outside the law but with the apparent consent of the Government."

Another op-ed from 3/24/2014: "Critical Situation: The so-called President has decided to establish himself as a fourth-rate dictator."

Another one from 3/20/2014 says, "One can't keep playing around with Maduro's assassin government and its insincere calls for peace."

This is far from an exhaustive sampling. *Ultimas Noticias* also features pro-government opinion and news reports, but to claim that fiercely anti-government voices are shut out of the media is a flagrant lie. You should sample Venezuela's media directly, especially if you read Spanish, and see for yourself.[38]

Cadiz responded the same day:

> Thanks for your detailed email and your concerns about my opening lead in the article. I've looked at your links and greatly appreciate you sending them to me. I was not aware of *Ultimas Noticias*, but thanks for pointing this newspaper out. I will have to update/retract the statement about media censorship.
>
> I will discuss further with my senior editors to correct this issue.
>
> Thanks for your concern.

The following clarification was appended to the end of the article four days later:

> This story originally said, "With the government also censoring media coverage, citizens have turned to social media to organize

and inform the world about the extreme measures the government has taken." The story did not mean to imply that the government was employing blanket censorship. While the government has taken steps to discourage reporting of some events in news and social media, both pro- and anti-government reports have continued to appear in the nation's news media, and publicly accessible social media tools have continued to work inside the country.

This clarification was better than nothing, but it came buried underneath an article that flatly contradicted it. The headline, subhead—"Venezuela an online battleground for Canadians backing protests: Canadians part of an effort to overcome crackdown on local news"—above an image of a masked protester all conveyed that Canadians in general were allied with protesters in a noble battle for press freedom.

Cadiz also relied heavily on two anti-Maduro sources. One was Ana Maria Roa, whom Cadiz said was "a Toronto resident of 22 years, [who] came to Canada when she was 18 and makes regular visits to Venezuela" and "participated in protests in her hometown of San Cristobal." Another source was "Yorman Urdaneta, originally from the Zulia state of Venezuela, who has been living in Canada for four years." Cadiz quoted her as saying, "Eventually there is going to be a social explosion in Venezuela, and I believe there is going to be a lot of blood on the streets. But the only way the people are going to get their country back is to fight."

Cadiz was not even familiar with Venezuela's largest newspaper, so it's reasonable to guess he was not aware that the opposition was defeated decisively in municipal elections only two months before the protests began. One reason for that defeat was the mentality of opposition people like his source, Urdaneta, who have consistently proved willing to see "a lot of blood on the streets" to annul their electoral defeats.

In April 2013, Venezuela's overseas voters cast 93.1 percent of their votes for Capriles. Any article that relies on Venezuelan expatriates would be completely unrepresentative of Venezuelan public opinion.[39]

But it's a fair guess that Cadiz wasn't aware of this either. It's quite easy to understand why, by 2014, a well-intentioned journalist would report the way Cadiz did. The Western media had been laying the propaganda groundwork since 2001. Venezuelan-Canadians—attractive sources for the CBC because they speak English or French and are easier to contact than people in Venezuela—were overwhelmingly pro-opposition.[40] And consider what prominent NGOs were saying about Venezuela's media.

In 2014, Reporters without Borders (RSF) ranked Venezuela 116 out of 179 in its "freedom of expression" index (and Canada 18th).[41] On February 20, the Committee to Protect Journalists (CPJ) made the absurd claim that "nearly all TV stations in Venezuela are either controlled or allied with the government of Maduro and have ignored the nationwide protests."

It was child's play to refute this nonsense if you actually spent some time looking at the content of Venezuela's TV media during the protests. But it was much easier (and no doubt invited less flak) if you simply took the word of supposedly reputable NGOs and Venezuelans living in Canada. Examples are listed below of significant protest coverage on Venezuelan TV, including interviews with hardline opposition leaders of the protests, among them the future Trump-recognized "interim president" Juan Guaidó:

- Interview with Henrique Capriles on Venevisión (Feb, 20).
- Venevisión coverage of opposition protests (Feb, 18).
- Globovisión report on student protests (Feb, 12).
- Interview with Juan Guaidó on Globovisión (Feb, 22).
- Venevisión interview with Tomás Guanipa, leader of the opposition Primero Justicia (Justice First) party (Feb. 20).
- Globovisión interview with María Corina Machado (Feb, 17).[42]

Commenting on Machado's interview with Globovisión, the U.S. economist Mark Weisbrot observed that she

> accuses the government of torturing students, and defends the

most controversial aspect of the ongoing protests: she argues that the people have a right to overthrow the democratically elected government. (This is something that would not appear on TV in most countries in the world in a situation like the current one in Venezuela, where threats to overthrow the government have been carried out and attempted repeatedly in the past 12 years). This interview is on *Globovisión*, the station that the ... *New York Times* report complains has "softened its news coverage."[43]

Comparing Two New York Times *Editorials on the Question of "Democratic Norms"*

On March 14, 2014, the *New York Times* editorial board stated:

> In the month since mass demonstrations began in Venezuela, at least 25 people have died in the protests. No end to the crisis is in sight, and each day the grievances grow, the arrests multiply, positions harden and moderates retreat.[44]

The protesters were in fact responsible for more deaths than the government, but the editorial linked to a *Times* article that conveyed the opposite by relying on pro-opposition sources. The editorial continued:

> There is no easy solution. The government of President Nicolás Maduro still commands strong loyalty from followers of the populist revolutionary Hugo Chávez, who died a year ago, while the opposition is divided and lacking in a common platform beyond despair over the economic mess left behind by "Chavismo." This is not a "Venezuelan Spring" to be resolved by the exit of a discredited tyrant. Though Mr. Maduro lacks his predecessor's charisma, his narrow victory in the presidential election last April is not in dispute, and no elections are scheduled before 2015. This is a bitterly divided population in urgent need of mediated dialogue.

The editorial board was guilty of a few drastic bits of historical revisionism. First, contrary to what the editorial claimed, Maduro's electoral victory *was* still disputed by the leaders of the protests. Their violent attempts to overturn the 2013 presidential election results were written out of existence. López and Machado never accepted the validity of Maduro's victory; López had even stated that the 2013 protests should have continued until Maduro was overthrown. The opposition knew it could count on U.S. support no matter how violently and intransigently it behaved. Rather than pressure its own government to stop giving the opposition that confidence, the editorial dismissed the blame that Maduro put on the United States.

The editorial also ignored the opposition's big defeat in nationwide municipal elections only two months before the 2014 protests began. Chavistas were probably better prepared to campaign than they were when Maduro was elected earlier that year, shortly after the death of Chávez. Also, despite problems, the economy had continued to grow. Oil prices remained high and would not collapse for almost another year. The editorial stated that opposition barricades "make life harder." Actually, those barricades *ended* several lives, and damaged the economy. And yet the editorial still claimed that the protesters were "driven to despair" by economic problems and mainly concerned with "restoring democratic norms."

Compare this editorial with one the *Times* published only five months later, on August 6, 2014, about Israel's bombing of Gaza (Operation Protective Edge) which, like the protests in Venezuela, lasted for about two months.[45] The key passage singled out Hamas for vastly harsher condemnation than Israel, the government that was actually responsible for the slaughter:

> In too many cases, Israel launched weapons that hit schools and shelters and failed to adequately protect Palestinian citizens. But Hamas knowingly targeted Israeli civilian centers in violation of any civilized standard and launched weapons from populated

areas in what looks like a deliberate effort to draw Israeli fire on innocents.

Israel attacked Palestinians in Gaza with nearly complete impunity. According to figures in the editorial, Israel's firepower killed 1,800 Palestinians (408 of them children) in about two months. That's 96 percent of the dead in what the *New York Times* outlandishly called a "war." It was also about one hundred times more people than the Maduro government and its supporters could credibly be accused of killing months earlier. The editorial board also mentioned in passing Israel's "blockade that has kept Gazans confined to the strip, and deprived them of imports, exports and jobs." This grossly understates the impact of the blockade that by itself kills thousands of Palestinians every year.[46]

The editorial claimed U.S. relations were "strained" by Israel's actions, but that's a lie. A few weeks before this editorial was published, the U.S. Senate unanimously passed a resolution expressing complete unqualified support for Israel's "right to defend its citizens and ensure the survival of the State of Israel."[47]

Unlike Hamas, the lavishly U.S.-funded Israeli government did not get accused by the *New York Times* of perpetrating terrorist attacks even as it clearly terrorized Palestinians.[48] "Failed to adequately protect" is the most the *Times* can muster when Palestinian corpses pile up embarrassingly high.[49]

The editorial showed no concern that Israel was violating the "democratic norms" (which are nonexistent under Israel's military occupation) that, in Venezuela, supposedly concern the U.S. government and the *New York Times* editorial board. There can be no doubt that the Western media would also give a U.S.-approved government in Venezuela a free hand to murder. After all, a U.S.-backed government in Caracas received flattering press coverage after its security forces killed hundreds, possibly thousands, of people in five days during the Caracazo Massacre of 1989.[50]

Radically different standards for concepts such as "democratic norms," "peaceful protest," and "self-defense" apply to U.S.-backed governments or protest movements. An extraordinary threat to democracy and human rights around the world—the one posed by Washington and its many accomplices—therefore goes undetected by the people who could do something about it.

9

Buildup to the Fifth Coup Attempt

Venezuela's GDP growth recovered for at least two quarters after the defeat of the fourth coup attempt in 2014. But at the end of the year, a collapse in oil prices—combined with President Nicolás Maduro's refusal to reform the exchange rate system—caused a recession that kept getting worse.

The chart below shows West Texas Intermediate (WTI) oil prices during the period between Maduro's election on April 14, 2013, and the end of the violent protests in 2017. WTI is a cheaper type of oil than Brent, which is often referred to in news articles about oil prices, and are closer in price to those of Venezuelan oil.[1] After oil prices collapsed during the fourth quarter of 2014, they fluctuated around $50 per barrel for years, and often went far lower, defying the predictions of experts.

The table below shows several oil price predictions cited by Mark Weisbrot and Jake Johnston in a 2012 report for the Center for Economic and Policy Research.[3] All these predictions grossly overestimated what the average price of oil would be in 2015 and 2020.

Maduro's failure to overhaul the fixed exchange rate system can be partially explained by the two coup attempts he had already survived in April 2013 and in February–April 2014. Maduro inherited the

Figure 9.1: WTI Oil Prices (from Maduro's Election to August 1, 2017)

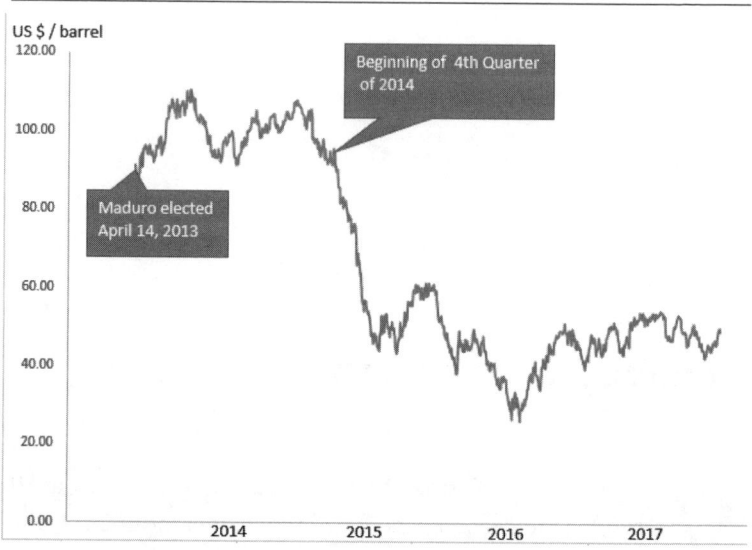

Source: Federal Reserve Bank of St. Louis.[2]

exchange rate system implemented by Chávez in February 2003 after the oil strike. Unfortunately, many Chavistas credited that system, in which the government sets official exchange rates, as being essential to Venezuela's economic success under Chávez.[4] Maduro was inhibited from making changes that could alienate his activist support base. He probably also hoped that notoriously unpredictable oil prices would return to 2013 levels.[5] Reduced oil revenues made U.S. dollars scarcer, which caused the black-market rate for dollars to rise even faster. The expanding black market was the main cause of inflation, even though it represented a small percentage of all transactions for dollars.

The government increasingly imposed price controls in an effort to slow inflation. But this mainly expanded a black market in price-controlled goods—and created long lines outside stores where price-controlled items were sold. Maduro insisted that Venezuela's chief problem was economic sabotage by his opponents—what he called an "economic war." But many voters were not persuaded,

TABLE 9.1: Projection of Oil Prices 2015–2035 (2010 dollars per barrel)

	2015	2020	2025	2030	2035
AEO2012	116.91	126.68	132.56	138.49	144.98
AEO2011	95.41	109.05	118.57	124.17	126.03
EVA	82.24	84.75	89.07	94.78	102.11
IEA	106.30	118.10	127.30	134.50	140.00
INFORUM	91.78	105.84	113.35	117.83	116.76
IHSGI	99.16	72.89	87.19	95.65	98.08
Purvin & Gertz	98.75	103.77	106.47	107.37	107.37
SEER	94.20	101.57	107.13	111.26	121.94

Source: U.S. Energy Information Administration (2012).

and the opposition was able to rebound from its defeat in the 2014 municipal elections. On December 6, 2015, it won control of the National Assembly.

After President Donald Trump deepened the U.S. sanctions regime in August 2017, Venezuela did face a true economic war. But in 2015, "economic war" was not a strong explanation for the recession.[6] With better economic policy, Maduro could have won two vastly better years for Venezuela despite the fall in oil prices. It would not have been easy, and the needed reforms would have been assailed by some critics from the left, as well as from the right (however hypocritically in the latter case). But the example of Evo Morales in Bolivia, who was overthrown in a U.S.-backed coup in November 2019 despite very solid economic policy and popular support, is highly instructive. No amount of economic success or democratic legitimacy will by itself prevent a U.S.-backed coup. And regardless of what might have been done better by Maduro during his first two years in office, after 2017 sanctions would have destroyed Venezuela's economy.[7]

The UNASUR Proposal

In July 2016, an economic team put together by the Union of South American Nations (UNASUR) proposed a detailed stabilization plan to the Venezuelan government.[8] The team consisted of Francisco Rodriguez, a longtime Chávez critic, but also Mark Weisbrot and Alex Main from the Center for Economic and Policy Research, an independent think tank based in Washington DC that had often debunked false claims about Venezuela. The UNASUR team estimated that Venezuela's indirect subsidies—such as the exchange rate system and very cheap gasoline—cost the government anywhere from 11 to 17 percent of GDP. To put that in perspective, health care expenditures in Latin American countries (public and private combined) averaged about 7 percent of GDP. The UNASUR plan would have replaced indirect subsidies with direct subsidies, such as an electronic discount card for low-income consumers of gasoline. Among its main recommendations was a clean float of the bolivar: the currency was to be freely traded so that the exchange rate was set by supply and demand.[9]

The plan did not address long-term problems. Venezuela, like all countries in the Global South, needs to diversify its economy or its export performance will be at risk. Exports are crucial to economic development.[10]

Even a mild critic of Chavismo such as former UK Labour leader Jeremy Corbyn said that Venezuela's economic crisis was in part due to its failure to diversify.[11] Did Chavismo fail to diversify Venezuela's economy, as critics charge? Yes, but it's a charge that is much more fairly made against the U.S.-backed governments that ruled Venezuela during the period from 1930 to 1998. It's not a very reasonable charge to level against Chavismo, which did not gain full control of the state oil company until 2003 and always faced the threat of a coup—thanks to Washington's hostility.

Corruption is also regularly blamed for Venezuela's economic problems. One of the most successful examples of economic development took place in South Korea from 1960 to 1996, almost entirely under corrupt U.S.-backed dictatorships.[12] Even with U.S. support, successful diversification and development took decades: South Korea's child mortality rate went from being three times higher than that of the United States in 1960 to being equal to it by 1996.[13] South Korea's example dramatically exposes the inadequacy of "corruption" as an explanation for a country's failure to develop. It also shows how beneficial freedom from Western hostility can be—in addition to some well-thought-out, state-directed policies.

December 6, 2015: The Opposition's Biggest Electoral Win

At the state and local level, Venezuela's opposition was able to score electoral victories even while Chavismo had overwhelming popular support—basically throughout the entire period of 1998 to 2014.

But with the exception of a very narrow win in the 2007 constitution referendum, victory at the national level eluded the opposition. As Venezuela's recession deepened, polls pointed to the opposition winning the 2015 legislative elections. Despite grumblings from hard-liners who wanted to abstain from the elections, the opposition participated and won 56 percent of the vote. The government's party, the United Socialist Party of Venezuela (PSUV), won 41 percent. In terms of seats, the opposition's victory was even larger. It won a two-thirds majority in the Assembly.[14] Recall that the disparity between the percentage of votes and seats was used by the opposition to attack the legitimacy of the 2010 National Assembly elections, when Chávez's party won 49 percent of the vote, giving it 59 percent of the seats.[15] Just before the 2015 elections, the *Washington Post* editorial board complained that the voting districts had been "gerrymandered" in the government's favor.[16] Predictably, that objection was forgotten when the opposition won a much higher percentage of seats than votes.

Anyone who knew about the opposition leadership's ample access to the mass media in Venezuela would be unsurprised that they could win.[17] Outside Venezuela, supporters of the opposition would casually claim that it was shut out of the media—with no need to worry about rebuttals.[18]

Months before the election, on August 7, 2015, a *New York Times* editorial stated in its headline, "Venezuela Tries to Silence Critics."[19] The editorial didn't mention Venezuela's media directly, but cited the jailing of Leopoldo López and the fact that Maria Corina Machado was barred from running. It concluded: "Whether the opposition will get to compete fairly, though, is in doubt." It referred to Machado and López as "critics" who "refrained from endorsing acts of violence."

How would the *New York Times* editorial board have described "critics" like Machado and López in the United States had they been involved with multiple foreign-backed efforts to overthrow the U.S. government? We get a good idea from a *Times* editorial published on April 11, 2019, which praised the Trump Justice Department for charging Julian Assange, who was responsible simply for doing journalism, not plotting coup attempts.[20]

On November 22, 2015, two weeks before the National Assembly elections, the *Washington Post* ran an editorial titled "Venezuela's Dirty Election Approaches."[21] The editorial cited Organization of American States president Luis Almagro, who also aggressively impugned the elections in advance by stating:

> The opposition is coming to the elections with its main leaders disqualified or in detention, with limited ability to access the media, under the scrutiny of the country's intelligence system, and under the burden of the country's legal framework interpreted against them.

Thus, falsely portrayed as oppressed underdogs with a system hopelessly rigged against them, the opposition went on to leverage its money (including U.S. funds), media access, and the recession into a huge win at the polls—one that gave them a two-thirds majority of seats despite winning only 56 percent of the vote.[22]

On January 15, 2016, Nicolás Maduro gave his State of the Union address in front of the now opposition-controlled National Assembly. It was broadcast on "*cadena nacional*"—that is, on all TV stations in Venezuela—along with a thirty-minute rebuttal by Henry Ramos Allup, the first National Assembly president chosen by the opposition.[23] It was a bizarre spectacle when seen in light of the assertion, made relentlessly by the likes of the *Washington Post* and so many others, that Maduro's opponents were silenced.

BUILDUP TO THE FIFTH COUP ATTEMPT

Maduro sits as Henry Ramos rebuts his speech (*Telesur*).

Of course, opposition politicians like Henry Ramos have always had ample access to huge audiences. In 2015, according to data from CONATEL, the Venezuelan government's media regulator, a record high 68 percent of Venezuelan households had access to subscription TV (either through satellite or cable), where anti-government pundits and politicians regularly appeared.[24] That does not include illegally obtained access, which would drive the percentage much higher.[25] Only two years earlier, in 2013, the top three private networks in Venezuela—Venevisión, Televen, and Globovisión—had about a 70 percent combined audience share for news and, years later (despite what were essentially wartime conditions imposed by crippling U.S. sanctions and threats) were still very balanced between pro and anti-government coverage.[26]

But if you believed what Chavismo's detractors had been saying for over a decade, then watching Henry Ramos rebut Maduro in a thirty-minute speech broadcast on all TV stations in January 2016 had to seem remarkable. This was happening in a country that the Western media had for many years depicted as having a thoroughly silenced opposition.[27]

The most outrageous part of Ramos's rebuttal was when he explained why portraits of Simón Bolívar had been removed from the building when the opposition took over. The portraits were digital renderings of Bolívar's face created through a government-funded study of his remains, which Chávez unveiled in 2012.²⁸ Ramos insisted that the portraits made Bolívar look less white than he had really been—that Bolívar's features had been "mulaticized," as he put it. He put his racist concern with the degree of Bolívar's whiteness on display in a speech he knew was being aired on every TV network in Venezuela. That he did so in the middle of an economic crisis added even more to the absurdity.

About ten minutes after commenting on Bolívar's whiteness, Henry Ramos turned to Maduro to verify that his remarks were still being broadcast on "*cadena nacional.*" They were. About ten minutes later, Maduro jokingly reminded Ramos again that he was still on "*cadena nacional.*"

The Western media apparently missed Ramos's prime-time bigotry. One exception was the anti-Chavista *Caracas Chronicles* blog, which seemed a bit embarrassed by his outburst. It briefly commented in a live blog of the speech: "Ramos Allup is still harping on the Bolívar portraits! #LetItGoHenry."²⁹ The opposition's racism had always been ignored by its international cheerleaders. That racism would manifest itself in gruesome ways during the fifth coup attempt.

Months after his televised rebuttal of Maduro, at a rally on August 27, Ramos publicly lamented the failure of the military coup of April 2002.³⁰ He said the coup had pulled Chávez's pants down and revealed that he didn't have male parts.³¹ At the rally, Ramos also said he was getting "a flood" of information leaked to him by military men who were fed up with Maduro. Ramos mockingly claimed that Maduro was "terrified" that an upcoming opposition march on September 1 in Caracas could have the same consequences as the infamous march that briefly led to Chávez's overthrow in 2002.

Two months later, a 10,000-word *New Yorker* article titled "Venezuela, A Failing State" by William Finnegan flattered Ramos extravagantly.³² Finnegan provided a firsthand account of the march on September 1, which Ramos said had Maduro "terrified" of another coup. Finnegan wrote that Ramos was "calm, worldly, almost professorial," a "mensch" with "good comedic timing," "the public's first choice for President, far ahead of Maduro. Now I could see why." To seem a bit less of a fanboy, Finnegan added vaguely that Ramos "can be fierce, and he has a long history to live down." The result was that Finnegan had transformed an unabashed bigot, who had all but admitted to fomenting another military coup, into a charming democrat.

A U.S. Embassy cable published by Wikileaks, long before Finnegan's article appeared, showed how the U.S. ambassador to Venezuela, William Brownfield, privately assessed Ramos in 2006.[33] Brownfield called him "unimaginative, overconfident, and even repellent." It's impossible to disagree, but adjectives at least as harsh also apply to Brownfield, who in 2019 called for intensifying the already murderous sanctions on Venezuela without even bothering to pretend that they weren't lethal.[34]

The cable revealed that Ramos and officials from his party were constantly begging U.S. officials for money and favors.[35] Think of how deeply imperial double standards are ingrained. A political leader in the United States who behaved like Ramos—who made no secret of his desire to see a coup, and who had been caught soliciting funds from a foreign government that supported previous coup attempts—would be in prison.

In December 2015, after the elections, the lame-duck Chavista-dominated Assembly replaced thirteen Supreme Court judges whose twelve-year terms had expired.[36] Before the appointments were made, the Supreme Court had ruled that it was constitutional to make the changes before the new Assembly was sworn in on January 5.

That day, Henry Ramos Allup announced that Maduro would be ousted within six months.[37] Unsatisfied with the high level of impunity the U.S.-backed opposition had enjoyed until then (thanks, in part, to the wide-ranging amnesty that Chávez granted opposition leaders in 2007), the new Assembly quickly drafted an "amnesty law" aimed at freeing those imprisoned as a result of the four coup attempts since 2002.

The institutional struggle began when the National Electoral

Council (CNE) said that four of the legislative elections may have to be rerun because they were tainted by vote-buying.[38] (The Supreme Court soon backed this announcement with a ruling on December 30, 2015.) One Chavista and three opposition legislators from the state of Amazonas were suspended. As the journalist Rachael Boothroyd-Rojas explained in an article for VenzuelAnalysis.com, the suspensions removed the opposition's two-thirds supermajority, which would have given it more power; for example, the power to remove judges in cases of "gross misconduct." Even with a supermajority, however, the National Assembly's powers were checked by the "Citizens Power" branch, which the constitution defines as the "Ombudsman, the General Prosecutor [Attorney General] and the General Comptroller." The Citizens Power branch would determine if something qualifies as "gross misconduct," enabling the removal of a judge by the National Assembly. In short, while a supermajority certainly gave the National Assembly more power, it was not going to allow it to easily trample the other branches of government. Nevertheless, the constitutional standoff that went on during the following months continued to lay the groundwork for the fifth coup attempt.[39]

On January 6, the suspended legislators were sworn in despite the CNE's decision and its backing from the Supreme Court. On January 11, the Supreme Court escalated the dispute further by declaring the entire National Assembly "in contempt" for swearing in the three suspended legislators.[40] The Assembly was therefore unable to pass laws until two days later, when the opposition backed down. The three members in the disputed seats were formally "disincorporated" on January 13, meaning that their swearing-in ceremonies were annulled.[41]

Supreme Court Thwarts National Assembly

Over the ensuing months, the Assembly attempted to pass a number of laws and block Maduro's decrees but was repeatedly thwarted by the Supreme Court (with the exception of one law that was upheld by the court on April 28).⁴² The court overruled a January 22 vote by the National Assembly that would have blocked Maduro's "Economic Emergency" decree. The court then approved an extension of the decree in March.⁴³

In March, the Assembly also passed a statement asking OAS president Luis Almagro to help invoke the organization's "Democratic Clause" against Venezuela. The charter empowers member states to sanction a government by suspending it from the OAS if it has been judged to have violated democratic norms.⁴⁴ The real threat in this case would be providing legal and political cover for intensified U.S. sanctions. Early in that month, opposition legislators unveiled their plan to oust Maduro before the end of his six-year term. It involved passing a law that would retroactively reduce the presidential term from six years to four, pursuing a recall referendum, and other tactics.⁴⁵

The retroactive presidential term shortening proposal was thrown out by the Supreme Court on April 26.⁴⁶ The opposition's proposed "amnesty law" was struck down by the court in April.⁴⁷

One of the new Assembly's first proposed laws would have privatized social housing built under Chavista governments. The Supreme Court shot it down in May on the grounds that it infringed on a constitutional right to housing. The court also expanded Maduro's economic emergency decree powers which, among other things, allocated more resources to the recently created Local Production and Distribution Committees (CLAPs) that distributed food directly to households through communal councils. In September, the emergency decree was extended again.⁴⁸

In June, the Supreme Court struck down a proposed law dealing with foreign international aid.⁴⁹ It would have allowed foreign aid groups to operate in Venezuela without the invitation of the president and, according to the court, given the aid groups "the power to decide what the cooperation consists of, what quality and on what conditions it would be delivered." The court said that the law infringed on the "powers of the Executive branch with respect to states of emergency and in regards to the management of foreign relations."

On July 19, the court blocked the Assembly's attempt to remove the thirteen Supreme Court justices who had been appointed in December. The journalist Lucas Koerner reported:

> The high court cited Article 265 of the Venezuelan Constitution, which specifies that the removal of TSJ justices can "only be done by the National Assembly through a two-thirds majority in cases of grave misconduct, as authorized by the Citizens Power" branch of government.
>
> Venezuela's Citizen's Power branch, which is composed of the attorney general, the national ombudsman, and the comptroller, has yet to recommend an investigation of any of the TSJ justices.[50]

On July 28, the Assembly voted to defy, as it briefly had in January, the Supreme Court's suspension of three opposition legislators who were accused of vote buying. The court announced that any votes it took while it defied that suspension would be "null."[51]

One of the Assembly's multipronged strategies to oust Maduro was based on the claim that he was Colombian. This charge was inspired by rumors, including the possibility that Maduro's mother may have been born in Colombia. The Supreme Court ruled in October that Maduro was indeed Venezuelan. Lucas Koerner explained at the time that even Colombia's government, which was hostile to Maduro, undermined the opposition's effort.[52]

In October, the Supreme Court also ruled that, given the Assembly's status of being "in contempt," Maduro could bypass it for the purpose of getting his budgets approved. Three opposition mayors broke with Accion Democratica, the political party led by Henry Ramos, and signed a document supporting the budget—and were, in turn, expelled from their party.[53]

On November 15, 2016, the three opposition legislators the Supreme Court had suspended after their elections were called into question submitted a letter to Henry Ramos saying they were "willing to be disincorporated" from the National Assembly. It appeared that the standoff between the National Assembly, the Supreme Court, and President Maduro might soon be resolved. But the legislators did not follow through on this, and they were never actually "disincorporated," as the Supreme Court had ordered back on January 11. The Supreme Court pointed this out in a November 21 ruling.[54]

The Saga of the Failed Recall Referendum Drive

If a recall referendum had been held before January 10, 2017, an opposition victory would have triggered a fresh presidential election. The Venezuelan constitution says that one recall vote is allowed after the midway point of the president's six-year term. But if a recall vote is won in the fourth year, then the vice president simply takes over for the remainder of the term. In a recall referendum held before January 10, 2017, then, an opposition victory would have triggered a fresh presidential election. It was therefore very important to the opposition that a recall vote be held in 2016.[55]

The opposition did not officially launch its signature drive until April 26, 2016, because they were working on other strategies simultaneously. One that they were excited about was retroactively shortening the presidential term to four years.[56] In a recall referendum, the opposition would have to win with more votes than Maduro received in April 2013. However, a referendum on the "term shortening" amendment to the constitution provided a lower threshold: no requirement to win with more votes than Maduro received in 2013. The Supreme Court had reasonable grounds for quashing that idea. By insisting that the amendment apply to Maduro's current term, the opposition was effectively trying to bypass the constitutionally established procedure for cutting Maduro's current term short: the recall referendum.

Henrique Capriles wanted to pursue the recall vote process immediately. But it wasn't until early March 2016 that the notoriously divided opposition coalition announced a four-pronged approach to ousting Maduro: reducing his term to four years, organizing street protests, rewriting the constitution through a constituent assembly, and carrying out a recall referendum.[57]

According to Venezuelan law, gathering signatures from 1 percent of the electorate starts the recall referendum process, and then gathering—and having the national electoral council (CNE) verify—signatures representing 20 percent of the electorate triggers a vote. During the recall attempt in 2004, eight months had elapsed between the end of November 2003, when the opposition submitted signatures representing 20 percent of the electorate, and the recall vote held in August 2004.[58] In May 2016, however, when the opposition was eight months away from the crucial January 10 deadline, it had not collected enough signatures required for a recall vote. It had only gathered enough signatures for the CNE to begin the process.

The opposition did not help itself by staging protests, which turned violent, outside CNE offices in May. This gave the CNE grounds for suspending its work for weeks.[59] A Eurasia Group flowchart of the process showed that January 10 would have been a tight deadline even if Maduro's allies on the CNE had not engaged in deliberate foot dragging—as they certainly did.[60]

In late October, courts in four states issued injunctions against the petition drive based on fraud allegations. The CNE again suspended its work, thereby ensuring, as was already obvious, that the crucial January 10 deadline would be missed.[61]

The National Assembly voted to obey the Supreme Court and disincorporate the three opposition legislators on January 11—*after* first electing a new president, Julio Borges, on January 5, who presided over the vote. But the court refused to recognize the January 11 vote because it had ordered the Assembly to formally disincorporate the legislators *before* it would recognize any other vote the Assembly took. Henry Ramos, as the last Assembly president the court recognized as legitimate, would have to preside over the vote. The opposition refused that condition and therefore remained in contempt.[62]

The Assembly then invoked Article 233 of the constitution to make the argument that Maduro had abandoned his post—the same absurd claim that Juan Guaidó would use in 2019 to declare himself interim president. On January 30, 2017, the Supreme Court rejected the Assembly's arguments. Even opposition writer Francisco Toro conceded the absurdity of the argument in an October 26, 2016, blog post (but justified making it anyway, claiming that Maduro was guilty of worse constitutional violations).[63]

In March, the Supreme Court announced that it would fill in for the National Assembly (while the Assembly remained in contempt) for the purpose of negotiating contracts for the state oil company. The opposition and its supporters abroad, such as CNN, claimed that the National Assembly had been "dissolved." A significant consequence of this ruling, one that turned the constitutional battle into a full-blown coup attempt, was that the Chavista attorney general, Luisa Ortega Díaz, publicly denounced the ruling as a "rupture of the constitutional order." It was soon clear that she had flipped to the opposition's side, which was an especially critical development because she was part of the key Citizen Power branch of government mentioned above.[64]

It's important to note what the journalists Rachael Boothroyd-Rojas and Ryan Mallett-Outtrim mentioned about the Supreme Court ruling in an analysis piece:

> Although Article 336.7 of the constitution does give the TSJ [Supreme Court] the authority to "declare an unconstitutional default in the national, state or municipal legislature . . . and establish, if necessary, corrective measures," the exact "measures" open to the court aren't specifically elaborated on.
>
> Do they include allowing the TSJ to take over the daily affairs of the AN [National Assembly]? There's certainly no precedent for it under the current constitution; but then again, the constitution does establish the TSJ as the ultimate legal body in the country for interpreting the Magna Carta.[65]

On April 1, the Supreme Court backed down and reversed its ruling. But by April 4, the fifth coup attempt was underway.[66]

The Constitutional Blame Game

To what extent did Maduro's government trample democracy, judicial independence, and the constitution during this institutional standoff? All things considered, not enough to warrant being called a dictatorship or even particularly "authoritarian."

These terms were not applied to Brazil, for example, when President Dilma Rousseff was ousted by the Senate in 2016, based on an indefensible pretext: the breaching of budget rules that had nothing to do with perpetrating a crime, which is the constitutional requirement for impeachment. Two years later, ex-president Lula da Silva was imprisoned in what was obviously a politically driven case, and therefore disqualified from running for president in 2018. Both these acts were undemocratic power grabs by Brazil's right wing and welcomed by Washington.[67]

More dramatically, the Áñez government in Bolivia was not called a dictatorship by the likes of Human Rights Watch and the Western media, even though it was installed after a military coup that ousted President Evo Morales. In fact, HRW's America's director explicitly referred to Bolivia under Áñez as a "democracy."[68]

Additionally, there is no valid democratic principle that requires an elected government to let itself be overthrown by the proxies of a hostile foreign power. The very first article of the Venezuelan constitution states:

> The Bolivarian Republic of Venezuela is irrevocably free and independent, basing its moral property and values of freedom, equality, justice and international peace on the doctrine of Simón Bolívar, the Liberator. Independence, liberty, sovereignty, immunity, territorial integrity and national self-determination are unrenounceable rights of the Nation.[69]

Citizens of the world's most powerful states, especially the United States, may understandably take their country's "independence," "sovereignty," "self-determination," and "territorial integrity" for granted. They do not worry about foreign governments overthrowing their own, unless they believe the ravings of people like John Bolton (who not only claimed that Iraq had weapons of mass destruction but also that Cuba posed a biological weapons threat to the United States) or Rachael Maddow (who urged her audience to worry that Russia might be able to disable "all the natural gas lines that service Sioux Falls" in the middle of winter).[70]

But for much of the world, being targeted for destruction by the United States is an all too realistic concern. And the threat to Venezuela from the United States and its proxies long predates both Venezuela's economic crisis and the 2015 National Assembly elections. It is hardly "authoritarian" that Venezuela's CNE didn't make a recall petition process quick and easy for an insurrectionist opposition.[71]

That said, consider two of the opposition's more valid complaints during this standoff.

One involved the way vote-buying allegations were handled with respect to three Assembly seats won by the opposition in the state of Amazonas. Based on taped phone conversations, there certainly was a plot to pay people *who could show* (through a photo of the voting receipt that is provided after voting electronically) that they voted for opposition candidates in that state.[72] But with witnesses from all sides present inside voting centers during the elections, it seems unlikely that this scheme could have been carried out on any significant scale. There were clearly grounds for fining, and maybe even jailing, some of the people involved, but annulling the results should arguably require reasonable grounds that the violations may have changed the outcome of the election. Otherwise the door is opened, or thrown further open, to all kinds of frivolous electoral complaints. Venezuela had already been plagued for years by the opposition doing just that. The CNE and the Supreme Court were indeed using somewhat uncompelling legal grounds to deprive the opposition of the few seats it needed for a supermajority in the National Assembly, which would have given it more power. On the other hand, the law had regularly been bent (or often disregarded entirely) in favor of opposition leaders such as Henry Ramos since 2002, simply because they were rich and allied with the United States. Ramos had not only been exposed seeking money and favors from a hostile foreign government, but in March 2017, he boasted about using his position as National

Assembly president to make Venezuela's economic crisis worse.[73] An "authoritarian" government would not have allowed Ramos any role in public life by 2015, much less recognize him, as the Supreme Court did, as the legitimate National Assembly president.

Another one of the opposition's valid complaints during the standoff involved the Supreme Court's decision to rule the *entire* National Assembly in contempt for swearing in the three legislators accused of vote buying. That was disproportionate. There should have been a way to simply not count votes from those legislators until the issue was resolved. In fact, this was effectively the situation for about the first seven months of 2016, when the Assembly was not being held in contempt.

The opposition argued that during those months the Supreme Court was completely partial to Maduro (that is, not independent) and that it unjustifiably thwarted the Assembly's ability to legislate. But much of what the Assembly tried to pass could be placed in two general categories: the blatantly unconstitutional—retroactively shortening the presidential term, claiming that Maduro abandoned his post, and trying to get more impunity for past coup attempts through an amnesty law—and the highly questionable—using foreign aid groups to undermine the authority of the president, privatizing social housing. In short, the court's rulings against the opposition were mainly reasonable.

No doubt the Supreme Court was solidly Chavista, but that's because Chavistas had dominated almost every major election since 1998. If Republicans dominated all major elections in the United States for eighteen years, as Chavistas had done in Venezuela, then the U.S. Supreme Court would be lopsidedly Republican. No system will magically produce judges who deliver politically neutral judgments.[74]

Moreover, the very real national security concerns Venezuela faced also gave the Supreme Court strong reason to close ranks behind Maduro. The judiciary at all levels, however, was never under the thumb of the president or reflexively Chavista. And even purportedly Chavista public prosecutors were often obstructing efforts to hold enemies of the government accountable for grave crimes. It was a big problem going back to Chavismo's early years, but it came to the surface during the violent protests of 2017.

In Venezuela, the U.S.-backed opposition used a serious economic crisis brought about by a fall in export revenue, which was greatly aggravated by the government's errors, to gain popular support. (This strategy was similar to what happened in Brazil when Dilma Rousseff was ousted from the presidency in 2016.) After 2016, the Venezuelan Supreme Court's response to the opposition-controlled National Assembly was hardly beyond reproach. But even without missteps, another U.S.-backed coup attempt was going to come. Two coup attempts had already been made against Maduro before economic problems had made any dent in his level of popular support. In Bolivia, in 2019, the pretext for a military coup did not require any economic crisis at all to depose a very popular president, Evo Morales—it merely required bogus claims of electoral fraud, backed by the United States and, inevitably, the Western media.[75]

The opposition would increasingly lean on U.S. support and, closely related to that, the indefinite prolongation of economic crisis to try to seize power by force—even if it lost them popular support and inflicted hardships on their own country.

10

Fifth Coup Attempt: April 4–July 31, 2017

Between April 4 and July 31, 2017, violent protests erupted in Venezuela and claimed 126 lives. These protests were a fifth attempt to leverage U.S. support and oust the government by force. While this coup attempt failed, it paved the way for Donald Trump to dramatically escalate the severity of U.S. sanctions. Unlike the fourth coup attempt (the protests of 2014), the 2017 protests came after oil prices had collapsed, and after U.S. sanctions, imposed by President Obama in 2015, openly targeted the Maduro government. In 2014, the protests came as the economy, while struggling, was still growing and shortly after Maduro's allies had won a decisive victory in municipal elections. In 2017, by contrast, the protests came after Maduro's popular support had decreased due to an indisputably grave economic crisis. Like Maduro's opponents in Venezuela, by 2017 the Western media were similarly emboldened to be more aggressive. For example, months before the protests of 2017, in October 2016, the *New York Times* editorial board absolved the U.S.-backed protesters in advance for killing anyone:

> As the situation worsens, it is only logical that more Venezuelans

will be driven by desperation to rise up. If there is more bloodshed, Mr. Maduro will be responsible.[1]

This is quite a contrast with the *Times* editorial published two years earlier that rebuked Palestinians while Israel was in the process of slaughtering hundreds of them per week with close to one hundred percent impunity.[2] Absolution in advance is out of the question for Palestinians who must not even fire enhanced fireworks (so-called rockets) into empty fields. It's a blessing reserved for U.S. allies.[3]

The *New York Times* followed up with four more editorials about Venezuela between March 31 and August 30—just before and after four months of violent protests:

"Venezuela's Descent Into Dictatorship" (March 31)
"Pressuring Venezuela's Leader to Back Down" (April 4)
"Mr. Maduro's Drive to Dictatorship" (August 3)
"Exporting Chaos to Venezuela" (August 17)

None of the editorials had a harsh word to say about the opposition, even though it was not clear which side had killed more people during the protests. It was very clear, however, that protesters were responsible for some grisly atrocities. Also note the *Times*'s determination to stick the "dictator" label on Maduro. The August 3 editorial said that Maduro "belongs" in the same "rarefied company" as Bashar al-Assad and Kim Jong-un.[4] And even though the August 17 editorial expressed nervousness over the Trump administration's military threats against Venezuela, it continued to demonize Maduro's government—which is what made those threats possible.

In addition to the Western propaganda apparatus that always demanded impunity for U.S. allies in Venezuela, another force emerged from within Chavismo that was openly pushing the same line: Luisa Ortega Díaz, Venezuela's attorney general since 2003. In fact, she was praised in a *New York Times* editorial on March 31.

Ortega publicly broke with Maduro and the Supreme Court over a ruling in March that would have allowed the court to fill in for the

National Assembly while the latter was ruled in contempt. Ortega's position initially looked like sincere dissent against the ruling. However, as the fifth coup attempt, the violent protests of 2017, began and their death toll climbed (eventually taking 126 lives), it became clear that her objective was weakening Maduro, not enforcing the law or upholding the constitution. This became especially obvious after Maduro announced on May 1 that he was calling elections for a constituent assembly.

The journalist Lucas Koerner explained on June 16:

> In a shocking revelation, Ortega announced on May 24 that of 2,664 people indicted for crimes such as homicide, looting, grievous bodily harm, robbery, and arson, "only 284 have been jailed." "[This] confrontation . . . will not be resolved by putting people in jail," she said during the press conference.[5]

Edgar Marquez, the head of an organization representing Chavista protesters and bystanders who were killed or injured during the April 2002 coup, said that Ortega used typos in the case files and other frivolous excuses to justify setting people free. She also stopped returning the calls of organizations like his with whom she had always worked. Marquez said that after her break with the government, they discovered that she had lied to them for several years about cases she claimed to have been pushing through the courts. They did not suspect the worst about her, however, until 2017.[6]

Ortega also gave an interview to the *Wall Street Journal* on May 3, saying, "We can't demand peaceful and legal behavior from citizens if the state takes decisions that don't accord with the law."[7] It was a bold provocation. An inability to make U.S.-backed insurrectionists respect the law was among Venezuela's biggest problems since 2002. Neither Maduro nor Chávez could ever deal with prominent U.S.-backed subversives the way that the self-proclaimed "mature democracies" could. But here was Venezuela's attorney general inverting that reality in a U.S. newspaper, one that was especially hostile to

Chavismo; the article itself referred to the "authoritarian government she serves" and "the hard-line leftist regime."

Three years earlier, in 2014, Ortega was named by U.S. Senator Marco Rubio as one of the many Venezuelan officials he wanted sanctioned.[8] In February 2015, it appeared that Ortega was added to a list of Venezuelan officials hit with visa restrictions by President Obama. (The U.S. State Department said that it could not legally name anyone on the list.)[9] Three days later, Ortega announced on a public radio show that she was hiring a lawyer to sue the U.S. government.[10] The *Wall Street Journal* made no mention of this in its interview with Ortega. Reuters, the BBC, and Al Jazeera also published articles about Ortega around that time.[11] None mentioned that she had prepared to sue the U.S. government in 2014. When and why did she drop the idea?

As late as March 5, 2017, Ortega had tweeted, "Today we remember Hugo Chávez Frias, a tireless Venezuelan fighter for social and just causes."[12] On August 29, 2017, weeks after she had been fired on August 5, Ortega fled Venezuela to avoid prosecution for allegedly letting her husband use her office to run an extortion ring. On August 31, Reuters reported her decision to pass details about corrupt acts allegedly perpetrated by Maduro "to authorities in the United States, Spain, Mexico, Brazil and Colombia."[13] The opposition-controlled National Assembly refused to recognize her dismissal. By 2018, Ortega was trying cases before the opposition-appointed Supreme Court in Exile, whose members are based in the United States, Panama, Chile, and Colombia. They reportedly met weekly via Skype.[14] In July 2018, Ortega hinted that a hard-line opposition conspiracy theory that Chávez died in December 2012 rather than March 2013 may be true (though she later backed away from that).[15] She has also claimed to be investigating the (already debunked) theory that Maduro is not Venezuelan.[16] She immediately recognized the Trump-appointed Juan Guaidó as Venezuela's president in January 2019.[17] And on March 14, 2019, in an exclusive interview with the hard-line Pananpost.com, she attacked Chávez, whom she had always emphatically praised:

Look, I'm going to face whatever. I'm not afraid of anything. But those who say that, are those who have unfortunately been victims of Chavismo. Chavismo sowed hatred. Divide and conquer: that was the maxim. I do not know who said it, but it was very true.

Maduro and Chávez too! They created hatred between brothers, between neighbors.[18]

Ortega's about-face seemed calculated to avoid punishment, as a long-time Chavista official, at the hands of an opposition government that she assumed would soon take power. In an interview on February 1, 2018, she was asked by the Venezuelan journalist Isnardo Bravo if she had presidential ambitions. Her response was: "I don't know if one day I could think about or plan that but for now no."[19]

With a prosecutor like this, the question of why grave crimes against government supporters, and the government itself, went unpunished under the Chávez and Maduro governments, becomes easier to answer.

In 2011, the documentary filmmaker Edward Ellis made a film, *Tierras Libres*, about the assassination of hundreds of Chavista activists in the countryside since 2001. The murders strongly suggested the involvement of wealthy landowners opposed to land reform. Ellis's assessment of the Chavista legal system's failure to bring perpetrators to justice was scathing, but the Western media, despite constantly digging for anything negative to say about Venezuela under Chávez, took almost zero interest. The *Guardian* allowed Ellis an op-ed three months after a letter was sent to them protesting its complete lack of coverage of the murders, despite having a correspondent, Rory Carroll, living in Caracas for years.[20]

There is a prophetic ring to Ellis's remarks in a 2011 interview, when one considers that Luisa Ortega Díaz and a few other prosecutors turned completely against Chavismo several years later:

The legal system in Venezuela, despite the international media's misinterpretations, is still, in many cases, very much in the hands of the middle and upper classes. Most of these people have their roots in the power structures of Punto Fijismo—that's to say, the ancien regime.

The majority of lawyers and judges share the same cultural background and class origins as the landowners and latifundistas. They went to the same schools and universities, visit the same clubs and drink the same whisky regardless of whether or not they don a red hat at a rally. So what you have is a system run and controlled by money. If you have the resources to pay private lawyers who know how to manipulate the system, you have a much greater chance of walking free. And when it comes to the Attorney's General Office or Public Attorney's Office, they are notoriously ineffective and bureaucratic—many times filled with the same players.

In my opinion, the lack of accountability in the nation's Public Attorney's Office (Ministerio Publico) is the greatest obstacle to ending impunity in the countryside, if not the entire country. Specific policies need to be implemented to ensure the follow-up and investigation of cases but until we have people from the lower classes graduating as lawyers and becoming judges, I fear not much will change.[21]

Ellis's film undermined the story that the Western media and NGOs like Human Rights Watch were determined to push: that the judiciary was under Chávez's thumb. The international human rights NGOs had no interest in pressuring the government to root out corruption within its own ranks and reform the legal system *if the opposition would be weakened by it*. That explains why the case of Lourdes Afiuni, a judge imprisoned for corruption after she released a banker from custody, was transformed by the Western media into an "emblematic" case of alleged abuse under Chávez.[22]

Meanwhile, hundreds of Chavistas victimized by corrupt judges, prosecutors, and police in the rural areas were ignored. One such victim is Donella D'vies, whose husband Hermes Escalona was murdered in 2003. D'vies featured prominently in Edward Elllis's film, which reveals that she actually appeared once on Chávez's weekly TV show, *Alo Presidente*. On the show, Chávez promised her that he'd ask his own attorney to see what was going on with the case. The film followed up with D'vies, who tearfully said that nothing happened. "I never heard from that lawyer," she said, and added through tears, "For the poor there is no justice." Indeed, and no interest either, unless their plight can be weaponized in support of U.S. allies.[23]

An all too rare exception to this pattern was the case of assassinated Indigenous leader Sabino Romero. He struggled to have the government enforce the constitutional land rights of the Yukpa people. That effort pitted him against wealthy landowners whom activists allege decided to have him killed. Romero was murdered in 2013 by a hired assassin named Angel Antonio Romero Bracho, aka "Manguera," who was sentenced to thirty years in prison in 2015. A year earlier, five police officers who were Manguera's accomplices were given much lighter sentences (seven years). Nobody has been prosecuted for actually hiring Manguera, and activists say their pressure campaign was essential to getting any convictions at all. In 2016, these activists, led by Romero's wife, pressured Luisa Ortega after a prosecutor told them the case had been closed—to no avail.[24] As of 2020, Romero's supporters continued to demand that the intellectual authors of Romero's assassination be prosecuted.[25]

Ignacio Ramirez Romero, a lawyer who is the head of the National Federation for the Defense of Human Rights in Venezuela (FENADDEH), says he did not doubt Luisa Ortega's loyalty to Chavismo when she became a prominent prosecutor in 2002, but was not impressed with her ability: "I was very surprised when she was appointed Attorney General because she did not inspire confidence."[26] The remarkably inept prosecution of Leopoldo López by Luisa Ortega and other prosecutors, who later turned against Chavismo, also suggests that their lethargy and incompetence may have been significantly rooted in the corruption and professional class bias that filmmaker Edward Ellis denounced years earlier.[27]

FIFTH COUP ATTEMPT

Another Grim Tally

As it had done for the 2014 coup attempt, VenezuelAnalysis put together a detailed tally on the deaths during the fifth coup attempt in 2017.[28] Because the victims are far more numerous—126 in 2017, compared with 43 in 2014—the two graphics below summarize the data rather than providing an incident-by-incident summary.[29] The tally uses information from the attorney general's office as a baseline, which was then assessed against press reports and other sources.

Figure 10.1: Cause of Deaths, April 4–July 31, 2017

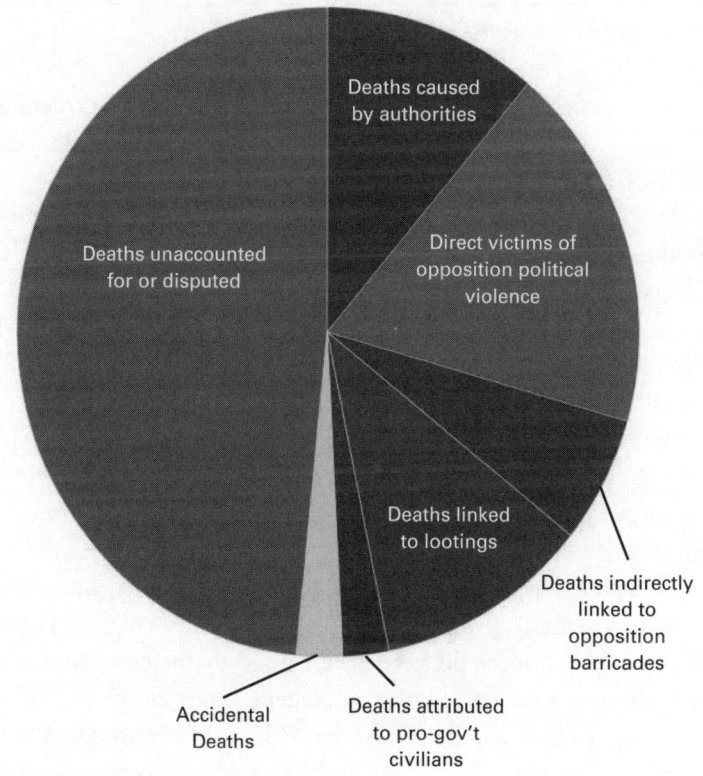

Source: Courtesy VenezuelAnalysis.

Figure 10.2: Who Died during Protests, April 4–July 31, 2017

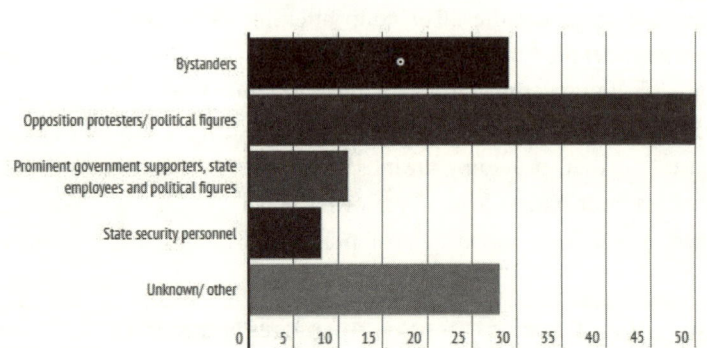

Source: Courtesy VenezuelAnalysis.

Given Luisa Ortega's open confrontation with Maduro throughout this period, this is not an approach that would underestimate deaths for which the government or its supporters were responsible.

At least a quarter of all 126 protest-related deaths were caused by the opposition, either directly or by hazards they created in the streets. That is very likely an underestimate, however, given that in about half the cases the information was too vague to conclude who was responsible. Considering only the cases for which responsibility is clear, about half the deaths were caused by the opposition.

Similar comments apply when one considers who died. About fifty victims could be clearly identified as opposition protesters or political figures, while nineteen were clearly members of the security forces or government supporters. Fifty-six victims were either bystanders or could not be reliably placed on either side of the political divide.

Anyone tempted to discard the possibility that a lot of the unknown or disputed deaths could have been caused by the opposition need only consider the case of Orlando Figuera. If not for the brazenness of the opposition protesters who killed him, his death could easily have ended up in the "unknown" or "disputed" categories, or perhaps dismissed as unrelated to the protests, because alleged criminals are often lynched in Venezuela.

FIFTH COUP ATTEMPT

Figuera's murder was not only gruesome, it was revealing in many ways that were ignored. On May 20, Figuera was stabbed six times, doused with gasoline, and set on fire by protesters in the wealthy Altamira neighborhood, which is in the opposition stronghold of Chacao, a municipality in East Caracas. (Leopoldo López was mayor of Chacao from 2000 until 2008; its mayors have always been from the opposition.) The assault on Figuera happened in broad daylight in front of a large crowd, in a neighborhood where many foreign journalists lived.[30] Figuera died in a hospital from his injuries two weeks after the assault.[31]

Unable to deny that anti-Maduro protesters had set Figuera on fire, Reuters tried to depoliticize and downplay the atrocity as much as possible. They interviewed their own photographer, Marco Bello, on May 22 (while Figuera was being treated in a hospital) who said, "All I heard throughout was that he was being accused of trying to steal from a woman. I didn't hear anyone accusing him of being a pro-government infiltrator."[32] Reuters added that "lynchings have become common, killing about one person every three days," according to a local NGO. On June 4, the day Figuera died from his injuries, a Reuters headline used the passive voice about his death. A man was "set ablaze"—by whom?[33] In the twelfth paragraph readers were finally informed that Figuera had been "set ablaze" by anti-government protesters. The article added:

> The government says Figuera was targeted for being "Chavista," or a supporter of late leftist Hugo Chávez, because he had dark skin and looked poor.
>
> But a Reuters witness on site said a group of mostly hooded protesters pursued Figuera, calling him a thief, after he was accused of trying to rob a woman.

Figuera's parents also accused the protesters of attacking him because they thought he was a Chavista.[34] Reuters ignored what the victim's family said and instead presented a variation of their patented "Maduro says" formulation, manipulating readers into deciding if

Maduro's government or a Reuters photographer was more credible.³⁵ Many readers would tend to believe the victim's family, certainly more than a relentlessly vilified government, but Reuters took away that option. Disputing the exact reason protesters murdered Figuera was a desperate bit of damage control.

Protesters—whom the Western establishment uncritically supported—had murdered him in broad daylight, in a neighborhood that was teeming with foreign journalists.³⁶ Two days before the assault on Figuera, another man, Carlos Ramirez, accused protesters from his hospital bed of setting him on fire because they thought he was a Chavista. It happened in the same neighborhood, Altamira. Ramirez survived.³⁷

In one of his lengthy articles for *The New Yorker*, Jon Lee Anderson mentioned Figuera's murder in passing without naming him: "Antigovernment activists had doused a chavista youth in gasoline and set him on fire." But Anderson quickly went on to assert that government forces had been "far more violent than the protesters."³⁸ In contrast to his brief mention of Figuera's case, Anderson spent paragraphs uncritically relaying the views of Roberto Patiño, an opposition protester who had been injured. Anderson seems to have concluded that the government was "far more violent" based on the claim that "a hundred and twenty protesters died in the fighting." But, as shown in the pie charts above, forty-eight deaths (about 40 percent) were bystanders, government supporters, or security forces. This means that, at most, seventy-eight protesters died, even if one assumes that all the "unknown" and "disputed" deaths were those of protesters.³⁹

Recall that, in the case of Israel, when almost one hundred percent of the dying is on the Palestinian side, and the death toll is in the thousands, the Western media often manages to depict Palestinians as the more violent party. At best, they are portrayed as equally violent and culpable.⁴⁰ Amnesty International and Human Rights Watch have descended to this false depiction as well.⁴¹

The Office of the UN High Commissioner for Human Rights (OHCHR), in a report it released in August 2017, sloppily claimed that Figuera died the same day he was attacked. In fact, he died from his injuries fifteen days later. The report also conspicuously failed to ask Trump to stop threatening Venezuela militarily, as he had begun to do. A credible human rights organization would never overlook that type of aggression.[42]

Needless to say, the murder of a poor Afro-Venezuelan by protesters supported by the Western media and big NGOs did not become an "emblematic" case, like that of the judge Lourdes Afiuni (who had been under house arrest since 2011, and was released in 2019).[43] Instead, Figuera's case was written off as an isolated case by the Western propaganda apparatus.

Why Did These Protesters Get Away with It?

Obvious questions about the Figuera case cried out to be asked, but never were. For instance, the June 4, 2017, Reuters article highlighted above quoted a local NGO, Foro Penal, to suggest that the government was going overboard with arrests as part of its "heavy-handed repression" of the protests. Reuters didn't say who had been arrested for Figuera's murder. In fact, nobody has been arrested by Venezuelan police in what became, certainly in Venezuelan state media, a very high-profile case. More than two years later, in September 2019, the Maduro government was trying to extradite one suspect from Spain.[44]

Enzo Franchini Oliveros, a Chacao resident and construction company owner, was publicly named as a suspect a month after the attack. He was identified thanks to video footage that showed the license plate of his motorcycle. In November 2019, Spain released him from custody, claiming that Venezuela's extradition paperwork was not in order. A Spanish newspaper, *La Razon*, published a sympathetic article about Franchini that ignored all the evidence against him.[45] Should it not have been very easy—especially for an alleged dictatorship—to quickly make numerous arrests in this case?

In March 2019, Figuera's mother had publicly expressed outrage that suspects had been able to leave the country.[46] Her frustration was understandable. Enzo Franchini had been in trouble with the law before but had managed to escape punishment. The class bias in the legal system that persisted under Chávez and Maduro is clearly a big factor in this case. It's a bias that the Western establishment has consistently *pressured Venezuela to maintain* by invoking "judicial independence" or other lofty pretexts. Figuera's killers also showed no fear of being outed to police by neighborhood residents. Were residents, including many foreign journalists, too afraid of the so-called peaceful protesters to get involved? In some cases, were they too much in sympathy with the killers?

In May, U.S. journalists Abby Martin and Mike Prysner filmed a short documentary about the protests that was aired in July by Telesur, a network funded by the Venezuelan government.[47] They showed that anyone living in Venezuela has good reason to fear doing honest firsthand reporting about anti-government protesters. Martin and Prysner began their film by interviewing numerous peaceful protesters who arrived early in the day, but then they began following the violent protesters who tended to arrive later on. These protesters set up flaming street barricades in Altamira, the neighborhood where Figuera was murdered. Martin and Prysner were at one point surrounded by hooded men who demanded to know which outlet they were with. Having U.S. accents and white skin probably saved their lives. The men assumed they would get the kind of coverage they wanted. Martin and Prysner followed the protesters to a major highway that the protesters had blocked by commandeering two large trucks. Protesters also began throwing rocks at an air force base.

The National Guard arrived and fired tear gas to clear the roads. This of course meant that the violent protesters had succeeded in producing images of supposed repression. Martin said that no arrests were made that night. Prominent opposition supporters, among them the hard-line Panampost.com, spread rumors that Martin and Prysner were working for Venezuela's intelligence services.[48] This is the kind of allegation that outrages big human rights NGOs when it is made by the Venezuelan government against the opposition.

Martin and Prysner were threatened because the opposition is not used to journalism that doesn't ape their perspective, no matter the facts. An extreme example of the latter type of journalist is the veteran British broadcaster Michael Crick. Confronted on Twitter with graphic images of Figuera's murder, he responded dismissively by saying that such things also happen in the United Kingdom.[49] We can imagine how quickly Venezuela would be bombed if its government was linked to protesters who burned people alive in the streets of London or Washington.

Trump Thinks He Can Overrule Maduro's Call for a Constituent Assembly

It's possible for a government to abuse its authority by calling for a vote (for example, one that would take universal rights away from racial or religious minorities), or, more obviously, by suppressing one. But with the support of the Western propaganda system, the United States has appointed itself judge of when a government in the Global South can hold a vote.

On May 1, 2017, Maduro called for the election of a Constituent Assembly (ANC) to rewrite the constitution. It was a way to break the institutional standoff with the National Assembly, because a constituent assembly has very broad powers under Venezuela's constitution. After the Constituent Assembly was elected on July 31, it allowed the government to replace Luisa Ortega Díaz. Her dismissal as attorney general, combined with the general exhaustion of the hard-line opposition, put an end to the fifth coup attempt.

There was a precedent for this development: a constituent assembly had been elected to write a constitution in 1999, and Venezuelans were asked to make very significant amendments to that constitution in referenda held in 2007 and 2009. At the end of 2013, Leopoldo López said in an interview that he was a strong believer that a constituent assembly was required to rewrite the constitution.[50] In fact, it was one of the strategies the opposition said they were working on in March of 2016.[51] But when Maduro called for the election of a constituent assembly, it was presented as an outrageous power grab. Trump dramatically intensified economic sanctions against Venezuela and began making military threats a few weeks after the Constituent Assembly was elected on July 31, 2017.[52]

The Western media, ignoring Venezuela's constitution, widely depicted the ANC as Maduro's creation, and gave the impression that the opposition was not allowed to run in the ANC elections. Nicholas Casey of the *New York Times* deceptively explained to readers on July 29, two days before the elections:

> Now, President Nicolás Maduro is pushing a radical plan to consolidate his leftist movement's grip over the nation: He is creating a political body with the power to rewrite the country's Constitution and reshuffle—or dismantle—any branch of government seen as disloyal.
>
> The new body, called a constituent assembly, is expected to grant virtually unlimited authority to the country's leftists.
>
> Venezuelans are going to the polls on Sunday to weigh in on the plan. But they will not have the option of rejecting it, even though some polls show that large majorities oppose the assembly's creation. Instead, voters will be asked only to pick the assembly's delegates, choosing from a list of stalwarts of Mr. Maduro's political movement.[53]

Casey's article never told readers that the opposition refused to run candidates. He seemingly preferred to let people assume that the opposition was not allowed to run. He also never explained that the sweeping powers of the ANC are defined in article 347 of the constitution, so it was not a "new body" that was Maduro's creation.[54] Later in the article, Casey included the vague statement that Hugo Chávez "oversaw the last rewrite of the Constitution, in 1999," but he failed to clarify that an ANC was elected to draft that constitution.[55]

Foreign media didn't always go to the deceptive extremes of the *New York Times*. An article in Al Jazeera by Elizabeth Melimopoulos, published on the day of the ANC elections, told readers that the opposition had refused to run candidates, also explaining:

In 1999, the then newly elected President Hugo Chávez and voters supported the initiative.

The difference this time is that Sunday's election was ordered by decree, with no referendum indicating that a majority wanted a change.[56]

But Article 348 of Venezuela's constitution does not say that an initial referendum is necessary. In 1999, Venezuela was transitioning away from the constitution that had been adopted in 1961. In 2017, Articles 347 and 348 of Venezuela's constitution defined, respectively, the powers of the ANC and how it could be convened. Article 348 stated:

> The initiative for calling a National Constituent Assembly may emanate from the President of the Republic sitting with the Cabinet of Ministers; from the National Assembly, by a two-thirds vote of its members; from the Municipal Councils in open session, by a two-thirds vote of their members; and from 15% of the voters registered with the Civil and Electoral Registry.

Reasonable arguments can be made that, given the sweeping powers of the ANC, an initiating referendum should have been held even if one wasn't explicitly stated as a requirement. But that is hardly grounds for declaring Venezuela a dictatorship. And there is no argument for expecting Venezuela's Supreme Court to follow Trump's orders on the matter.

Another objection to the ANC elections was that it was organized based on territorial and sectoral lines: that is, representatives were chosen for geographic regions but also for certain sectors, such as Indigenous people, pensioners, students, et cetera, in such a way that gave an advantage to the government. This was basically the "gerrymandering" objection that was made about the National Assembly elections of 2015—one that was forgotten when the alleged gerrymandering ended up favoring the opposition.

An analysis published on May 30, 2017, by government opponent

Francisco Rodriguez, estimated that the opposition could win control of the ANC if it received 60 percent of the vote.[57] To put it another way, Maduro's allies could win a majority in the ANC with 40 percent of the vote, a percentage that also often won majorities in Canadian and British parliamentary elections.

A Tale of Four Referenda

In July, the opposition organized an illegal—and therefore nonbinding—referendum that asked voters to reject the looming ANC elections. It claimed that on July 16 over seven million people (a bit over one-third of the electorate) voted against electing an ANC, only two weeks before the ANC elections were held. Ballots were burned to supposedly prevent government reprisals against voters.[58]

In the twenty-first century, the idea that burning paper records would do much to foil an alleged dictatorship from retaliating was a curious claim. Recent referenda elsewhere provide striking examples of Western hypocrisy—and the gaping holes in the stories the West sells about U.S. allies and adversaries.

Venezuelan Opposition Referendum—A Democratic Festival, Says Western Media

On the day of the illegal vote in Venezuela, Reuters reported: "There was a festive atmosphere under the Caribbean sun in most places, with people blasting music, honking car horns, waving Venezuelan flags, and chanting 'Yes we can!'"[59] One of the referendum questions was especially provocative. It asked if the military should obey the opposition-controlled National Assembly. But Maduro's government did not send security forces to stop voters from participating.[60]

Referendum in Spain Provokes EU-Approved Repression

But that's exactly what happened in Spain a few months later, in response to an illegal independence referendum in Catalonia. The elected Catalan government was then dissolved by the national government.[61] Its president, Carles Puigdemont, was arrested in Germany at Spain's request.[62] The EU, and Spain in particular, have since 2017 increasingly joined Trump in sanctioning Venezuela and hypocritically expressing concern over the state of its democracy.[63] In fact, even CNN showed images of Spanish national police attacking Catalan voters.[64]

Coup to Stop a Referendum in Honduras Had "Very Strong Argument," Says Clinton

In 2009, Honduran President Manuel Zelaya tried to ask the public the following question in a non-binding vote:

> Do you agree that in the general elections of November 2009 a fourth ballot box should be installed to decide whether to convene a National Constitutional Assembly that would approve a political Constitution?[65]

The Supreme Court said Zelaya couldn't hold the non-binding vote, but he proceeded to organize the vote anyway. Zelaya ended up being overthrown in a military coup on June 28, 2009. During a televised Democratic Party presidential primary debate in 2016, Hillary Clinton commented on Zelaya's ouster saying that, aside from throwing him out of the country, "they had a very strong argument that they had followed the constitution and the legal precedence."[66]

Hillary Clinton, who was the U.S. Secretary of State at the time, later boasted that she had been maneuvering behind the scenes to ensure that Zelaya's return would be rendered "moot."[67] Honduras is now one of the regional governments that supports U.S. attacks on Venezuela in the name of human rights and democracy.

Referendum in Ecuador Assaults Judicial Independence with Western Support

In Ecuador, in 2018, a body with the verbose name "Transitory

Council of Citizens Participation and Social Control" (CPCCS-T is the correspondingly clunky Spanish acronym) ended up assuming the sweeping powers of a Constituent Assembly (for example, by firing Ecuador's Constitutional Court) without its members ever being elected.[68] A referendum held in February 2018 gave President Lenín Moreno the power to handpick the CPCCS-T. Referendum questions are supposed to be approved by the Constitutional Court to ensure they are clear and do not trample basic rights. Moreno learned that the court was going to shoot down two of the seven unrelated questions in the referendum—one of which (in a very confusing way) proposed that he handpick the CPCCS-T. Moreno was enraged and publicly reprimanded the court, and then simply bypassed it. Disregarding the constitution, he issued a decree authorizing the referendum. Ecuador's right-wing private media were delighted with his behavior, and Moreno easily ensured that public media went along with him as well. Western media were similarly impressed.[69]

A *Washington Post* editorial board heaped praise on Moreno when the referendum was held.[70] José Miguel Vivanco, the Americas Division Director of Human Rights Watch, has been an enthusiastic fan of Moreno's government and the CPCCS-T in particular.[71]

The Fifth Coup Attempt Fails, the Opposition Implodes

Rather than run candidates in a high-stakes election given the broad powers of the ANC, the opposition opted to leverage its U.S. support to try to further delegitimize and ultimately overthrow the government. It therefore handed complete control of an extremely powerful body to Maduro's allies. But the coup attempt failed and, afterward, most of the opposition balked at the thought of losing another election. Opposition candidates participated in the comparatively low-stakes regional elections that were held a few months later, in October. These were the elections discussed earlier, in which the opposition performed disastrously, even though turnout (at 61 percent) was not low. Maduro simply had vastly more support than the opposition-aligned pollsters cared to admit.[72]

Four of the five opposition governors who won in those elections outraged and demoralized opposition hard-liners by being sworn in before the president of the ANC, Delcy Rodriguez. Henry Ramos Allup suddenly became a whipping boy for much of the opposition because all four governors were from Accion Democratica, the political party he leads. The *Miami Herald* pundit Andres Oppenheimer said that the United States should consider hitting Henry Ramos with sanctions, and that the four opposition governors should be sanctioned as well.[73]

Trump would have to intensify his already lethal and criminal effort to prop up his stumbling allies in Venezuela. The Juan Guaidó phase of Washington's extraordinary threat to Venezuela was fifteen months away from beginning. That was a major escalation, of course, but one that built on multiple U.S.-backed coup attempts that were made possible by the constant vilification of Chavismo by Western media and prominent NGOs, dating back to at least 2002. Confronting that history is required not only to remove the inexcusable threat posed by the United States and its allies to Venezuela, but to better understand the need for democratic reform, especially regarding control of public debate, within the world's richest countries.

PART III

Extraordinary Deceit (An Analysis)

11

Read Carroll and You've Read Them All (2006–2012)

The Irish journalist Rory Carroll's reporting for the *Guardian* from Venezuela is important for three reasons.

First, he was prolific. For years, his work dominated the *Guardian*'s Venezuela coverage. This London-based newspaper is an outlet that many people regarded as left-wing, so not one they'd suspect of being reflexively anti-Chávez. The British-Chilean documentary filmmaker Pablo Navarete remarked on Twitter, "I lived in Venezuela for two years between 2005 and 2007. When I arrived I thought the *Guardian* was a left-wing newspaper. By the time I left it was clear it wasn't. I felt almost ashamed at my naivety."[1]

Second, he was on the ground. Carroll was based in Venezuela for several years and this, understandably, was cited by Carroll himself and his many high-profile fans as evidence that he was credible.

Third, he was representative. His book about his years in Caracas, *Comandante: Hugo Chávez's Venezuela*, received rave reviews in high-profile publications across the accepted ideological spectrum.[2] *The Economist* named it among the "Books of the Year" for 2013, and it received glowing coverage from the *New York Times Book Review*, *Washington Post*, *The New Republic*, *Christian Science Monitor*, and many other publications.

Aside from its quantity, Carroll's reporting did not significantly impact the *Guardian*'s Venezuela coverage, which remained roughly the same—overwhelmingly hostile toward Chávez—in the years before and after Carroll was in Caracas. It's very unlikely that any other correspondent would have reported much differently for the *Guardian* had Carroll not been chosen for the job.

The journalist and scholar Alan MacLeod helped substantiate this last point in his book, *Bad News from Venezuela*. MacLeod interviewed numerous Western journalists reporting from the country and summarized some of his findings:

> Some may be surprised to learn that journalists who write for the most left-wing major newspaper in the English-speaking West [the *Guardian*], home of the far left, are close friends with people writing for the most conservative sources in the English-speaking world on the topic. However, media analysts have argued . . . the left-wing private media and the right-wing private media have long shared more opinions and interests in common than they have had disagreements and that they have a propensity to hunt in packs, spending a great deal of time together and developing a sense of group solidarity and resulting in the phenomenon of groupthink on many issues. This is particularly the case with foreign journalists.[3]

To illustrate the groupthink mentioned above, MacLeod analyzed articles in seven major Western newspapers during the two months following Chávez's death in 2013.[4] He compared this coverage to what appeared when Saudi Arabia's King Abdullah died two years later. His conclusion:

> Hugo Chávez, a man who had won multiple clean elections, dramatically reduced inequality, poverty and extreme poverty,

decreased unemployment and inflation, increased literacy rates, increased GNP per capita in Venezuela, a country where polls show that its citizens believe the country became substantially more democratic . . . was presented in a less favourable light than King Abdullah, an absolute monarch boasting one of the worst human rights records in history. The key difference in this instance was that Abdullah was an ally of the British and American states and of neoliberal globalization that big business pushed for, whereas Chávez was its foe.[5]

Oligarchs and the Professional Class

Corporate journalists such as Carroll, working as foreign correspondents for newspapers such as the *Guardian* or *New York Times*, are part of a professional class that capitalism does not reward with anything resembling the incomes of oligarchs who own media outlets—or even the lavish salaries of elite TV journalists.[6]

However, compared to the majority of workers, who do jobs that require no post-secondary education, professional journalists are rewarded with a significant amount of prominence and prestige, and can usually be relied on to attack political movements that oligarchs hate.[7] This is often true of the professional class even when they are struggling financially.[8] Chavismo's difficult relationship with much of Venezuela's professional class is unsurprisingly mirrored in the hostility of numerous professional journalists like Carroll. On top of the imperial assumptions correspondents like Carroll bring to their coverage of movements like Chavismo, professional class solidarity with their counterparts in poor countries is also a factor. Any political movement that is serious about attacking inequality will encounter strong resistance from segments of the professional class.[9]

A Useful NPR Interview

In April 2013, a month after the death of Hugo Chávez, Rory Carroll spoke to NPR about his years of reporting from Caracas:

Now, over time, when he [Chávez] became a bit more oppressive, shutting down television stations, and when the wheels were kind of beginning to come off the economy in some ways, I, in my own reporting, became very critical, just reflecting what I saw on the ground. And this prompted quite a debate, internal debate, in my newspaper, because a lot of editors then and to this day feel and felt that we should have supported Hugo Chávez because he was a standard-bearer for the left. Whereas I, very close up, I thought, well, no, actually. Because sadly, he's running the country into the ground and we have to report that.[10]

This NPR interview succinctly illustrates many of the distortions that plagued Carroll's reporting, which includes 250 Venezuela-related articles from 2006 to 2012. Over that same period, the two other *Guardian* writers who most frequently rebutted Carroll's perspective, Mark Weisbrot and Richard Gott, published twenty-one and seventeen Venezuela-related articles respectively.[11] Whatever debate there was within the *Guardian* about its Venezuela coverage, Rory Carroll and the editors who supported him prevailed. It was no contest.

When Carroll asserted to NPR that Chávez had "run the country into the ground," it was the message that he'd conveyed in article after article for several years.[12] The charts below demolish this claim. By the time Chávez left office, income poverty and extreme poverty had been reduced drastically. Income inequality, as measured by the Gini Coefficient, fell substantially and became the lowest in the region. Venezuela's rank in the UN Human Development Index—a composite measure of national income (GDP), access to education, and child mortality—rose from seventh in the region when Chávez first took office to fourth in the region by the time of his death in 2013. High inflation—which Carroll cited constantly in his articles (and in the NPR interview) as proof of economic mismanagement under Chávez—was a problem long before Chávez took office. The average inflation rate during the Chávez years was 22 percent. Over the eighteen-year period before he took office, it averaged 36 percent.[13] It also trended upward before Chávez and stayed comparatively flat while he was in office. (See Figure 11.1, below.)

Figure 11.2 (page 188) shows that Venezuela's Gini Coefficient went from 0.50 in the 2001–2003 period to about 0.40 in the 2009–2011 period. A lower Gini Coefficient means less income inequality. Costa Rica and the Dominican Republic are above the dashed line because their levels of inequality became worse between the two periods (their Gini Coefficients increased). Venezuela is the country farthest below the dashed line because its inequality deceased by the greatest amount between the two periods.

Figure 11.3 (page 189), showing poverty levels, reveals a big jump in both poverty and extreme poverty during the early Chávez years: the result of the opposition's first two attempts to drive Chávez from office by force. Carroll's book never mentions the spike in poverty caused by those attempts.[14]

Figure 11.1: Inflation, Pre-Chávez versus Chávez Years

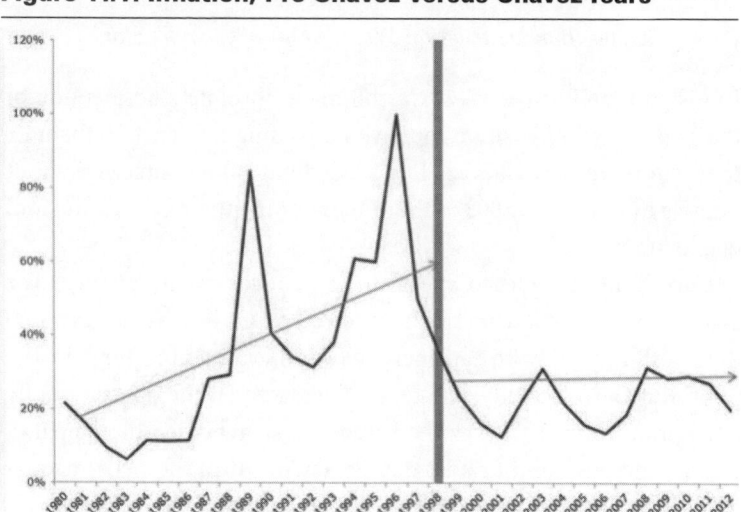

Source: Courtesy VenezuelAnalysis.

Figure 11.2: Gini Coefficient, 2001–2003, Latin America

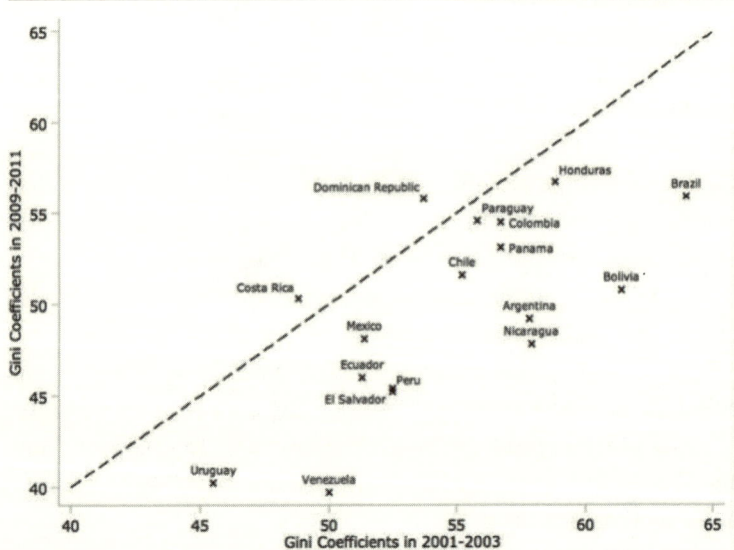

Source: Courtesy VenezuelAnalysis.

Opposition Destruction Written Out of Carroll's Story

In his entire NPR interview, Carroll made absolutely no mention of the Venezuelan opposition, not even a passing reference to them or their efforts to oust Chávez. That's like doing a long interview about politics in Iraq since 2003 without mentioning the U.S. invasion and occupation.

Carroll, in an effort to appear even-handed, readily gave Chávez credit for being charismatic: he referred to Chávez as "an extraordinary showman" with "an incredibly powerful connection" to the poor. But Carroll totally sidestepped the fact that the opposition, by attempting to oust Chávez, had waged a scorched earth campaign against the poor and against democracy. In turn, the poor made a logical decision to support Chávez against the repulsive opposition leadership.

Figure 11.3: Poverty and Extreme Poverty Rate

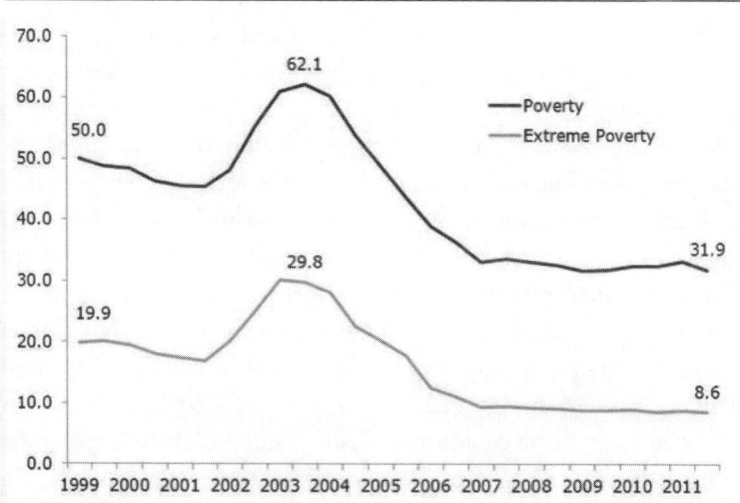

Source: Center for Economic and Policy Research.

TABLE 11.1: Selected Latin American Countries Ranked by UN's Human Development Index		
2000	2013	2015
Argentina	Chile	Chile
Chile	Argentina	Argentina
Uruguay	Uruguay	Uruguay
Mexico	Venezuela	Venezuela
Brazil	Mexico	Mexico
Peru	Brazil	Brazil
Venezuela	Ecuador	Peru
Ecuador	Peru	Ecuador
Colombia	Colombia	Colombia
Paraguay	Paraguay	Paraguay
Bolivia	Bolivia	Bolivia

Source: Compiled by the authors.

The facts don't support the theory that the poor were dazzled into irrationally supporting a talented "showman"—the shallow and patronizing insinuation made by Carroll and other corporate journalists.[15] A more credible explanation is that they took Chávez's side because they wagered, correctly, that his government intended to redistribute wealth and power in their direction, while his opponents had proved willing to do anything to prevent such a redistribution.

If the Chávez government were as "oppressive" (the term Carroll used to describe Chávez to NPR) as the government in the United Kingdom, where young men have been sentenced to years in prison for simply advocating riots through comments on Facebook, then most of Venezuela's top opposition leaders would have received lengthy prison terms by 2002.[16]

As an example he could use to justify calling Chávez "oppressive," Carroll mentioned Chávez "shutting down television stations." In 2007, five years after the coup—one that Venezuela's major broadcasters had all supported—the Chávez government refused to renew the license of one domestic broadcaster, RCTV. The non-renewal of RCTV's license in 2007 did not shut it down. It only meant that RCTV's broadcasts were no longer available free of charge, as the broadcasts of the other coup-supporting networks (Venevision, Globovision, and Televen) remain to this day in Caracas. RCTV continued to broadcast through cable and satellite until 2010, eight years after the coup, when another dispute with government regulators forced it off the air. But by April of 2013, when Maduro ran against Henrique Capriles to replace the recently deceased Chávez, data for TV coverage and audience share compiled by the Carter Center during the campaign showed no significant advantage for Maduro. But the decontextualized fuss made for years over RCTV by journalists like Carroll made such a finding seem impossible.[17]

A Privileged, "Close-Up" View of the Class Divide

NPR asked Carroll to describe the class divide in Caracas. He described the poor "clinging to the hillsides" in cheaply built houses. At lower elevations, he said, "the rich, the middle class tend to live." He might have added that the wealthier areas are in East Caracas. NPR also asked Carroll to state authoritatively if Chávez had improved the lives of the poor. Didn't the poor decide that for themselves by handing Chávez numerous electoral victories over fourteen years? Carroll was eager to stress that he saw Venezuela "close up," but he dismissed the perspective of the majority of Venezuelan voters who had always seen Venezuela close up—and not from a pricey East Caracas apartment.

According to Michael Fox, one of the authors of *Venezuela Speaks: Voices from the Grassroots*, Rory Carroll contacted him shortly after Carroll had arrived in Caracas in 2006.[18] Carroll was taking crash courses in Spanish and was generally trying to familiarize himself with Venezuela. He invited Fox to a party at his apartment in Altamira, an upper-class neighborhood and opposition stronghold in East Caracas.[19] Fox said that the "lavish" apartment "had the feel of a penthouse" and included an "amazing balcony" overlooking Altamira. Carroll was quite happy with it, according to Fox. A small group of journalists were there, including the British-Chilean documentary filmmaker Pablo Navarrete, who recalled on Twitter that "foreign correspondents + other 'expats' in the apt's expansive veranda sipped cocktails while the barrio lights glistened on the horizon."[20]

A party like Carroll's would not set an atypical scene. Foreign journalists in Caracas, with the exception of those like Fox who worked for small alternative media outlets like VenezuelAnalysis, overwhelmingly reside in East Caracas. As the *Miami Herald* journalist Jim Wyss told Alan MacLeod:

> I can see the house of the reporter for the *Guardian* from where I am sitting. . . . I think almost everybody is living in the wealthier area because it is really one of the few places that is safe to walk around. Security is a real issue in Venezuela.[21]

Lucas Koerner was based in Caracas reporting on the perspective of the Chavista grassroots for VenezuelAnalysis from 2015 until 2020.

He did not dismiss the physical safety of journalists as a problem, but explained why it was hardly an insurmountable one:

> While insecurity is undoubtedly a major problem in Caracas, it is mainly a barrier for multi-media teams reliant on ample quantities of expensive equipment. Print and photo journalists can freely navigate most of the city's barrios. It is simply a matter of taking the time to build local contacts and connections. Like everywhere else, journalism in Venezuela is all about cultivating relationships based on trust.[22]

And, like everywhere, it's easiest, professionally and personally, to stick to reporting the perspective of the most comfortable.

For Chávez, No "Benefit of the Doubt," Ever

Rory Carroll told NPR that any "right-thinking person" would have given Chávez the "benefit of the doubt" during his early years. But the *Guardian*'s news coverage certainly didn't. In 2002, when it mattered most, the *Guardian* reported from the perspective of the U.S.-backed opposition—an approach that Carroll would continue when he arrived in Venezuela four years later.[23] At that time, Michael Fox said, there was actually hope among international activists in Venezuela that Carroll might show less bias against the "Bolivarian process" because the *Guardian,* at the time, had a better reputation among leftists. Despite some terrible reporting on Venezuela, its "Comment Is Free" section offered some balance and hope that its reporting might someday improve. Also, Carroll himself, while trying to learn Spanish and get familiar with his new beat, seemed initially interested in hearing pro-Chávez views.[24]

It must be stressed that during Carroll's years reporting from Caracas, Venezuela was making rapid progress in poverty reduction. When oil prices collapsed in late 2014 and Venezuela entered into an economic depression, editorial standards dropped even further—to the point where military intervention by the United States was being discussed openly in articles about Venezuela.[25] The vilification of a U.S. enemy need not wait for economic difficulties to arrive. (The U.S.-backed coup in Bolivia against the very successful Evo Morales in November 2019 is another example.) It is wise, from the imperial perspective, to vilify an undesirable government while it is doing well. This lays the foundation for more destructive demonization if and when problems arrive. Carroll's reporting did that during Chavismo's most successful years.

In 2007, a headline to one of Carroll's articles blared, "Venezuela Scrambles for Food Despite Oil Boom."[26] A photo underneath the headline showed people lined up outside a government-run supermarket that sells subsidized food and other items at low prices.

Headlines are important: only 40 percent of readers in the United States said they read beyond the headlines, according to a study conducted by the Media Insight Project.[27] The selection of headlines, photos, and topics crucially shapes how readers perceive foreign governments. In the case of Carroll's article, all of these elements conveyed the impression that things were generally getting worse in Venezuela, when the country was in fact undergoing a period of rapid poverty and inequality reduction. The photo and the headline, tweaked to replace the word "Boom" with "Wealth," would easily fit among articles written while Maduro was in office as well.

It is unlikely that Carroll chose the headline, which is typically done by editors, but people who read beyond the headline to the rest of the article found this claim: "Up to a quarter of staple food supplies have been disrupted, according to Datanalisis, a public opinion and economic research group." Here Carroll presents the anti-Chávez polling firm Datanalisis as an impartial "research group." Recall that one of its directors, Gil Yepes, almost certainly signed the Carmona Decree after Chávez was briefly overthrown in April 2002.[28]

Another striking example, from December of 2007, is an article by Carroll that ran with the headline "Chávez loses bid to rule until 2050."[29] In 2007, Venezuelan voters narrowly rejected a slew of constitutional amendments proposed by Chávez, 51 to 49 percent. One of the amendments would have abolished presidential term limits. The unsubtle intent of the *Guardian*'s headline to Carroll's article about this vote—"Chávez loses bid to rule until 2050"—was to suggest that an audacious power grab had been foiled, as if Chávez had tried to delay the next presidential election until 2050.

It was an especially dumb headline considering that the *Guardian* is based in the United Kingdom, which does not have term limits for elected officials. Carroll's editors should not have found the concept difficult to grasp.

Chávez had once mocked his opponents by saying that he would stay in office until 2050—obviously, by winning elections. Carroll can't be blamed for the headline. Indeed, his very first sentence refuted it: "The Venezuelan president, Hugo Chávez, has lost a referendum that would have allowed him to run for re-election indefinitely and enshrined socialism in the country." But that makes the headline even more inexcusable. In an opinion piece published on the *Guardian*'s website the very same day, the writer and aid worker Conor Foley falsely stated that "voters narrowly rejected his [Chávez's] proposals for constitutional reform which would have enabled him to stay in power until 2050."[30] Foley's piece showed that this falsehood spread by the *Guardian* wasn't restricted to a flawed headline.

Opposition's Racist Attacks Ignored by Carroll

Even though Carroll's article refuted its own misleading headline, it still contained many lies of omission, as was common in his reporting. He said that Chávez had labeled his opponents "fascists, traitors and mental retards," and that he had called U.S. President George W. Bush "a donkey, an alcoholic and a war criminal." But Chávez's opponents also called him (and his supporters) names. More significantly, they tried to overthrow him. But in Carroll's account, Chávez was presented as irrationally abusive. A related insinuation was that Chávez's opponents were earnest democrats whom Chávez assailed with unprovoked abuse.

Carroll said nothing in the article about the two U.S.-backed attempts, one of them briefly successful, to overthrow Chávez. He also ignored the racist nature of the attacks on Chávez and his supporters by the opposition media. A cursory glance at the prolific output of former *El Universal* cartoonist Rayma Suprani illustrates the prevalence and vehemence of those racist attacks.[31]

For many years, Suprani routinely deployed flagrantly racist images of Chávez and Chavistas in one of Venezuela's leading newspapers. Such images would never have been published by the *Guardian*, Carroll's employer, given its liberal pretensions.[32] In one cartoon, Suprani depicts animals watching the struggle for political power on TV while the opposition seemed to have Chávez on the ropes (during the first days of the oil strike in December 2002). The animals don't look happy. One animal asks the "score of the game." Another answers: "Civilization 3, Barbarism 1."[33]

In 2014, shortly after Rayma Suprani was fired, Z. C. Dutka wrote about her work for VenezuelaAnlysis.com: "Rayma's cartoons, which have been rejected as racist and classist by countless government supporters, often depicted chavistas as overgrown, brutish gorilla-like figures in red shirts, chained to their political party in shackles." Dutka's article showed two examples: one in which an ape-like Chávez figure leaves a trail of bananas for his supporters, and another in which his supporters are drawn as identical red-colored brutes (their faces unmistakably meant to caricature Chávez) all chained together and marching in unison under a caption that reads "the Independence Day parade." In another Suprani cartoon, government-built homes for poor people are depicted as dog houses, and the inhabitants are directly attacked as idiots who don't realize that they are living like dogs: "They promised us a house and they delivered," reads the caption.[34]

Suprani's cartoons were representative of the opposition's pervasive racism. And yet, in his 293-page book, Carroll devotes one full sentence to the opposition's racist attacks on Chávez: "They made racist jokes that 'mi comandante' really means 'mico mandante' monkey ruler."[35] Carroll also claimed in the book that Chávez invited abuse through "calculated, measured provocations," "a trap that exposed their [the opposition's] arrogance, economic power and sense of entitlement." But Chavistas in general, not just Chávez, were targeted with racist abuse—an obvious problems with his "measured provocation" theory.[36] How did the poor provoke the opposition's abuse? By existing, and voting for Chávez who took their side against racists?

Did a Wikileaks Document Show that Oil Giants Had Chávez by the Throat?

On December 9, 2010, one of Carroll's articles ran with the headline, "WikiLeaks Cables: Oil giants squeeze Chávez as Venezuela struggles."[37] Carroll's opening sentence stated that "Venezuela's tottering economy is forcing Hugo Chávez to make deals with foreign corporations to save his socialist revolution from going broke."

What sets Wikileaks apart as a media outlet is that it publishes primary sources, which allows readers to check for themselves what journalists write about the documents it releases. The cables Carroll cited said nothing at all about Venezuela's government going broke, and, in any case, such a claim would have been absurd. At the time, Venezuela had very low levels of public debt and ample foreign exchange reserves.[38]

What allowed Carroll to make this claim? He asserts that the Italian ambassador "Luigi Maccotta told his US counterpart that Italian oil company ENI squeezed PDVSA over an Orinoco Belt deal in January this year knowing it had no one else to turn to." But Carroll also writes that "foreign oil companies still in Venezuela stay largely silent lest they anger the government and find themselves locked out of the Western Hemisphere's biggest energy reserves," which contradicts the central claim of the article. Why would foreign investors care about angering Chávez if their position was as strong as Carroll claimed?

Carroll also failed to mention that even U.S. officials were not completely sold on Luigi Maccotta's version of events. The cable said:

> It is unclear what bonus Eni really paid PDVSA, but it is interesting that regardless of the figure, PDVSA likely will not see any cash flow in the immediate future due to its $1 billion debt to the Italian company.

Based on U.S. officials engaging in dubious speculation about PDVSA's cash flow situation in 2010, Carroll jumped to the Chávez government being at the mercy of foreign businessmen. His book says nothing about foreign companies ever having Chávez by the throat, even though he does mention Eni once, giving him the opportunity to do so, and it says absolutely nothing about the U.S. diplomatic cables released by Wikileaks—which can be taken as an admission that his sensationalist reporting did not stand up.[39]

Chomsky Blasts Carroll's "Quite Deceptive" Reporting of His Views

Carroll's deceptive approach didn't only apply to Venezuelan sources and events, but was also evident when he wrote about prominent foreign observers.

In 2011, Carroll conducted an interview for the *Observer* with the famous left-wing intellectual Noam Chomsky. The *Observer* is a Sunday-only newspaper that is owned by the Guardian Media Group, and its content is hosted on the *Guardian* website. Carroll reported that "speaking to the *Observer* last week, Chomsky has accused the socialist leader [Hugo Chávez] of amassing too much power and of making an 'assault' on Venezuela's democracy."[40] The original headline read, "Noam Chomsky denounces old friend Hugo Chávez for 'assault' on democracy." The article closed with an open letter Chomsky wrote to Chávez asking for clemency in the case of Judge María Lourdes Afiuni, who had been in prison from 2009 to 2011 while facing corruption charges, and was moved to house arrest earlier that year.

Carroll had always taken a highly selective interest in Chomsky's views on Latin America. In 2008, when Chomsky signed an open letter critical of Nicaraguan president Daniel Ortega, Rory Carroll pounced on it. At about the same time, Chomsky signed an open letter to Colombian president Alvaro Uribe about far graver matters, but this letter was ignored. The letter to Uribe asked him to stop right-wing paramilitaries from assassinating and threatening academics in Colombia. The one to Ortega objected to allegedly unfair use of technicalities to bar two political parties from municipal elections.[41]

Very shortly after the article appeared in the *Observer*, Chomsky was scathing in his assessment of the way Carroll had summarized their conversation. He said Carroll had been "quite deceptive" and had excluded "much of relevance that I stressed throughout, including the fact that criticisms from the US government or anyone who supports its actions can hardly be taken seriously, considering Washington's far worse record without any of the real concerns that Venezuela faces, the Manning case for one, which is much worse than Judge Afiuni's." Asked about one obvious insinuation from Carroll's article, if he believed Chávez had made Venezuela less democratic, Chomsky replied, "I don't think so, and never suggested it."[42]

Chomsky's criticism, and a backlash from readers, prompted the *Guardian* to release a full transcript of the interview. It also tweaked the headline to replace the word "denounces" with "criticizes."[43] Two years later, Carroll mentioned the Chomsky interview in his book *Comandante* (essentially to argue that the Afiuni case marked a turning point in the level of support Chávez could receive from the international left) but neglected to include Chomsky's harsh criticism of the interview.[44] In fact, exactly as Chomsky claimed, the transcript showed several key comments that Carroll left out of both his book and his original account of the interview for the *Observer*:

> My suspicion is that the judiciary is not as independent as it should be. We may compare it to Colombia next door. Colombia's human rights record is incomparably worse....
>
> And I should say that the United States is in no position to complain about this. Bradley Manning has been imprisoned without charge, under torture, which is what solitary confinement is. The president [Obama] in fact intervened.

Chomsky's criticism of the Chávez government was far from a "denunciation," and was not meant to suggest that Venezuela had less right to call itself a democracy than the United States or Colombia (the closest U.S. ally in Latin America). His qualified statement contradicted a view of the Chávez government that Carroll relentlessly insinuated in his reporting: that Venezuela fell short of being a democracy, unlike (by tacit assumption) the United States or United Kingdom. Carroll claims explicitly in *Comandante* that Venezuela in the Chavista era had become "an authoritarian democracy, a hybrid system of personality cult and one-man rule that permitted opposition parties, free speech, and free, not entirely free elections."[45] Elsewhere in the book he refers to the Chávez government as an "authoritarian regime."[46] Carroll never refers to the United States or United Kingdom in that manner—governments that, as Chomsky has often noted, seriously constrain democracy despite not being confronted with an extraordinary threat, such as foreign governments that are trying to overthrow them, and are powerful enough to pull it off.

Carroll's Book: Covering Details with Imperial Moss

Carroll's book *Comandante* provides an almost total whitewash of the U.S. role in efforts to overthrow Chávez. The book's complete silence about the explosively revealing U.S. diplomatic cables released by Wikileaks in 2010 is a great illustration of how determined Carroll was to provide a whitewash. Those cables reveal a U.S. government obsession with weakening the regional influence of the Chávez government. The cables show that the United States trained and assisted Venezuelan opposition leaders long after they had disgraced themselves by participating in the 2002 coup, while pressuring regional governments to resist Chavista influence. For example, in 2006 the U.S. ambassador to Honduras, Charles Ford, wrote in a cable that "[President] Zelaya is no Chávez, but if left unchanged, circumstances could make him complicit in advancing Chávez's influence in the region." The cables show that Ford tried and, after some initial success, ultimately failed to persuade Zelaya to shun Chávez's Petrocaribe initiative, which provided generous repayment options for oil that Venezuela sold to Honduras. In 2009, the democratically elected Zelaya was overthrown in a military coup. U.S. officials under Obama maneuvered to undermine the regional response to the coup.

The cables reveal that U.S. Embassy officials lobbied several regional governments to recognize Honduran elections even if Zelaya was not allowed to finish his term.[47]

In order to whitewash the role of the United States in the coup that briefly ousted Chávez in 2002, Carroll's book ignored information that was in the public domain long before the cables published by Wikileaks. Carroll's book said the following regarding the coup of April 2002:

> The CIA, its own documents later showed, knew a coup plot had been bubbling. The US ambassador said he warned Chávez a coup was imminent and that the president shrugged it off, saying he knew about the plot. Whatever the truth of that, the opposition felt emboldened by US antipathy to the comandante, and the Bush administration smirked when he fell. But there was little evidence, as Chávez would later insist, that Washington pulled the strings.
>
> An Irish documentary, *The Revolution Will Not Be Televised*, became an influential advocate overseas for Chávez's version, casting him as a romantic hero. The coup entered folklore, guilt and innocence tangled in the veins, details covered by moss.[48]

Note how Carroll says nothing about U.S. funding and training for the coup perpetrators. Neither does he address U.S. willingness to back up the coup-plotters' version of events, to ensure immediate IMF loans, and to continue funding the opposition after the coup failed. Moreover, Carroll's claim that there is "little evidence that Washington pulled the strings" is a standard evasion: it ignores ample U.S. support for the coup's perpetrators by focusing on the question of whether or not the United States had micromanaged the coup. A few months after the coup, an internal U.S. government investigation said Washington had "provided training, institution building, and other support to individuals and organizations understood to be actively involved in the brief ouster of the Chávez government."[49] Carroll's story about the coup would easily be seen as preposterous if the situation had been reversed: if Venezuela's government admitted to having assisted the perpetrators of a coup in the United States, welcomed it while it was successful, but later tried to absolve itself by saying it had warned Washington.

Opposition Impunity, Cubans, and Kernels of Truth

Remarkably, *Comandante* never mentions the amnesty Chávez granted in December 2007 to participants in the 2002 coup and the oil strike that followed. Carroll does discuss two high-profile participants in those coup attempts, Henrique Capriles and Leopoldo López, but says nothing about their participation. That's especially striking in the case of Capriles, a two-time presidential candidate, because Carroll discusses him in some detail as a candidate. Carroll praised Capriles's athletic physique, mentioned that he dated models, said he received homophobic and anti-Semitic abuse, and talked about his electoral victories in the state of Miranda, but never mentioned that Capriles (with López) led the arrest of a Chavista minister during the April 2002 coup and also participated in a mob siege of the Cuban Embassy.[50] The book also never says a word about the hundreds of Chavista peasants who were assassinated since 2001, most likely by wealthy landowners opposed to land reform. Carroll would have been aware of this wave of murders: in 2011, the *Guardian* published a short letter, signed by Chomsky, John Pilger, and many others, deploring the newspaper's Venezuela coverage, which was dominated by Carroll, and had completely ignored the issue.[51] And yet, the murdered peasants are mentioned nowhere in the book Carroll published two years later.

Elsewhere in *Comandante*, Carroll depicts Chávez as ruthlessly bullying judges to keep opponents in line. But the truth is that Chávez largely failed to keep them, or even state prosecutors, from undermining his government.[52] Alarmingly often, the legal system let his most dangerous opponents off the hook even when they murdered or grievously harmed poor people within his electoral base, or flouted the rule of law. By making these key omissions, Carroll's book erases the huge challenges that Chávez faced. It is true that the Chávez government had shortcomings, as does any government. But had Chávez not faced an insurrectionist opposition staunchly backed by a superpower, he could have placed less emphasis on political loyalty and more on technical competence when appointing people to key posts. He could have moved more aggressively against corruption and sabotage within the government's own ranks without fear of providing more defectors to a dangerous U.S.-backed opposition. Those factors do not absolve Chávez of responsibility for every problem, but they were huge contributing factors that Carroll simply buried.[53]

Foreign correspondents like Carroll do not only bring an imperial bias to their work, but also a bias in favor of the professional class to which they belong. That's important in the case of Venezuela because fierce resistance to Chávez's efforts to empower poor people did not come only from the highest levels (oligarchs) but from the professional class: specialized workers like doctors, lawyers, engineers, journalists, administrators. Intelligence officers may even be included among them.

In the most insightful passages of *Comandante,* Carroll describes how poor people derived dignity from their participation in communal councils, whose development Chávez supported all over the country. Carroll describes a communal council meeting he attended with a security guard, "Luis," whom he befriended, perhaps in his Altamira apartment building. In the pre-Chávez era, poor people in neighborhood assemblies informally organized to try to solve problems. Under Chávez, these groups evolved into the communal councils (generally consisting of 200 to 400 families in cities and 20 to 50 in rural areas) that were given legal recognition and government funding. As of 2019, there were 47,000 registered communal councils, involving millions of people.[54] Carroll correctly observes that the councils acted as a buffer against Chávez's failings. They certainly give people a way to direct their anger and frustration at lower-level government officials and bureaucrats, and of course to pressure them to do their jobs properly, including by having the people take on tasks themselves.

Luis, the security guard, with whom Carroll attended a communal council meeting, had a hard life. In 2010, his beloved grandson was murdered, a victim of Venezuela's infamously high violent crime rate. But Luis's support for the government was not shaken. This was evident even in Carroll's predictably uncharitable and mocking account of the meeting, in which he nevertheless conceded that the councils "breathed life into grassroots government: planting trees in plazas, distributing subsidized food, fixing houses and roads, liaising with government agencies."[55] Carroll wrote of Luis:

> At work, he was nobody, one of a million anonymous, barely acknowledged security guards. But back in El Valle, he was part of the revolution, an active and respected member of the communal council.[56]

But for the professional class, and not just in Venezuela, dignity is often derived from serving an unjust social order; for Western journalists, this means serving the U.S.-led imperial order. Carroll is probably sincere in expressing his mystification at some of Chávez's early moves against Venezuela's professional class. He uses the more nebulous term "middle class" and includes within it everyone from teachers to Catholic bishops: "The puzzle was not Chávez's attacks on the plutocrats—when he accused them of looting the nation's oil wealth, he was essentially correct—but his alienation of the middle class."[57]

In many Latin American countries, professional-class prestige often comes with a hefty dose of racial privilege. The racist attacks on Chávez first erupted when the private media turned the professional class against him.[58] Similar to what the economist Dean Baker has long advocated for segments of the professional class in the United States (for example, exposing U.S. doctors to competition from equally qualified, lower-paid doctors from Europe and elsewhere), Chávez exposed Venezuela's professional class to foreign competition by making deals with Cuba. Cuban doctors, nurses, teachers, technicians, and intelligence specialists began taking up positions in Venezuela. In addition to providing essential services to people who would not have otherwise received them, the Cubans' presence also effectively undermined the ability of Chavismo's professional-class enemies to subvert the revolutionary process—including from within.[59] Chávez also bypassed (and therefore enraged) the medical establishment by having thousands of Venezuelans trained in Cuba.[60]

The Norwegian journalist Eirik Vold, who lived in Venezuela for years while Chávez was in office, wrote about the way Chavista *"misiones,"* various types of social programs initiated by Chávez, including the provision of basic medical services to the poor, were distorted by his opponents: "The established commercial media had treated *las misiones* with a combination of crass criticism and concealment. The first time I heard about the Cuban doctors, for example, was in an *El Universal* article that described that scandal of a child who died from alleged malpractice at the hands of a Cuban doctor."[61]

The Venezuelan Medical Federation (FMV in its Spanish acronym) launched strikes against Chávez beginning in 2001, and boycotted a government program that would pay Venezuelan doctors to serve the poorest communities. It then tried to block the government from using Cuban doctors, through an agreement that was initiated in February 2003 by the Chavista mayor of the Libertador municipality.[62] In August 2003, a Venezuelan court ruled in support of a lawsuit brought by the FMV seeking to outlaw the use of Cuban doctors by invoking licensing procedures. The Chávez government appealed to the Supreme Court (initially without success) and disregarded the court rulings while it continued to file appeals.[63] But Chávez also issued a decree in December 2003 expanding the Libertador program to the entire country. Subsequent changes to the judiciary (including the 2004 court-packing law that Human Rights Watch equated to a coup attempt), combined with the immense popularity of the program that Chávez dubbed Misión Barrio Adentro, rendered the FMV's legal victories in 2003 irrelevant.[64] Though *Comandante* acknowledges the popularity of the Cuban doctors, it says nothing about the war Venezuela's medical establishment waged on them through the courts and the private media.[65] As of 2020, the president of the FMV, Dr. Douglas León Natera, who has been its president for decades, was still decrying the "supposed doctors" from Cuba and calling their work in Venezuela "illegal."[66] He was also a signer of the Carmona Decree in April 2002.[67]

Unlike plutocrats or oligarchs who have no justification to exist, a professional class—workers with above average training and experience requirements to do their jobs—is necessary in any modern economy.[68] Dealing with elitism within this class therefore poses a unique challenge. In addition to bringing in Cuban competitors, Chávez also attempted to address this challenge by giving working-class communities greater access to higher education. Public universities were created to bypass the so-called autonomous universities that were opposition strongholds. But, as with efforts to expand worker-run industries, performance standards in the universities were compromised by short-term political calculations: some students weren't failed in courses when they should have been, just as some worker-run cooperatives were not forced to pay back government loans. Writers sympathetic to Chavismo such as Eirik Vold have acknowledged this, while also saying the problems were "often rather exaggerated."[69]

If the Chávez government could be cast as an "authoritarian regime," or as some kind of hybrid that falls short of being a democracy, even though it clearly had majority support and was reducing poverty, it should be no surprise that the government could be more effectively demonized after serious economic problems emerged. Numerous foreign correspondents like Rory Carroll spent years waging a propaganda war on Chavismo. Despite the *Guardian*'s left-wing reputation, correspondents such as Carroll are still part of the professional class, as well as citizens of the leading imperial states. Carroll's reporting conformed with those perspectives, which helps explain the accolades his book received across the Western media spectrum. Carroll diligently produced the propaganda that, in later years, allowed the United States to dramatically escalate the threat it posed to Venezuela.

12

The Human Rights Fraud

For the past twenty years, Human Rights Watch (HRW) has been particularly aggressive in attacking Chavismo. Recall its appalling response to the coup that briefly ousted Chávez in 2002.[1] While a knee-jerk dismissal of everything HRW reports about U.S. enemies is unadvisable, knee-jerk acceptance is more dangerous. This outfit does not hide that it is essentially the U.S. Empire's human rights group. If westerners accept HRW's claims uncritically, they will become complicit with the U.S. government and its close allies terrorizing much of the world, including, of course, Venezuela. This can be seen most clearly by taking a wider view of HRW's work.

In 2014, one hundred scholars, including three Nobel Peace Prize laureates, published an open letter to HRW asking it to close its "revolving door" with U.S. officials. HRW's reply to the petition dismissed their concerns and said that, "on balance, the United States has played a constructive role at the [United Nations] Human Rights Council."

In 2015, Ken Roth, HRW's executive director went even further. He wrote:

> For all its faults, the U.S. government remains the most powerful

THE HUMAN RIGHTS FRAUD

proponent of human rights, and the Human Rights Watch base in the United States gives the organization special access to Washington.[2]

A very incomplete list of U.S. "faults" in this century alone highlight what a scandalous statement this is coming from the head of a human rights group:

- Launching a war of aggression in Iraq based on lies that left at least half a million Iraqis dead. In fact, wars fought by the U.S. since 2001 have displaced at least 37 million people.[3]
- Providing ample material support for Israeli atrocities and repression in Palestine and for Saudi atrocities in Yemen.
- Directly overthrowing Haiti's democratically elected president Jean-Bertrand Aristide in 2004 and installing a dictatorship that killed about four thousand Aristide loyalists by 2006.
- Showering Colombia's government with financial, military, and propaganda support as its military (and paramilitary allies) murdered 39,000 to 53,000 civilians between 2000 and 2011.[4]
- Ignoring European and Canadian support for these crimes, Roth has also hailed Western governments in general as "the strongest traditional allies of the human rights cause."[5]

"Rescues" by Aggressors Must Not Get a "Bad Name"?

When Roth called the United States the "world's most powerful proponent of human rights," he added that "much of the world is rightly suspicious of the U.S. government's agenda, so Human Rights Watch is careful to maintain our independence from U.S. foreign policy (we regularly report on and criticize it)."

Widespread disgust with the U.S.-led invasion of Iraq in 2003 clearly pressured HRW to show some "independence from U.S. foreign policy." Almost a year *after* the invasion, HRW published an essay arguing that the war could not be called a "humanitarian intervention."[6] It said the piece was written because "the Iraq war and the effort to justify it even in part in humanitarian terms risk giving humanitarian intervention a bad name." It worried that such a development "could be devastating for people in need of future rescue." HRW wanted the world's most powerful states to carry out "future rescues." HRW also clarified that "our purpose is not to say whether the U.S.-led coalition should have gone to war for other reasons."

So almost a year *after* the WMD pretext was exposed as fraudulent, and even while rejecting a humanitarian pretext, HRW still refused to take an antiwar position on Iraq.

Haitian Lives Do Not Matter to HRW

The United States has been deeply involved with countless military coups in the Americas, but in 2004 it openly perpetrated one. On February 29, 2004, U.S. troops flew Haiti's democratically elected president, Jean-Bertrand Aristide, out of Haiti in the early hours of the morning. The coup received crucial support from France, Canada, and eventually Brazil and Uruguay, both of which contributed a large number of troops to MINUSTAH—the French acronym for the UN mission stationed in Haiti in June 2004 to consolidate the dictatorship of Gérard Latortue. That dictatorship would rule Haiti for two years.[7]

In 2010, MINUSTAH's negligence spread cholera throughout Haiti's water supply. The ensuing epidemic killed about 10,000 Haitians. It is easy to verify from HRW's website that it took several years for it to say anything that resembled a demand for the UN to accept full responsibility.

In 2014, HRW official Amanda Kessling wrote a commentary for CNN titled "Why Water Access Matters to Poverty Reduction." Her piece mentioned Haiti's cholera epidemic—and the death toll, which by then was 8,700—but she did not mention the UN's responsibility for it.[8]

The evidence of UN guilt was so obvious that by 2011 the cholera victims' political battle with the UN was well underway despite an initial lack of support from foreign NGOs working in Haiti. The journalist and activist Yves Engler reported that foreign NGOs based in

Haiti—such as Doctors without Borders and Oxfam—were publicly dismissive of the victims' struggle during its early stages.[9] In 2016, a report by a UN Special Rapporteur, Philip Alston, also said that scientific evidence of MINUSTAH's guilt was "overwhelming" and that the arguments the UN used to evade accountability were "legally indefensible."[10] Nevertheless, Obama administration lawyers represented the UN in New York where they successfully helped it evade responsibility—a routine victory for the world's "most powerful proponent of human rights."[11]

Four months later, the outgoing UN Secretary General, Ban Ki-moon, half apologized by saying that the UN "simply did not do enough with regard to the cholera outbreak and its spread in Haiti." Philip Alston observed, "He apologizes that the UN has not done more to eradicate cholera, but not for causing the disease in the first place."[12] Ban also promised that the UN would do more for the victims, but by 2018, very little was happening on that front. The Institute for Justice and Democracy in Haiti, which led the legal battle for the victims, sent a letter to the UN demanding that it quit dragging its feet.[13] The letter was signed by sixty organizations, including Amnesty International. HRW, conspicuously, was *not* one of them.

The U.S.-Led "Rescue" of Notorious Killers that HRW Had Once Denounced

Under the U.S.-backed dictatorship of Gerard Latortue, about 4,000 people were killed in pro-Aristide strongholds by the Haitian police or by armed anti-Aristide groups, according to a scientific survey published in *The Lancet*. The study, which found 8,000 homicides overall (including the 4,000 noted above), was done in the Greater Port-au-Prince area, not all of Haiti.[14]

Table 12.1 (page 210) shows the study's findings (expressed as a death rate) as well as scientific estimates for Iraq during the bloodiest years after the 2003 invasion. Data for Venezuela is also included. Iraq has been invoked to make absurd comparisons to both Haiti and (much more frequently) Venezuela. For example, unscientific and

TABLE 12.1: Violent Death Rates: Various Countries and Years[17]

	Violent Deaths (thousands)	Population (millions)	Violent Death Rate (per 100,000/yr.)
Venezuela (2016)	16.7	29.8	56
Greater Port-au-Prince (22 months)	8.0	2.1	206
All of Iraq (2003–2006)	151–601	26.1	170–720

Source: Compiled by the authors.

incomplete counts of Iraq's violent death toll (compiled by Iraq Body Count) have been used to claim that Venezuela under Chávez was more dangerous than Iraq.[15] In the case of Haiti, Iraq Body Count figures have been used to suggest that the mortality study published in *The Lancet* about Haiti could not possibly be accurate[16]

Sympathy for the Dictatorship's Police in Haiti, None for Its Victims

In May 2005, while killings were underway in Haiti, José Miguel Vivanco, HRW's Americas Director, wrote an open letter to the UN Security Council asking for more armed personnel (that is, firepower) for MINUSTAH.[18] In the letter, Vivanco blamed "gangs claiming affiliation with former President Jean-Bertrand Aristide" for "much of the violence." Vivanco's letter referred to the U.S.-installed Latortue dictatorship as the "Interim Government of Haiti." HRW never referred to Latortue as a dictator. By contrast, Vivanco has spent years calling Maduro a dictator.[19]

Two months before Vivanco wrote his letter, researchers with Harvard Law School concluded that "MINUSTAH has effectively provided cover for the police to wage a campaign of terror in Port-au-Price's slums." They implored MINUSTAH to "address" the "persecution" of Aristide's supporters and to counteract the rampant "impunity for the perpetrators of political violence."[20]

But Vivanco's almost exclusive concern was that Haitian police were "highly vulnerable" and "outgunned by former military and criminals." He therefore asked for additional forces for MINUSTAH, and that these troops be "explicitly authorized to use the force necessary to protect the civilian population and stop violent attacks"—implying that they weren't violent enough already. He threw in a brief acknowledgment that police should be restrained from using "lethal force unnecessarily against demonstrators" but made no mention of extrajudicial executions. Vivanco wanted to see MINUSTAH empowered to kill more people in poor neighborhoods where Aristide's political movement (Lavalas) had always been extremely popular and organized.[21] This organized support went back decades and was the reason Aristide and his allies were able to rout his opponents in elections, even though his supporters endured horrors after Aristide was first overthrown in a 1991 coup. Vivanco expressed absolutely no concern that Aristide's supporters were "highly vulnerable" (as he described the police) while they were being killed by the thousands.

Vivanco's letter was also shocking because, days before it was published, Latortue's dictatorship had acquitted the Haitian death squad leader Jodel Chamblain, whose atrocities against Aristide supporters HRW had documented in the early 1990s.[22] In 2004, Chamblain had marched triumphantly into Port-au-Prince with Dominican Republic–based paramilitaries.[23] In addition to this, months before Vivanco's letter came out, the dictatorship announced that it would be providing back pay to Haiti's former military. HRW had also documented the atrocities of Haiti's military during the early 1990s after the first coup that overthrew Aristide. Could Vivanco, who has been HRW's Americas Director since 1994, have forgotten everything HRW had written about the Haitian military's crimes, and Chamblain's?[24]

In 1994, the Clinton government ordered the military men who had seized power in 1991 to let Aristide finish his term.[25] Thousands of U.S. troops entered Haiti to oversee the dictatorship's exit. After some embarrassing incidents during which U.S. troops stood by as Aristide's supporters were murdered, they eventually provided some security to Aristide and his supporters. The troops also protected the Haitian elite from popular outrage, stemmed migration to the United States (a key reason that Clinton supported Aristide's return), and took the opportunity to seize evidence of U.S.-citizen collaboration with the death squad for which Jodel Chamblain was a top commander. Restored to office, Aristide defied U.S. objections and disbanded Haiti's military in 1995. Until 1997, HRW had repeatedly demanded that the U.S. government return the stolen documents to Haiti to help with the ongoing prosecution of criminals like Chamblain. But by 2004, HRW was basically feigning ignorance about its own reports from the 1990s so it could disregard the murderous campaign against Aristide's supporters—and even request more firepower for MINUSTAH to do the Latortue dictatorship's work.[26]

TABLE 12.2: MINUSTAH Deaths from "Malicious Acts"

Year	No. of Deaths
2005	6
2006	5
2007	0
2008	1
2009	1
2010	0
2011	1
2012	0
2013	0
2014	0
2015	1
2016	0
2017	0
Average	**1.15**

Source: United Nations[29]

In the first year and a half of MINUSTAH's occupation of Haiti, the most dangerous period of its battle against so-called gangs, the number of troops it lost to acts of violence remained in the single digits.[27] They were more likely to be killed in accidents. Over its thirteen-year existence, MINUSTAH's losses from "malicious acts" in Haiti averaged about one per year, according to its own figures. In many years, the number was zero.[28]

Two months after Vivanco's letter was published, a MINUSTAH raid in a poor neighborhood killed twenty-three people. A few weeks after the massacre, a MINUSTAH spokesperson said it "deeply regrets any injuries or loss of life during its operation." It could openly acknowledge and take responsibility for the deaths because it knew there would be no legal consequences.[30]

THE HUMAN RIGHTS FRAUD

As for the Haitian police force that Vivanco described as "highly vulnerable," it was in fact much smaller than many police forces in the world, relative to the size of Haiti's population. But, by that measure, the security forces propping up Latortue's dictatorship were several times *less* vulnerable than the ones on which Aristide had to rely. That was mainly because Latortue also had MINUSTAH working for him. The table below shows the violent death rate for armed personnel in Haiti, Venezuela, Iraq, and the United States during different time periods. Those death rates in part reflect how much violence there was in each country (i.e., how dangerous it was in general), but they also reflect how numerous were the armed personnel relative to the population. Hence, the number of police (or troops) relative to population is also included in the table.

Haiti still has a small police force relative to its population. As of 2018, it had roughly 60 percent of the number of police per person as the United States.[32] When Aristide was overthrown in 2004, it had less than 15 percent. Moreover, as HRW itself documented in 1995, Haiti's police force was penetrated by anti-Aristide officers with murderous track records, thanks to U.S. efforts. After the 2004 coup, the United States inserted hundreds of the insurgents and former military

TABLE 12.3: Police/Troop Death Rates in Selected Countries and Time Periods[31]

	No. of Police Troops	Armed Personnel per million inhabitants	Violent Deaths of Armed Personnel	Deaths per 100,000 Personnel
Haitian Police: Feb. 2003–04 (before Aristide ousted)	2500–3000	278–333	40	1,333–1,600
Haitian Police and MINUSTAH forces: Feb. 2004–05 (year after Aristide ousted)	10,000–10,500	1,100–1,200	38	362–366
Haitian Police (2018–19)	15,000	1,350	17–34	113–227
Police in U.S. (2011–15)	724,690	2,300	27–72	4–10
Venezuelan Police (2015–17)	175,000	5,900	157–351	90–201
U.S. Troops in Iraq (2004–07)	130,600–148,300	5,000–5,300	656–755	456–549

Source: Compiled by the authors.

members who helped overthrow Aristide into Haiti's police force.[33]

Given that the police in Haiti were not only scarce but infiltrated by U.S.-backed criminals, poor people began arming for self-defense. No doubt, informally armed groups can devolve into being criminal gangs (as can the police). One reason Aristide was vilified by the international media was that he refused to demonize all poor people who, quite understandably under these conditions, organized to defend themselves.[34] But Vivanco had no inhibition about demonizing them while a dictatorship openly backed the armed actors who had always terrorized the poor.

In the time leading up to the coup, Vivanco ignored Aristide's dire shortage of police. HRW instead criticized Aristide in a published statement that appeared only sixteen days before U.S. troops kidnapped him.[35] While insurgents, who had been given safe haven in the neighboring Dominican Republic for years, were killing and scattering his few police, HRW declared that "Aristide Should Uphold Rule of Law."[36] It demanded that he "take immediate, constructive steps to reestablish the rule of law and rebuild the country's democratic institutions." In his book *Damming the Flood*, Peter Hallward sarcastically commented on HRW's demands:

> Once Aristide's puzzling failure to do these things had facilitated his removal from office, rather than call for the immediate restoration of the elected government or even press for an inquiry into the circumstances of its removal, HRW urged, instead, the speedy dispatch of more foreign troops.[37]

The Nobel laureates who had asked HRW to close its revolving door with Washington were also dismayed by its stance on Haiti: "In the face of what were likely the worst human rights abuses of any country in the Western Hemisphere at the time, HRW barely lifted a finger."[38]

HRW essentially treated the U.S.-perpetrated coup in Haiti and its bloody aftermath as a "humanitarian rescue" that must not get a "bad name." Its failure to act as a credible human rights advocate was matched by the Western media's dismal performance. It is easy to anticipate how HRW's attitude toward the police in Venezuela would be completely transformed after some kind of U.S.-orchestrated "humanitarian rescue": the "*colectivos*," organized Chavistas in poor neighborhoods who are sometimes armed, would be cast in the same role as the pro-Aristide "gangs" that Vivanco demonized in Haiti.[39] But as long as Venezuela's police work for a government that the United States is trying to overthrow, they are unreservedly, and often recklessly, denounced by HRW.

By Contrast, Outrage at Police in Venezuela, for Now

On September 19, 2019, HRW issued a brief report titled "Venezuela: Extrajudicial Killings in Poor Areas: Pattern of Serious Police Abuse Goes Unpunished." The report said:

> Interior Minister Néstor Reverol reported in December 2017 that there were 5,995 such cases in 2016 and 4,998 in 2017. Venezuelan security forces killed nearly 7,000 people in incidents they claimed were cases of "resistance to authority" in 2018 and the first five months of 2019, according to the government figures.[40]

Relative to population (Haiti in 2004–06 had roughly a third of Venezuela's 2019 population), the numbers above are very similar to the number of people killed per year by the armed actors serving Latortue's dictatorship in Haiti. But in Venezuela's case, HRW was eager, on the basis of skimpy evidence, to imply widespread politically motivated killings by police. The report quoted Vivanco saying that "authorities are resorting to egregious abuses in low-income communities that no longer support the Maduro regime."[41]

By HRW's own account, then, these killings were *not* taking place in bastions of organized opposition to the government that went back decades—as they were in Haiti under Latortue, who represented the U.S.-backed elite that Aristide had trounced in the elections. In Venezuela's case, those bastions of opposition to Chavista governments are middle- and upper-class neighborhoods. And of course, HRW never referred to Latortue's dictatorship as a "regime," nor did it ever speculate or express interest in Latortue's popularity level in the poor neighborhoods his security forces attacked.

HRW also showed no concern about Venezuelan police vulnerability as it had in Haiti in 2005 (when, *after* Aristide was overthrown, it became Vivanco's primary concern), even though the dangers of policing in Venezuela have been widely reported. Closely related to that problem is Venezuela's notoriously high homicide rate, one of the highest in the Americas—as the Western media has constantly reminded us for decades. But this was easily forgotten when it was not useful to the story HRW wanted to tell.

From 2015 to 2017, the violent death rate for Venezuelan police as a group ranged from 90 to 201 per 100,000 personnel (see the table above). The homicide rate for all Venezuelans as of 2017 was 57 per 100,000 inhabitants, according to the UN.[42] Unlike Haiti (which has fewer police per person than the United States), Venezuela has about two and a half times more police per person than the United States. Despite their much higher numbers relative to the population, Venezuelan police are (at least) ten times more likely to be killed on duty than U.S. police.[43]

Under Maduro, Venezuela has shifted to a *mano dura* (hard-handed) approach to crime.[44] Nobody should endorse this approach, given that it inevitably encourages police impunity in the poorest communities. Unfortunately, that approach has popular support throughout the region.[45] Under Chávez, however, a much more progressive approach to policing, combined with rapid poverty and inequality reduction, failed to have much positive impact on the homicide rate. Homicides plateaued during Chávez's last four years in office, after an alarming increase that began years before he was first elected. There is widespread agreement that the homicide rate has fallen since 2016, for reasons that are unclear.[46]

In fact, Chávez was accused of deliberately weakening the police at the expense of public safety. Western media didn't shrink from blaming him for the country's high homicide rate. In 2012, the *Los*

Angeles Times reported the following in an article with the headline, "In Venezuela, killings of Caracas police are on rise":

> Observatory director and criminologist Roberto Briceno-Leon believes that the violent tone set by Chávez in promoting his socialist Bolivarian Revolution is partly responsible for rising crime rates—a belief that he says is shared by 58% of Venezuelans polled by his university group.
>
> "Chávez has promoted the idea that violence forms part of the class struggle against the rich and the landowners, and so it's not so bad," Briceno-Leon said. "He has always rationalized high crime by saying the problem exists on every country on Earth, and that it's the fault of poverty and capitalism. He won't hire more police because he sees it as a right-wing policy."[47]

Under both Chávez and Maduro, notwithstanding their different approaches to policing, the criminal justice system overall, including prosecutors and judges, remained stacked against poor people. The assassinations of Chavistas in the countryside and widespread impunity for the violent opposition are the most striking manifestations of this fact.

But Chávez should have been widely praised for resisting the temptation to support heavy-handed policing. By itself, this was a positive aspect of his years in office. Instead, he was absurdly accused of having sinister motives for doing so. Brian Nelson's book *The Silence and the Scorpion* (an apologia for the 2002 coup that briefly ousted Chávez) suggests that Chávez's efforts to curb the power of police were actually intended to benefit Colombian FARC rebels operating in Venezuela.[48] Chávez *should* be criticized for not making the sweeping changes required to ensure that most prosecutors and judges did their jobs properly. And yet, had he done so, the response of groups like HRW would have been to scream that judicial independence was being trampled.[49]

HRW's radically different approach to police violence in Haiti and Venezuela illustrates how shamelessly the group adopts any stance that will help the United States justify overthrowing the governments it doesn't like and keeping in power the dictatorships it supports. The death of Chávez provided another revealing example of HRW acting as if it were the U.S. government's human rights group.

Dramatic Imperial Bias Revealed by Death of Chávez

Within two hours of Chávez's death on March 5, 2013, HRW put out a statement attacking his legacy. It was titled "Chávez's Authoritarian Legacy: Dramatic Concentration of Power and Open Disregard for Basic Human Rights." The statement chose not to say a single positive thing about Chávez's time in office. HRW does not limit itself to only criticizing governments or political leaders. It also hands out effusive praise. In addition to flattering the world's most powerful states (the United States and its European allies), HRW has applauded low-level U.S. allies as well, such as Ecuador under Lenín Moreno.

There was nothing in the statement about how Venezuela had achieved a huge reduction in poverty and inequality under Chávez. (But when those trends reversed under Maduro, HRW took the decline as a stick with which to beat the government constantly.) There was nothing about drastically increased voter turnout under Chávez. There was no recognition that Chávez admirably resisted pressure from the opposition to resort to heavy-handed policing in order to bring down Venezuela's very high homicide rate.

There was no praise for Chávez strongly opposing the U.S. bombing of Afghanistan in 2001, as well as its invasion of Iraq, the 2004 coup in Haiti, the 2009 coup in Honduras, NATO's bombing of Libya, the catastrophic militarization of the conflict in Syria, and Israel's aggression in Lebanon and Palestine. None of that drew Chávez any applause from HRW.

Instead, as examples of Chávez "embracing abusive governments," HRW highlighted Libya under Muammar al-Gaddafi, Syria, Iran, and Cuba—all governments the United States has targeted for destruction.[50] HRW did not mention the U.S.-backed government of Colombia even though, for a time, Chávez had warm relations with the far-right and extremely abusive Alvaro Uribe.[51] In 2008, their relationship rapidly went sour.⁵² But Chávez quickly repaired relations with Colombia after Juan Manuel Santos took office in 2010. Santos (who attended Chávez's funeral) was Uribe's Minister of Defense from 2006 to 2009, and is therefore deeply implicated in the large-scale crimes of armed actors in Colombia, both military and paramilitary.⁵³ Chávez also had warm relations with the right-wing Haitian President Michel Martelly, whose sham election in 2011 was the direct result of U.S. and OAS bullying. But, for obvious reasons, none of these relationships provoked outrage or even a mention from HRW.⁵⁴

Moreover, it's impossible to see how any government in the Global South, unless it's suicidal, avoids relationships with abusive governments. Consider the most obvious example: Venezuela's relationship with the United States.

Should we condemn Chávez for continuing to sell oil to the United States despite its abusive government? Of course not. To do so would have inflicted hardships on the most vulnerable Venezuelans and indiscriminately punished people in the United States.

Countries of the Global South should try to unite to resist the arbitrary rule of the strong, even if doing so sometimes means defending bad governments. This is analogous to saying that the basic civil rights of criminals must be defended in any society that rejects arbitrary rule.

For example, Chávez supported Libya's Gaddafi—rhetorically, since Venezuela was not in a position to do much else. But the United States got its way in Libya. Gaddafi was overthrown and savagely murdered by U.S. proxies. Venezuela's support was hardly going to prevent that—unfortunately, because the United States and its NATO allies managed to make Libya far worse today than it was under Gaddafi.

HRW officials would also never give Chávez credit for his achievement of surviving U.S.-backed efforts to overthrow him.⁵⁵ Had those efforts succeeded, they would have resulted in a Latortue-style campaign to murderously eradicate Chavismo as an organized political force. We know from what happened in Haiti that HRW's responses would have ranged from silence to outright support for a brutal dictatorship. This became clear once more after a military coup ousted Evo Morales in Bolivia in 2019. In May 2020, Vivanco explicitly referred to the U.S.-backed Añez dictatorship in Bolivia as a "democracy."[56]

HRW's statements about other prominent political leaders who have died, considered alongside its statement regarding Chávez, dramatically expose its double standards. HRW has deplored the bigotry of Donald Trump, but it hailed an overtly racist warmonger, the late U.S. Senator John McCain. Ken Roth, HRW's executive director, tweeted that McCain "will be remembered for his firm, principled opposition to torture, especially by Bush, a member of his own party." Its Americas director, José Miguel Vivanco, tweeted (in Spanish) that McCain was "a giant in North American politics and an ally in the defense of human rights." Sarah Margon, HRW's Washington director, tweeted that McCain's death "feels exceptionally tough for those of us who have fought for human decency and basic rights alongside and with him." Dinah PoKempner, HRW's general counsel, retweeted an article that called McCain a "war hero."[57]

McCain's "war hero" status comes from participating in the slaughter in Vietnam that most likely killed three million people—or "gooks" as McCain unapologetically preferred to call them.[58] He was taken prisoner after his plane was shot down during his twenty-third bombing mission and then he was tortured by the North Vietnamese.[59] How many people did McCain kill during those missions? Was it hundreds? Thousands? It's inexcusable that he was tortured, but it does not justify what he was doing in Vietnam—which was criminal, not heroic. His ordeal as a prisoner cannot erase the humanity of *his* victims or justify the racist slurs he used against them. Despite the death toll of millions of Vietnamese, McCain complained in his 1989 book *Faith of My Fathers* about "frustratingly limited bombing targets." In 1998, McCain's arguments for a "winnable" Vietnam War were poorly veiled regrets that the slaughter was not worse: "Had we taken the war to the North and made full, consistent use of air power in the North, we ultimately would have prevailed."[60] HRW also published an official statement after McCain's death saying that he "was

THE HUMAN RIGHTS FRAUD 221

for decades a compassionate voice for US foreign and national security policy."[61] McCain strongly supported the Contra terrorists armed by Ronald Reagan in the 1980s to bring Nicaragua's democratically elected government to its knees—the first democracy Nicaragua had after seven decades of brutal dictatorship backed (and for a time directly imposed) by Washington.[62] How could that—or the fact that McCain joked about bombing Iran—evade the notice of a serious human rights group?[63]

Himself a sponsor of terrorists, McCain tried to have the Chávez government placed on the U.S. "sponsors of terrorism" list.[64] U.S. journalist Max Blumenthal wrote of McCain, "In Libya and Syria, he cultivated affiliates of Al Qaeda as allies, and in Ukraine, McCain courted actual, sig-heiling neo-Nazis."[65] McCain also supported the wars in Iraq and Afghanistan.[66] In its statement following his death, HRW vaguely conceded that there "were certainly times when McCain didn't live up to his own aspirations." But it then hastened to add that McCain had a "deep commitment to human rights."

The group's praise for McCain's anti-torture rhetoric is also interesting. Why was the use of torture even being debated in a country that Ken Roth proclaimed the "world's most powerful proponent of human rights"? McCain's opposition to torture, putting aside the watered-down legislation he actually supported, is much more indicative of a regressive political culture than of virtue on his part.[67] In the twenty-first century, are we also to cheer U.S. politicians for being anti-slavery and pro-universal suffrage? Regardless, even if the U.S. political culture does include people who are worse than McCain on some issues, how does that excuse a human rights group showering him with praise?

HRW's statement published in 2015 after the death of staunch U.S. ally King Abdullah of Saudi Arabia was titled "Saudi Arabia: King's Reform Agenda Unfulfilled: New Leadership Should Prioritize Improving Country's Human Rights Record."[68] It found positive things to say about a man who ran perhaps the most brutal and backward dictatorship on earth.[69] It said that, under Abdullah, there had been "a marginally expanded public role for women" and other "concrete gains for women." It noted that "internet and social media empowered Saudi citizens to speak openly," and that Abdullah was a "great champion of religious dialogue outside the kingdom."

Its criticism of Saudi Arabia was embarrassingly muted. It said that "some written laws promulgated during King Abdullah's reign curtailed basic rights." Another sentence blandly observed that Saudi judges "continue to jail and sentence people for 'sorcery' and 'sowing discord.'" In fact, Abudullah's government beheaded people for those things.[70]

HRW's hopeful tone regarding alleged progress in Saudi Arabia has been a staple of U.S. establishment propaganda for several decades. Abdullah Al-Arian, an assistant professor of history at Georgetown University, put together a collection of *New York Times* headlines from 1953 to 2017 that all hyped "reform" in Saudi Arabia.[71] The U.S. media critic Adam Johnson has mocked this endless spin for the Saudi rulers as the "71,500-year reform plan" that congratulates them for "moving their country toward the 19th century every five years or so."[72]

HRW's beloved John McCain reacted to Abdullah's death by calling him an "important voice for reform in Saudi Arabia," a "vocal advocate of peace," and a "critical partner in the war on terror." President Obama, former President George H. W. Bush, Vice President Joe Biden, and Secretary of State John Kerry all made similar remarks.[73]

Western support for the Saudi dictatorship (often referred to by the romanticized term "kingdom") has gone far beyond public flattery. In September 2016, Reuters estimated that "Obama's administration has offered Saudi Arabia more than $115 billion in weapons, other military equipment and training, the most of any U.S. administration in the 71-year U.S.-Saudi alliance."[74] Canada and the UK have also supplied its military.[75]

The horrors that Saudi Arabia has inflicted on Yemen since 2015 with Western-supplied military hardware and training, combined with the murder of *Washington Post* columnist Jamal Khashoggi on October 2, 2018, by Saudi agents, led to an unprecedented public relations problem.[76] By 2019, Trump was forced to use his veto in order to

THE HUMAN RIGHTS FRAUD   223

keep supporting the Saudi atrocities in Yemen. On May 2, 2019, the U.S. Senate failed to override the veto.[77]

HRW still found positive things to say about the Saudi government in a statement on November 4, 2019—proving that its commitment to the "71,500-year reform plan" was very strong indeed. It said that "important social reforms enacted under Saudi Crown Prince Mohammed bin Salman have been accompanied by deepening repression and abusive practices meant to silence dissidents and critics."[78] It was still willing to give more credit to a notoriously barbaric U.S. ally than it did to Chávez when he died.

13

Colombia's U.S.–Approved Horror Show Could Come to Venezuela

After two decades of coup attempts, ever-tightening economic strangulation, and tens of thousands of deaths from preventable disease, it could be tempting to assume that Venezuela's surrender to U.S. dictates would be better than the status quo. Since 2016, Venezuela's economic collapse has sparked an exodus of Venezuelans into Colombia and other countries. According to one widely cited group of anti-Maduro academics, nearly one million per year left Venezuela for other countries between 2017 and 2019.[1] What if the sanctions ended and those millions of people could go home?[2]

In the real world, controlled experiments are impossible. But Venezuela's neighbor, Colombia, offers a glimpse into what the future holds for Venezuelans should Chavismo fall to the right-wing opposition. A U.S. victory in Venezuela—the overthrow of Maduro—would bring an end to sanctions. But whatever relief that brings could be completely canceled by the ravages of low-intensity war, the likes of which Colombia has endured as the price for keeping its oligarchy in power.

More than 220,000 have died in Colombia's fifty-seven-year-old civil war.[3] Its population of internally displaced people was about 7 million in 2016, and had consistently been similar to Syria's between

2011 to 2016.⁴ As of 2015, there were hundreds of thousands of Colombian refugees living in Venezuela, but barely any Venezuelan refugees living in Colombia.⁵ Colombia's government was never targeted for economic strangulation by the United States: it has been a recipient of U.S. financial and military support. Similarly kind treatment has been dispensed to Colombia's government by the western media. For example, in 2014, the *New York Times* editorial board said: "Colombia, Brazil and other Latin American countries should lead an effort to prevent Caracas from representing the region [on the UN Security Council] when it is fast becoming an embarrassment on the continent." The *Times* actually singled out Colombia's government as one of the regional good guys.⁶

On April 18, 2009, at the Summit of the Americas in Trinidad, Hugo Chávez handed a copy of *Open Veins of Latin America* by Eduardo Galeano to the new U.S. president and repository of great hopes, Barack Obama. Galeano is one of Latin America's most respected writers, and *Open Veins* is a devastating single-volume history of the carnage wrought by various empires on the continent. But the book didn't have much of an impact on Obama or lead to any change in how the United States related to Venezuela. Had Obama cracked the book open, he could have learned about the system of plunder that has afflicted the continent for the past five hundred years.

In its history of exploitation, Venezuela shares much with other countries in the region, and has many special connections to its neighbor, Colombia. In the time of Simón Bolívar, during the early nineteenth century, Venezuela was part of Gran Colombia. Panama seceded from Colombia in 1903 at the behest of the United States, while other countries, including Venezuela, split off at different times. Colombia today has roughly twice Venezuela's population and covers a bigger territory.

Their shared histories go through the boom-and-bust commodity cycles of the twentieth century and the armed struggles of the 1960s. When Colombia's FARC, ELN, and M-19 fought their leftist armed struggles against the state, Venezuela had its own armed struggles in the hillsides. The U.S. counterinsurgency strategy, brought to

Colombia by U.S. General William P. Yarborough in the 1960s, envisioned Latin America's military officers trained in the United States to fight these local insurgencies on behalf of multinational corporations and local landowners. Among their tools: the creation of auxiliary forces, armed civilians working with the military, which used indiscriminate attacks on civilians and showy violence to terrorize would-be guerrilla sympathizers. If rural guerrilla fighters followed Mao Zedong's doctrine of being "fish" swimming among the rural population, the U.S.-backed counterinsurgents would "drain the swamp" by displacing peasants from their villages and depopulating the countryside. The counterinsurgency strategy was generalized and applied to Venezuela, to build up the security state and a counterinsurgency.

U.S. oil politics in Latin America could not but focus on Venezuela. Colombia also has oil, as do Ecuador and Bolivia. U.S.- and UK-backed sanctions against the Mexican government in the 1930s were a punishment for nationalization.[7]

Both countries were founded on the exploitation of African slaves, the theft of Indigenous lands, and an unequal, plantation-based economy with concentrated land-ownership and cities built to export commodities to the metropoles of the world. They diverged in the specific commodities they specialized in, with Colombia focusing on coffee and Venezuela becoming a major petroleum exporter in the early twentieth century. In the 1970s, the global economy of illegal drugs changed, and the U.S. market for cocaine, produced from the coca leaf grown in the Andes (Colombia, Bolivia, and Peru), expanded dramatically. Apart from being illegal, the business functions like other commodity-based businesses: raw materials are produced in the Global South, and sellers and consumers in the Global North capture most of the value, placing their profits in U.S. and European banks. But in the propaganda system, Colombia came to be portrayed as the source of the world's drug problems, as opposed to what it was, a source for the primary commodities, coca and poppy, from which profits and power were derived mainly by the elites of the United States and Europe (whose masses also consumed the finished product).

COLOMBIA'S HORROR SHOW COULD COME TO VENEZUELA

The Cuban Revolution in 1959 inspired leftist guerrillas throughout the hemisphere. In Colombia, the pre-emption of a liberal reform movement through the assassination of the presidential candidate Jorge Eliécer Gaitán in 1948 started a guerrilla war that has continued in various forms until today. In addition to problems shared with Brazil, Venezuela, Ecuador, and its other neighbors, from land concentration to an inability to protect its own industries or welfare state from penetration by U.S. corporations and privatization pressures, Colombia has borne this special burden of a permanent civil war. Because of this, the United States has since the 1960s treated Colombia as its laboratory for counterinsurgency in the Americas—including paramilitarism, the use of the drug trade to finance counterinsurgency, aerial fumigation, surveillance, and other activities.

The permanent civil war has also provided Colombia's elites with cover for the violent suppression of popular movements and demands for social reform. The Colombian state has identified unions, peasant associations, Indigenous people, and Afro-Colombians with the guerrillas and has therefore treated them as civil war belligerents. In the countryside, this has led to mass displacement and an internal refugee crisis. In the cities, it takes the form of the assassination of union and social movement leaders. These killings are done by paramilitary death squads who are organized and financed by elites, sometimes privately but usually through the state, which allows them to operate with impunity.

All of these dynamics are seen in other Latin American countries, but they have dominated and shaped Colombia's history to a greater extent.

Venezuela evolved somewhat differently. The political class developed a power-sharing arrangement to maintain democratic trappings while keeping the country and the all-important oil company in elite hands and under U.S. hegemony. And though guerrillas did take up arms in the 1960s, Colombia-style dirty-war methods kept the disruption of business-as-usual to a minimum. But when Hugo Chávez arrived on the Venezuelan scene and upset this rigid political order, promising to include the masses in the benefits of the oil economy, the dirty-war methods were expanded. In particular, Venezuelan peasants trying to assert their rights were murdered in large numbers, like their counterparts in Colombia.

When Chavismo became a political force in 1998, there were some wait-and-see moments as the United States tried to determine what Chavismo was and how it would affect oil politics globally. Colombian analyst Hector Mondragon believed that Plan Colombia, a multi-billion-dollar package of military and anti-narcotics co-operation announced in 2000, had a lot to do with having a bigger U.S. military presence in Colombia to better target Venezuela (and Ecuador).[8] The entire decade of 2000–2010 was one of continuous escalation of the Colombian civil war, as President Álvaro Uribe, who held office from 2002 to 2010, kept ramping the conflict up, promising victory against the guerrillas. When victory proved elusive, Uribe blamed Colombia's neighbors Ecuador and Venezuela, and tried to inflame wars against them.

A series of Colombia-Venezuela incidents were manufactured to maintain a continuous sense of threat against the reform process underway in Venezuela.

The first such incident: In February 2003, the Colombian consulate and Spanish Embassy in Caracas were bombed. The Colombian government immediately insinuated that Chávez was behind the bombings, but no further conflict between Colombia and Venezuela followed. By November, Venezuela's public prosecutor, Danilo Anderson, issued arrest warrants accusing anti-Chávez National Guard general Felipe Rodriguez and two lieutenants in the bombings.[9] Rodriguez, who was one of the leaders of the April 2002 coup against Chávez, went into hiding, but was apprehended in 2005. Less than a year before, Anderson, who had brought the charges against him, was assassinated by a car bomb.[10] In 2008, a Venezuelan court convicted Rodriguez and sentenced him to ten years and six months in prison[11] for planning the bombings to destabilize the government.[12] He received early release on March 4, 2011.[13]

The next incident occurred at a regional security summit in Bogotá, in mid-March 2003. There, the Colombian government (with its U.S.

COLOMBIA'S HORROR SHOW COULD COME TO VENEZUELA 229

patron behind it) pointed fingers at every single neighboring country. Panama was blamed for being a route by which arms and people are transported. Ecuador came in for criticism as a drug trafficking route as well. Brazil was asked to send troops to Colombia for a "multilateral force against terrorism." (In January of that year, Uribe had asked for a U.S. intervention in his own country.)

Venezuela was singled out for special criticism. Colombia's representatives at the summit claimed that Venezuela was training and supporting one of Colombia's guerrilla organizations, the FARC. Because the FARC was already on the U.S. State Department's list of "terrorist organizations," a deft combination of the Bush doctrine, of overthrowing states accused of supporting terrorism, and the Rumsfeld doctrine, "the absence of evidence is not the evidence of absence," would have been enough to justify an intervention against Venezuela.

Colombia's rant at the summit was a bold inversion of reality for multiple reasons. It was Colombia's army-backed paramilitaries who had crossed the border into Panama in January 2003 to murder four Indigenous leaders—the mayors and commissioner of the Kuna Paya village, who were shot and hacked apart with machetes. And it was the Colombian army that would soon engage in cross-border terrorism by attacking Venezuela and testing its defenses.

On March 31, 2003, Chávez announced on Venezuelan radio: "A short while ago, I ordered an air force operation and we bombed an area where we detected the presence of a group" of Colombian irregular forces along the border. The Colombian irregulars had attacked a Venezuelan military post. Chávez stressed that Caracas would not tolerate Colombian armed groups entering Venezuela. "Neither paramilitaries nor rebels nor the armed forces of Colombia have authorization, nor will they have it, to be on Venezuelan territory," he said.[14]

Another Colombian raid occurred in May 2004. Some eighty-eight Colombian paramilitaries were apprehended on Sunday, May 9, at a ranch, El Hatillo, near Caracas.[15] These eighty-eight were part of a larger group of 130 who had entered Venezuela. According to the testimony of one of the captured Colombians, the group was training and preparing for yet another operation to overthrow the Venezuelan government:

> The terrorist plan consisted of attacking a military installation in Caracas this week, possibly the Urban Security Command of the National Guard. On Monday, the paramilitaries were to be taken to another ranch, where they would receive final training with arms and ammunition, and do the assault on Wednesday. "We were going to attack a military base that has tunnels underneath containing arms," said the presumed paramilitary. The purpose, according to one of the anti-Chávez "generals," was to steal arms from the base to give to a 3,000 strong paramilitary group who were to come to Venezuela in 8 days.[16]

The ranch belonged to Robert Alonso, an anti-Castro Cuban, high-profile member of the Venezuelan opposition, and brother of the actor Maria Conchita Alonso. There were also, according to Venezuelan authorities, active members of Venezuela's military involved in the plot, which included not only plans to take over the state but to carry out terrorist attacks.

One of the Colombians who was caught gave anonymous, on-camera testimony while wearing a mask. The man, a Colombian army reservist, had been given the impression that he would be going to do agricultural work in the countryside, but, along with the others, was then informed that he would be training for a major military operation. "When we learned what was really going on," he said, "more than one Colombian wanted to escape. One Colombian tried, but they caught him after 100 metres, and told him the next time they would kill him, and they took our papers."

Chávez framed the issue in explicitly anti-terrorist terms. "We've struck a blow against coup-plotters, destabilizers, and terrorists, in this endless struggle against terrorism, destabilization, and the enemies of democracy and the people." He described the whole operation as an assassination attempt: "They came to kill me."

Richard Boucher, the State Department's spokesperson, said: "I know there are some accusations that all this is part of some US conspiracy to overthrow the Chávez government. We categorically reject these declarations and shameful accusations."[17]

Next, the Venezuelan opposition finally tried to use the constitution to get rid of Chavismo by gathering signatures for a recall referendum, scheduled for August 2004. But as the referendum campaign ramped up that summer, Uribe announced a new "border brigade," with forty-six tanks supplied from Spain, to be deployed to the Venezuelan border.[18] The Venezuelan military expressed concern; Chávez went to work on a diplomatic solution. Spain, which had elected a socialist government, cancelled the deal. The tanks never arrived, and the whole topic became a friendly joke between Uribe and Chávez at a later summit, during a brief period of cordial relations.

The opposition's referendum failed as well, with Venezuelans voting overwhelmingly to keep Chávez in office. But in December 2004, Colombia made another daring provocation: the arrest of a high-profile spokesman for the Colombian guerrillas, Rodrigo Granda, in Venezuela. The Colombian government received support from suborned Venezuelan police and military agents as it smuggled Granda out of Caracas. He was taken to a Colombian prison and released three years later in a multilateral negotiation with France. The whole incident was also a statement from Uribe (and the United States) against Chávez's attempts to work with Cuba to facilitate a negotiated solution to the Colombian civil war. In response, Chávez closed the Colombia-Venezuela border.

Around the time of Granda's release in 2007, Chávez pushed for another major effort to negotiate an end to the Colombian civil war. The hope was for a humanitarian exchange of prisoners, which would address the FARC's most unpopular tactic, kidnapping. Uribe eventually scuttled the deal and initiated military operations in FARC zones instead.[19]

From 2007 forward, Uribe kept ramping up the aggression against FARC locally and against Venezuela internationally. In March 2008, Colombia assassinated the commander of the FARC, Raúl Reyes, in an air raid.[20] Reyes was in Ecuador. The cavalier air attack on another country nearly led to war with both Ecuador and Venezuela—which may well have been the point.

At the end of Chavismo's glory years, from 2006 to 2012, the Colombia-Venezuela border again became the focus of the assault on Chavismo. A smuggling economy developed as people began taking subsidized staples out of Venezuela—fuel, food, toilet paper, and other products available through Venezuelan government programs. Destabilizing Venezuela's economy by making staple items difficult to get, border smuggling proved a more effective weapon against Chavismo than outright military attack. Colombia never had the internal stability required to make foreign conquest a viable option. Its military's primary enemy has been civilians and, as a distant second, the FARC.

During one phase of the most recent coup attempt in Venezuela, Juan Guaidó pulled his aid stunt on the Colombian border. Some of the Venezuelans who defected to his side ended up miserable and hopeless in Colombia. "We are adrift; we do not have the support of anybody. We want Juan Guaidó to come to talk to us face to face," their spokesman said from a UN refugee camp weeks later.[21] Some Venezuelan defectors even ended up in ICE detention centers in the United States. The Empire, from its own immoral perspective, is probably wise not to reward failure.[22]

In contrast with Venezuela's apparently uniquely bad human rights situation, we have Colombia, which is portrayed as fighting the good fight against terrorism. The facts reveal horrors committed by Colombia's rulers that Venezuela's elite and its U.S. sponsors have so far been prevented from inflicting on Venezuela.

At the beginning of Colombia's peace process in 2013, a state body produced an estimate of 220,000 deaths that were caused by the conflict between 1958 and 2013. Between 1996 and 2005, there was a kidnapping every eight hours and an anti-personnel mine killed someone every single day. Between 1980 and 2012, there were 1,982 massacres, most of which were committed by the state and paramilitaries.[23]

These paramilitary death squads have become a part of the political leadership of the country.[24] Their crimes are the most horrific of any actors in the conflict and also the largest in scale. Over the course of various demobilization initiatives, during which paramilitaries could surrender and confess their crimes, the state collected evidence: "1,926 confessions of demobilized paramilitary members have been taken; 32,909 crimes confessed—the vast majority murders; 2,666 victim remains exhumed, and 257,089 victims registered."[25] (These figures were reported in a 2009 State Department cable and published by Wikileaks.) The paramilitary campaign was particularly genocidal against Colombia's Indigenous people, bringing thirty-four groups to the verge of extinction.[26]

Post-peace process, the killings keep going. The grim statistics are documented by Colombian human rights organizations such as the Lawyer's Collective (Colectivo de Abogados). Human rights defenders were killed in large numbers: 133 in 2016, 126 in 2017, and 178 in 2018.[27] The UN's Office of the High Commissioner for Human Rights documented 108 killings of human rights defenders in 2019.[28] Murders of peasant leaders, union leaders, and so-called social-cleansing murders of LGBTQ, homeless people, sex workers, and others targeted by right-wing paramilitaries, also abound.

But the scandal that dominated headlines for years in Colombia was the "false positives" scandal, in which the army killed 10,000 or more completely innocent noncombatants to boost the death toll they could report of guerrillas. The false positives program went on throughout Uribe's rule from 2002 to 2010.[29] The scandal broke in 2008. There were over 5,000 military men involved in the killings, and a few hundred have been imprisoned for it.[30] Uribe is still a senator in Colombia and recognized as the power behind the current president, Ivan Duque. In addition to the false positive murders, thousands of Colombians were disappeared during each year of Uribe's rule: 15,732 in 2002, 12,577 in 2003, and 9,759 in 2004, until the number slowly declined to below 1,000 in 2013 under President Santos. During the war, somewhere around seven million Colombians became internal refugees or internally displaced people.[31]

The point of all this isn't simply to say, "Imagine if Chavismo's human rights record had resembled that of Uribismo?"—although the contrast should be clear by now. The significance of this comparison is to show that Colombia's nightmare of a permanent war against social movements is precisely what is planned for Venezuela should the opposition's coup attempts finally succeed.

In September 2014, *New York Times* editors singled out Colombia as a country that should "lead an effort to prevent Caracas from representing the region when it is fast becoming an embarrassment."[32] The editors registered zero "embarrassment" when U.S. General John Kelly told Congress, "The beauty of having a Colombia—they're such good partners, particularly in the military realm, they're such good partners with us. When we ask them to go somewhere else and train the Mexicans, the Hondurans, the Guatemalans, the Panamanians, they will do it almost without asking. And they'll do it on their own. They're so appreciative of what we did for them. And what we did for them was, really, to encourage them for 20 years and they've done such a magnificent job."[33]

If the United States succeeds in Venezuela, the success will look something like Colombia: a multigenerational civil war, the exclusion of the majority, the murder of social leaders, and the reconfiguration of the economy for the benefit of the United States and the local elite. The only compensation for the tragedy unfolding for the country will be better media coverage. No one who wishes Colombians or Venezuelans well can accept their own government's contributing to such a future.

Acknowledgments

We could not have written this book without the work of independent researchers and journalists, many of whom have lived for several years in Venezuela. We are especially indebted to the journalists of VenezuelAnalysis and the researchers at the Center for Economic and Policy Research. To say they have punched above their weight against establishment journalists would be an understatement. We are especially grateful to those who have taken the time to interact directly with us over the years: Lucas Koerner, Rachael Boothroyd, Ricardo Vaz, Paul Dobson, Greg Wilpert, Michael Fox, Tamara Pearson, Ryan Mallett-Outtrim, Mark Weisbrot, Alex Main, Dan Beeton, David Rosnick.

We are also very grateful to have interacted over the years with Andrew Cawthorne, Francisco Rodriguez, Temir Porras, Ignacio Ramirez, Edgar Marquez, Vladimir Villegas, Maria Paez Victor and Eirik Vold.

We thank the Monthly Review Press team for publishing our book, and for their diligent work editing it.

Most of all, we are thankful to Chavista voters who showed up consistently at the polls since 1998 to show us all that the world's most dangerous empire and it propaganda organs are not omnipotent. We owe them thanks, but mostly our sincerest apologies for our inability to stop the harm that our government, in collaboration with other key U.S. allies, has inflicted on them.

Chronology: Six Coup Attempts

1. **April 11–14, 2002**: President Hugo Chávez deposed in a military coup. Constitution of 1999 annulled. Dictatorship under Pedro Carmona recognized by the United States. Carmona Decree dismisses the Supreme Court and elected officials countrywide. The coup results in seventy-nine violent deaths: sixty-eight Chávez government supporters (Chavistas), seven opposition supporters, and five bystanders. Two days later, Chávez is restored to power by massive protests and a revolt against the coup by segments of the military.

2. **December 2002–February 2003**: Management-led shutdown of state oil company, PDVSA. Combined with impact of April coup, it causes loss of 29 percent of GDP; income poverty increases from 48 to 62 percent. After shutdown fails to topple the government, almost half of PDVSA employees are fired.

3. **April 2013**: Nicolás Maduro wins election following Chávez's death in March. United States refuses to recognize election results. Violent protests led by losing candidate Henrique Capriles attempts to have election annulled. Nine deaths, all Maduro supporters (Chavistas), one possibly the result of crime unrelated to protests.

4. **February–April 2014**: Opposition suffers defeat in nationwide municipal elections in December 2013. Two months later, violent protests led by Leopoldo López again aimed at ousting Maduro. Forty-three deaths: twenty-two strongly indicate responsibility of opposition protesters, sixteen strongly indicate government's responsibility (security forces or supporters). Responsibility for three deaths is unclear; two additional deaths are accidental and cannot be blamed on either side.[1]

5. **April–July 2017**: Opposition wins control of National Assembly in December 2015. Maduro prevails in legal battles with Assembly. In April 2017, violent protests aimed at ousting Maduro erupt again. One hundred and twenty-six deaths: fifty opposition supporters, twenty-nine bystanders, nineteen government supporters or police, and twenty-eight unknown or disputed.[2]

6. **January 2019–ongoing**: Juan Guaidó recognized as interim president by United States and many of its allies. Trump administration intensifies economic sanctions, blocking revenues from oil sales to the United States from going to Maduro government. U.S. threats of military attack increase in frequency while U.S. officials make direct appeals to Venezuelan military to oust Maduro.

Notes

1. The Extraordinary Threat to Venezuela

1. Natalie Obiko Pearson and Ian James, "Venezuela Offers Billions to Countries in Latin America," Associated Press, August 28, 2007, https://venezuelanalysis.com/news/2571.
2. Mark Weisbrot and Jeffrey Sachs, "Economic Sanctions as Collective Punishment: The Case of Venezuela," Center for Economic and Policy Research, April 2019, http://cepr.net/images/stories/reports/venezuela-sanctions-2019-04.pdf.
3. "FACT SHEET: Venezuela Executive Order," The White House (Office of the Press Secretary), Mar. 9, 2015, https://obamawhitehouse.archives.gov/the-press-office/2015/03/09/fact-sheet-venezuela-executive-order.
4. William Neuman, "Obama Hands Venezuelan Leader a Cause to Stir Support," *The New York Times*, March 11, 2015, https://www.nytimes.com/2015/03/12/world/americas/venezuela-nicolas-maduro-obama.html.
5. *The Economist* once stated, "It is now widely accepted that monetary policy is best set by an independent central bank, insulated from political pressures. But fiscal policy still remains in the hands of politicians . . . The idea of an independent fiscal authority deserves serious consideration. It may seem radical and undemocratic. But that, remember, is what many governments once said of demands to make their central banks independent." See "Fiscal flexibility: Could finance ministers learn a few tricks from central bankers?" *The Economist*, Nov. 25, 1999.
6. "Julian Assange arbitrarily detained by Sweden and the UK, UN expert

panel finds," UN Human Rights, Office of the High Commissioner, https://www.ohchr.org/EN/NewsEvents/Pages/DisplayNews.aspx?NewsID=17013&LangID=E.
7. *United States v. Julian Paul Assange*, March 6, 2018, https://www.justice.gov/usao-edva/press-release/file/1153481/download; "Collateral Murder-Wikileaks-Iraq," Youtube, April 3, 2010, https://www.youtube.com/watch?v=5rXPrfnU3G0.
8. International Crimes Database, "United States v. William L. Calley Jr.," International Crimes Database, http://www.internationalcrimesdatabase.org/Case/1131.
9. Joe Emersberger, "Amnesty International still doesn't recognise Chelsea Manning as a Prisoner of Conscience," *The Canary*, April 5, 2019, https://www.thecanary.co/us/us-analysis/2019/04/05/amnesty-international-still-doesnt-recognise-chelsea-manning-as-a-prisoner-of-conscience/.
10. "Assange Arrest—Part 2: 'A Definite Creep, A Probable Rapist,'" *Media Lens*, April 18, 2019, http://www.medialens.org/index.php/alerts/alert-archive/2019/901-assange-arrest-part-2-definite-creep-probable-rapist.html.
11. The rebellion against police violence in the wake of George Floyd's murder in June 2020 was still ongoing as we finished writing this book. See "#SayHerName: Protests Demand Justice for Sandra Bland & Black Teen Found Dead in Jail 1 Day Later," *Democracy Now!*, July 23, 2015, https://www.democracynow.org/2015/7/23/sayhername_new_case_of_black_girl; Jorge Barrera, "Families still waiting to hear from Thunder Bay police on fate of 9 cases recommended for reinvestigation," CBC News, March 25, 2019, https://www.cbc.ca/news/indigenous/thunderbay-cases-oiprd-1.5067443.
12. The United States and the gang of wealthy countries allied with it function more like a *mafia*. Originally applied to Sicilian organized crime, the word *mafia* connotes organizations—businesses—that conduct illegal and violent activities. The word *mafia* captures the sordid, violent nature of most of what is done and the moral squalor of journalism that covers for it. The way the Syriza government in Greece was ruthlessly bullied in 2015 by the European Central Bank, EU Commission, and IMF suggests that the gangster tactics applied to poor and middle-income countries may even have been used against Greece had its government not capitulated.
13. We are not fond of the term "regime change" since it appears to implicitly label a government targeted by Washington as a "regime." The word "regime" (despite having a morally neutral meaning in academic work as an existing political or social order) in mass media usage is like the similarly pejorative terms "strongman" or "authoritarian leader":

put-downs that mean a little more than "governments or heads of state we don't like."

14. For discussion of some more indirect intervention to undermine progressive governments in Brazil, Paraguay, and Argentina in this century, see Joe Emersberger's essay "The Empire's Media and the Quest for Veto Authority in the Americas," FAIR, June 6, 2018, https://fair.org/home/the-empires-media-and-the-quest-for-veto-authority-in-the-americas/.
15. Lucas Koerner, "U.S. Presidential Hopeful Bernie Sanders Slams Chávez in Reposte to Clinton Attack," VenezuelAnalysis, Sep. 17, 2015, https://venezuelanalysis.com/news/11511.
16. "Candidates Answer CFR's Questions," Council on Foreign Relations, July 30, 2019, https://www.cfr.org/article/bernie-sanders.
17. Joe Emersberger, "Amnesty International Replied to Questions about Venezuela," Z Blogs, Feb. 24, 2018, https://zcomm.org/zblogs/amnesty-international-replied-to-questions-about-venezuela/.
18. Josh Katz and Kevin Quealy, "Which Country Is America's Strongest Ally? For Republicans, It's Australia," *The New York Times*, Feb 3, 2017, https://www.nytimes.com/interactive/2017/02/03/upshot/which-country-do-americans-like-most-for-republicans-its-australia.html.
19. "Coalition troops in Iraq," BBC News, July 20, 2004, http://news.bbc.co.uk/2/hi/middle_east/3873359.stm.
20. "Donald Trump has shown a surprising enthusiasm for sanctions," *The Economist*, Nov. 28, 2019, https://www.economist.com/united-states/2019/11/28/donald-trump-has-shown-a-surprising-enthusiasm-for-sanctions.
21. See Weisbrot and Sachs, "Economic Sanctions as Collective Punishment." Francisco Rodriguez, while somewhat critical of the paper, nevertheless said in a private email to Emersberger that he had estimated that about a third of the increased mortality in 2018 could be attributed to U.S. sanctions.
22. Ricardo Vaz and Lucas Koerner, "US to Mobilize Military Reservists in 'Anti-Drug' Operation Against Venezuela," VenezuelAnalysis, April 30, 2020, https://venezuelanalysis.com/news/14857.
23. "New Oil Sanctions on Venezuela: 'Would Destroy What's Left of its Economy,'" Mark Weisbrot interviewed by Sharmini Peres, Jan. 30, 2019, https://therealnews.com/stories/new-oil-sanctions-on-venezuela-would-destroy-whats-left-of-its-economy.
24. Joe Emersberger, "Study Linking US Sanctions to Venezuelan Deaths Buried by Reuters for Over a Month," FAIR, June 14, 2019, https://fair.org/home/study-linking-us-sanctions-to-venezuelan-deaths-buried-by-reuters-for-over-a-month/.

25. Nick Cohen, "Blair's just a Bush Baby," *The Guardian*, March 10, 2002, https://www.theguardian.com/politics/2002/mar/10/politicalcolumnists.comment.
26. "Resilience Testing," Torino Economics (a Torino Capital Group Company), March 25, 2019.
27. Frea Lockley, "A US senator issues a mafia-style threat against government supporters in Venezuela," *The Canary*, Feb. 2, 2019, https://www.thecanary.co/trending/2019/02/21/a-us-senator-issues-a-mafia-style-threat-against-government-supporters-in-venezuela/.
28. See chapter 3 for details.
29. Tulsi Gabbard tweet, Feb. 10, 2019, https://twitter.com/TulsiGabbard/status/1094604724354142208.
30. Ben Jacobs, "Trump threatens 'military option' in Venezuela as crisis escalates," *The Guardian*, Aug. 12, 2017, https://www.theguardian.com/world/2017/aug/11/donald-trump-venezuela-crisis-military-intervention.
31. "John Bolton's cryptic note raises eyebrows at briefing," Fox News Channel, Jan. 29, 2019, available on Youtube at https://www.youtube.com/watch?v=jcMZilW56QM/.
32. "US coup in Venezuela motivated by oil and corporate interests," *The Grayzone* citing a Fox News Channel clip, Jan. 29, 2019, available on Youtube at https://www.youtube.com/watch?v=O_yHo9efvO8.
33. "Today in Energy," U.S. Energy Information Administration, October 16, 2018, https://www.eia.gov/todayinenergy/detail.php?id=37253.
34. Reuters reported Venezuela's oil exports to average 500,000 barrels per day in 2018. Early in 2020, Reuters reported that those exports had fallen to an average of 43,030 barrels per day. See Devika Krishna Kumar and Collin Eaton, "Venezuelan oil exports to U.S. still a primary source of cash," Reuters, Jan. 25, 2019, https://www.reuters.com/article/us-venezuela-politics-usa-oil-graphic/venezuelan-oil-exports-to-u-s-still-a-primary-source-of-cash-idUSKCN1PJ2CT; and Marianna Parraga, "Venezuelan oil exports fell by a third in 2019 as U.S. sanctions bit," Reuters, Jan. 7, 2020, https://www.reuters.com/article/us-venezuela-oil-exports/hit-by-sanctions-venezuela-lost-a-third-of-its-oil-exports-last-year-data-idUSKBN1Z627P.
35. Timothy Gardner and Makini Brice, "U.S. allows Chevron to drill for oil in Venezuela for three more months," Reuters, October 21, 2019, https://www.reuters.com/article/us-usa-venezuela-chevron/trump-administration-renews-three-month-license-for-chevron-in-venezuela-idUSKBN1X0270.
36. Girish Gupta, "Kimberley-Clark looks to begin arbitration against Venezuela," Reuters, April 20, 2018, https://www.reuters.com/

article/us-venezuela-kimberlyclark/kimberley-clark-looks-to-begin-arbitration-against-venezuela-idUSKBN1HR20X.
37. Noam Chomsky, "The Threat of a Good Example," excerpted from *What Uncle Sam Really Wants* (1992), https://chomsky.info/unclesam01/.
38. In chapter 11, we look at the coup the United States perpetrated in Haiti in 2004 and discuss how Human Rights Watch portrayed the Latortue dictatorship's security forces as desperately requiring international support while they were clearly waging a murderous campaign against the dictatorship's opponents in poor neighborhoods that were strongholds of support for the deposed Aristide government. See also Joe Emersberger, "Wikileaks releases 3rd cable from Haiti," *Z Blogs*, Jan. 30, 2011, https://zcomm.org/zblogs/wikileaks-releases-3rd-cable-from-haiti-by-joe-emersberger/.
39. Dan Beeton, Jake Johnstone, and Alexander Main, "Venezuela," *The Wikileaks Files: The World according to US Empire* (London and New York: Verso, 2015), 527–528.
40. "Statement from President Donald J. Trump Regarding the Resignation of Bolivian President Evo Morales," Nov. 11, 2019, https://www.whitehouse.gov/briefings-statements/statement-president-donald-j-trump-regarding-resignation-bolivian-president-evo-morales/.
41. Greg Grandin, "What 'The New York Times' Got Wrong on Bolivia," *The Nation*, Dec. 18, 2019, https://www.thenation.com/article/bolivia-times-morales-coup/.
42. HRW executive director Ken Roth tweeted the rightwing *Economist* magazine's take as if it were sage analysis. See https://twitter.com/KenRoth/status/1196133917247655939.
43. Bernie Sanders told Univision journalist Jorge Ramos, "I think Morales did a very good job in alleviating poverty, in giving the Indigenous people of Bolivia a voice they never had before . . . at the end of the day it was the military that intervened . . . when the military intervenes, Jorge, in my view that's called a coup." See https://youtu.be/2BMV3lnVrTQ.
44. Joe Emersberger, "Reuters Shields OAS Over False Claims That Sparked Bolivia Coup," FAIR, Dec. 17, 2019, https://fair.org/home/reuters-shields-oas-over-false-claims-that-sparked-bolivia-coup/. See chapters 6 and 11 for more discussion of the coup in Bolivia.

2. Yes, Maduro Is a Duly Elected Leader

1. Ricardo Vaz, "Venezuelan Opposition Leader Guaidó Declares Himself President, Recognized by US and Allies," VenezuelAnalysis, January 23, 2019, https://venezuelanalysis.com/news/14244; Jessica Donati and Vivian Salama, "Pence Pledged U.S. Backing Before Venezuela Opposition Leader's Move," *Wall Street Journal*, January 25, 2019,

https://www.wsj.com/articles/a-call-from-pence-helped-set-an-uncertain-new-course-in-venezuela-11548430259.

2. Paul Dobson, "Venezuela: Self-Proclaimed 'Interim President' Released After 'Irregular' Detention," VenezuelAnalysis, January 14, 2019 https://venezuelanalysis.com/news/14218; George Ciccariello-Maher, "Venezuela's Slow Coup Continues," Al Jazeera, February 1, 2019, https://www.aljazeera.com/opinions/2019/1/29/venezuelas-slow-coup-continues.

3. Naky Soto, "Why Juan Guaidó Can't Become President Right Away," *Caracas Chronicles*, January 16, 2019, https://www.caracaschronicles.com/2019/01/16/why-juan-guaido-cant-become-president-right-away/.

4. Naky Soto, "Why Juan Guaidó Can't Become President Right Away," *Caracas Chronicles*, January 16, 2019, https://www.caracaschronicles.com/2019/01/16/why-juan-guaido-cant-become-president-right-away/.

5. After the 2013 election, it obviously would not have made any sense for the opposition to try to get Diosdado Cabello (president of the National Assembly at the time and a close Maduro ally) to invoke article 233.

6. "¡Oposición sin liderazgo! 81 % de los venezolanos no sabe quién es Juan Guaidó (+ Encuesta)," *Con el Mazo Dando*, January 20, 2019, https://www.conelmazodando.com.ve/oposicion-sin-liderazgo-81-de-los-venezolanos-no-sabe-quien-es-juan-guaido-encuesta.

7. Christopher Sabatini and Kenneth Frankel, "An interview with Francisco Rodríguez, Managing Director and Chief Economist of Torino Economics," *Global Americans*, January 25, 2019, https://theglobalamericans.org/2019/01/an-interview-with-francisco-rodriguez-managing-director-and-chief-economist-of-torino-economics/.

8. Joe Emersberger, "Remembering Henri Falcon's May 2018 Presidential campaign in Venezuela," *Znet*, May 2, 2002, https://zcomm.org/zblogs/remembering-henri-falcons-may-2018-presidential-campaign-in-venezuela/.

9. Lucas Koerner, "Venezuela's Maduro Wins Reelection with 67.7% of Vote, Falcon Cries Fraud," VenezuelAnalysis, May 21, 2018, https://venezuelanalysis.com/news/13830.

10. Brian Ellsworth, "A Venezuelan paradox: Maduro's critics long for change but won't vote," Reuters, May 16, 2018, https://www.reuters.com/article/us-venezuela-election-abstention-insight/a-venezuelan-paradox-maduros-critics-long-for-change-but-wont-vote-idUSKCN1IH1J8; Alexandra Ulmer, "Venezuelan leader's popularity inches up to 25 percent: poll," Reuters, March 24, 2015, https://www.reuters.com/

article/us-venezuela-maduro/venezuelan-leaders-popularity-inches-up-to-25-percent-poll-idUSKBN0MK2B420150324.
11. See discussion in chapter 8 of Alan MacLeod's research showing how overwhelmingly Venezuela's media has been depicted as "caged."
12. Luis Vicente León, "El secuestro de Lucía," *Prodavinci*, September 24, 2017, http://historico.prodavinci.com/blogs/el-secuestro-de-lucia-por-luis-vicente-leon1/.
13. Luis Vicente Leon, "Los escenarios venezolanos," *El Universal*, November 4, 2018, http://www.eluniversal.com/el-universal/24838/los-escenarios-venezolanos.
14. "Entrevista Venevision: Luis Vicente Leon, Presidente de Datanalisis," *Venevision,* October 31, 2018. The remarks highlighted here are taken from the 12:50 point of the interview on https://www.youtube.com/watch?v=N2RcrK92yK8&feature=youtu.be.
15. Jose Antonio Gil Yepes, "Uno que entendió," *El Universal*, October 25, 2018, https://www.eluniversal.com/el-universal/23984/uno-que-entendio; also, in July 2002, three months after Hugo Chávez was briefly ousted in a U.S.-backed military coup, the *Los Angeles Times* reported that Gil Yepes had said of Chávez, "He has to be killed."
16. Gil Yepes signing the decree is mentioned in: "Jesse Chacon: El sistema judicial siempre ha tenido altos niveles de corrupcion," *El Impulso*, May 14, 2012, https://www.elimpulso.com/2012/05/14/jesse-chacon-el-sistema-judicial-siempre-ha-tenido-altos-niveles-de-corrupcion/. His name is also listed as one of the signers at about the 1:22:22 point in the documentary "Se Llama Abril Y Esta Es Su Historia," April 13, 2014, https://www.youtube.com/watch?v=iQQUDhqMPTU. His second last name (in what was probably a transcription error) was spelled "Yepez" instead of "Yepes." He did not reply to tweets asking him to confirm if he had signed. Luis Vicente León, very oddly, told Emersberger by email on May 13, 2019, that he did not know if Gil Yepes, his fellow director and longtime colleague, signed the infamous decree, and that the firm does not "monitor" the "private" acts of its directors. Luis Vicente León made no further reply after being asked if he could pass along our question to Gil Yepes.
17. See chart in Joe Emersberger, "Western Media Shorthand on Venezuela Conveys and Conceals So Much," FAIR, April 23, 2018, https://fair.org/home/western-media-shorthand-on-venezuela-conveys-and-conceals-so-much/.
18. Joe Emersberger, "Interview with Edward Ellis, Director of 'Tierras Libres,'" VenezuelAnalysis, August 22, 2011, https://venezuelanalysis.com/analysis/6438.
19. Dorothy Kronick and Francisco Rodríguez, "15O: Fraud or Fatigue?,"

WOLA, October 26, 2017, https://venezuelablog.org/15o-fraud-fatigue/.
20. In an October 2, 2017 report for Torino Capital entitled "Unintended Consequences," Rodriguez predicted, based on Datanalisis polls, that the opposition would win 18 of the governorships and that the government would receive only 21.1% of the vote nationwide—a bit less than half of what it predicted the opposition would receive, 44.7%.
21. Kronick and Rodrguez, "150: Fraud or Fatigue?"
22. Katrina Kozarek, "CLAP: Venezuela's Latest Food Distribution and Production Initiative," VenezuelAnalysis, March 22, 2017, https://venezuelanalysis.com/video/12993.
23. Kronick and Rodrguez, "150: Fraud or Fatigue?"
24. We'll discuss those policy failures in chapters 6 and 10.
25. Lucas Koerner, "Venezuelan Opposition Backs US Sanctions amid International Condemnation," VenezuelAnalysis, August 29, 2017, https://venezuelanalysis.com/news/13333.
26. Ben Jacobs, "Trump threatens 'military option' in Venezuela as crisis escalates," *The Guardian*, August 12, 2017, https://www.theguardian.com/world/2017/aug/11/donald-trump-venezuela-crisis-military-intervention.
27. The Carter Center put out a statement (https://www.cartercenter.org/news/pr/venezuela-020419.html) in February 2019 complaining that Maduro had "misused" his praise in 2012 as a broader validation of the Venezuelan electoral system. No doubt, as the U.S. electoral system illustrates, elections can be unfair in ways that have nothing to do with the actual counting of ballots. The fact remains that Venezuela has an excellent system for counting ballots. The Carter Center statement said it had not "formally observed" a Venezuelan election since 2004. In fact, the Carter Center did an extensive report on the April 2013 presidential election. See https://www.cartercenter.org/resources/pdfs/news/peace_publications/election_reports/venezuela-pre-election-rpt-2013.pdf.
28. Joe Emersberger, "On Venezuela's Regional Elections: Some Elephants in the Room," VenezuelAnalysis, October 24, 2017, https://venezuelanalysis.com/analysis/13464.
29. Ricardo Vaz, "Venezuela Regional Elections: Chavismo in Triumph, Opposition in Disarray and Media in Denial," VenezuelAnalysis, October 20, 2017, https://venezuelanalysis.com/analysis/13456.
30. The demoralized state of the opposition and its internal disputes intensified when four of the five winning governors from the opposition side swore themselves in before the Constituent Assembly that had been elected in July. Violent protests that cost 126 lives were launched

against Maduro's decision to elect that assembly—the fifth U.S.-backed effort to oust the government by force. See Chapter 10.
31. Laura Silver, Courtney Johnson, and Kyle Taylor, "Venezuelans have little trust in national government, say economy is in poor shape," Pew Research, January 25, 2019 https://www.pewresearch.org/fact-tank/2019/01/25/venezuelans-have-little-trust-in-national-government-say-economy-is-in-poor-shape/.
32. Federal Election Commission, "Federal Elections 2016," Federal Election Commission USA, December, 2017, https://transition.fec.gov/pubrec/fe2016/federalelections2016.pdf.
33. 42% of the vote on 68% turnout: UK Parliament, "General Election 2017: full results and analysis," House of Commons Library, January 29, 2019, https://researchbriefings.parliament.uk/ResearchBriefing/Summary/CBP-7979#fullreport.
34. 37% of the vote on 66% turnout: "Elections 2015 Results," BBC, https://www.bbc.com/news/election/2015/results.
35. Daniel Schwartz, "Federal election voter turnout 68.3 per cent, highest in 22 years: official vote count," CBC, November 5, 2015, https://www.cbc.ca/news/politics/multimedia/federal-election-voter-turnout-68-3-per-cent-highest-in-22-years-official-vote-count-1.3302064.
36. Ana Vanessa Herrero and Megan Specia, "Venezuela Is in Crisis. So How Did Maduro Secure a Second Term?" *The New York Times*, January 10, 2019, https://www.nytimes.com/2019/01/10/world/americas/venezuela-maduro-inauguration.html.
37. Other high profile figures in the United States, such as Secretary of State Tillerson and Senator Marco Rubio, were openly trying to incite the Venezuelan military to perpetrate a coup. In February 2018, Emersberger asked Amnesty International for a comment. Amnesty replied that it "believes that a responsible discussion on the current state of human rights in Venezuela should not be focused on statements made by parties outside the country and context, but on the urgent need to address, without further delay, the serious crisis situation which the country is facing." Apparently nobody at Amnesty was familiar with the human rights records of governments in Latin America installed by U.S.-backed military coups. Joe Emersberger, "Amnesty International Replied to Questions About Venezuela," *Znet*, February 24, 2018, https://zcomm.org/zblogs/amnesty-international-replied-to-questions-about-venezuela/.
38. Gregory Wilpert, "Election Observers Submit First Reports on Venezuelan Presidential Election," VenezuelAnalysis, December 15, 2006, https://venezuelanalysis.com/news/2139; Ewan Robertson, "Chávez Wins Venezuelan Presidential Election with 54% of the

Vote," *Venzuelanalysis*, October 7, 2012, https://venezuelanalysis.com/news/7331.
39. Ricardo Vaz, "Venezuelan Elections: Chavismo Still in Power, US Still Belligerent, Media Still Dishonest," VenezuelAnalysis, June 4 2018, https://venezuelanalysis.com/analysis/13852.
40. Lucas Koerner, "The Global Left and the Danger of a Dirty War in Venezuela," VenezuelAnalysis, February 25, 2019, https://www.mintpressnews.com/global-left-danger-dirty-war-venezuela/255501/.
41. Kiraz Janicke, "Venezuelan President's Amnesty for Coup Participants is Praised and Criticised," VenezuelAnalysis, January 3, 2008, https://venezuelanalysis.com/news/3030.
42. Vivian Sequera and Andrew Cawthorne, "Venezuela's Maduro defies foreign censure, offers 'prize' to voters," Reuters, May 3, 2018, https://www.reuters.com/article/us-venezuela-election/venezuelas-maduro-defies-foreign-censure-offers-prize-to-voters-idUSKBN1I41KK.
43. Ricardo Vaz, "Venezuelan Elections: Chavismo Still in Power, US Still Belligerent, Media Still Dishonest," VenezuelAnalysis, June 4, 2018, https://venezuelanalysis.com/analysis/13852.
44. Gaby J. Miller, "The Perfect Blackmail," *Caracas Chronicles*, December 11, 2017, https://www.caracaschronicles.com/2017/12/11/the-perfect-blackmail/.
45. "El voto es secreto," *El Nacional*, November 11, 2015, http://www.el-nacional.com/noticias/historico/voto-secreto_42710.
46. The 61 percent turnout in the October 2017 regional election demolishes a Latinobarometro poll that claimed that as of 2017 only 45 percent in Venezuela believe their votes are secret. See https://t.co/lqTEHMGmki.
47. The General Electoral Accompaniment Reports are archived at VenezuelAnalysis: https://venezuelanalysis.com/files/generalelectoralac companimentreportmay20181pdf, https://venezuelanalysis.com/file/10529/, https://venezuelanalysis.com/file/10530/, https://venezuel analysis.com/file/10531/.
48. "CEELA: Tribunal Electoral de Honduras, responsable de crisis política," TeleSUR, December 7, 2017, https://youtu.be/UhHj9eWNES4.
49. Lucas Koerner, "Venezuelan Opposition Protests Proposed UN Electoral Observer Mission," VenezuelAnalysis, March 13, 2018, https://venezuelanalysis.com/News/13717.
50. https://twitter.com/Ademocratica/status/973345076490457088.
51. In February 2006 in Haiti René Preval won the presidency in an election despite the fact that he announced his candidacy at the last moment and could barely campaign due to threats from U.S.-backed paramilitaries. Preval's victory technically ended two years of U.S.-imposed dictatorship.

52. For more detail see Joe Emersberger, "Remembering Henri Falcon's May 2018 Presidential campaign in Venezuela," *Znet*, May 2, 2002, https://zcomm.org/zblogs/remembering-henri-falcons-may-2018-presidential-campaign-in-venezuela/.
53. In other chapters we will address with other reasons that have been given to say that the Maduro government is not legitimate—in particular its dispute with the National Assembly after 2015.
54. Corina Pons and Vivian Sequera, "Leader of Venezuela Congress says he is prepared to assume presidency," Reuters, January 11, 2019, https://www.reuters.com/article/us-venezuela-politics-idUSKCN1P51U6.
55. Very similarly, after the November 10, 2019 military coup in Bolivia, Reuters published well over 100 articles about the political situation in Bolivia without ever mentioning the extensive expert criticism OAS election monitors received for impugning the election won by Evo Morales. See Joe Emersberger, "Reuters Shields OAS over false claims that sparked Bolivia coup," FAIR, December 18, 2019, https://fair.org/home/reuters-shields-oas-over-false-claims-that-sparked-bolivia-coup/.

3. The Guaidó Era as a Sixth, Very Long Coup Attempt

1. Torino Capital estimates Venezuela's GDP as $116 billion in 2018. The IMF estimated it as $96 billion. See https://www.imf.org/external/pubs/ft/weo/2018/02/weodata/weorept.aspx?pr.x=53&pr.y=7&sy=2016&ey=2023&scsm=1&ssd=1&sort=country&ds=.&br=1&c=299&s=NGDPD%2CLUR&grp=0&a=; for regional health care spending as a share of GDP, see https://data.worldbank.org/indicator/SH.XPD.CHEX.GD.ZS?locations=ZJ.
2. Francisco Rodriguez, "Crude Realities: Understanding Venezuela's Economic Collapse," WOLA, September 20, 2018, https://venezuelablog.org/crude-realities-understanding-venezuelas-economic-collapse/; Rodriguez later presented his data (similar to what we do above) in tabular form to refute claims that a graph he presented was misleading. See Mark Weisbrot and Jeffrey Sachs, "Economists Use 'Fuzzy Graphs' to Challenge Data on the Human Cost of Trump Sanctions on Venezuela," CEPR, May 6, 2019, https://cepr.shorthandstories.com/venezuela-sanctions-response/index.html.
3. Due to U.S. sanctions, PDVSA and CITGO severed ties in 2019. See Anya Parampil, "Blockbuster oil bribery scandal exposes corrupt double-dealing of Guaidó 'attorney general,'" *The Grayzone*, July 14, 2020, https://thegrayzone.com/2020/07/14/bribery-scandal-courts-corrupt-forces-guaidos-coup/.
4. Marianna Parraga and Catherine Ngai, "Exclusive: Venezuela state

oil firm's credit woes spread to U.S. unit Citgo," Reuters, September 14, 2017, https://www.reuters.com/article/us-oil-citgo-pete-credit-exclusive/exclusive-venezuela-state-oil-firms-credit-woes-spread-to-u-s-unit-citgo-idU.S.KCN1BP2P2.

5. Torino Capital: "Venezuela Red Book: Hard landing," January 9, 2018, p. 22. "All foreign-currency bonds are denominated in dollars, and all are governed by New York law."
6. See "Crude Realities."
7. That's very different from a government "losing" revenue in local currency that it's able to print.
8. Mark Weisbrot, "Trump's Other 'National Emergency': Sanctions That Kill Venezuelans," CEPR, February 28, 2019, http://cepr.net/publications/op-eds-columns/trump-s-other-national-emergency-in-the-americas-with-sanctions-that-kill.
9. This figure came from unpublished data Francisco Rodriguez of Torino Capital supplied to Weisbrot and Sachs for their paper: Mark Weisbrot and Jeffrey Sachs, "Economic Sanctions as Collective Punishment: The Case of Venezuela," CEPR, April 2019, http://cepr.net/images/stories/reports/venezuela-sanctions-2019-04.pdf.
10. Personal communication with Rodriguez on June 26, 2019.
11. Katrina Kozarek, "CLAP: Venezuela's Latest Food Distribution and Production Initiative," VenezuelAnalysis, May 22, 2017, https://venezuelanalysis.com/video/12993.
12. Joshua Goodman, "As Venezuelans go hungry, Trump targets food corruption," Associated Press, September 24, 2018, https://apnews.com/48fd9d59e3d74ffb9de25d3ab0550afc.
13. "Encovi: 7,3 millones de hogares se benefician de las cajas Clap," *Version Final*, December 3, 2018, http://versionfinal.com.ve/ciudad/encovi-73-millones-de-hogares-se-benefician-de-las-cajas-clap/.
14. Amy Goodman, "Allan Nairn: Trump's Venezuela Envoy Elliott Abrams Is a War Criminal Who Has Abetted Genocide," *Democracy Now!*, January 30, 2019, https://www.democracynow.org/2019/1/30/allan_nairn_trump_s_venezuela_envoy.
15. Joe Emersberger, "Francisco Rodriguez answers some questions I asked about Venezuela," *Znet*, December 16, 2019, https://zcomm.org/zblogs/francisco-rodriguez-answers-some-questions-i-asked-him-about-venezuela/.
16. FACT SHEET: Venezuela Executive Order, The White House (Office of the Press Secretary), March 9, 2015, https://obamawhitehouse.archives.gov/the-press-office/2015/03/09/fact-sheet-venezuela-executive-order.
17. Alan Gomez and Christal Hayes, "First lawsuits filed against President Donald Trump's national emergency order," *USA Today*,

February 15, 2019, https://www.usatoday.com/story/news/politics/2019/02/15/donald-trump-national-emergency-border-wall-lawsuits/2882729002/.
18. Courtney Vinopal, "3 legal arguments that could challenge Trump's national emergency," PBS, February 15, 2019, https://www.pbs.org/newshour/politics/how-trumps-national-emergency-could-be-challenged-in-court.
19. OAS Charter, https://www.oas.org/en/sla/dil/inter_american_treaties_A-41_charter_OAS.asp#Chapter_XV.
20. UN Charter, https://www.un.org/en/sections/un-charter/chapter-i/index.html.
21. Andrew Knoll, Patricia Torres, and Steve Kenny, "Trump Alarms Venezuela With Talk of a 'Military Option,'" *The New York Times*, August 12, 2017, https://www.nytimes.com/2017/08/12/world/americas/trump-venezuela-military.html; Trump: Scott Smith, "Venezuelan Socialist President Easily Toppled," *US News and World Report*, September 25, 2018, https://www.usnews.com/news/world/articles/2018-09-25/us-puts-sanctions-on-venezuela-first-lady-other-officials; "Tillerson says Venezuelan military may turn on Maduro," BBC, February 2, 2018, https://www.bbc.com/news/world-latin-america-42913191; Ben Norton, "VIDEO: CIA Director Mike Pompeo Hints U.S. Is Working with Mexico and Colombia to Push Regime Change in Venezuela," *AlterNet*, July 26, 2017, https://www.alternet.org/2017/07/cia-venezuela-us-mike-pompeo-coup-opposition/.
22. Search of Bolton's twitter timeline for "Venezuela" and "military" since January 23, 2019, https://twitter.com/search?l=&q=Venezuela%20military%20from%3AAmbJohnBolton%20since%3A2019-01-23&src=typd&lang=en; https://twitter.com/AmbJohnBolton/status/110556109829 8769415, accessed January 9 2020.
23. Hugh Hewitt, "National Security Adviser Ambassador John Bolton, interview with Hugh Hewitt," Hugh Hewitt, February 1, 2019, http://www.hughhewitt.com/national-security-adviser-ambassador-john-bolton/.
24. Roberta Rampton, "Move over ayatollahs: Bolton turns tweets and talons on Maduro," Reuters, February 27, 2019, https://www.reuters.com/article/us-venezuela-politics-bolton/move-over-ayatollahs-bolton-turns-tweets-and-talons-on-maduro-idU.S.KCN1QG25V.
25. Lesley Wroughton, "U.S. envoy warns Maduro that actions against Guaido would be 'foolish,'" Reuters, January 30, 2019, https://www.reuters.com/article/us-venezuela-politics-usa-diplomacy/u-s-envoy-warns-maduro-that-actions-against-guaido-would-be-foolish-idU.S.KCN1PO2SJ.

26. Paul Dobson, "Guaido Sets Date for Attempted Aid Entry as UN Reiterates Call for Dialogue," VenezuelAnalysis, February 13, 2019, https://venezuelanalysis.com/news/14323.
27. Ricardo Vaz, "Venezuela: Maduro Leads Military Exercises as Guaido Appeals to Armed Forces," VenezuelAnalysis, January 28, 2019, https://venezuelanalysis.com/news/14266.
28. "U.S. warns against new Gaza flotilla plans," Reuters, June 24, 2011, https://www.reuters.com/article/idUSTRE75N4A620110624.
29. Jim Wyss, "Venezuela aid organizers imagine a 'river of people' overwhelming Maduro's blockade," *Miami Herald*, February 8, 2019, https://www.miamiherald.com/news/nation-world/world/americas/venezuela/article225996580.html.
30. See previous note.
31. Stephanie Nebehay, Brian Ellsworth, "U.N. approves $9 million in aid for crisis-stricken Venezuela," Reuters, November 26, 2018, https://www.reuters.com/article/us-venezuela-politics-un-idUSKCN1NV2AR; Paul Dobson, "Maduro Calls on UN to Help Break U.S.-led Blockade, Supply Medical Equipment," VenezuelAnalysis, November 14, 2019, https://venezuelanalysis.com/news/14147.
32. Stephanie Nebehay, Brian Ellsworth, "U.N. approves $9 million in aid for crisis-stricken Venezuela," Reuters, November 26, 2018, https://www.reuters.com/article/us-venezuela-politics-un-idUSKCN1NV2AR.
33. Matt Spetalnick and Luc Cohen, "U.S. looking for ways to get aid into Venezuela: envoy," Reuters, February 14, 2019, https://www.reuters.com/article/us-venezuela-politics-aid-abrams/u-s-looking-for-ways-to-get-aid-into-venezuela-envoy-idU.S.KCN1Q32FW; other Reuters articles had similarly deceitful headlines around the time of the aid stunt, e.g. "Brazil has 200 tons of aid for Venezuela, trucks cannot cross border," "'Disgusting' that Venezuela's Maduro would close borders to aid, says UK."
34. "How a bridge between Colombia and Venezuela became part of a propaganda fight," CBC, February 15, 2019, https://www.cbc.ca/news/world/venezuela-bridge-aid-pompeo-1.5018432.
35. "Fight over food aid a high-stakes battle in Venezuela as hunger hits hard," CBC, February 8, 2019, https://www.cbc.ca/news/world/fight-over-food-aid-a-high-stakes-battle-in-venezuela-as-hunger-hits-hard-1.5010878.
36. Joe Emersberger, "Venezuela gets foreign aid with Maduro's consent. Canadian state media is 'comfortable' denying it," *The Canary*, February 19, 2019, https://www.thecanary.co/global/world-analysis/2019/02/19/venezuela-gets-foreign-aid-with-maduros-consent-canadian-state-media-is-comfortable-denying-it/.

37. https://twitter.com/kgosztola/status/1091848921771638785 accessed January 11, 2020; "Aide Says U.S. Planes Carried Contra Arms," Associated Press, August 15, 1987 https://www.nytimes.com/1987/08/15/world/aide-says-us-planes-carried-contra-arms.html.
38. David Edwards and David Cromwell, "Outrageous Omissions—How the Press Has Buried the Truth of Iraqi Disarmament," *Media Lens*, February 28, 2003, https://www.medialens.org/2003/outrageous-omissions-how-the-press-has-buried-the-truth-of-iraqi-disarmament/; David Edwards and David Cromwell, "Blair's Betrayal Part 1—The Newsnight Debate—Dismantling The Case For War," *Media Lens*, February 10, 2003, https://www.medialens.org/2003/blairs-betrayal-part-1-the-newsnight-debate-dismantling-the-case-for-war/; David Edwards and David Cromwell, "It wasn't just Blair; the media also duped us," *New Statesman*, https://www.newstatesman.com/node/194752.
39. https://twitter.com/AmbJohnBolton/status/1098043058766123013.
40. https://twitter.com/marcorubio/status/1098411474261811201.
41. https://twitter.com/marcorubio/status/1099726515292508162.
42. Glenn Greenwald, "NYT's Exposé on the Lies About Burning Aid Trucks in Venezuela Shows How U.S. Government and Media Spread Pro-War Propaganda," *The Intercept*, March 10, 2019, https://theintercept.com/2019/03/10/nyts-expose-on-the-lies-about-burning-humanitarian-trucks-in-venezuela-shows-how-us-govt-and-media-spread-fake-news/.
43. Twitter statistics cited by Francisco Rodriguez in LATam this Week, Torino Capital, March 25, 2019.
44. https://twitter.com/SenSanders/status/1099380342018912257.
45. Lucas Koerner, "Democrats and Death Squads in Venezuela," VenezuelAnalysis, March 15, 2019, https://venezuelanalysis.com/analysis/14390.
46. "Sanders on Venezuela—Does His Critique of US Policy Go Far Enough?" The Real News Network, March 4, 2019, https://therealnews.com/stories/sanders-on-venezuela-does-his-critique-of-us-policy-go-far-enough.
47. Lucas Koerner, "U.S. Presidential Hopeful Bernie Sanders Slams Chávez in Riposte to Clinton Attack," VenezuelAnalysis, September 17, 2015, https://venezuelanalysis.com/news/11511.
48. Camilo Montoya-Galvez, "Pressed on socialism, Sanders distances himself from Venezuela's Maduro in Democratic debate," CBS, September 13, 2019, https://www.cbsnews.com/news/bernie-sanders-distances-himself-from-venezuela-president-nicolas-maduro-when-pressed-on-socialism-at-debate/.

49. *New York Times* editorial board interview of Bernie Sanders, January 13, 2020, https://www.nytimes.com/interactive/2020/01/13/opinion/bernie-sanders-nytimes-interview.html. In the interview sanders refers to Ortega as an "exception" who became a "dictator." Asked if Maduro was also an "exception," Sanders said he was.
50. "End Venezuela Sanctions Says Rep. Ro Khanna and 15 Progressive Democrats," The Real News Network, March 8, 2019, https://web.archive.org/web/20190309230954/https://therealnews.com/stories/end-venezuela-sanctions-says-rep-ro-khanna-and-15-progressive-democrats.
51. Mark Weisbrot, "Trump's Other 'National Emergency': Sanctions That Kill Venezuelans," CEPR, February 28, 2019, http://cepr.net/publications/op-eds-columns/trump-s-other-national-emergency-in-the-americas-with-sanctions-that-kill.
52. Khanna claimed the Carter Center offered to "supervise" but Maduro refused. We asked the Carter Center directly to confirm this and received no reply. See chapters 2 and 5 for more about the Carter Center.
53. "Venezuela: Hunger, punishment and fear, the formula for repression used by authorities under Nicolás Maduro," Amnesty International, February 20, 2019, https://www.amnesty.org/en/latest/news/2019/02/venezuela-hunger-punishment-and-fear-the-formula-for-repression-used-by-authorities-under-nicolas-maduro/.
54. George Ciccariello-Maher, "Collective Panic in Venezuela," *Jacobin*, June 2014, https://www.jacobinmag.com/2014/06/collective-panic-in-venezuela/.
55. Joe Emersberger, "Amnesty International Replied to Questions about Venezuela," *Znet*, February 24, 2018, https://zcomm.org/zblogs/amnesty-international-replied-to-questions-about-venezuela/.
56. Signatories, "Amnesty International Should Oppose U.S. Economic Sanctions and Incitement of a Military Coup in Venezuela," *Mint Press News*, January 26, 2019, https://www.mintpressnews.com/ask-amnesty-international-oppose-us-economic-sanctions-incitement-military-coup-venezuela/254217/.
57. Joe Emersberger, "Amnesty International modifies its position on U.S. sanctions and threats against Venezuela," *Znet*, February 8, 2019, https://zcomm.org/zblogs/amnesty-international-modifies-its-position-on-us-sanctions-and-threats-against-venezuela/.
58. "Statement by UN High Commissioner for Human Rights Michelle Bachelet 40th session of the Human Rights Council," March 20, 2019,https://www.ohchr.org/EN/NewsEvents/Pages/DisplayNews.spx?NewsID=24374&LangID=E.

59. Alfred de Zayas, "UN Human Rights Expert: Statement on Venezuela & Ecuador," VenezuelAnalysis, December 13, 2017, https://venezuelanalysis.com/analysis/13548.
60. Human rights in the Bolivarian Republic of Venezuela* Report of the United Nations High Commissioner for Human Rights on the situation of Human rights in the Bolivarian Republic of Venezuela, OHCHR, Jul 5, 2019, https://www.ohchr.org/EN/HRBodies/HRC/RegularSessions/Session41/Documents/A_HRC_41_18.docx.
61. This analogy (which was a modified version of one used by Caitlin Johnson) was used in an article for FAIR.org by Emersberger; https://twitter.com/caitoz/status/1121584572964073472; Joe Emersberger, "Study Linking U.S. Sanctions to Venezuelan Deaths Buried by Reuters for Over a Month," FAIR, June 14, 2019, https://fair.org/home/study-linking-us-sanctions-to-venezuelan-deaths-buried-by-reuters-for-over-a-month/.
62. https://twitter.com/marcorubio/status/1129115646007099392. We added the red underlining of key words to the screenshot of Rubio's tweet.
63. Paul Dobson, "Venezuelan Government Announces Arrests over Electrical Blackouts," VenezuelAnalysis, April 24, 2019, https://venezuelanalysis.com/news/14442.
64. Lucas Koerner and Ricardo Vaz, "Washington Escalates Venezuela Sanctions into Full-Fledged Embargo," VenezuelAnalysis, August 6, 2019, https://venezuelanalysis.com/news/14615.
65. Anya Parampil, "U.S. sanctions 'carpet bombed Venezuela's economy': opposition advisor & economist Francisco Rodríguez interviewed by Anya Parampil," Reddit, December 21, 2019, https://www.reddit.com/r/venezuela/comments/eeg0db/us_sanctions_carpet_bombed_venezuelas_economy/.
66. Lisa Lambert and Daphne Psaledakis, "Pompeo says U.S. will help prevent Latin American protests becoming riots," Reuters, December 2, 2019, https://www.reuters.com/article/us-usa-venezuela-pompeo/pompeo-says-u-s-will-help-prevent-latin-american-protests-becoming-riots-idU.S.KBN1Y61QC; "Almagro denuncia 'patrón' de desestabilización de Venezuela y Cuba en la región," AFP, Oct 25, 2019, https://www.voanoticias.com/a/luisalmagro-oea-venezuela-cuba-latinoamerica/5140013.html; https://twitter.com/jguaido/status/1181397848258162688; https://twitter.com/JulioBorges/status/1185590850987974657; "Juan Guaidó: 'Nicolás Maduro financia las protestas y el vandalismo en los países latinoamericanos para desestabilizar la región,'" *infobae*, October 22, 2019, https://www.infobae.com/america/venezuela/2019/10/22/juan-guaido-nicolas-

maduro-financia-las-protestas-y-el-vandalismo-en-los-paises-latinoamericanos-para-desestabilizar-la-region/.
67. "Maduro se burla de Lenín Moreno por culparlo de las protestas en Ecuador," *El Periodico*, October 9, 2019, https://www.elperiodico.com/es/internacional/20191009/maduro-burla-lenin-moreno-protestas-ecuador-7673095.
68. Alan MacLeod, "With People in the Streets Worldwide, Media Focus Uniquely on Hong Kong," FAIR, December 6, 2019, https://fair.org/home/with-people-in-the-streets-worldwide-media-focus-uniquely-on-hong-kong/.
69. Daniel Ramos, "Bolivia's interim government charges Morales with sedition and terrorism," Reuters, November 22, 2019, https://www.reuters.com/article/bolivia-politics/bolivias-interim-government-charges-morales-with-sedition-and-terrorism-idUKL2N2820Z5.
70. Jorge Martin, "Venezuela: Guaidó's Botched Coup—What Does It Mean and What's Next?," VenezuelAnalysis, May 2, 2019, https://venezuelanalysis.com/analysis/14459.
71. Paul Dobson, "Venezuela: Pompeo Exposes Frustration Over Opposition Divisions as China, Russia Call for Non-Interference," VenezuelAnalysis, June 6, 2019, https://venezuelanalysis.com/news/14525.
72. Orlando Avendaño, "Enviados de Guaidó se apropian de fondos para ayuda humanitaria en Colombia," *Pan-Am Post*, June 14, 2019, https://panampost.com/orlando-avendano/2019/06/14/enviados-de-guaido-se-apropian-de-fondos-para-ayuda-humanitaria-en-colombia/.
73. "Venezuela's Guaido calls for probe into funds for military defectors," Reuters, June 16, 2019, https://www.reuters.com/article/us-venezuela-politics/venezuelas-guaido-calls-for-probe-into-funds-for-military-defectors-idU.S.KCN1TG0NK.
74. Lucas Koerner and Ricardo Vaz, "Venezuela: Guaido Embattled as Opposition Splits over New Corruption Scandal," VenezuelAnalysis, December 5, 2019, https://venezuelanalysis.com/news/14739; a version of the Armando.info article can be read at the following link, https://web.archive.org/web/20191205210331/https://armando.info/reportajes/Details/2614.
75. Orlando Avendaño, "Calderón Berti: 'Nuestros grandes errores han sido responsabilidad de Leopoldo López'," *Pan Am Post*, December 3, 2019, https://es.panampost.com/orlando-avendano/2019/12/01/calderon-berti-nuestros-grandes-errores-han-sido-responsabilidad-de-leopoldo-lopez/.
76. Jim Wyss, "Poll shows Venezuela's Guaidó is losing popularity and has sunk to Maduro level," *Miami Herald*, December 4, 2019,

https://www.miamiherald.com/news/nation-world/world/americas/article238040219.html; Angus Berwick, Mariela Nava, "'Missed his moment': opposition corruption scandal undermines Venezuela's Guaido," Reuters, December 3, 2019, https://www.reuters.com/article/us-venezuela-politics-analysis/missed-his-moment-opposition-corruption-scandal-undermines-venezuelas-guaido-idU.S.KBN1Y72BB.

77. See also Anya Parampil, "The CITGO Conspiracy: Opposition figures accuse Guaidó officials of 'scam' to liquidate Venezuela's most prized international asset," *The Grayzone*, September 3, 2019, https://thegrayzone.com/2019/09/03/the-citgo-conspiracy-opposition-figures-accuse-guaido-officials-of-scam-to-liquidate-venezuelas-most-prized-international-asset/.

78. Joe Emersberger, "Remembering the Venezuelan National Assembly vote lost by Guaidó in January 2019," *Znet*, July 11, 2020, https://zcomm.org/zblogs/remembering-the-venezuelan-national-assembly-vote-lost-by-guaido-in-january-2019/.

79. Lucas Koerner and Ricardo Vaz, "Venezuela: Guaido Replaced as Parliament Head in Disputed Vote," VenezuelAnalysis, January 5, 2020, https://venezuelanalysis.com/news/14755.

80. Joe Emersberger, "Media Struggle to Defend Washington's Cruelty Toward Venezuela and Iran as Coronavirus Spreads," FAIR, March 25, 2020, https://fair.org/home/media-struggle-to-defend-washingtons-cruelty-toward-venezuela-and-iran-as-coronavirus-spreads/.

81. "Why the spread of covid-19 in Venezuela is a particularly frightening prospect," *The Washington Post* editorial, March 20, 2020, https://www.washingtonpost.com/opinions/global-opinions/why-the-spread-of-covid-19-in-venezuela-is-a-particularly-frightening-prospect/2020/03/19/47d94d20-693f-11ea-9923-57073adce27c_story.html.

82. "Treasury Targets Additional Russian Oil Brokerage Firm for Continued Support of Maduro Regime," U.S. Department of the Treasury, March 12, 2020, https://home.treasury.gov/news/press-releases/sm937.

83. Lucas Koerner and Ricardo Vaz, "Corporate Media Cover for U.S. Mob Threats Against Venezuela," FAIR, April 15, 2020, https://fair.org/home/corporate-media-cover-for-us-mob-threats-against-venezuela/.

84. "Bachelet calls for easing of sanctions to enable medical systems to fight COVID-19 and limit global contagion," https://www.ohchr.org/en/NewsEvents/Pages/DisplayNews.aspx?NewsID=25744&LangID=E.

85. Ricardo Vaz and Lucas Koerner, "US Investigating Ex-Green Beret, Denies 'Direct' Involvement in Failed Venezuela Coup," VenezuelAnalysis, May 7, 2020, https://venezuelanalysis.com/news/14867.

86. Lucas Koerner, "Trump Claims to Have Venezuela 'Surrounded' as Iranian Tankers Approach," VenezuelAnalysis, May 21, 2020, https://venezuelanalysis.com/news/14883; "Iran complains to U.N., summons envoy over U.S. threat on Venezuela shipment," Reuters, May 17, 2020, https://www.reuters.com/article/us-iran-us-venezuela-fuel/iran-complains-to-un-summons-envoy-over-us-threat-on-venezuela-shipment-idUSKBN22T0NI.
87. https://twitter.com/rosendo_joe/status/1273821472675389440.
88. Leonardo Flores, "Biden's vision for Venezuela is virtually indistinguishable from Trump's," *The Grayzone*, July 9, 2020, https://thegrayzone.com/2020/07/09/bidens-venezuela-indistinguishable-trumps/.

4. How Could Chavismo Flourish in "Once Prosperous," Democratic Venezuela?

1. State of the Union 2019: Read the full transcript, https://www.cnn.com/2019/02/05/politics/donald-trump-state-of-the-union-2019-transcript/index.html.
2. The article describes a "confidential plea" that was "compiled by a consortium of United Nations agencies and local nongovernmental organizations." Apparently, $109 was requested—a sum that would offset less than 1.7% of the $6 billion worth of damage done in only one year by the financial sanctions the Trump administration imposed in August 2017. The "confidential plea" was obviously addressed to the wrong people. It needed to be sent to the U.S. government, and not confidentially. Sharmini Peries, "We are Swimming in an Ocean of Lies on Venezuela," The Real News Network, March 26, 2019, https://therealnews.com/stories/we-are-swimming-in-an-ocean-of-lies-on-venezuela.
3. Joe Emersberger, "Venezuela and Poverty: Has the International Media's Foolishness Reached an All-Time High?," VenezuelAnalysis, November 30, 2015, https://venezuelanalysis.com/analysis/11730.
4. Search conducted April 5, 2019. "Once the wealthiest" and "once the richest" produced 79 and 222 hits respectively.
5. Jason Mitchell, "Corbyn's blueprint," *The Spectator*, February 18, 2017, https://www.spectator.co.uk/article/corbyn-s-blueprint.
6. Jake Johnston and Sara Kozameh, "Venezuelan Economic and Social Performance Under Hugo Chávez, in Graphs," CEPR, March 7, 2013, http://cepr.net/the-americas-blog/venezuelan-economic-and-social-performance-under-hugo-chavez-in-graphs; Greg Wilpert, "The Origins of Venezuela's Economic Crisis," The Real News Network, April 2, 2019, https://therealnews.com/stories/the-origins-of-venezuelas-

economic-crisis; Hannah Ritchie and Max Roser, "Fossil Fuels," *Our World in Data*, 2017, https://ourworldindata.org/fossil-fuels#oil.
7. "Venezuela Crushes Army Coup Attempt," Associated Press, February 5, 1992, https://www.nytimes.com/1992/02/05/world/venezuela-crushes-army-coup-attempt.html.
8. Net National Income—which is Gross Domestic Product (GDP) minus the depreciation of capital goods—would be a better measure, but economists typically track GDP and its growth.
9. "GDP per capita (constant LCU)—Venezuela, RB," World Bank, 2014, https://data.worldbank.org/indicator/NY.GDP.PCAP.KN?locations=VE.
10. GDP data adjusted for purchasing power parity was found through searches on the IMF World Economic outlook database (October 2018 version). https://www.imf.org/external/pubs/ft/weo/2018/02/weodata/index.aspx. Dean Baker explains, "Purchasing power parity calculations of GDP attempt to measure all the goods and services produced by a country with a common set of prices. This means we add up all the cars, tables, haircuts, knee surgeries etc. produced in both the US and China and assume that each item costs the same in both countries." See Dean Baker, "China as number one: the relative size of the U.S. and Chinese economies," CEPR, March 29, 2018, https://cepr.net/china-as-number-one-the-relative-size-of-the-u-s-and-chinese-economies/.
11. Infant mortality data from the UNICEF website.
12. See note 16.
13. TeleSUR English, "Venezuela's Caracazo: State Repression and Neoliberal Misrule," VenezuelAnalysis, March 1, 2016, https://venezuelanalysis.com/analysis/11868.
14. Aashiq Thawerbhoy, "Los Angeles to Caracas: Examining Neo-liberal Policies Leading Toward Rebellion," VenezuelAnalysis, October 2, 2009, https://venezuelanalysis.com/analysis/4833.
15. George H. W. Bush Presidential Library and Museum, https://bush41library.tamu.edu/files/memcons-telcons/1989-03-03—Pérez.pdf; Peter T. Kilborn, "U.S. planning role in $2 billion loan to aid Venezuela," *The New York Times*, March 4, 1989, https://www.nytimes.com/1989/03/04/world/us-planning-role-in-2-billion-loan-to-aid-venezuela.html; Clifford Krause, "Bush Visit to Highlight Caracas Chief's Role," *The New York Times*, November 26, 1990, https://www.nytimes.com/1990/11/26/world/bush-visit-to-highlight-caracas-chief-s-role.html.
16. "Venezuela Crushes Army Coup Attempt," Associated Press, February 5, 1992, https://www.nytimes.com/1992/02/05/world/venezuela-crushes-army-coup-attempt.html. Dan Kovalik compares the very different reaction by the Western media to the Tiananmen Square

17. Bart Jones, *Hugo! The Hugo Chávez Story from Mud Hut to Perpetual Revolution* (Steerforth Press, 2007), 160: "The coup left fourteen soldiers, five police, and one civilian dead. Dozens were injured."
18. Bart Jones, *Hugo!*, 174. At least 40 of the deaths were inmates of a Caracas prison where a revolt took place the day of the coup attempt, but it was not the prison where Chávez was being held at the time: Todd Robberson, "Gunfire Keeps Caracas Tense," *The Washington Post*, November 29, 1992, https://www.washingtonpost.com/archive/politics/1992/11/29/gunfire-keeps-caracas-tense/67b2b2aa-8db2-4808-934f-e8c12624e315/.
19. Bart Jones, *Hugo!*, 157.
20. Bart Jones, *Hugo!*, 190.
21. George Ciccariello-Maher, *We Created Chávez: A People's History of the Venezuelan Revolution*, (Duke University Press, 2007), 23; Bart Jones, *Hugo!*, 32, 69, 70.
22. Gregory Wilpert, *Changing Venezuela by Taking Power: The History and Policies of the Chávez Government* (Verso, 2006), 12; 268n8. The name of this residence should not be confused with a town with the same name in the state of Falcon.
23. George Ciccariello-Maher, *We Created Chávez*, 23.
24. Rachael Boothroyd, "Venezuela's Transition to Democracy: Latin America's Best Kept Secret," VenezuelAnalysis, November 26, 2014, https://venezuelanalysis.com/analysis/11040.
25. Bart Jones, *Hugo!*, 38, 39.
26. Ciccariello-Maher, *We Created Chávez*, 76, 100.
27. Bart Jones, *Hugo!*, 297.
28. Gregory Wilpert, *Changing Venezuela*, 20.
29. While one can quibble with any term, we feel "professional class" is more appropriate than the vague "middle class." See discussion in chapter 7.
30. Gregory Wilpert, *Changing Venezuela*, 20.
31. Gregory Wilpert, *Changing Venezuela*, 268n20, 269.
32. Gregory Wilpert, *Changing Veneuzela*, 21.

5. First Coup Attempt: April 2002

1. Greg Wilpert's thorough April 7, 2013, essay in VenezuelAnalysis, "The 47-Hour Coup That Changed Everything," is a key source for this chapter. It has a complete list of what the decree did. See https://venezuelanalysis.com/analysis/2336.
2. Wilpert is co-founder of VenezuelAnalysis and still a member of its team. See https://venezuelanalysis.com/about.

3. This happened with a coup attempt against Haitian President Jean Bertrand Aristide in December 2001. See Jeb Sprague, *Paramilitarism and the Assault on Democracy in Haiti* (Monthly Review Press, 2012), 153–156.
4. Correo del Orinoco, "What You Need to Know About the Enabling Law," VenezuelAnalysis, August 19, 2013, https://venezuelanalysis.com/analysis/9955.
5. Gregory Wilpert, "Venezuela's Enabling Law Could Also Enable the Opposition," VenezuelAnalysis, February 6, 2007, https://venezuelanalysis.com/analysis/2213.
6. Bart Jones, *Hugo! The Hugo Chávez Story* (Steerforth, 2007), 305. Chávez used the powers given to him by an "enabling law" passed by the National Assembly and that was about to expire.
7. "Coronel venezolano rechazó su baja y se declaró en rebeldía," Emol.com, February 21, 2002. https://www.emol.com/noticias/internacional/2002/02/21/79294/coronel-venezolano-rechazo-su-baja-y-se-declaro-en-rebeldia.html. We believe Article 350 to be dangerously vague and therefore unwise.
8. Bart Jones, *Hugo!*, 166–67, 312–13, 321; Ciccariello-Maher writes that Peña was disliked and distrusted by the Afro-Venezuelan Network "in part due to his unabashed racism" long before his break with Chávez. George Ciccariello-Maher, *We Created Chávez* (Duke University Press, 2013), 158–9; Juan Forero, "A Brash Rival for Venezuela's President," *The New York Times*, December 10, 2001, https://www.nytimes.com/2001/12/10/world/a-brash-rival-for-venezuela-s-president.html.
9. See note 1.
10. "Hace 19 años se transmitió el primer Aló Presidente," https://www.youtube.com/watch?v=-W92bDoVAp0&feature=youtu.be.
11. See also Joe Emersberger, "Remembering Henri Falcon's May 2018 Presidential campaign in Venezuela," *Znet*, May 2, 2002, https://zcomm.org/zblogs/remembering-henri-falcons-may-2018-presidential-campaign-in-venezuela/; chapter 2 also provides example of the high profile media access available to Datanalisis directors Luis Vicente Leon and Antonio Gil Yepes.
12. Regarding those nineteen deaths, Francisco Toro, an opposition writer and *Washington Post* op-ed writer who founded the Caracas Chronicles website, was willing to concede in 2004 that "Today, we know that there were deaths on both sides." Tellingly, Toro describes all the people killed (up to 50 in his account) in the uprising to restore Chávez as "looters." Toro admits the private media imposed a complete blackout on news coverage to try to keep Carmona in power, but was in denial about the purpose of the blackout. Why was it needed if, as

Toro claims, "Chávez did not return because the crowds came out, the crowds came out because they realized Chávez was about to return. The key decisions—both to remove Chávez and to reinstate them—were taken behind closed doors by high-ranking military men"? There was nothing much for the media to hide in Toro's account; Francisco Toro, "The Untold Story of Venezuela's 2002 April Crisis," *Caracas Chronicles*, April 14, 2004, https://www.washingtonpost.com/people/francisco-toro/?utm_term=.f42630bbbd01; https://www.caracaschronicles.com/2004/04/14/the-untold-story-of-venezuelas-2002-april-crisis/. Toro also gives the false impression that the Chávez government had not paid reparations to the victims of the 1989 Caracazo Massacre as the IACHR ordered it to do in August of 2002. Wilpert debunked that claim. See "The 47 hour coup." See also Lucas Koerner, "Venezuelan Government Announces Further Reparations for Victims of Caracazo," VenezuelAnalysis, March 2, 2015, https://venezuelanalysis.com/news/11244.

13. Bart Jones, *Hugo!*, 364. Jones describes a final attempt to get a signed resignation letter; two years later, in Haiti, the United States had Aristide sign a resignation letter, then quickly flew him very far away from Haiti—to the Central African Republic.
14. Bart Jones, *Hugo!*, 343.
15. Bart Jones, *Hugo!*, 358.
16. Greg Wilpert, "The 47-Hour Coup That Changed Everything," VenezuelAnalysis, August 13, 2007, https://venezuelanalysis.com/analysis/2336.
17. *The Revolution Will Not Be Televised / Chávez: Inside The Coup* (2003), Kim Bartley and Donnacha O'Brian, February 2003, https://www.youtube.com/watch?v=7ulE1AYhqTw. For more discussion of this documentary, and attacks that were made on it, see Joe Emersberger, "Attempts to whitewash the military coup of April 2002 in Venezuela," *Znet*, May 17, 2020, https://zcomm.org/zblogs/attempts-to-whitewash-the-military-coup-of-april-2002-in-venezuela/. Another forensic analysis of the events of Puente Llaguno is presented in Angel Palacios's 2004 documentary film, *Puente Llaguno: Claves de una massacre*, https://vimeo.com/154420688.
18. Eirik Vold, *Hugo Chávez: The Bolivarian Revolution Up Close* (Irene Publishing, 2016), 71.
19. "... networks showed cartoons, cooking shows, and Hollywood movies like *Pretty Woman*." See Bart Jones, *Hugo!*, 356.
20. Patria Grande, "Memorias del apagón mediático: Los editoriales de El Universal, El Nacional y Tal Cual los días del golpe," *Aporrea*, April 12, 2011, https://www.aporrea.org/actualidad/n178889.html; Ivan Oliver

Rugeles, "Los documentos del golpe," *Aporrea*, April 12, 2009, https://www.aporrea.org/medios/a76016.html.
21. Bart Jones, *Hugo!*, 344.
22. "U.S. Papers Hail Venezuelan Coup as Pro-Democracy Move," FAIR, June 1, 2002, https://fair.org/extra/u-s-papers-hail-venezuelan-coup-as-pro-democracy-move/.
23. Joe Emersberger, "Why Venezuela Reporting Is So Bad: Review of Alan MacLeod's Bad News From Venezuela," FAIR, June 27, 2018, https://fair.org/home/why-venezuela-reporting-is-so-bad/.
24. Scott Wilson, "Clash of Visions Pushed Venezuela Toward Coup," *The Washington Post*, April 21, 2002, https://www.washingtonpost.com/archive/politics/2002/04/21/clash-of-visions-pushed-venezuela-toward-coup/7e18ff12-a04a-40a7-80d5-a67a17b6394b/.
25. See data in Table 2.2 of Alan Macleod, *Bad News From Venezuela: Twenty Years of Fake News and Misreporting* (Routledge, 2018). We organized and formatted the data differently than MacLeod.
26. Alex Bellos, "Chávez rises from very peculiar coup," *The Guardian*, April 15, 2002, https://www.theguardian.com/world/2002/apr/15/venezuela.alexbellos.
27. Lee Salter, "A Decade of Propaganda? The BBC's Reporting of Venezuela," VenezuelAnalysis, December 14, 2009, https://venezuelanalysis.com/analysis/5003.
28. Press Briefing by Ari Fleischer, White House press secretary, April 12, 2002, https://georgewbush-whitehouse.archives.gov/news/releases/2002/04/20020412-1.html.
29. "A Review of U.S. Policy Toward Venezuela November 2001–April 2002," Report Number 02-OIG-003, July 2002, United States Department of State and the Broadcasting Board of Governors Office of Inspector General, https://web.archive.org/web/20090204221116/http://www.oig.state.gov/documents/organization/13682.pdf.
30. Mark Weisbrot, "Bush Administration Tries to Hide Role in Venezuela Coup," CEPR, August 9, 2002, https://cepr.net/bush-administration-tries-to-hide-role-in-venezuela-coup/.
31. See Appendix 2 of Weisbrot's testimony to Congress in 2004, https://cepr.net/democracy-venezuela/.
32. Scott Wilson on U.S. involvement in Venezuela coup, https://www.youtube.com/watch?v=KzSnH4_p0PY&feature=youtu.be. This video clip was used in Oliver Stone's documentary *South of the Border*.
33. Joe Parkin Daniels, "Venezuela: Is a U.S.-backed 'military option' to oust Maduro gaining favour?" *The Guardian*, September 13, 2018, https://www.theguardian.com/world/2018/sep/12/venezuela-trump-nicolas-maduro-military-option. The earlier version stated: "It later

emerged that the administration of George W. Bush had known about the coup plot, although did not support it. That did not stop Chávez from painting the action as another imperialistic intervention."

34. Mark Weisbrot, "The IMF's Lost Influence in the 21st Century and Its Implications," CEPR, September 15, 2016, https://cepr.net/the-imf-s-lost-influence-in-the-21st-century-and-its-implications/; Mark Weisbrot, "IMF and World Bank Face Declining Authority as Venezuela Announces Withdrawal," CEPR, May 1, 2007, https://cepr.net/imf-and-world-bank-face-declining-authority-as-venezuela-announces-withdrawal/. IMF bio for Thomas C. Dawson II, https://www.imf.org/external/np/bio/eng/td.htm.

35. For discussion of how other human rights organizations responded to the coup, see Joe Emersberger, "Disgraceful yet illuminating reactions to the 2002 coup that briefly ousted Hugo Chávez: IACHR, CPJ and RSF," *Znet*, May 18, 2020, https://zcomm.org/zblogs/disgraceful-yet-illuminating-reactions-to-the-2002-coup-that-briefly-ousted-chavez-iachr-cpj-and-rsf/.

36. "Restore Rule of Law, Protect Rights in Venezuela," Human Rights Watch, April 11, 2002, https://www.hrw.org/news/2002/04/11/restore-rule-law-protect-rights-venezuela. The press release actually appears to have been written (or perhaps updated) on April 12—some time after Carmona seized power but before the Carmona Decree was issued.

37. From articles 233, 234 of the 1999 constitution, it would appear that legal arrest of the president could only happen through a Supreme Court ruling.

38. "Human Rights Watch Questions and Answers about Venezuela's Court Packing Law," Human Rights Watch, July 2004, https://www.hrw.org/legacy/backgrounder/americas/venezuela/2004/QnA_venezuela.pdf.

39. Bart Jones, *Hugo!*, 369.

40. Wilpert, *Changing Venezuela* (2006), 48.

41. Interview with legal scholar Oswaldo Ruiz Chiriboga, who said at one point: "There are organizations that I considered to be serious in the past but they are now supporting Moreno. I am talking specifically about Human Rights Watch (the Americas division). The Americas head [Jose Miguel Vivanco] is applauding Moreno for what he is doing." Joe Emersberger, "Ecuadorian President Lenin Moreno's Assault on Human Rights and Judicial Independence," *Counterpunch*, October 12, 2018, https://www.counterpunch.org/2018/10/12/ecuadorian-president-lenin-morenos-assault-on-human-rights-and-judicial-independence/.

42. We discuss this in more detail at the end of chapter 11; Darren Ell, "Haiti: The Damage Done," *The Dominion*, March 14, 2007, http://www.dominionpaper.ca/articles/1070.

43. Mario Canipa Vargas, "Vivanco, de HRW: 'Penalizar la opinion de gobiernos dictatoriales, no de una democracia como la de Bolivia," *Brujula Digital*, May 15, 2020, https://brujuladigital.net/politica/vivanco-de-hrw-penalizar-la-opinion-es-de-gobiernos-dictatoriales-no-de-una-democracia-como-la-de-bolivia. See also https://twitter.com/KenRoth/status/1196248843848945664 and https://twitter.com/KenRoth/status/1194055888539140097. Under constitutional reforms voters ratified while Morales was in office, Constitutional Court judges were elected to a six year term: Daniel Ramos, "Bolivians spoil ballots in judicial vote to protest Morales," Reuters, December 4, 2017, https://fr.reuters.com/article/us-bolivia-politics-idUSKBN1DY2I5. HRW, in its attack on Chávez's law, stresses that FDR did not follow through on his threats. FDR was dealing with obstruction to relief for people suffering through the Great Depression. Chávez was dealing with an even more dangerous situation—a court flagrantly collaborating with the perpetrators of a military coup in order to block efforts to alleviate crushing poverty.
44. Matt Mathers, "AOC urges Biden to pack Supreme Court, says GOP doesn't think Democrats have the 'stones to play hardball,'" *The Independent*, October 27, 2020, https://www.independent.co.uk/news/world/americas/us-politics/aoc-urges-biden-pack-supreme-court-amy-coney-barrett-confirmation-b1374277.html. As noted in the article, even much more conservative Democrats like Nancy Pelosi were open to the idea.
45. James Suggett, "Venezuela Dismisses Human Rights Watch's Demand to Clarify FARC Relationship," VenezuelAnalysis, June 4, 2008, https://venezuelanalysis.com/news/3527.
46. "Venezuela: A human rights agenda for the current crisis," Amnesty International, January 2003, https://www.amnesty.org/download/Documents/104000/amr530012003en.pdf. "Venezuela: step back from the brink—an urgent appeal to Venezuelan society and the international community," Amnesty International, December 19, 2002, https://www.amnesty.org/download/Documents/116000/amr530182002en.pdf.
47. Duncan Campbell, "Chávez film puts staff at risk, says Amnesty," *The Guardian*, November 22, 2003, https://www.theguardian.com/world/2003/nov/22/film.venezuela.
48. Francisco Toro, an opposition supporter and writer, bristled at Amnesty's excuse for pulling the film: "Knowing, as I do, some of the AI staffers in Caracas, this story always seemed a bit outlandish to me. Is some opposition radical really going to attack Fernando M. Fernandez over TRWNBT [*The Revolution Will Not Be Televised*]?! Just doesn't seem likely . . ." Francisco Toro, "Away . . . ," *Caracas Chronicles*,

February 16, 2004, https://www.caracaschronicles.com/2004/02/16/away-2/.

49. A twitter thread compiling many of these eyebrow-raising tweets by Fernandez in 2019: https://twitter.com/rosendo_joe/status/1132346808112488448.

50. Fernandez was the author of this 2018 Amnesty International Report about the human rights situation in Venezuela: "Bajo el Imperio de la Violencia Letal: Estado de derecho y Homicidios en Venezuela: Causas Y Efectos de las Disfunciones, Acciones y Omisiones de la Administración de Justicia Penal." The report cites PROVEA and COFAVIC; https://www.amnistia.org/media/4214/ai_sc_librillo2.pdf.

51. Before Amnesty landed on "safety" as an excuse to pull the film, another Amnesty official and organizer of the film festival, Don Wright, gave a political reason, telling *Democracy Now!*, "When we choose films we strive to choose films that are nonpartisan and nonpolitical to reflect the mandate of our organization." See Amy Goodman, "*The Revolution Will Not Be Televised*—Why is Amnesty Not Screening a New Documentary About the Failed 2002 Coup in Venezuela?," *Democracy Now!*, November 6, 2003, https://www.democracynow.org/2003/11/6/the_revolution_will_not_be_televised.

52. See this video: https://www.youtube.com/watch?feature=player_embedded&v=-Q8m0AXGCYE. In another, López told another reporter that "President Carmona" was updated about the arrest (see 19-second point): https://www.youtube.com/watch?v=gvewm8UDJbQ; see also https://www.youtube.com/watch?feature=player_embedded&v=KdMM793V-Hk.

53. Villegas Poljak, "Abril, Golpe Adentro. Venezuela 2002," 170–171; on López and the arrest see notes 93, 94; https://vdocuments.mx/abril-golpe-adentro-venezuela-2002.html.

54. When we questioned him about this incident directly via Twitter, Fernando Fernandez did not reply.

55. Jennifer McCoy, "Chávez's Second Chance," *The New York Times*, April 18, 2002, https://www.nytimes.com/2002/04/18/opinion/chavez-s-second-chance.html. The Carter Center was established by former U.S. president Jimmy Carter and his wife Rosalynn. It often monitors elections in various countries.

6. Second Coup Attempt: Oil Strike, December 2002–February 2003

1. Juan Forero, "Protesters Shot Dead in Venezuela; Oil Deliveries Slowed," *The New York Times*, December 7, 2002, https://www.nytimes.com/2002/12/07/world/protesters-shot-dead-in-venezuela-oil-

deliveries-slowed.html; Lopez's participation in the April 2002 coup was discussed in chapter 5.
2. "Chávez supporters protest coup ruling," CNN, August 14, 2002, https://www.cnn.com/2002/WORLD/americas/08/14/venezuela.unrest/.
3. Other high ranking military men cleared were General Efrain Vaquez Velasco, Vice Admiral Hector Ramirez Perez, and General Pedro Antonio Pereira Olivares. See Sarah Wagner, "Venezuela's Attorney General Asks Court to Review Exoneration of Coup Plotters," VenezuelAnalysis, December 2004, https://venezuelanalysis.com/news/820.
4. On Plaza "liberation" see Bart Jones, *Hugo!* (Steerforth, 2007), 372–374; for discussion of U.S. embassy cables published by Wikileaks which exposed U.S. efforts to weaken and divide the Chavista movement, see chapter 18 of Wikileaks, *The Wikileaks Files: The World According to US Empire* (Verso, 2016).
5. As the weeks passed and the strike lost momentum some opposition leaders banked on the referendum proposal but the Supreme Court squashed it on January 24. Leopoldo López called it the "death of justice"; "Opposition to stage symbolic referendum on 2 February," BBC Monitoring Americas, January 25, 2003.
6. James Dao, "U.S. Urges Early Elections in Venezuela," *New York Times*, December 13, 2002, https://www.nytimes.com/2002/12/13/international/us-urges-early-elections-in-venezuela.html. Emphasis added.
7. Bart Jones, *Hugo!*, 375.
8. Bart Jones, *Hugo!*, 375.
9. Juan Forero, "Protesters Shot Dead in Venezuela; Oil Deliveries Slowed," *The New York Times*, December 7, 2002, https://www.nytimes.com/2002/12/07/world/protesters-shot-dead-in-venezuela-oil-deliveries-slowed.html.
10. "Esposa de Chávez le pide que oiga al pueblo y evite violencia," Reuters, December 10, 2002, https://www.eluniverso.com/2002/12/10/0001/14/9AC79F616E9845188CE2721B0B0CE897.html. In 2007, her father and various other family members opposed her anti-Chávez stance: See "Family of President's Ex-Wife Declares Support for Reform, Against Her," *YVKE Mundial*, November 30, 2007, https://venezuelanalysis.com/newsbrief/2936.
11. Juan Forero, "In Venezuela's General Strike, the Pinch Becomes Pain," *The New York Times*, December 10, 2002, https://www.nytimes.com/2002/12/10/world/in-venezuela-s-general-strike-the-pinch-becomes-pain.html.

12. Paul Dobson, "Trump Renews Venezuela Emergency Decree as Maduro Dismisses Guaido Threat," VenezuelAnalysis, March 6, 2019, https://venezuelanalysis.com/news/14369.
13. Francisco Dominguez, "Ricardo Hausmann—A Reliable Commentator for the *Guardian* on Venezuela?," VenezuelAnalysis, March 4, 2013, https://venezuelanalysis.com/analysis/8013.
14. See chapter 2 for discussion of Datanalisis bias and track record.
15. Eirik Vold, *Hugo Chávez: The Bolivarian Revolution from up close* (Lulu.com, 2016), 87.
16. Joe Emersberger, "New Book Offers Timely Rejoinder to Hugo Chávez Bashing in Media," VenezuelAnalysis, April 7, 2017, https://venezuelanalysis.com/analysis/13037.
17. Juan Forero, "Venezuelan May Consider Early Election," *The New York Times*, December 11, 2002, https://www.nytimes.com/2002/12/11/world/venezuelan-may-consider-early-election.html. Emphasis added.
18. Juan Forero, "Venezuela's Oil: Wellspring of Bad Blood," *The New York Times*, December 17, 2002, https://www.nytimes.com/2002/12/17/world/venezuela-s-oil-wellspring-of-bad-blood.html. Emphasis added.
19. Bart Jones, *Hugo!*, 380.
20. Bart Jones, *Hugo!*, 387.
21. Juan Forero, "Venezuelan News Outlets Line Up with the Foes of Chávez," *The New York Times*, December 22, 2002, https://www.nytimes.com/2002/12/22/world/venezuelan-news-outlets-line-up-with-the-foes-of-chavez.html.
22. Bart Jones, *Hugo!*, 382–3.
23. Juan Forero, "Strike Frays in Venezuela as Foes of Chávez Retreat," *The New York Times*, February 2, 2003, https://www.nytimes.com/2003/02/03/world/strike-frays-in-venezuela-as-foes-of-chavez-retreat.html.
24. Juan Forero, "Chávez Still on Top in Venezuela after Tough Year," *The New York Times*, April 13, 2003, https://www.nytimes.com/2003/04/12/world/chavez-still-on-top-in-venezuela-after-tough-year.html.
25. Bart Jones, *Hugo!*, 386.
26. Taken from: Jake Johnston and Sara Kozameh, "Venezuelan Economic and Social Performance under Hugo Chávez, in Graphs," CEPR, March 7, 2013, https://cepr.net/venezuelan-economic-and-social-performance-under-hugo-chavez-in-graphs/.
27. Chart showing real GDP adapted (we added note pointing to end of "oil strike") from Figure 1 in Mark Weisbrot and Jake Johnston, "Venezuela's Economic Recovery: Is It Sustainable?," CEPR, September 2012, https://cepr.net/documents/publications/venezuela-2012-09.pdf.

28. Juan Forero, "Venezuela: Labor Chief Who Led Crippling Strike Is Arrested," *The New York Times*, March 2, 2005, https://www.nytimes.com/2005/03/02/world/world-briefing-americas-venezuela-labor-chief-who-led-crippling.html; Juan Forero, "Venezuela Union Leader Guilty of Treason," *The New York Times*, December 15, 2005, https://www.nytimes.com/2005/12/15/world/americas/venezuela-union-leader-guilty-of-treason.html; Steven Mather, "Venezuelan Officials Arrest 14 National Guardsmen over Prison Escape," VenezuelAnalysis, August 17, 2006, https://venezuelanalysis.com/news/1891; Kiraz Janicke, "Peru Gives Political Asylum to Leader of Venezuelan Oil Industry Shutdown," VenezuelAnalysis, September 4, 2007, https://venezuelanalysis.com/news/2583; "CTV llamó a los venezolanos a mantenerse en las calles en apoyo a Guaidó," *El Nacional*, February 4, 2019, http://www.el-nacional.com/noticias/politica/ctv-llamo-los-venezolanos-mantenerse-las-calles-apoyo-guaido_269402.
29. Ernesto Villegas, *Abril Golpe Adentro* (2012), 375–377.
30. Ernesto Villegas, *Abril Golpe Adentro*, 370; https://twitter.com/VillegasPoljak/status/799691194544615424.
31. Mark Weisbrot and Jake Johnston, "Venezuela's Economic Recovery: Is It Sustainable?," September 2012, https://cepr.net/documents/publications/venezuela-2012-09.pdf.
32. Venezuela is hardly the only place where the IMF has made horrible predictions to promote its right wing agenda: "when Latvia began its 'internal devaluation' in 2008, the IMF projected a 5% drop in GDP for 2009; it came in at more than 18%." See Mark Weisbrot, "Greece should look before it leaps," *The Guardian*, May 18, 2010, https://www.theguardian.com/commentisfree/cifamerica/2010/may/18/greece-latvia.
33. Mark Weisbrot, "Can The Venezuelan Economy Be Fixed?", *Huffington Post*, October 26, 2016, https://www.huffpost.com/entry/can-the-venezuelan-econom_b_12647100; Juan Forero, "Venezuela Imposes Currency Controls to Shore Up Economy," *The New York Times*, February 6, 2003, https://www.nytimes.com/2003/02/06/business/worldbusiness/venezuela-imposes-currency-controls-to-shore-up.html.
34. Weisbrot on dollars issued to the private sector: "These were reduced by half in October of 2012 and practically eliminated in February. This meant more importers had to purchase increasingly expensive dollars on the black market. This is where the burst of inflation came from." The government may have made a misguided attempt to punish importers who diverted dollars into the black market, or made a disastrous attempt to promote "import substitution." See Mark

Weisbrot, "Venezuela Is Not Greece," CEPR, May 6, 2010, https://cepr.net/venezuela-is-not-greece/.

35. The effective exchange rate is a weighted average of the official and black market exchange rates, so the skyrocketing black market rate eventually became a huge factor in determining the effective rate.

36. Chart taken with permission from Mark Weisbrot, "Venezuela's Black Market Dollar Plummets on News of New Exchange Rate Mechanism," CEPR, March 24, 2014, https://www.cepr.net/venezuelas-black-market-dollar-plummets-on-news-of-new-exchange-rate-mechanism/.

37. The stabilization plan proposed by UNASUR's technical team in 2016 (see chapter 10) argues that the exchange rate system, in addition to propelling the devaluation-inflation spiral, actually subsidized capital flight by making dollars cheap to acquire for those who then moved them abroad.

38. Weisbrot wrote in 2010, "A managed, or 'dirty' float—in which the government does not set a target exchange rate but intervenes when necessary to preserve exchange rate stability—would suit the Venezuelan economy much better than the current fixed rate." See Mark Weisbrot, "Venezuela Is Not Greece," CEPR, May 6, 2010, https://cepr.net/venezuela-is-not-greece/.

39. Weisbrot commented in 2014, "the Morales government has kept the Bolivian exchange rate very stable for seven years . . . Venezuela's fixed exchange rate system, by contrast, has been much less stable and ran into serious trouble in the past year-and-a-half." See Mark Weisbrot, "FiveThirtyEight Gets It Wrong on Venezuela," CEPR, April 4, 2014, https://cepr.net/five-thirty-eight-gets-it-wrong-on-venezuela/.

40. Hernán Luis Torres Núñez, "Paralysed Venezuela vs Thriving Bolivia: Two Faces of Socialism," VenezuelAnalysis, October 14, 2014, https://venezuelanalysis.com/analysis/10961.

41. Joe Emersberger, "A rebuttal to Torres Núñez: Bolivia-Venezuela comparisons should be helpful to the most radical Chavistas," TeleSUR English, October 18, 2014, https://www.telesurenglish.net/opinion/Bolivia-Venezuela-Comparisons-Should-be-Very-Helpful-to-Radical-Chavistas-20141018-0026.html.

42. According to Mark Weisbrot, Rafael Ramírez, a former head of PDVSA, pushed hard for reform of the exchange rate system. Ramírez had long been accused of corruption by the opposition. In 2017, Maduro's government also accused him. Ramírez went into hiding.

7. Third Coup Attempt: Fatalities over Frivolous Claims, April 2013

1. Ewan Robertson, "Maduro Proclaimed Venezuelan President Elect Amid Opposition Claims of 'Illegitimacy,'" VenezuelAnalysis, April 16, 2013, https://venezuelanalysis.com/news/8640.

2. "Maduro sigue aventajando a Capriles," *El Nuevo Diario*, April 11, 2013, https://www.elnuevodiario.com.ni/internacionales/282859-maduro-sigue-aventajando-capriles/.
3. Ewan Robertson, "Maduro Proclaimed Venezuelan President Elect Amid Opposition Claims of 'Illegitimacy,'" VenezuelAnalysis, April 16, 2013, https://venezuelanalysis.com/news/8640.
4. Economists, "Economists Call on Media to Report Overwhelming Evidence Regarding Venezuelan Election Results," CEPR, https://truthout.org/articles/economists-call-on-media-to-report-overwhelming-evidence-regarding-venezuelan-election-results/.
5. Mark Weisbrot and David Rosnick, "A Statistical Note on the April 14 Venezuelan Presidential Election and Audit of Results," CEPR, May 9, 2013, https://cepr.net/report/a-statistical-note-on-the-april-14-venezuelan-presidential-election-and-audit-of-results/.
6. See chapter 2 for Carter's disingenuous response to Maduro citing this remark years later.
7. Only four months before Maduro's victory, Capriles won the election for Miranda state governor by four percentage points: in absolute terms, he won by 47,000 votes, a much smaller victory than the 272,000 vote margin for Maduro. A loss in that Miranda state election (only months after his defeat to Hugo Chávez in the 2012 presidential election) might have finished Capriles politically. But there was no 100 percent audit of the results in Miranda either. See Ewan Robertson, "Venezuela's 2012 State Election: Lessons for Chavismo and the Opposition," VenezuelAnalysis, December 18, 2012, https://venezuelanalysis.com/analysis/7564.
8. Ewan Robertson, "Maduro Proclaimed Venezuelan President Elect Amid Opposition Claims of 'Illegitimacy,'" VenezuelAnalysis, April 16, 2013, https://venezuelanalysis.com/news/8640.
9. Ewan Robertson, "Maduro Proclaimed Venezuelan President Elect Amid Opposition Claims of 'Illegitimacy,'" VenezuelAnalysis, April 16, 2013, https://venezuelanalysis.com/news/8640.
10. "Anuncio de Auditoria del CNE al proceso electoral 14A y Respuesta de Capriles Radonsky," Globovision broadcast uploaded to Youtube April 19, 2013, http://www.youtube.com/watch?v=wwkchXTPtn4.
11. Peter Wilson, "Venezuela opposition to boycott vote audit," *USA Today*, April 25, 2013, https://www.usatoday.com/story/news/world/2013/04/25/venezuela-opposition-protest-election/2113113/?sf12125123=1.
12. "Mesa inició en España gira europea en busca de apoyos," *El Universal*, April 23, 2013, https://web.archive.org/web/20130430124058/http://www.eluniversal.com/nacional-y-politica/130423/mesa-inicio-en-espana-gira-europea-en-busca-de-apoyos.

13. Dan Beeton, "U.S. Media Continues to Treat Capriles' Complaints Seriously Despite Lack of Evidence," CEPR, May 20, 2013, https://cepr.net/us-media-continues-to-treat-capriles-complaints-seriously-despite-lack-of-evidence/.
14. Lesley Wroughton and Mike McDonald, "Kerry to push for OAS reform, broad debate on drug policy," Reuters, June 4, 2013, https://web.archive.org/web/20130605092207/http://www.reuters.com/article/2013/06/05/us-usa-oas-idUSBRE95403920130605.
15. In his book (p. 291) Rory Carroll summed things up much like Reuters had: "Capriles claimed fraud and demanded a recount. Maduro agreed, then balked."
16. Dan Beeton and Stephan Lefebvre, "A Timeline of Venezuelan Opposition Reactions to the Recent Elections," CEPR, June 18, 2013, https://cepr.net/a-timeline-of-venezuelan-opposition-reactions-to-the-recent-elections/.
17. Dan Beeton, "U.S. Media Continues to Treat Capriles' Complaints Seriously Despite Lack of Evidence," CEPR, May 20, 2013, https://cepr.net/us-media-continues-to-treat-capriles-complaints-seriously-despite-lack-of-evidence/.
18. Alasdair Baverstock, "Venezuela's Maduro still waiting on Washington's recognition," *Christian Science Monitor*, May 17, 2013, https://www.csmonitor.com/World/Americas/2013/0517/Venezuela-s-Maduro-still-waiting-on-Washington-s-recognition.
19. Dan Beeton, "Unreasonable Doubt: Despite the CNE's Many Audits, Capriles Remains Dissatisfied," VenezuelAnalysis, June 14, 2013, https://venezuelanalysis.com/analysis/9705; Christopher Toothaker, "Venezuela council's election audit backs outcome," *Washington Examiner*, June 9, 2013, https://www.washingtonexaminer.com/venezuela-councils-election-audit-backs-outcome; Eugenio G. Martinez, "CNE no podrá entregar datos exigidos por Capriles antes de septiembre," *El Universal*, May 17, 2013, https://web.archive.org/web/20130607165346/http://www.eluniversal.com/nacional-y-politica/130517/cne-no-podra-entregar-datos-exigidos-por-capriles-antes-de-septiembre.
20. "Técnicos internacionales validan auditoría de duplicidad de huellas: CNE," *Panorama*, September 11, 2013, https://www.aporrea.org/actualidad/n236089.html.
21. "Study Mission of The Carter Center 2013 Presidential Elections in Venezuela," Carter Center, https://www.cartercenter.org/resources/pdfs/news/peace_publications/election_reports/venezuela-final-rpt-2013-elections.pdf, 8–9. See chapter 5 for more discussion of the Carter Center. Among high profile NGOs it has stood out in its willingness to contradict some of the lies about Venezuela, but it was always firmly

within the U.S. imperial camp.
22. Mark Weisbrot and David Rosnick, "A Statistical Note on the April 14 Venezuelan Presidential Election and Audit of Results," CEPR, May 9, 2013, https://cepr.net/report/a-statistical-note-on-the-april-14-venezuelan-presidential-election-and-audit-of-results/.
23. Dan Beeton, "Does Capriles Have a Plausible Claim, or Is He 'Venezuela's Sore Loser'?," VenezuelAnalysis, May 6, 2013, https://venezuelanalysis.com/analysis/9080.
24. White House Press Briefing, April 15, 2013, https://web.archive.org/web/20130418064354/http://www.whitehouse.gov/photos-and-video/video/2013/04/15/press-briefing#transcript; White House Press Briefing, April 19, 2013, https://web.archive.org/web/20130419131623/http://www.state.gov/r/pa/prs/dpb/2013/04/207598.htm.
25. On ICG funding in 2013, see "Who Supports The International Crisis Group," International Crisis Group, May 15, 2013, https://web.archive.org/web/20130515174223/http:/www.crisisgroup.org/en/support/who-supports-crisisgroup.aspx; Mark Weisbrot, "International Crisis Promotion from the 'International Crisis Group,'" CEPR, May 17, 2013, https://cepr.net/international-crisis-promotion-from-the-international-crisis-group/.
26. A few years later, farcical legal proceedings led to the ouster of Brazilan President Dilma Rousseff, the imprisonment of former President Lula da Silva, and the election of the fascist Jair Bolsonaro—finally producing the U.S.-Brazil alliance against Venezuela that the ICG desired. See Glenn Greenwald, "Watch: Glenn Greenwald Explains the Political Earthquake in Brazil Caused by Our Ongoing Exposes," *The Intercept*, June 15, 2019; Brasil Wire, *Year of Lead* (Sumare Editions, 2019); Petra Costa, *The Edge of Democracy* (Netflix, 2019), https://www.netflix.com/ca/title/80190535.
27. "Venezuela: Respect Free Speech and Assembly," HRW, April 17, 2013, https://www.hrw.org/news/2013/04/17/venezuela-respect-free-speech-and-assembly.
28. Diego Ore, "Recriminations over post-vote violence stoke Venezuela tensions," Reuters, May 8, 2013, https://www.reuters.com/article/us-venezuela-politics/recriminations-over-post-vote-violence-stoke-venezuela-tensions-idUSBRE94710I20130508. The article said a third protector of the health center, Johny Pacheco, was killed when thieves attempted to steal his car.
29. "62 FOTOS de daños a Centros de Salud (CDI), telecomunicaciones, viviendas y partidos políticos," ALBA Ciudad, April 21, 2013, https://albaciudad.org/2013/04/62-fotos-de-danos-a-centros-de-salud-cdi-telecomunicaciones-viviendas-y-partidos-politicos/.

30. Rory Carroll wrote a flattering article about Bocaranda a year earlier which said Bocaranda's work had "become a must-read for politicians, voters, diplomats, investors and others." Rory Carroll, "Meet Nelson Bocaranda, Venezuela's unofficial information minister," *The Guardian*, March 15, 2012, https://www.theguardian.com/world/2012/mar/15/nelson-bocaranda-venezuela-information. But a State Department cable showed that Bocaranda had acted as a U.S. government agent. Wikileaks, "Colombian guerrillas reportedly met with GBRV officials in Caracas," November 20, 2009, https://wikileaks.org/plusd/cables/09CARACAS1485_a.html. The words "strictly protect" applied to Bocaranda in a U.S. Embassy cable mean, according to an Obama administration spokesman, "to 'strictly protect' their identities because the information is very sensitive, and the source is taking an extreme risk by providing it to the United States": see P. J. Crowley, "Wikileaks's Harmful New Dump Increases Risk to U.S. Information Sources," *Daily Beast*, August 31, 2011, https://www.thedailybeast.com/wikileaks-harmful-new-dump-increases-risk-to-us-information-sources.
31. Six years later, a *New York Times* article rehashed the allegations that Bocaranda had spread. Lucas Koerner and Ricardo Vaz wrote a superb response to it for FAIR.org: Lucas Koerner and Ricardo Vaz, "Pathological Deceit: The NYT Inverts Reality on Venezuela's Cuban Doctors," FAIR, https://fair.org/home/pathological-deceit-the-nyt-inverts-reality-on-venezuelas-cuban-doctors/.
32. See chapter 7 for some details on the medical establishment's battles with the Chávez government since 2001.
33. The IACHR was similarly mute about the immorality of Bocaranda's tweet and the way Provea covered for attacks on medical centers. In a report that mentioned Bocaranda's tweet it showed no concern for the doctors Bocaranda put at risk or the people who were killed for defending them: see Inter American Commission on Human Rights (IACHR), "Annual Report 2013," IACHR, http://www.oas.org/en/iachr/docs/annual/2013/docs-en/AnnualReport-Chap4-Venezuela.pdf.
34. Ernesto Emilio Villegas Poljak, "Venezuela e Historia: Efemerides notables de Venezuela," Venezuela e Historia, April 28, 2019, http://venezuelaehistoria.blogspot.com/2019/04/ernesto-emilio-villegas-poljak.html.
35. Yves Engler, "Canadian Government Funds Venezuelan Opposition," VenezuelAnalysis, December 13, 2010, https://venezuelanalysis.com/analysis/5853.
36. Foro Itinerante de Participacion Popular, "Victimas de la Arrechera: La violencia fascista en Venezuela del 15 al 19 abril de 2013," Expediente 15A, https://web.archive.org/web/20130809184836/; http://www.

sibci.gob.ve/wp-content/uploads/2013/06/VICTIMAS-DE-LA-ARRECHERA-WEB.pdf.
37. Brian Ellsworth and Diego Ore, "Venezuela opposition challenges Maduro's win in court," Reuters, May 2, 2013, https://www.reuters.com/article/us-venezuela-election/venezuela-opposition-challenges-maduros-win-in-court-idUSBRE94118W20130503.
38. William Neuman, "Venezuelan Court Rejects Challenge to Presidential Election Results," *The New York Times*, August 7, 2013, https://www.nytimes.com/2013/08/08/world/americas/venezuelan-court-rejects-challenge-to-presidential-election-results.html?searchResultPosition=2.
39. Noam Chomsky, "The Corporate Takeover of U.S. Democracy," *In These Times*, January 24, 2010, https://chomsky.info/20100124/.
40. An AP article mentioned Capriles's press baron family connections by saying "Cadena Capriles' founding owners aren't directly related to the politician who shares their last name"; Fabiola Sanchez, "Venezuela's president tightens grip on media," Associated Press, December 7, 2013,https://news.yahoo.com/venezuela-39-president-tightens-grip-media-050209180.html?.
41. "Preliminary Report Study Mission of the Carter Center, Presidential Elections in Venezuela, April 14, 2013," July, 2013, 47, 54–60, http://www.cartercenter.org/resources/pdfs/news/peace_publications/election_reports/venezuela-pre-election-rpt-2013.pdf.
42. See chapter 5 for a discussion of a ridiculous op-ed the Carter Center's Americas director, Jen McCoy, wrote in *The New York Times* shortly after the 2002 coup.
43. Alan MacLeod, 70: "The 'caged' frame represented any time a story implied or stated that the Venezuelan media were coerced or cowed by the government." In *Comandante*, Carroll portrays the opposition media as all but muted by 2006: "However, after 2006 opponents started toning down their aggressive rhetoric, while the president not only continued but escalated his, raining abuses year after year upon increasingly mute targets." See 92.
44. "Critics of Venezuelan Government Detained," Amnesty International, April 1, 2010, https://web.archive.org/web/20101206224911/http://www.amnesty.org/en/library/asset/AMR53/004/2010/en/3c325d52-0c98-4b05-87f3-a98c1b575406/amr530042010en.html.
45. Joan E. Greve, "Hillary Clinton hints Russia is grooming Tulsi Gabbard as third-party candidate," *The Guardian*, February 18, 2019, https://www.theguardian.com/us-news/2019/oct/18/hillary-clinton-hints-russia-is-grooming-tulsi-gabbard-as-third-party-candidate.
46. López said that to Venezuela opposition writer Juan Nagel. In the same interview, López said he firmly supported convening a constituent

assembly, but when Maduro called for one in 2017 it became the pretext for the fifth coup attempt. Juan Cristobal Nagel, "Leopoldo, Unleashed," *Caracas Chronicles*, December 18, 2013, http://web.archive.org/web/20150805140337/http:/caracaschronicles.com/2013/12/18/leopoldo-unleashed/.

47. Julio "Coco" Jimenez ("Capriles MAMAGUEVO"), Pero Tenemos, May 7, 2016, https://www.youtube.com/watch?v=BdBEsX-JiXg.
48. Joe Emersberger, "Reuters Shields OAS Over False Claims That Sparked Bolivia Coup," FAIR, December 17, 2019, https://fair.org/home/reuters-shields-oas-over-false-claims-that-sparked-bolivia-coup/.

8. Fourth Coup Attempt: February to April 2014

1. Data in this chart was downloaded from Venezuela's Central Bank: http://www.bcv.org.ve/sites/default/files/cuentas_macroeconomicas/5_2_4_trim.xls. A discussion of the exact starting point of the recession that developed into catastrophe can get a bit technical. It depends heavily on seasonally adjusting quarterly data, and on which year is taken as a starting point for doing so. See Joe Emersberger, "When did Venezuela's economic crisis begin?," *Znet*, June 6, 2020, https://zcomm.org/zblogs/when-did-venezuelas-economic-crisis-begin/.
2. Patricia Velez and Andrew Cawthorne, "Venezuelan socialists win 54 percent of mayors' vote," Reuters, December 13, 2013, https://www.reuters.com/article/us-venezuela-election/venezuelan-socialists-win-54-percent-of-mayors-vote-idUSBRE9BC0XT20131213.
3. Leopoldo López, 12 de Febrero, Nos veremos en la calle que es nuestro terreno, de forma no violenta, es nuestra estrategia, February 11, 2014, https://web.archive.org/web/20170621115917/, https://www.eluniversal.com/opinion/140211/12-de-febrero.
4. Juan Nagel, "#LaSalida is not a strategy," *Caracas Chronicles*, February 11, 2014, https://www.caracaschronicles.com/2014/02/11/lasalida-is-not-a-strategy/.
5. "Coups, Media and Stalemates: What Violent Protests Mean for Venezuela," VenezuelAnalysis, February 14, 2014, https://venezuelanalysis.com/analysis/10353.
6. Andrew Disiderio, Lara Siligman, and Natasha Bertrand, "Impeachment trial to keep National Guard troops at Capitol," https://www.politico.com/news/2021/01/24/impeachment-trial-national-guard-trump-capitol-461805; Kevin Breuninger, "Biden asks agencies for threat assessment on domestic terrorism after deadly Capitol riot," https://www.cnbc.com/2021/01/22/biden-asks-for-threat-assessment-on-domestic-terrorism.html.
7. Jose Manzaned, "162 Attacks on Cuban Doctors in Venezuela Ignored

by Media," VenezuelAnalysis, April 28, 2014, https://venezuelanalysis.com/analysis/10651.
8. "Oscar Lopez Rivera to be freed after 36 years in US prison," Telesur, June 17, 2017, https://www.telesurenglish.net/news/Oscar-Lopez-Rivera-To-Be-Freed-After-36-Years-in-U.S.-Prison-20170117-0029.html; Maggie Astor, "Puerto Rico: What Other Americans Should Know," *The New York Times*, September 25, 2017,https://www.nytimes.com/2017/09/25/us/puerto-rico-hurricane-american.html.
9. The fairness of his conviction has been strongly contested. Supporters claim he was never linked to violent acts: "Puerto Rico's Debt Is Not Financial, It's Colonial: The Political Imprisonment of Oscar Lopez Rivera," The Real News, July 1, 2015, https://therealnews.com/stories/valba0702prisoner. The most notorious attack killed four people in New York: see Neil MacFarquhar, "Clemency Opens Old Scars For Sons of Bombing Victim," *The New York Times*, April 23, 1999, https://www.nytimes.com/1999/08/23/nyregion/clemency-opens-old-scars-for-sons-of-bombing-victim.html?searchResultPosition=44. We do not trust the U.S. justice system, especially in this case, but have not looked closely at the details. We therefore suspend judgment on his guilt or innocence.
10. Glenn Greenwald, "Obama Killed a 16-Year-Old American in Yemen. Trump Just Killed His 8-Year-Old Sister," *The Intercept*, January 30, 2017, https://theintercept.com/2017/01/30/obama-killed-a-16-year-old-american-in-yemen-trump-just-killed-his-8-year-old-sister/.
11. Helen Carter, "England riots: pair jailed for four years for using Facebook to incite disorder," *The Guardian*, August 16, 2011, https://www.theguardian.com/uk/2011/aug/16/uk-riots-four-years-disorder-facebook.
12. Michael White, "Retribution for the riots? Why not?," *The Guardian*, August 18, 2011, http://www.theguardian.com/politics/blog/2011/aug/18/retribution-for-riots-why-not.
13. Joyce Purnick, "Why Bloomberg evicted Occupy Wall Street," Reuters, November 16, 2011, http://blogs.reuters.com/great-debate/2011/11/16/why-bloomberg-evicted-occupy-wall-street/; Richard Kim, "We Are All Human Microphones Now," *The Nation*, October 3, 2011, https://www.thenation.com/article/we-are-all-human-microphones-now/; Ray Sanchez, "More than 700 arrested in Wall Street protest," Reuters, October 1, 2011, https://www.reuters.com/article/us-wallstreet-protests/more-than-700-arrested-in-wall-street-protest-idUSTRE7900BL20111002.
14. Josmar Trujillo, "The 'Total Anarchy' of Wet Cops," FAIR, July 26, 2019, https://fair.org/home/the-total-anarchy-of-wet-cops/.

15. Protesters interrupted the first minutes of the second Democratic debate with calls to fire the NYPD officer who put Eric Garner in a fatal chokehold. Jason Silverstein, "Protesters interrupt Democratic debate calling for Daniel Pantaleo, NYPD officer in Eric Garner case, to be fired," CBS, August 1, 2019, https://www.cbsnews.com/news/democratic-debate-hecklers-fire-pantaleo-chanting-at-debate-mayor-de-blasio-protesters-interrupt-cory-booker-eric/.
16. Ryan Wilson, "Obama on Kaepernick protest: 'I want everybody to listen to each other,'" CBS, September 29, 2016, https://www.cbssports.com/nfl/news/obama-on-kaepernick-protest-i-want-everybody-to-listen-to-each-other/; Josh Ruebner, "US House of Representatives condemns boycotts for Palestinian rights," Electronic Intifada, July 24, 2019, https://electronicintifada.net/blogs/josh-ruebner/us-house-representatives-condemns-boycotts-palestinian-rights.
17. See Introduction for more discussion.
18. Eric Ting, "Kamala Harris: Kaepernick backlash was 'not a thing' until Russian bots 'started taking it on,'" *SFGate*, July 13, 2019, https://m.sfgate.com/politics/article/Kamala-Harris-Kaepernick-backlash-Russian-bots-14093564.php?sfns=mo.
19. William Neuman, "In Venezuela, Surrounded by Dark Plots (Real or Not)," *The New York Times*, September 10, 2013, https://www.nytimes.com/2013/09/11/world/americas/in-venezuela-surrounded-by-dark-plots-real-or-not.html.
20. Consider the U.S. overthrow of Aristide in Haiti in 2004 or the U.S.-led efforts in Nicaragua to overthrow Ortega in the 1980s and again in 2018.
21. Ewan Robertson, "Where Is Venezuela's Political Violence Coming From? A Complete List of Fatalities from the Disturbances," VenezuelAnalysis, April 5, 2014, https://venezuelanalysis.com/analysis/10580.
22. This differs slightly from the Venezuelan government which said there were 43 deaths. According to an opposition source, three deaths occurred after March 29 (not listed in our table): one police officer who was shot on April 9 and two opposition protesters who died from injuries weeks after the protests ended. "Uno por uno, estos son los 43 muertos en las protestas contra el regimen de Maduro en Venezuela," infobae, February 12, 2015, https://www.infobae.com/2015/02/12/1626403-uno-uno-estos-son-los-43-muertos-las-protestas-contra-el-regimen-maduro-venezuela/.
23. "Video muestra que joven Jimmy Vargas habría muerto accidentalmente al caer de una platabanda," Alba ciudad, February 24, 2014,https://albaciudad.org/2014/02/video-muestra-que-joven-tachirense-

jimmy-vargas-murio-al-caer-accidentalmente-de-una-platabanda/. Reuters once reported it as follows: "Witnesses said he was hit with a tear gas canister and fell from a balcony overlooking the protest." See Brian Ellsworth, "Protests, barricades bring Venezuela's 'Cordial City' to a halt," Reuters, February 27, 2014, https://www.reuters.com/article/us-venezuela-protests-sancristobal/protests-barricades-bring-venezuelas-cordial-city-to-a-halt-idUSBREA1Q1WA20140227; Daniel Wallis and Diego Ore, "New battle rages over death toll from Venezuela crisis," Reuters, March 31, 2014, https://uk.reuters.com/article/uk-venezuela-protests-deaths/new-battle-rages-over-death-toll-from-venezuela-crisis-idUKBREA2U0M820140331.

24. Daniel Wallis and Diego Ore, "New battle rages over death toll from Venezuela crisis," Reuters, March 31, 2014, https://uk.reuters.com/article/uk-venezuela-protests-deaths/new-battle-rages-over-death-toll-from-venezuela-crisis-idUKBREA2U0M820140331. In the following article no breakdown of 34 deaths is provided: Diego Ore and Brian Ellsworth, "Venezuela death toll rises to 34 as troops and protesters clash," Reuters, March 22, 2014, https://www.reuters.com/article/us-venezuela-protests/venezuela-death-toll-rises-to-34-as-troops-and-protesters-clash-idUSBREA2L0LK20140323.

25. Peter Hart, "Who Is Dying in Venezuela? A Revealing NYT Correction," FAIR, March 26, 2014, https://fair.org/home/who-is-dying-in-venezuela-a-revealing-nyt-correction/.

26. Mark Weisbrot, "New York Times Corrects False Statement on Venezuela," CEPR, February 27, 2014, https://cepr.net/new-york-times-corrects-false-statement-on-venezuela/.

27. "Venezuela: Tipping Point," International Crisis Group, May 21, 2014, https://web.archive.org/web/20140625060411/http://www.crisisgroup.org/~/media/Files/latin-america/venezuela/b030-venezuela-tipping-point.pdf.

28. In an attempt to justify this, the ICG mentions allegations that a government supporter shot and killed a policeman at an opposition barricade. But government officials also claimed that some opposition protesters had been shot by their own side. That hardly makes the evidence against the government in those cases "weak."

29. The ICG report made the astounding remark that the opposition merely lacked "concrete proof" of fraud in the 2004 recall referendum by referring to arguments based on "statistical anomalies." The Carter Center hired a team of specialized statisticians—not simply Jennifer McCoy as the ICG very sloppily suggested whose only job was to assess those arguments. A key point made by the statisticians was that there was no credible explanation how the government could have

perpetrated fraud such that the random audit of the results would have failed to expose it.

30. "OAS Permanent Council Approved Declaration on the Situation in Venezuela," March 7, 2014, http://www.oas.org/en/media_center/press_release.asp?sCodigo=E-084/14.

31. Nate Singham, "The Role of the OAS and UNASUR in Mediating Inter-Regional Conflicts," CEPR, March 10, 2014, https://www.cepr.net/the-role-of-the-oas-and-unasur-in-mediating-inter-regional-conflicts/.

32. Willian Neuman, "In Venezuela, Conciliatory Talk but Combative Tactics," *The New York Times*, March 14, 2014, http://www.nytimes.com/2014/03/15/world/americas/in-venezuela-conciliatory-talk-but-combative-tactics.html.

33. "La Unión Europea confía en que la misión de Unasur logre aliviar tensiones en Venezuela," Noticias24, March 24, 2014, https://web.archive.org/web/20140329002842/http://www.noticias24.com/venezuela/noticia/230163/canciller-de-paraguay-participara-de-mision-de-unasur-en-venezuela-2/.

34. Andrew Cawthorne, "Venezuela's foreign minister calls Kerry 'murderer,'" Reuters, March 14, 2014, http://www.reuters.com/article/2014/03/14/us-venezuela-protests-idUSBREA2D1J020140314?feedType=RSS.

35. Esteban Israel and Deisy Buitrago, "Soldiers storm Venezuelan protesters' stronghold," Reuters, March 16, 2014, http://uk.reuters.com/article/2014/03/17/uk-venezuela-protests-idUKBREA2F0XQ20140317.

36. MacLeod concluded that 100 percent of the UK and U.S. newspaper articles in his sample depicted the Venezuelan media as "caged" by the government. About 90 percent falsely depicted the state as dominating Venezuela's media landscape. See *Bad News from Venezuela*, 70–71.

37. Mark Cadiz, "Venezuela an online battleground for Canadians backing protests," CBC, March 27, 2014, https://www.cbc.ca/news/world/venezuela-an-online-battleground-for-canadians-backing-protests-1.2586074 .

38. *Ultimas Noticias* shifted its content decidedly in the government's favor in subsequent years but that hardly left the opposition marginalized. See Lucas Koerner and Ricardo Vaz, "There's Far More Diversity in Venezuela's 'Muzzled' Media than in US Corporate Press," FAIR, May 20, 2019, https://fair.org/home/theres-far-more-diversity-in-venezuelas-muzzled-media-than-in-us-corporate-press/.

39. Tamara Pearson, "Auditing Process Begins in Venezuela amid Opposition Claims of 'Lies' and 'Persecution,'" VenezuelAnalysis, April 30, 2013, http://venezuelanalysis.com/news/8946.

40. Emersberger, who has family in Ecuador, was contacted by the CBC

and asked for a comment when a huge earthquake struck the country in April of 2016.
41. Press Freedom index 2014, Reporters without Borders, https://rsf.org/en/world-press-freedom-index-2014.
42. https://web.archive.org/web/20140228213038/http://www.noticierovenevision.net/videos/politica/2014/febrero/21/90148=capriles-llama-a-orientar-la-protesta-pacifica-hacia-el-descontento-por-las-politicas-aplicadas; https://web.archive.org/web/20140816122752/http://www.noticierovenevision.net/videos/politica/2014/febrero/18/89751=multitud-se-hizo-presente-este-martes-en-la-plaza-brion-de-chacaito-en-caracas; https://web.archive.org/web/20140227222913/http://globovision.com/articulo/marcha-de-estudiantes-esta-desvinculada-de-partidos-politicos-segun-fcu; https://web.archive.org/web/20140306233416/http://globovision.com/articulo/diputado-guaido-detencion-de-lopez-es-injustahttps://web.archive.org/web/20140306233416/http://globovision.com/articulo/diputado-guaido-detencion-de-lopez-es-injusta; https://web.archive.org/web/20160505231433/http://www.noticierovenevision.net/politica/2014/febrero/20/89967=entrevista-venevision-tomas-guanipa,-secretario-general-de-primero-justicia; https://web.archive.org/web/20140221100455/http://globovision.com/articulo/maria-corina-machado-ofrecera-detalles-sobre-convocatoria-para-este-martes.
43. Mark Weisbrot, "Does Venezuelan Television Provide Coverage That Opposes the Government?," VenezuelAnalysis, February 24, 2014, https://venezuelanalysis.com/analysis/10400.
44. *New York Times* Editorial Board, "The Blame Game in Venezuela," *The New York Times*, March 14, 2014, https://www.nytimes.com/2014/03/15/opinion/the-blame-game-in-venezuela.html.
45. *New York Times* Editorial Board, "Making the Gaza Cease-Fire Last," *The New York Times*, August 6, 2014, https://www.nytimes.com/2014/08/07/opinion/making-the-gaza-cease-fire-last.html.
46. As of 2018, UNICEF said Israel's child mortality rate was 3.6 per 1000 live births compared to 20.9 in the neighboring Palestinian lands it has occupied for over fifty years. There were 3190 Palestinian child deaths in 2018 in the occupied lands, about 2600 more than would have taken place if the child mortality rate were not five times higher than in Israel.
47. "U.S. Senate Unanimously Approves Resolution Giving Full Support of Israel on Gaza," *Haaretz*, July 20, 2014, https://www.haaretz.com/u-s-senate-unanimously-approves-resolution-giving-full-support-of-israel-on-gaza-1.5256107. 113th CONGRESS 2d Session H. CON. RES. 107, http://org.salsalabs.com/o/641/images/H. Con. Res. 107.pdf.
48. The editorial said nothing about lavish U.S. support that has flowed to

Israel for decades. See Rania Khalek, "Obama hands Israel the largest military aid deal in history," Electronic Intifada, September 14, 2016, https://electronicintifada.net/blogs/rania-khalek/obama-hands-israel-largest-military-aid-deal-history.

49. "Rocket attacks into Israel by Hamas and other extremist groups must stop, along with other terrorist attacks," thundered the *New York Times* editorial. There were twelve Israeli civilians killed inside Israel by Palestinians in all of 2014, and only five killed by rockets fired from the occupied territories. The vast majority of the fatalities that Palestinians inflicted on Israel in 2014 were soldiers: 41 killed in Gaza and 24 in Israel. But *New York Times* editors demanded that the side enduring nearly 100 percent of the deaths also have a perfect record of sparing civilians. See "Israeli security force personnel killed by Palestinians in the Gaza Strip, since Operation Cast Lead," B'Tselem, https://www.btselem.org/statistics/fatalities/after-cast-lead/by-date-of-event/gaza/israeli-security-force-personnel-killed-by-palestinians.

50. See discussion of Caracazo Massacre in chapter 4. See also Mark A. Uhlig, "Venezuela Unrest: Lesson for Leader," *The New York Times*, March 6, 1989, https://www.nytimes.com/1989/03/06/world/venezuela-unrest-lesson-for-leader.html. The Uhlig article oozes sympathy for Perez and concludes, "And it remains to be seen whether Mr. Perez can preserve his influence abroad at a time when his troubles at home are on painful display." Venezuela's security forces had just perpetrated a gruesome massacre but it was "his [Perez] troubles" was the sympathetic perspective the author used.

9. Buildup to the Fifth Coup Attempt

1. See https://www.oil-price.net/.
2. See https://fred.stlouisfed.org/series/DCOILWTICO.
3. Mark Weisbrot and Jake Johnston, "Venezuela's Economic Recovery: Is It Sustainable?," CEPR, September 2012, https://cepr.net/documents/publications/venezuela-2012-09.pdf; also note that on September 5, 2014, an op-ed by two opposition economists (Ricardo Hausmann and Miguel Angel Santos) said that Venezuela may default on foreign debt when oil prices were still at $90 per barrel. They said nothing about oil prices being about to collapse. See Ricardo Hausmann and Miguel Angel Santos, "Should Venezuela Default," *Project Syndicate*, September 5, 2014, https://www.project-syndicate.org/commentary/ricardo-hausmann-and-miguel-angel-santos-pillory-the-maduro-government-for-defaulting-on-30-million-citizens—but-not-on-wall-street?barrier=accesspaylog.
4. See last section of chapter 6, "The Forgotten Currency Float."

5. We asked Dean Baker, who saw that U.S. housing price increases in the 2000s were unsustainable, why oil prices were not similarly predictable. He replied, "new finds of oil are hard to predict. And, the technology that made fracked oil affordable was also a new story. There is nothing like this in housing. Demand also fluctuates hugely with the business cycle, which economists have not been good at predicting. A further complication is that the spread of electric cars is likely to become a big deal in the next decade."
6. It's plausible that the U.S. government and Saudi Arabia contributed to the fall in oil prices as a way to pressure Russia, Iran, and Venezuela. Trump has been unusually open about the fact that the U.S. government pressures the Saudis to set production levels to suit U.S. interests. However, other factors, like technological developments, may have depressed prices anyway.
7. Jeff Mason and Roberta Rampton, "U.S. declares Venezuela a national security threat, sanctions top officials," Reuters, March 9, 2015, https://www.reuters.com/article/us-usa-venezuela/u-s-declares-venezuela-a-national-security-threat-sanctions-top-officials-idUSKBN0M51NS20150309.
8. Joe Emersberger, "Chavismo must stop the economic bleeding," TeleSUR English, July 19, 2016, https://www.telesurenglish.net/opinion/Chavismo-Must-Stop-the-Economic-Bleeding-20160719-0039.html.
9. In a managed float the government intervenes at times to buy or sell currency to stabilize the exchange rate. This was done very successfully by Bolivia under its left-wing president, Evo Morales, for several years. See chapter 6.
10. Economist Ha Joon Chang stated in a 2009 paper, "To put it bluntly, economic development is impossible without good export performance. Economic development requires importation of advanced technologies, in the form of either machines or technology licensing, which need to [be] paid for with foreign currencies." See Ha Joon Chang, "Industrial Policy: Can We Go Beyond an Unproductive Confrontation?" 2009, ABCDE Conference, Seoul, South Korea, https://web.archive.org/web/20090805034532/http://siteresources.worldbank.org/INTABCDESK2009/Resources/Ha-Joon-Chang.pdf.
11. For about 8:50 min point of video segment: Jon Snow, "Jeremy Corbyn—full Jon Snow interview on Brexit, Venezuela, and anti-Semitism," Channel 4 News, September 26, 2017, https://www.youtube.com/watch?v=7v7LHgxvCnY.
12. Ha Joon Chang, "South Koreans worked a democratic miracle. Can they do it again?," *The New York Times*, September 14, 2017, https://www.nytimes.com/2017/09/14/opinion/south-korea-social-mobility.

html. We do not dismiss the brutality of the South Korean dictatorships after 1960, but the worst crimes took place in the 1950s. There were, for example, perhaps 100,000 executions in 1950 alone: Charles J. Hanley and J. S. Chang, "Summer of Terror: At least 100,000 said executed by Korean ally of US in 1950," *Asia Pacific Journal*, July 2, 2008, https://apjjf.org/-Charles-J.-Hanley/2827/article.html.
13. UNICEF (2018).
14. Gabriel Hetland, "The End of Chavismo? Why Venezuela's Ruling Party Lost Big, and What Comes Next," VenezuelAnalysis, December 10, 2015, https://venezuelanalysis.com/analysis/11768; Z. C. Dutka, "Venezuelan Opposition Gains 2/3 Super Majority in National Assembly Elections," VenezuelAnalysis, December 8, 2015, https://venezuelanalysis.com/news/11762.
15. Greg Wilpert, "A New Opportunity for Venezuela's Socialists," VenezuelAnalysis, October 1, 2010, https://venezuelanalysis.com/analysis/5683.
16. With no irony about the fact that gerrymandering (which we oppose) is a basic feature of U.S. electoral politics.
17. See chapter 8 discussion of data on media coverage gathered by the Carter Center in 2013, and chapter 9 discussion of Venezuelan media coverage of protests of 2014.
18. We are not including rebuttals by the vilified Maduro government. The Western media similarly allowed statements by Saddam Hussein and his officials denying Iraq had WMD in 2002.
19. *New York Times* Editorial Board, "Venezuela Tries to Silence Critics," *The New York Times*, August 7, 2014, https://www.nytimes.com/2015/08/08/opinion/venezuela-tries-to-silence-critics.html.
20. *New York Times* Editorial Board, "'Curious Eyes Never Run Dry,'" *The New York Times*, April 11, 2019, https://www.nytimes.com/2019/04/11/opinion/assange-wikileaks-arrest.html; Joe Emersberger, "Assange's 'Conspiracy' to Expose War Crimes Has Already Been Punished," FAIR, April 12, 2019, https://fair.org/home/assanges-conspiracy-to-expose-war-crimes-has-already-been-punished/.
21. *Washington Post* Editorial Board, "Venezuela's Dirty Election Approaches," *The Washington Post*, November 22, 2015, https://www.washingtonpost.com/opinions/venezuelas-dirty-election-approaches/2015/11/22/5cd4bc7a-8d5f-11e5-acff-673ae92ddd2b_story.html.
22. Five million dollars was budgeted for 2014 alone by U.S. government to "strengthen Venezuelan civil society and democratic institutions"; Congressional Budget Justification, Volume 2—Fiscal year 2014, U.S. State Department, 126, https://web.archive.org/web/20130713144919/http://www.state.gov/documents/organization/208290.pdf.

23. "Video completo del discurso de Henry Ramos Allup y las caras que no pudiste ver, solo por VIVOplay," VIVO play, January 16, 2016, https://www.youtube.com/watch?v=bPh7urGq9tw.
24. "INFORME DE LAS CIFRAS DEL SECTORII TRIMESTRE 2018," Conatel, May 12, 2018, http://www.conatel.gob.ve/wp-content/uploads/2018/12/Presentacion-de-cifras-II-2018_05-12-2018.pdf.
25. By 2019, an opposition pollster said 87.7 percent of households had access if one includes illegal access. This figure was provided confidentially to us by an opposition source with access to the polling data. Given the way opposition pollsters bias their sampling of the population, we believe that figure is an overestimate.
26. See chapter 8, "The Carter Center Quietly Drops a Bomb." See also Joe Emersberger, "Detailed notes on Venezuelan newscast on the private network Venevision," *Znet*, August 20, 2019, https://zcomm.org/zblogs/notes-on-venezuelan-newscast-on-venevision-august-20-2019/.
27. Alan MacLeod, *Bad News from Venezuela: Twenty Years of Fake News and Misreporting* (2018).
28. Daniel Wallis, "Venezuela's Chávez unveils 3D image of hero Bolivar," Reuters, July 24, 2012, https://www.reuters.com/article/us-venezuela-chavez-bolivar-idUSBRE86N1F120120724.
29. Francisco Toro, "Memoria y Cuenta Live Blog," *Caracas Chronicles*, January 15, 2016, https://www.caracaschronicles.com/2016/01/15/memoria-y-cuenta-liveblog/.
30. The speech in which Ramos did this was reported in passing by Reuters in early September: Andrew Cawthorne, "Venezuela opposition says blocked from meeting near summit," Reuters, September 10, 2016, https://www.reuters.com/article/us-venezuela-politics-idUSKCN11G0QV.
31. "Ramos Allup en San Cristobal el 27 de agosto de 2016," Luigino Bracci Roa—Situacion en Venezuela, September 3, 2016, https://youtu.be/9WZUiyG6cXI.
32. William Finnegan, "Venezuela, A Failing State," *The New Yorker*, November 7, 2016, https://www.newyorker.com/magazine/2016/11/14/venezuela-a-failing-state.
33. "Accion Democratica: A Hopeless Case: Brownfield," April 17, 2006, https://wikileaks.org/plusd/cables/06CARACAS1026_a.html.
34. The Intercept reported Brownfield saying, "And if we can do something that will bring that end quicker, we probably should do it, but we should do it understanding that it's going to have an impact on millions and millions of people who are already having great difficulty finding enough to eat, getting themselves cured when they get sick, or finding clothes to put on their children before they go off to school. We don't get to do this and pretend as though it has no impact there. We have to

make the hard decision—the desired outcome justifies this fairly severe punishment." See Jeremy Scahill, "Pox Americana: Vijay Prashad on Venezuela, India, Mexico, Congo, and U.S. Hegemony," *The Intercepted Podcast*, February 10, 2019, https://theintercept.com/2019/02/10/intercepted-podcast-vijay-prashad-venezuela-india/.

35. The cable suggests Ramos and his people did not have a high success rate getting money and other favors at the time because Brownfield viewed them as unpopular and incompetent. He said of one Ramos ally, "He calls different sections of the Embassy *if* [our emphasis] he does not receive what he requests."

36. Jonas Holldack, "Venezuelan National Assembly Approves New Supreme Court Magistrates and Historic Grassroots Seed Law," VenezuelAnalysis, December 23, 2015, https://venezuelanalysis.com/news/11788.

37. Z. C. Dutka, "Venezuela's Socialists Walk Out after Incoming Opposition Legislators Violate Procedures," VenezuelAnalysis, January 5, 2016, https://venezuelanalysis.com/news/11801.

38. Rachael Boothroyd Rojas, "Venezuelan Supreme Court Suspends Swearing in of 4 Incoming Legislators," VenezuelAnalysis, January 2, 2016, https://venezuelanalysis.com/news/11796.

39. Rachael Boothroyd Rojas, "Venezuelan Supreme Court: 'National Assembly Is Void,'" VenezuelAnalysis, January 12, 2016, https://venezuelanalysis.com/news/11813. Dr. Francisco Dominguez, "Right Wing Majority in Venezuela's National Assembly: The Constitutional and Political Stakes," VenezuelAnalysis, February 2, 2016, https://venezuelanalysis.com/analysis/11846.

40. Rachael Boothroyd Rojas, "Venezuelan Supreme Court: 'National Assembly Is Void,'" VenezuelAnalysis, January 12, 2016, https://venezuelanalysis.com/news/11813.

41. "Tribunal Supremo de Venezuela declara 'en desacato' a la Asamblea Nacional de mayoría opositora," BBC Mundo, January 11, 2016, https://www.bbc.com/mundo/noticias/2016/01/160111_venezuela_tsj_descato_asamblea_dp; Jonas Holldack, "Venezuelan Opposition Accepts Supreme Court Ruling, Introduces Law Privatizing Housing Mission," VenezuelAnalysis, January 14, 2016, https://venezuelanalysis.com/news/11817; Luana Cabrera, "Asamblea Nacional desincorpora a diputados del estado Amazonas," January 13, 2016, https://politikaucab.files.wordpress.com/2016/01/converted_file_671882de.pdf.

42. "TSJ: Ley de bono de alimentación para pensionados debe tener presupuesto," ALBA Ciudad, April 30, 2016, https://albaciudad.org/2016/04/tsj-ley-de-bono-de-alimentacion-para-pensionados-debe-tener-presupuesto/.

43. Rachael Boothroyd Rojas, "Economic Emergency in Effect in Venezuela, as Supreme Court Rules in Favour of Executive," VenezuelAnalysis, February 15, 2016, https://venezuelanalysis.com/news/11854; Ryan Mallett-Outtrim, "Venezuela's Supreme Court Approves Maduro's Decree Power Extension," VenezuelAnalysis, March 18, 2016, https://venezuelanalysis.com/news/11893.
44. Luis Almagro, "How Venezuela can avoid suspension from the OAS," *The Globe and Mail*, March 23, 2017, https://www.theglobeandmail.com/opinion/how-venezuela-can-avoid-suspension-from-the-oas/article34385819/.
45. Rachael Boothroyd Rojas, "Venezuelan Parliament Defies Supreme Court, Petitions OAS to Intervene," VenezuelAnalysis, March 5, 2016, https://venezuelanalysis.com/news/11874; Lucas Koerner, "Venezuelan Opposition Announces Plan to Oust Maduro, Faces Constitutional Roadblocks," VenezuelAnalysis, March 9, 2016, https://venezuelanalysis.com/news/11880.
46. Lucas Koerner, "Venezuelan Supreme Court: Amendment Shortening Presidential Term Not Retroactive," VenezuelAnalysis, April 26, 2016, https://venezuelanalysis.com/news/11948.
47. "TSJ: Ley de bono de alimentación para pensionados debe tener presupuesto," ALBA Ciudad, April 30, 2016, https://albaciudad.org/2016/04/tsj-ley-de-bono-de-alimentacion-para-pensionados-debe-tener-presupuesto/; Lucas Koerner, "Venezuela's Supreme Court Strikes a Blow to the Impunity of Liberal Terror," VenezuelAnalysis, April 22, 2016, https://venezuelanalysis.com/analysis/11943.
48. Lucas Koerner, "Venezuelan Supreme Court Blocks Housing Privatization Law," VenezuelAnalysis, May 9, 2016, https://venezuelanalysis.com/news/11965; The CLAPs were officially founded in April of 2016: "Clap: Organización popular para el abastecimiento y la producción," Ministerio del Poder Popular para la comminucacion e informacion, June 19, 2016, https://web.archive.org/web/20160620214426/http://www.minci.gob.ve/2016/06/CLAP-organizacion-popular-para-el-abastecimiento-y-la-produccion/; Jeanette Charles, "Venezuelan Supreme Court Extends Economic Emergency State of Exception," VenezuelAnalysis, September 23, 2016, https://venezuelanalysis.com/news/12685.
49. Jeanette S. Charles, "Supreme Court Strikes Down Opposition Health Law, Declares AN's May Activities Invalid," VenezuelAnalysis, June 16, 2016, https://venezuelanalysis.com/news/12038.
50. Lucas Koerner, "Venezuelan Supreme Court Blocks Parliamentary Motion to Remove Justices," VenezuelAnalysis, July 20, 2016, https://venezuelanalysis.com/news/12090.

51. "Venezuela: Asamblea Nacional incorpora a diputados indígenas suspendidos por el Tribunal Supremo de Justicia," BBC Mundo, July 28, 2016, https://www.bbc.com/mundo/noticias-america-latina-36919544.
52. Lucas Koerner, "Venezuelan Supreme Court: Maduro is not Colombian," VenezuelAnalysis, October 31, 2016, https://venezuelanalysis.com/news/12762.
53. Rachael Boothroyd-Rojas, "Venezuelan Opposition Expels Mayors for Signing 2017 Budget," VenezuelAnalysis, October 24, 2016, https://venezuelanalysis.com/news/12739.
54. Jeanette Charles, "Amazonas Legislators Resign After Dialogue with Bolivarian Government," VenezuelAnalysis, November 16, 2016, https://venezuelanalysis.com/news/12788; a copy of the letter is here https://twitter.com/HectoRodriguez/status/798630555495661569; "Sentencia nº 952 de Tribunal Supremo de Justicia—Sala Constitucional de 21 de Noviembre de 2016," https://vlexvenezuela.com/vid/nicolas-maduro-653861161.
55. Maduro was elected in April of 2013, which suggests that the deadline should be April of 2017. However, due to Chávez's health crisis in early 2013, Maduro was acting president as of January 2013. Hence the January 10, 2017, deadline.
56. Rachael Boothroyd Rojas, "Venezuela's Future Uncertain as Opposition Launches Recall Referendum Petition," VenezuelAnalysis, April 28, 2016, https://venezuelanalysis.com/news/11951.
57. Lucas Koerner, "Venezuelan Opposition Announces Plan to Oust Maduro, Faces Constitutional Roadblocks," VenezuelAnalysis, March 9, 2016, https://venezuelanalysis.com/news/11880.
58. In fact, Chávez could have used valid legal arguments to avoid a recall referendum, but didn't. Eirik Vold (138) discusses leaked recordings that emerged in 2004 in which a prominent opposition journalist (Teodoro Petkoff) conceded that massive fraud took place in the signature collection process for the 2004 presidential recall referendum. The private media's strength at the time prevented the revelations from having as much impact as they otherwise would have had.
59. Ryan Mallett-Outtrim, "The Curious Case of Venezuela's Recall Referendum: Murder . . . or Suicide?," VenezuelAnalysis, January 9, 2017, https://venezuelanalysis.com/analysis/12875.
60. "Venezuela—Government Stability," Eurasia Group, April 27, 2016, https://eurasiagroup.bluematrix.com/docs/html/f6443b8d-b428-435d-a3d4-40db00a077ff.html.
61. Ryan Mallett-Outtrim, "Venezuela's Opposition Calls Protests Against Recall Postponement, Appeals to Military," VenezuelAnalysis, October 21, 2016, https://venezuelanalysis.com/news/12736; "Venezuela

Election Body: Recall Referendum Will Be in 2017," Telesur English, August 10, 2016, https://venezuelanalysis.com/news/12123.
62. "TSJ de Venezuela declara nulas nuevas acciones del Parlamento," Telesur, January 11, 2017, https://www.telesurtv.net/news/TSJ-de-Venezuela-declara-nulas-nuevas-acciones-del-Parlamento-20170111-0057.html.
63. Rachael Boothroyd-Rojas, "Venezuelan Supreme Court: The President Has Not Abandoned His Post," VenezuelAnalysis, January 31, 2017, https://venezuelanalysis.com/news/12912; Francisco Toro, "'Juicio Político' is not Impeachment (and 'abandono del cargo' is a stretch)," Caracas Chronicles, October 26, 2016, https://www.caracaschronicles.com/2016/10/26/quick-note-juicio-politico-article-222/.
64. Rafael Romo, "Venezuela's high court dissolves National Assembly," CNN, March 30, 2017, https://edition.cnn.com/2017/03/30/americas/venezuela-dissolves-national-assembly/; Ryan Mallett-Outtrim, "Venezuela's Attorney General Accuses Supreme Court of Violating the Constitution," VenezuelAnalysis, March 31, 2017, https://venezuelanalysis.com/news/13014.
65. Rachael Boothroyd-Rojas and Ryan Mallett-Outtrim, "Has Maduro Really Dissolved the National Assembly in Venezuela?," VenezuelAnalysis, March 31, 2017, https://venezuelanalysis.com/analysis/13018.
66. Rachael Boothroyd Rojas, "Venezuela's Supreme Court Annuls Controversial Decisions on Legislature," VenezuelAnalysis, April 1, 2017, https://venezuelanalysis.com/news/13019.
67. For details on Rousseff's ouster and Lula's disqualification see Mark Weisbrot, "Is Human Rights Watch Too Closely Aligned with US Foreign Policy?," The Nation, September 23, 2016, https://www.thenation.com/article/is-human-rights-watch-too-closely-aligned-with-us-foreign-policy/. See also Glenn Greenwald's explosive exposés on prosecutorial misconduct that led, among other things, to Lula's imprisonment: "Secret Brazil Archive," https://theintercept.com/series/secret-brazil-archive/.
68. Alan MacLeod, "The Bolivian Coup Is Not a Coup—Because US Wanted It to Happen," FAIR, November 11, 2019, https://fair.org/home/the-bolivian-coup-is-not-a-coup-because-us-wanted-it-to-happen/; "Vivanco, de HRW: 'Penalizar la opinión es de gobiernos dictatoriales, no de una democracia como la de Bolivia,'" Brujuladigital, May 15, 2020, https://brujuladigital.net/politica/vivanco-de-hrw-penalizar-la-opinion-es-de-gobiernos-dictatoriales-no-de-una-democracia-como-la-de-bolivia.
69. "Constitution—Title I: Fundamental Principles (Art. 1-9)," https://venezuelanalysis.com/constitution/title/1.
70. "Cuba Poses Biological Threat to U.S., Bolton Says," NTI, April 1, 2004,

https://www.nti.org/gsn/article/cuba-poses-biological-threat-to-us-bolton-says/; Shane Ryan, "Has Rachel Maddow Entered Her Infowars Period?," *Paste*, January 31, 2019, https://www.pastemagazine.com/articles/2019/01/has-rachel-maddow-entered-her-infowars-period.html.
71. The recall process in California's 2003 recall election took 7–8 months depending on how you define the start of the petition drive. Wisconsin's in 2012 took 6–7 months. Would there ever be an international campaign demanding that the United States speed up its recall process?
72. "Elecciones a la Asamblea Nacional 2015," CNE Poder Electoral, December 6, 2015, http://www.cne.gob.ve/resultado_asamblea2015/r/0/reg_220000.html; "PSUV pide investigar compra de votos de la oposición," Telesur, December 16, 2015, https://www.telesurtv.net/news/Gobierno-venezolano-revela-delitos-electorales-de-la-oposicion-20151216-0035.html.
73. Caracas Chronicles Team, "Henry Ramos Allup Explains the Supreme Tribunal Ruling Shutting Down the Legislative Branch," *Caracas Chronicles*, March 30, 2017, https://www.caracaschronicles.com/2017/03/30/henry-ramos-allup-explains-supreme-tribunal-ruling-shutting-legislative-branch/.
74. If Supreme Court judges were elected with help from a political party that wins other elections (however fairly), then concerns about political independence still arise. There is no easy solution.
75. Joe Emersberger, "Reuters (Unsurprisingly) Looks Away as Ecuador Tries to Outlaw Opposition Parties," FAIR, August 17, 2020, https://fair.org/home/reuters-unsurprisingly-looks-away-as-ecuador-tries-to-outlaw-opposition-parties/.

10. Fifth Coup Attempt: April 4–July 31, 2017

1. *New York Times* Editorial Board, "A Dangerous Standoff in Venezuela," *The New York Times*, October 26, 2016, https://www.nytimes.com/2016/10/27/opinion/a-dangerous-standoff-in-venezuela.html.
2. *New York Times* Editorial Board, "Making the Gaza Cease-Fire Last," *The New York Times*, August 6, 2014 https://www.nytimes.com/2014/08/07/opinion/making-the-gaza-cease-fire-last.html.
3. Israel's fifty-two-year military occupation of Palestinian lands should completely disqualify it as a democracy. Abby Martin remarked during Israeli elections in September 2019, "Nearly 5 million Palestinians whose lives are entirely dictated by Israel are unable to vote today."
4. *New York Times* Editorial Board, "Venezuela's Descent Into Dictatorship," *The New York Times*, March 31, 2017, https://www.nytimes.com/2017/03/31/opinion/venezuelas-descent-into-dictatorship.html;

New York Times Editorial Board, "Pressuring Venezuela's Leader to Back Down," *New York Times*, April 4, 2017, https://www.nytimes.com/2017/04/14/opinion/pressuring-venezuelas-leader-to-back-down.html; *New York Times* Editorial Board, "Mr. Maduro's Drive to Dictatorship," *The New York Times*, August 3, 2017, https://www.nytimes.com/2017/08/03/opinion/nicolas-maduro-sanctions.html; *New York Times* Editorial Board, "Exporting Chaos to Venezuela," *The New York Times*, August 17, 2020, https://www.nytimes.com/2017/08/17/opinion/venezuela-trump-maduro-military-threat.html.
5. Lucas Koerner, "Venezuelan Attorney General Skips Court Hearing, Alleges 'Coup,'" VenezuelAnalysis, July 4, 2017, https://venezuelanalysis.com/analysis/13191.
6. Interview was conducted with Emersberger June 7, 2019.
7. Anatoly Kurmanaev and Kejal Vyas, "Venezuela Attorney General Luisa Ortega Criticizes Regime She Serves," *The Wall Street Journal*, May 3, 2017, https://www.wsj.com/articles/venezuela-attorney-general-luisa-ortega-criticizes-regime-she-serves-1493846392.
8. "Senator Rubio Lists 23 Human Rights Violators That Should Be Sanctioned," Rubio's website, May 8, 2014, https://www.rubio.senate.gov/public/index.cfm/fighting-for-florida?ID=7d296759-5922-414f-944e-4a812a945419.
9. "Additional Visa Restrictions Against Human Rights Abusers, Individuals Responsible for Public Corruption, and Their Family Members in Venezuela," U.S. State Dept., February 2, 2015, https://2009-2017.state.gov/r/pa/prs/ps/2015/02/237077.htm.
10. "Fiscal general venezolana nombrará abogado para defenderse de sanción de EE.UU.," EFE, February 5, 2015, https://www.efe.com/efe/america/politica/fiscal-general-venezolana-nombrara-abogado-para-defenderse-de-sancion-ee-uu/20000035-2529464.
11. Deisy Buitrago, Alexandra Ulmer, "Venezuela's dissident state prosecutor expects to be fired," Reuters, July 4, 2017, https://www.reuters.com/article/us-venezuela-politics-idUSKBN19P20L; "Venezuela crisis: Attorney general refuses to attend court summons," BBC, July 5, 2017, https://www.bbc.com/news/world-latin-america-40504879; "Venezuela's attorney general refuses court summons," Al Jazeera, July 4, 2017, https://www.aljazeera.com/news/2017/07/venezuela-attorney-general-refuses-court-summons-170704222410423.html.
12. She also said in May 2017 that it would be impossible to improve the 1999 constitution that was written by an overwhelmingly Chavista Constituent Assembly. See https://www.infobae.com/america/venezuela/2017/05/19/la-fiscal-chavista-luisa-ortega-diaz-

volvio-a-rebelarse-y-rechazo-la-invitacion-de-maduro-a-debatir-la-constituyente/.
13. Rachael Boothroyd Rojas, "Venezuela's ANC Names New Attorney General & National Ombudsman," VenezuelAnalysis, August 12, 2017, https://venezuelanalysis.com/news/13292; Ryan Mallett-Outtrim, "Venezuelan Authorities Raid Former Ex-Prosecutor's Home in Corruption Case," VenezuelAnalysis, August 17, 2017, https://venezuelanalysis.com/news/13314; "Former Venezuelan prosecutor meets Mexican attorney general," Reuters, August 31, 2017, https://www.reuters.com/article/us-venezuela-politics-mexico/former-venezuelan-prosecutor-meets-mexican-attorney-general-idUSKCN1BC3M1.
14. Leila Miller, "Venezuelan judges work from abroad and await Maduro's ouster," *The Los Angeles Times*, May 7, 2019, https://www.latimes.com/world/la-fg-venezuela-supreme-court-judges-20190507-story.html.
15. Nathaly Quiroga, "Desde el exilio, el Tribunal Supremo de Justicia de Venezuela inició juicio contra Nicolás Maduro por corrupción," *France24*, August 3, 2018, https://www.france24.com/es/20180803-venezuela-tribunal-supremo-justicia-juicio-maduro; "Luisa Ortega Díaz reveló que Diosdado Cabello la llamó al morir Chávez," *El Nacional*, July 12, 2018, https://www.elnacional.com/venezuela/politica/luisa-ortega-diaz-revelo-que-diosdado-cabello-llamo-morir-chavez_243720/; In one interview she said that she assumes Chávez indeed died in March 2013: "Isnardo 20/20 Personal—Entrevista a la Fiscal General Luisa Ortega Diaz," Vpltv, February 1, 2018, https://youtu.be/mZVuJPkBRRU.
16. About 4:18 point of interview: "Isnardo 20/20 Personal—Entrevista a la Fiscal General Luisa Ortega Diaz," Vpltv, February 1, 2018, https://youtu.be/mZVuJPkBRRU.
17. "Luisa Ortega Díaz: Apoyemos al nuevo presidente Juan Guaidó," *El Nacional*, January 23, 2019, https://www.elnacional.com/venezuela/politica/luisa-ortega-diaz-apoyemos-nuevo-presidente-juan-guaido_267712/.
18. Orlando Avendaño, "Luisa Ortega Díaz: Chávez Is Responsible for the Tragedy in Venezuela," *Pan Am Post*, March 14, 2019, https://panampost.com/orlando-avendano/2019/03/14/luisa-ortega-diaz-chavez-is-responsible-for-the-tragedy-in-venezuela/?cn-reloaded=1; the Panampost.com is so extreme that it publishes articles claiming Henry Ramos Allup was never really an opponent of Chavismo. Orlando Avendaño, "El histórico partido «opositor» venezolano y su vinculación económica con el chavismo," Pan Am Post, August 26, 2019, https://es.panampost.com/orlando-avendano/2019/08/23/el-historico-partido-opositor-venezolano-y-su-vinculacion-economica-con-el-chavismo/.

19. She says this at about the 1:34 point of this interview: "Isnardo 20/20 Personal—Entrevista a la Fiscal General Luisa Ortega Diaz," Vpltv, February 1, 2018, hhttps://youtu.be/mZVuJPkBRRU.
20. Edward Ellis, "Murder of the campesinos," *The Guardian*, October 2, 2011, https://www.theguardian.com/commentisfree/2011/oct/02/venezuela-land-rights-chavez-farmers; "Abuses in Venezuela," letter, *The Guardian*, August 4, 2011, https://www.theguardian.com/world/2011/aug/04/abuses-in-venezuela-human-rights.
21. Joe Emersberger, "Interview with Edward Ellis, Director of 'Tierras Libres,'" VenezuelAnalysis, August 22, 2011, https://venezuelanalysis.com/analysis/6438.
22. Reuters referred to her case as "emblematic": Stephanie Nebehay, "Venezuela releases judge, journalist, 20 students—U.N.", Reuters, July 5, 2019, https://www.reuters.com/article/venezuela-un-prisoners/venezuela-releases-judge-journalist-20-students-u-n-idUSL8N24623I.
23. Joe Emersberger and Jeb Sprague, "Impunity for Venezuela's big landowners," Al Jazeera, November 13, 2011, https://www.aljazeera.com/indepth/opinion/2011/11/201111810548458225.html;Emma Kreyche, "Taking On Venezuela's Latifundios," *NACLA*, August 16, 2011, https://nacla.org/article/taking-venezuela%E2%80%99s-latifundios.
24. Lucía Martínez Romero, "We Want Justice: A Letter to Venezuelan Attorney General Luisa Ortega Díaz," VenezuelAnalysis, June 28, 2016, https://venezuelanalysis.com/analysis/12056; Lucas Koerner, "Murderer of Sabino Romero Given Maximum Sentence in Historic Ruling," VenezuelAnalysis, August 17, 2015, https://venezuelanalysis.com/news/11476; "Campesinos Defending Chávez's Project: A Conversation with Andres Alayo, Cira Pascual Marquina," VenezuelAnalysis, August 31, 2019, https://venezuelanalysis.com/analysis/14638.
25. "Lucia Martinez viuda del cacique Sabino Romero exige enjuiciar a los autores intelectuales del asesinato del lider yukpa," G. Martinez, *Aporrea*, March 3, 2020, https://www.aporrea.org/ddhh/n352867.html.
26. Remarks from Ignacio Ramirez come from taped conversation with Ramirez on August 18, 2019.
27. Joe Emersberger, "Reassessing the Leopoldo López trial of 2014–15," *Znet*, December 20, 2020, https://zcomm.org/zblogs/reassessing-the-leopoldo-lopez-trial-of-2014-15/.
28. "In Detail: The Deaths So Far," VenezuelAnalysis, July 11, 2017, https://venezuelanalysis.com/analysis/13081.
29. Graphics reprinted with permission from VenezuelAnalysis.com.
30. "Man set on fire during protest in Venezuela's capital," Thomson

Reuters, May 21, 2017, https://www.cbc.ca/news/world/venezuela-nicolas-maduro-demonstration-man-on-fire-1.4126317.
31. Alexandra Ulmer, Deisy Buitrago, "Venezuela eyes assembly vote in July; man set ablaze dies," Reuters, June 4, 2017, https://www.reuters.com/article/us-venezuela-politics-vote/venezuela-eyes-assembly-vote-in-july-man-set-ablaze-dies-idUSKBN18V0XL.
32. "Man set on fire during Venezuela protests," Reuters, May 22, 2017, https://www.reuters.com/article/us-venezuela-politics-image/man-set-on-fire-during-venezuela-protests-idUSKBN18I2HF.
33. Alexandra Ulmer and Deisy Buitrago, "Venezuela eyes assembly vote in July; man set ablaze dies," Reuters, June 4, 2017, https://www.reuters.com/article/us-venezuela-politics-vote/venezuela-eyes-assembly-vote-in-july-man-set-ablaze-dies-idUSKBN18V0XL.
34. Youtube, https://youtu.be/EaUfU4vm86Y.
35. Alexandra Ulmer and Deisy Buitrago, "Venezuela eyes assembly vote in July; man set ablaze dies," Reuters, June 4, 2017, https://www.reuters.com/article/us-venezuela-politics-vote/venezuela-eyes-assembly-vote-in-july-man-set-ablaze-dies-idUSKBN18V0XL.
36. Alan MacLeod, *Bad News from Venezuela*, 129, explains that while foreign journalists are often criticized for not leaving certain big cities like London, England, in Venezuela it is one municipality of Caracas, Chacao, that journalists seldom leave.
37. Video of interview supplied on Twitter account of Ernesto Villegas, Venezuela's Minister of Popular Power, May 22, 2017, https://twitter.com/VillegasPoljak/status/866810546259185664. See also "Noticias > Latinoamérica y el Caribe 'Tiene que morir por ser chavista,' le decían opositores a joven quemado vivo," Telesur, May 22, 2017, https://www.telesurtv.net/news/Tiene-que-morir-por-ser-chavista-le-decian-opositores-a-joven-quemado-vivo-20170522-0055.html.
38. Jon Lee Anderson, "Nicolas Maduro's Accelerating Revolution," *The New Yorker*, December 11, 2017, https://www.newyorker.com/magazine/2017/12/11/nicolas-maduros-accelerating-revolution.
39. Even an OHCHR report (see page 12) that was heavily biased in favor of the opposition concluded that 42 victims were security forces, bystanders killed in accidents caused by the opposition barricades, people killed directly by opposition protesters, or people killed in lootings not directly related to the protests. See https://www.ohchr.org/Documents/Countries/VE/HCReportVenezuela_1April-31July2017_EN.pdf.
40. When the death toll can't justify that kind of position in support for a U.S. ally then other metrics are used—like the number of "rockets" fired.
41. See Norman Finkelstein, *Gaza: An inquest into its martyrdom* (University of California Press, 2018).

42. OHCHR op cit.
43. Stephanie Nebehay, "Venezuela releasing judge, journalist, 20 students—U.N.," July 5, 2019, https://www.reuters.com/article/us-venezuela-un-prisoners/venezuela-frees-judge-journalist-20-students-u-n-idUSKCN1U016V.
44. "Detenido en España Enzo Franchini Oliveros: Indiciado de quemar vivo a Orlando Figuera en el 2017," *Correo del Orinoco*, July 10, 2019, http://www.correodelorinoco.gob.ve/detenido-espana-enzo-franchini-oliveros-indiciado-de-quemar-vivo-a-orlando-figuera-en-el-2017/.
45. "Identificado presunto responsable de asesinato de Orlando Figuera," *Correo del Orinoco*, June 20, 2017, http://www.correodelorinoco.gob.ve/identificado-presunto-responsable-de-asesinato-de-orlando-figuera/; Esther S. Sieteiglesias, "Primer día de libertad para Enzo Franchini," *La Razon*, November 5, 2019, https://www.larazon.es/internacional/20191106/kzp3rirduzae3cjnn7fdx73dl4.html.
46. "¿Quién protege a asesino identificado de Orlando Figuera?," *La Tabla*, March 20, 2019, http://la-tabla.blogspot.com/2019/03/quien-protege-asesino-identificado-de.html.
47. "Empire Files: Abby Martin Meets the Venezuelan Opposition," July 3, 2017, https://youtu.be/ig6yFP8HjVQ.
48. Twitter https://twitter.com/PanAmPost_es/status/870060011099181062.
49. Twitter https://twitter.com/rosendo_joe/status/913490320960163840.
50. Juan Nagel, "Leopoldo Unleashed: Juan Nagel interviews Lopez for Caracas Chronicles," *Caracas Chronicles*, December 18, 2013, http://web.archive.org/web/20150805140337/http://caracaschronicles.com/2013/12/18/leopoldo-unleashed/.
51. Lucas Koerner, "Venezuelan Opposition Announces Plan to Oust Maduro, Faces Constitutional Roadblocks," VenezuelAnalysis, March 9, 2016, https://venezuelanalysis.com/news/11880.
52. ANC stands for Asamblea Nacional Constuyente.
53. Nicholas Casey, "As Venezuela Prepares to Vote, Some Fear an End to Democracy," *The New York Times*, July 29, 2017, https://www.nytimes.com/2017/07/29/world/americas/venezuela-nicolas-maduro-constituent-assembly.html.
54. The Venezuela Solidarity Campaign, "Q & A: The National Constituent Assembly in Venezuela," VenezuelAnalysis, July 24, 2017, https://venezuelanalysis.com/analysis/13260.
55. Similarly, William Finnegan, referring to Hugo Chávez in the *New Yorker* article we discussed above, claimed, "He soon rewrote the constitution, concentrating power in the executive."
56. Elizabeth Melimopoulos, "Venezuela: What is a National Constituent Assembly?," Al Jazeera, July 31, 2017, https://www.aljazeera.

com/indepth/features/2017/07/venezuela-maduro-constituent-assembly-170729172525718.html.
57. Venezuela this Week, May 30–June 4, 2017: Bond Wars, Tornio Capital (Francisco Rodriguez).
58. "¡PIRÓMANOS! La MUD incendió todas las actas del plebiscito ilegal," *Lechiguinos*, July 17, 2017, http://www.lechuguinos.com/mud-incendio-actas-plebiscito/.
59. Corina Pons and Brian Ellsworth, "Venezuela opposition says 7 million vote in anti-Maduro poll," Reuters, July 16, 2017, https://www.reuters.com/article/us-venezuela-politics/venezuela-opposition-says-7-million-vote-in-anti-maduro-poll-idUSKBN1A104O.
60. Opposition supporters appear to have done more to intimidate voters on July 31 (day of the ANC elections) than government supporters did during the July 16 referendum. See Ryan Mallett-Outtrim, "Venezuelans to Re-Vote for ANC in Violence-Stricken Areas," VenezuelAnalysis, August 4, 2017, https://venezuelanalysis.com/news/13285.
61. "'Not unrealistic' for Catalan leader to get asylum in Belgium: minister," Reuters, October 29, 2017, https://www.reuters.com/article/us-spain-politics-catalonia-belgium/not-unrealistic-for-catalan-leader-to-get-asylum-in-belgium-minister-idUSKBN1CY07I.
62. Patrick Johnson, "Carles Puigdemont: The man who wants to break up Spain," BBC, March 26, 2018, http://www.bbc.com/news/world-europe-41508660.
63. Robin Emmott, "EU to impose arms embargo on Venezuela, lays basis for sanctions: diplomats," Reuters, November 8, 2017, https://www.reuters.com/article/us-venezuela-politics-eu/eu-to-impose-arms-embargo-on-venezuela-lays-basis-for-sanctions-diplomats-idUSKBN1D82CD.
64. Vasco Cotovio, Isa Soares, and Hilary Clarke, "Hundreds injured as Spain cracks down on Catalan referendum," CNN, October 1, 2017, https://www.cnn.com/2017/10/01/europe/catalonia-spain-independence-referendum-vote/index.html.
65. "This Revolution will NOT be Televised," *Honduras Coup 2009*, June 29, 2009, http://hondurascoup2009.blogspot.com/2009/06/this-revolution-will-not-be-televised.html.
66. Karen Attiah, "Hillary Clinton's dodgy answers on Honduras coup," *The Washington Post*, April 19, 2016, https://www.washingtonpost.com/blogs/post-partisan/wp/2016/04/19/hillary-clintons-dodgy-answers-on-honduras-coup/.
67. See chapter 5.
68. Unlike Venezuela's constitution, article 444 of Ecuador's constitution very clearly specifies that an initial referendum is required before

a constituent assembly is elected and that the referendum must outline the rules for the elections. See http://pdba.georgetown.edu/Constitutions/Ecuador/english08.html.

69. Joe Emersberger, "Western Media Hail Ecuador's Cynical President Moreno," FAIR, February 4, 2018, https://fair.org/home/western-media-hail-ecuadors-cynical-president-moreno; Moreno gave the National Assembly 20 days to choose seven standing and seven alternates from a shortlist of 21 names he provided them. Any not chosen from that list within 20 days would be automatically filled from Moreno's shortlist in the order they were listed; see "Lenín Moreno presentó los 21 nombres de las ternas para el Cpccs transitorio," El Comercio, February 19, 2018, https://www.elcomercio.com/actualidad/presidente-leninmoreno-ternas-cpccs-consulta.html. See also Joe Emersberger, "Ecuadorian President Lenin Moreno's Assault on Human Rights and Judicial Independence: Emersberger interviews Oswaldo Ruiz," *Counterpunch*, October 12, 2018, https://www.counterpunch.org/2018/10/12/ecuadorian-president-lenin-morenos-assault-on-human-rights-and-judicial-independence/.

70. Joe Emersberger, "Deconstructing a *Washington Post* Editorial on Ecuador," *Counterpunch*, February 9, 2018, https://www.counterpunch.org/2018/02/09/deconstructing-a-washington-post-editorial-on-ecuador/.

71. On twitter, Vivanco posted a picture of himself proudly embracing the head of Moreno's CPCCS-T, https://twitter.com/JMVivancoHRW/status/1001147649716834304.

72. The regional election results also weaken the claim that the turnout figure for the ANC elections that the opposition boycotted must have been inflated by Venezuela's CNE. See also the rebuttal of this claim that Ricardo Vaz wrote before the regional elections took place: Ricardo Vaz, "Venezuela in the Media: Double Standards and First Impressions," *Counterpunch*, September 4, 2017, https://www.counterpunch.org/2017/09/04/venezuela-in-the-media-double-standards-and-first-impressions/.

73. Andres Oppenehimer, "U.S. should mull sanctions against some Venezuelan opposition leaders—they deserve it," *Miami Herald*, October 25, 2017, https://www.miamiherald.com/news/local/news-columns-blogs/andres-oppenheimer/article180836336.html.

11. Read Carroll and You've Read Them All

1. See https://twitter.com/pablonav1/status/1088724996782993408.
2. Throughout this chapter, we refer to the paperback edition published in the United States in 2013 by The Penguin Press, New York.

3. MacLeod, 109.
4. MacLeod, 46. Chávez died on March 5, 2013. MacLeod looks at articles from March 1 to May 1.
5. MacLeod, 51.
6. MSNBC's Rachael Maddow makes $7 million per year, modest compared to top CEO salaries in the United States that were $50–100 million per year in 2018. But even those ridiculous salaries are dwarfed by the billions of dollars per year that have been made by people such as Warren Buffett, Bill Gates, Jeff Bezos, and Mark Zuckerberg. See, e.g., Kamila Rivero, "How Much Is Rachel Maddow Worth, and What Is Her Salary?," Cheatsheet.com, January 9, 2019, https://www.cheatsheet.com/entertainment/how-much-is-rachel-maddow-worth-and-what-is-her-salary.html/; Heather Landy, "The 10 highest-paid CEOs at US public companies," QZ.com, October 12, 2018, https://qz.com/work/1422134/the-10-highest-paid-ceos-at-us-public-companies/; Julia La Roche, "Here's How Much 10 of the Richest People in the World Made Per Minute in 2013," *Business Insider*, December 19, 2013, https://www.businessinsider.com/what-warren-buffett-makes-per-hour-2013-12.
7. TED: The Economics Daily: 37 percent of May 2016 employment in occupations typically requiring postsecondary education, US Bureau of Labor Statistics, June 28, 2017, https://www.bls.gov/opub/ted/2017/37-percent-of-may-2016-employment-in-occupations-typically-requiring-postsecondary-education.htm.
8. Thomas Frank, in a *Harper's* essay on the state of U.S. journalism wrote, "Here in the capital city, every pundit and every would-be pundit identifies upward, always upward. We cling to our credentials and our professional-class fantasies, hobnobbing with senators and governors, trading witticisms with friendly Cabinet officials, helping ourselves to the champagne and lobster. Everyone wants to know our opinion, we like to believe, or to celebrate our birthday, or to find out where we went for cocktails after work last night." See Thomas Frank, "Swat Team," *Harper's Magazine*, November 2016, https://harpers.org/archive/2016/11/swat-team-2/7/.
9. This highlights a serious problem with the "We are the ninety-nine percent" slogan introduced by Occupy Wall Street. Dean Baker, in his book *Rigged* (CEPR, 2016), and Thomas Frank, in his book *Listen Liberal* (Picador, 2017), have done excellent work addressing the problem of professional class bias among U.S. "progressives."
10. "'Comandante' Chávez Still Revered by Some, Despite Failings," NPR, April 10, 2013, http://www.npr.org/2013/04/10/176706001/comandante-hugo-chavez-still-revered-despite-his-failings.

11. This is from a direct search on the *Guardian* website. The period is from October 2006 until the end of 2012.
12. Charts showing Gini coefficient, poverty, and inflation taken from Jake Johnston and Sara Kozameh, "Venezuelan Economic and Social Performance Under Hugo Chávez, in Graphs," CEPR, March 7, 2013, https://cepr.net/venezuelan-economic-and-social-performance-under-hugo-chavez-in-graphs/; table showing UN Human Development Index ranking taken from Joe Emersberger, "A note about Venezuela's 'humanitarian crisis,'" *Znet*, March 30, 2017, https://zcomm.org/zblogs/a-note-about-venezuelas-humanitarian-crisis/.
13. IMF, World Outlook Database, April 2020; average of data from 1980 to 1998.
14. On page 94 of his book, Carroll said the oil strike caused "nationwide pain," "cost billions," "would destroy livelihoods," but never cited the readily available figures showing the big spike in poverty and extreme poverty that had taken place by 2003 as a result of the two major efforts to overthrow Chávez.
15. A particularly obnoxious example of this appeared in a *New Yorker* piece by Jon Lee Anderson, who wrote, "They gave him power in one election after another: they are victims of their affection for a charismatic man, whom they allowed to become the central character on the Venezuelan stage, at the expense of everything else." See Joe Emersberger, "On Jon Lee Anderson's 'slumlord' article on Venezuela," *Z Blogs*, January 28, 2013, https://zcomm.org/zblogs/on-john-lee-andersons-slumlord-article-on-venezuela-by-joe-emersberger/.
16. Helen Carter, "England riots: pair jailed for four years for using Facebook to incite disorder," *The Guardian*, August 16, 2011, https://www.theguardian.com/uk/2011/aug/16/uk-riots-four-years-disorder-facebook.
17. See chapter 8 for details on the Carter Center data.
18. Carlos Martinez, Michael Fox, and Jojo Farrell, *Venezuela Speaks: Voices from the Grassroots* (PM Press, 2010).
19. Personal communication with Fox about the party in Carroll's apartment.
20. https://twitter.com/pablonav1/status/1088723949326921730.
21. MacLeod, 108.
22. Personal communication with Koerner.
23. Chapter 5 discusses some wretched reporting Alex Bellos did for the *Guardian* at the time of the April 2002 coup.
24. The book *Venezuela Speaks* dispels caricatures of grassroots Chávez supporters among the poor as blindly devoted to their leader or passive recipients of petrodollars. The activists cited in the book identify

Chávez as a key ally in the "Bolivarian Process"—a project aimed at a deep transformation of Venezuela beyond simply the elimination of poverty. Carlos Martinez, Michael Fox, and Jojo Farrell, *Venezuela Speaks: Voices from the Grassroots* (PM Press, 2010).
25. Matt Kwong, "Why U.S. military intervention in Venezuela is 'possible'—but improbable," CBC, May 3, 2019, https://www.cbc.ca/news/world/venezuela-uprising-military-intervention-1.5120858.
26. Rory Carroll, "Venezuela scrambles for food despite oil boom," *The Guardian*, November 14, 2007, https://www.theguardian.com/world/2007/nov/14/venezuela.international.
27. "How Americans get their news," American Press Institute, March 17, 2014, https://www.americanpressinstitute.org/publications/reports/survey-research/how-americans-get-news/.
28. See chapter 5.
29. Rory Carroll, "Chávez loses bid to rule until 2050," *The Guardian*, December 3, 2007, https://www.theguardian.com/world/2007/dec/03/venezuela.usa.
30. Conor Foley, "A good day for democracy," *The Guardian*, December 3, 2007, https://www.theguardian.com/commentisfree/2007/dec/03/agooddayfordemocracy.
31. "Conozca las caricaturas de Rayma denunciadas por su xenofobia e irrespeto a los símbolos patrios," Venezuela Ministry of Popular Power, September 17, 2014, https://albaciudad.org/2014/09/conozca-las-caricaturas-de-rayma-que-trascendieron-por-su-xenofobia-e-irrespeto-a-simbolos-patrios/.
32. Z. C. Dutka, "Fired Political Cartoonist Claims Censorship in Venezuela, Colleagues Weigh In," VenezuelAnalysis, October 1, 2014, https://venezuelanalysis.com/news/10938.
33. This one was cited in a 2004 academic article about racism in Venezuela: Luis Duno-Gottberg, "Mob outrages: Reflections on the media construction of the masses in Venezuela April 2000–January 2003," *Journal of Latin American Cultural Studies*, 2004, https://www.academia.edu/5472298/Mob_outrages_Reflections_on_the_media_construction_of_the_masses_in_Venezuela_April_2000January_2003.
34. "Conozca las caricaturas de Rayma denunciadas por su xenofobia e irrespeto a los símbolos patrios," Venezuela Ministry of Popular Power, September 17, 2014, https://albaciudad.org/2014/09/conozca-las-caricaturas-de-rayma-que-trascendieron-por-su-xenofobia-e-irrespeto-a-simbolos-patrios/.
35. Carroll, 61. Also on pages 71 and 94 he makes passing reference to opposition leaders referring to Chávez as "the monkey."
36. Carroll, 93.

37. Rory Carroll, "WikiLeaks cables: Oil giants squeeze Chávez as Venezuela struggles," *The Guardian*, December 9, 2010, https://www.theguardian.com/world/2010/dec/09/wikileaks-oil-giants-squeeze-chavez.
38. Wikileaks, "Venezuela: Italian Ambassador Briefs on Eni Oil Deals," https://wikileaks.org/plusd/cables/10CARACAS163_a.html. As of September 2010, the Center for Economic and Policy Research (CEPR) reported that Venezuela's debt-to-GDP ratio was a very low 18 percent—far lower than in most European countries. Venezuela's foreign public debt was only 10.8 percent of GDP. It also had foreign exchange reserves of $28 billion which at the time covered at least half a year's worth of imports (double what the IMF recommends). See Mark Weisbrot and Rebecca Ray, "Update on the Venezuelan Economy," CEPR, September 2010, http://www.cepr.net/documents/publications/venezuela-2010-09.pdf. On EU debt levels in 2010, see Buttonwood, "More debt rankings," *The Economist*, February 2, 2010, http://www.economist.com/blogs/buttonwood/2010/02/debt_deficits_and_growth.
39. Carroll says on page 217, "Thus the comandante and chief executives from Chevron, Eni and other corporations played out charades of grand announcements, signing ceremonies and ribbon cuttings for projects that shimmered like mirages."
40. Rory Carroll, "Noam Chomsky criticises old friend Hugo Chávez for 'assault' on democracy," *The Guardian*, July 3, 2011, https://www.theguardian.com/world/2011/jul/03/noam-chomsky-hugo-Chávez-democracy?INTCMP=SRCH.
41. Joe Emersberger, "Rory Carroll's selective interest in Chomsky's views," *Media Lens*, July 3, 2011, https://web.archive.org/web/20111205104512/https://www.medialens.org/forum/viewtopic.php?p=11270.
42. Joe Emersberger, "Chomsky Says UK Guardian Article 'Quite Deceptive' about his Chávez Criticism," VenezuelAnalysis, July 4, 2011, https://venezuelanalysis.com/analysis/6323.
43. "Noam Chomsky on Venezuela—the transcript," *The Guardian*, July 4, 2011, https://www.theguardian.com/world/2011/jul/04/noam-chomsky-venezuela?intcmp=239. The original headline is still shown in some online reprints of the article—for example on Commondreams.org and Rabble.ca. See https://www.commondreams.org/news/2011/07/03/noam-chomsky-denounces-old-friend-hugo-Chávez-assault-democracy and http://www.rabble.ca/babble/international-news-and-politics/noam-chomsky-denounces-hugo-Chávez-assault-democracy.
44. Carroll, 248–50. In the book, Carroll wrote that "He [Chomsky] was not

going to explicitly denounce his ardent friend"—apparently forgetting that the original headline his newspaper gave the piece about Chomsky was "Noam Chomsky denounces old friend Hugo Chávez for 'assault' on democracy."

45. Carroll, 18.
46. Carroll, 264.
47. Wikileaks, *The Wikileaks Files: The Word according to US Empire* (Verso, 2016), chapter 18, 515–545.
48. Carroll, 82, 83.
49. "A Review of U.S. Policy Toward Venezuela, November 2001–April 2002, Report Number 02-OIG-003," July 2002, United States Department of State and the Broadcasting Board of Governors Office of Inspector General, https://web.archive.org/web/20090204221116/http://www.oig.state.gov/documents/organization/13682.pdf.
50. Carroll, 275, 285–6, 291.
51. "Abuses in Venezuela," *The Guardian*, August 4, 2011, https://www.theguardian.com/world/2011/aug/04/abuses-in-venezuela-human-rights. *The Guardian* removed reference to Carroll from the version of the letter it published on the grounds that it is "collectively responsible" for its news articles. Carroll never mentioned that letter in his book. A few months after the letter was published, the *Guardian* ran a piece by Edward Ellis about the peasants: Edward Ellis, "Murder of the campesinos," *The Guardian*, October 2, 2011, https://www.theguardian.com/commentisfree/2011/oct/02/venezuela-land-rights-chavez-farmers.
52. For discussion, see Joe Emersberger, "Interview with Edward Ellis, Director of 'Tierras Libres,'" VenezuelAnalysis, August 2, 2011, https://venezuelanalysis.com/analysis/6438.
53. Carroll (100) uncritically cites an anonymous former intelligence officer alleging that "the Cubans took us over." It never seems to occur to Carroll that an anonymous backstabber saying that to a foreign journalist adds to the evidence that it was a wise move to use Cuban personnel. The point generalizes to the medical establishment. Carroll (173) was also critical of Chávez ending cooperation with the DEA over (very reasonable) suspicions of espionage. "U.S. agents good, Cubans bad" sums up Carroll's perspective.
54. Federico Fuentes, "Venezuela's Crisis: A View from the Communes," VenezuelAnalysis, May 10, 2019, https://venezuelanalysis.com/analysis/14478.
55. Carroll, 257.
56. Carroll, 253.
57. Carroll, 59, 60.

58. Greg Wilpert, *Changing Venezuela by Taking Power* (Verso, 2006), 20.
59. See Dean Baker, "Professional Protectionists," CEPR, September 9, 2003, http://cepr.net/documents/publications/protectionists.PDF. Similarly, a key battle in the struggle for universal public healthcare in Canada was won in 1961 when Tommy Douglas, the premier of Saskatchewan, used foreign doctors to defeat a doctors' strike. See "The Fight for Medicare," CBC, https://www.cbc.ca/history/EPISCONTENTSE1EP15CH2PA4LE.html.
60. Wilpert, 163.
61. Eirik Vold, *Hugo Chávez: The Bolivarian Revolution Up Close* (Lulu.com, 2016), 148.
62. "Barrio Adentro: Derecho a la salud e inclusión social en Venezuela," Organización Panamericana de la Salud, Caracas, Venezuela, July 2006, 23, 24, 127, https://www.paho.org/Spanish/DD/PUB/BA.pdf.
63. Wilpert, 134.
64. See chapter 5 for discussion of Human Rights Watch's criticism of the court packing law passed in 2004.
65. Carroll, 102.
66. Ligia Perdomo, "¿Médicos cubanos ejercen en Venezuela sin hacer reválida como lo establece la Ley?," Espaja, August 10, 2020, https://espaja.com/fact-checking/medicos-cubanos-ejercen-en-venezuela-sin-hacer-revalida-como-lo-establece-la-ley. In 2009, Natera met with the U.S. Embassy in Venezuela. See Wikileaks, "Venezuela's Medical System in Disarray as GBRV Shifts Resources to Barrio Adentro," 2009, https://www.wikileaks.org/plusd/cables/09CARACAS1541_a.html.
67. The names of the people who signed the Carmona Decree are listed in this documentary and Natera's appears at the 1:21:55 point; see https://www.youtube.com/watch?v=iQQUDhqMPTU.
68. Despite Bernie Sanders's grave deficiencies, which we've discussed, we are heartened that any U.S. politician is at least willing to state the obvious: that "billionaires should not exist." See https://twitter.com/BernieSanders/status/1176481898685710337.
69. Sympathetic analysts like Vold have conceded that point. See Vold, 316, 317, regarding problems of low academic standards at the "Bolivarian University."

12. The Human Rights Fraud

1. See chapter 5.
2. Ken Roth, "Peter Slezkine Round Table: The Two Paths That Converged in Human Rights Watch," *Humanity Journal*, January 4, 2015, http://humanityjournal.org/blog/the-two-paths-that-converged-in-human-rights-watch/.
3. John Ismay, "At Least 37 Million People Have Been Displaced by

America's War on Terror," *New York Times*, September 8, 2020, https://www.nytimes.com/2020/09/08/magazine/displaced-war-on-terror.html. Ken Roth tweeted out this finding on Twitter, apparently forgetting what he said in 2015 or, worse, seeing no contradiction. See https://twitter.com/KenRoth/status/1303548990349365248.

4. Those figures include targeted assassinations and massacres, not collateral damage in the context of battles with armed guerrillas such as the FARC. It's a conservative estimate because it's based on a report funded by the U.S. and other allies of the Colombian government. See "¡BASTA YA! Colombia: Memorias de guerra y dignidad," Grupo de Memoria Histórica, 2013, http://www.centrodememoriahistorica.gov.co/descargas/informes2013/bastaYa/basta-ya-colombia-memorias-de-guerra-y-dignidad-2016.pdf.

5. "Twin Threats: How the Politics of Fear and the Crushing of Civil Society Imperil Global Rights," HRW World Report 2016, https://www.hrw.org/world-report/2016/twin-threats.

6. "War in Iraq: Not a Humanitarian Intervention," HRW, January 25, 2004, https://www.hrw.org/news/2004/01/25/war-iraq-not-humanitarian-intervention.

7. MINUSTAH officially ended its mission in October of 2017 and was replaced by a much smaller UN force. See Jake Johnston, "The UN's Legacy in Haiti: Stability, but for Whom?," *Haiti Liberte*, August 11, 2017, https://haitiliberte.com/the-uns-legacy-in-haiti-stability-but-for-whom/.

8. Amanda Klasing, "Why Water Access Matters to Poverty Reduction," March 21, 2014, https://www.hrw.org/news/2014/03/21/why-water-access-matters-poverty-reduction.

9. Yves Engler, "Minustah's filthy record in Haiti," *The Guardian*, September 11, 2011, https://www.theguardian.com/commentisfree/cifamerica/2011/sep/11/haiti-unitednations-minustah-cholera.

10. Kim Ives, "New Internal Report Slams UN Cholera Cover-Up," *Haiti Analysis*, August 24, 2016, http://haitianalysis.blogspot.com/2016/09/as-appeals-court-upholds-immunity-plea.html.

11. Rick Gladstone, "Court Hears Suit Against U.N. on Haiti Cholera Outbreak," *New York Times*, March 1, 2016, http://www.nytimes.com/2016/03/02/world/americas/court-hears-suit-against-un-on-haiti-cholera-outbreak.html?ref=world&_r=1; Joe Emersberger, "A Great Month For Impunity In US Courts," TeleSUR English, September 19, 2016, https://www.telesurenglish.net/opinion/A-Great-Month-for-Impunity-in-US-Courts-20160919-0017.html.

12. Kim Ives, "THE UN'S INCOMPLETE APOLOGY TO HAITI," *Popular Resistance*, December 8, 2016, https://popularresistance.org/the-uns-incomplete-apology-to-haiti/.

NOTES TO PAGES 209–210

13. "Human Rights Organizations Call on UN Secretary General to Engage Victims as Partners in the New Approach Plan," IJDH, July 16, 2018, https://www.ijdh.org/2018/07/resources/human-rights-organizations-call-on-un-secretary-general-to-engage-victims-as-partners-in-the-new-approach-plan/.
14. Athena R. Kolbe, Royce A. Hutson, "Human rights abuse and other criminal violations in Port-au-Prince, Haiti: a random survey of households," *The Lancet*, 2006, DOI:10.1016/S0140-6736(06)69211-8. http://www.ijdh.org/wp-content/uploads/2006/08/Lancet-Article-8-06.pdf.
15. An academic study in 2019 showed that most graduate students asked to use the internet to research mortality in Venezuela and four countries plagued by war (Syria, Yemen, Central Republic and Mali) erroneously concluded that Venezuela had the highest mortality rate: Mary Grace Flaherty and Leslie F. Roberts, "Internet searching produces misleading findings regarding violent deaths in crisis settings: short report," February 19, 2019, https://conflictandhealth.biomedcentral.com/articles/10.1186/s13031-019-0187-z.
16. Francisco Toro wrote, "from the time of the 2003 Iraq invasion until this January, while 116,705 civilians were killed in Iraq, according to the Iraq Body Count project, 124,221 Venezuelans were murdered, says Mármol García." Iraq Body Counts (IBC) figures are low because they relied largely on media reports and only counted civilian deaths. The fact that U.S. troops had a violent death rate several times higher than Venezuelan police (next table in this chapter) also highlights how low IBC figures are: see Francisco Toro, "Counting by Murders," *New York Times*, June 7, 2012, https://latitude.blogs.nytimes.com/2012/06/07/venezuelas-murder-rate-unmatched-among-middle-income-countries/.
17. Venezuela data taken from World Bank: https://data.worldbank.org/indicator/vc.ihr.psrc.p5https://data.worldbank.org/indicator/SP.POP.TOTL?locations=VE; Haiti data from the Kolbe and Hudson (note 18); Iraq Data from *The Lancet* and *The New England Journal of Medicine* (Table 4); http://web.mit.edu/humancostiraq/reports/human-cost-war-101106.pdf; https://www.nejm.org/doi/full/10.1056/NEJMsa0707782#t=articleTop. The scientific surveys for Iraq were designed to determine the death rate for all of Iraq. The Anbar governorate may have had a violent death rate drastically higher than what was found for Iraq as a whole. Anbar has only about 5 percent of Iraq's population but that's where a third of coalition troops died according to the data on the icasualties website: http://icasualties.org/.
18. Jose Miguel Vivanco, "Letter to the U.N. Security Council on

the Renewal of the Mandate of the U.N. Stabilization Mission in Haiti (MINUSTAH)," HRW, May 16, 2005, https://www.hrw.org/news/2005/05/16/letter-un-security-council-renewal-mandate-un-stabilization-mission-haiti-minustah.
19. Plenty of examples from Twitter can be seen in this search: https://twitter.com/search?q=Maduro%20dictator%20(from%3Ajmvivancohrw)&src=typed_query.
20. "Keeping the peace in Haiti?," Harvard Law School Advocates for Human Rights, March, 2005, http://www.ijdh.org/wp-content/uploads/2011/02/harvard-haiti-mar05.pdf. Quotes are from the executive summary and the conclusions.
21. Secretly commissioned polls by USAID in 2002 showed that Aristide was by far Haiti's most popular politician. René Preval's electoral victory in 2006 would also have been impossible unless Aristide remained popular: Preval had a history of very close association with him.
22. Joe Emersberger, "Haiti and Human Rights Watch," *Znet*, March 29, 2006 https://zcomm.org/znetarticle/haiti-and-human-rights-watch-by-joe-emersberger/.
23. In *Paramilitarism and the Assault on Democracy in Haiti* (256–62), Jeb Sprague discussed how U.S. and UN officials oversaw the insertion of paramilitaries who had fought alongside Chamberlain into the Haitian police force after the 2004 coup.
24. Vivianco bio: https://www.pbs.org/now/politics/vivanco.html.
25. By contrast, in the case of Juan Guaidó, Elliot Abrams (as if he were handing down a legitimate court ruling in Venezuela) declared that Guaidó's term as "interim president" would not officially begin until Maduro was ousted.
26. See Peter Hallward, *Damming the flood: Haiti, Aristide and the politics of containment* (Verso, 2010). Hallward explains that Aristide's movement lost the support of a "cosmopolitan elite" by 2004 whose contacts with foreign NGOs had been useful after the 1991 coup; for details on U.S. troops in Haiti in 1994, see Paul Farmer, *The Uses of Haiti* (third edition, Common Courage Press, 2005), 318–347; "A letter from HRW asking US government to return documents seized from Haiti," https://web.archive.org/web/20081217011117/https://www.hrw.org/legacy/english/docs/1997/10/16/haiti1520.htm.
27. "Canadian peacekeeper shot by Haitian gunmen," CBC News, December 20, 2005, https://www.cbc.ca/news/world/canadian-peacekeeper-shot-by-haitian-gunmen-1.539414.
28. United Nations Peacekeeping, "Fatalities by Year, Mission and Incident Type," UN, https://web.archive.org/web/20191010152658/https://peacekeeping.un.org/sites/default/files/statsbyyearmissionincidentty

pe_5a_30.pdf. About 100 troops were killed by the devastating 2010 earthquake. The 2010 earthquake, illness, and accidents account for almost all MINUSTAH deaths.

29. The UN does not give data for MINUSTAH deaths in 2004 but the numbers provided by a December 20, 2005, CBC article we cited suggests there either were no MINUSTAH deaths in 2004 or that they were incorporated into the 2005 data. MINUSTAH was first deployed in Haiti in June of 2004. MINUSTAH had 7400 armed personnel in Haiti in 2004 and that number increased steadily to almost 12,000 in 2010 and 2011. The numbers then declined to about 5000 in 2015 and 2016.

30. Amnesty International finally mentioned the massacre, in passing, six months later. See Joe Emersberger, "Amnesty International's Track Record in Haiti since 2004," *Znet*, February 7, 2007; https://zcomm.org/znetarticle/amnesty-internationals-track-record-in-haiti-since-2004-by-joe-emersberger/.

31. Where a range is given it represents the maximum and minimum during the time period. Data for Haiti taken from Hallward (218), the November 2004 report by the Center for the Study of Human Rights at the Miami School of Law (50), and the March 2005 report by the Harvard Law School Student Advocates for Human Rights (10), *Haiti Libre*, "34 PNH officers killed in 9 months, an increase of more than 200%," October 15, 2019, https://www.haitilibre.com/article-29013-haiti-flash-34-policiers-tues-en-9-mois-une-hausse-de-plus-de-200.html. We extrapolated 28 police deaths in the first 10 months after Aristide was overthrown (reported by Miami School of Law) to 34 for full year and assume 4 MINUSTAH deaths in the year after Aristide was overthrown. Data for Venezuela for 2017 taken from the study "Monitor del uso de la fuerza letal en América Latina"—article contributed by anti-Maduro academic Keymer Ávila, 147, footnote 45 (total officer deaths), https://www.researchgate.net/publication/335472147_Monitor_del_uso_de_la_Fuerza_Letal_en_America_Latina_un_estudio_comparativo_de_Brasil_Colombia_El_Salvador_Mexico_y_Venezuela?enrichId=rgreq-1f9a68164a0c47e179bb6a9a4a509189-XXX&enrichSource=Y292ZXJQYWdlOzMzNTQ3MjE0NztBUzo3OTcyMzc1ODQwNzI3MTNAMTU2NzA4NzY2MDk3Mg-%3D%3D&el=1_x_3&_esc=publicationCoverPdf. Avila says most police are killed off duty (60 percent in 2017 and 65 percent in 2016) but that is when they'd be more likely to be targeted for reprisals. In the same report (148), he says official figures put the total number of police (national, state, and municipal) at 175,000, an estimate he considers conservative. See also Table 4 of his 2016 report for a 2016

figure for officer deaths: 264. https://www.revistamisionjuridica.com/como-muere-la-policia-en-venezuela/. The 2015 figure for officer deaths was taken from another anti-Maduro writer: Pedro Pablo Peñaloza, who claimed a rapidly increasing trend in police deaths from 2013 to 2015. See https://www.univision.com/noticias/crisis-en-venezuela/los-policias-victimas-de-la-violencia-en-venezuela. Data for Iraq was taken from a 2009 Congressional Research Service report by Amy Belasco, https://fas.org/sgp/crs/natsec/R40682.pdf and the Icasualties website. U.S. police numbers taken from a 2016 BBC article that provided extensive data. Violent "in line of duty" deaths of police averaged 49.6 per year from 2005 to 2015, according to the article. As a rate (divided by the number of police officers in that period) that works out to roughly 7 per 100,000. The U.S. homicide rate averaged 5 per 100,000 in that period, according to numbers on the World Bank website. "US police shootings: How many die each year?" BBC, July 18, 2016, https://www.bbc.com/news/magazine-36826297; https://data.worldbank.org/indicator/VC.IHR.PSRC.P5?end=2017&locations=US&start=2000.

32. As of 2018–19, Haitian police have a violent death rate comparable to Venezuela's police. But (as also shown in the table) its police are about four times *less* numerous per person than Venezuela's. One cannot therefore conclude that Haiti's police operate in as dangerous an environment as Venezuela's. That said, the high death rate for Haitian police does suggest that the homicide rate reported in recent years for Haiti (the UNODC reports a value of 9.6 per 100,000 for 2016) may be much too low.

33. "Haiti: Security Compromised: Recycled Haitian Soldiers on the Police Front Line," HRW, March 1, 1995, https://www.hrw.org/report/1995/03/01/haiti-security-compromised/recycled-haitian-soldiers-police-front-line; Sprague, *Paramilitarism and the Assault on Democracy in Haiti*, 256–62.

34. Hallward (25) provides context for Aristide speeches that in a few instances encouraged poor people to fight back against death squads. Aristide, absurdly, was criticized over these remarks.

35. "Haiti: Aristide Should Uphold Rule of Law," HRW, February 13, 2004, https://www.hrw.org/news/2004/02/13/haiti-aristide-should-uphold-rule-law. HRW's expressed contempt toward Aristide was also rationalized by the lie that the 2000 legislative elections were "marred by serious fraud." For a thorough debunking of that lie, see Peter Hallward, "Option Zero in Haiti," *New Left Review*, 2004, https://newleftreview.org/issues/II27/articles/peter-hallward-option-zero-in-haiti.

36. Amnesty International was similarly idiotic. On January 20, 2004 it demanded Aristide make "every effort" to "protect peaceful demonstrators and bystanders." He could not even protect himself. See https://www.amnesty.org.uk/press-releases/haiti-attacks-demonstrators-must-be-fully-investigated.
37. Hallward, *Damming the Flood*, 155.
38. See note 4.
39. In Haiti, anti-Aristide people referred to "gangs" as "chimere" and Amnesty International reflexively used that partisan and pejorative term in its reports. Regarding Venezuela, the Western media and NGOs have used "colectivo" in a similar derogatory way. It is actually a term Chavistas have used to describe organized groups—not only those who are armed. Imagine the outrage if any NGO or newspaper used the term "escualidos" as if it were a neutral term for opposition supporters. It's a derogatory term used by Chavistas to describe them.
40. "Venezuela: Extrajudicial Killings in Poor Areas: Pattern of Serious Police Abuse Goes Unpunished," HRW, September 18, 2019, https://www.hrw.org/news/2019/09/18/venezuela-extrajudicial-killings-poor-areas.
41. Colin Brineman of CEPR observed that even the OHCHR "does not allege that many of these security-related killings were political in nature." See "A Tale of Two Policies: Trump's Hypocrisy and State Violence in Venezuela and Brazil," CEPR, August 27, 2019, https://cepr.net/a-tale-of-two-policies-trump-s-hypocrisy-and-state-violence-in-venezuela-and-brazil/.
42. See page 17 of this section of the 2019 UNODC report: https://www.unodc.org/documents/data-and-analysis/gsh/Booklet2.pdf. It was 81 per 100,000 in 2017 according to an anti-Maduro NGO. That figure was cited by *The Washington Post*: Mary Beth Sheridan, Mariana Zuniga, and Rachelle Krygier, "How bad is Venezuela's economy? Even the criminals are struggling to get by," *The Washington Post*, March 8, 2019, https://www.washingtonpost.com/world/how-bad-is-venezuelas-economy-even-the-criminals-are-struggling-to-get-by/2019/03/07/1ccb653e-3c75-11e9-b10b-f05a22e75865_story.html. But even some opposition writers have disputed that NGO's approach and argued that it overestimates the rate: see Dorothy Kronick, "How to Count Our Dead," *Caracas Chronicles*, July 1, 2016, https://www.caracaschronicles.com/2016/07/01/our-dead/.
43. We are using Keymer Avila's estimate that only 40 percent of Venezuelan police die on duty nationwide to adjust the figures in the table and compare to the U.S. police deaths which are "in line of duty." However, it would not be easy to know how often the murder of "off duty" police in Venezuela was directly related to their work.

44. Andrés Antillano and Héctor Bujanda, "Andrés Antillano: Economic Recession and Increased Repression Are the Spark for Social Explosions," *Contrapunto*, August 27, 2015, https://venezuelanalysis.com/analysis/11489.
45. Frances Jenner, "When 'mano dura' policing is not the only option," *Latin America Reports*, March 20, 2019: https://latinamericareports.com/when-mano-dura-policing-is-not-the-only-option/1450/. The article cites a UN poll showing 87 percent support for harsh measures against crime.
46. Daisy Galaviz, "The Hypothesis of the Decline of Crime," *Caracas Chronicles*, September 11, 2019, https://www.caracaschronicles.com/2019/09/11/the-hypothesis-of-the-decline-of-crime/; Dorothy Kronick, "How to Count Our Dead," *Caracas Chronicles*, July 1, 2016, https://www.caracaschronicles.com/2016/07/01/our-dead/.
47. Chris Kraul, "In Venezuela, killings of Caracas police are on rise," *Los Angeles Times*, September 4, 2012, https://www.latimes.com/world/la-xpm-2012-sep-04-la-fg-venezuela-cops-20120904-story.html.
48. Brian Nelson, *The Silence and the Scorpion* (Nation Books, 2012), 205.
49. In Ecuador, under left-wing President Rafael Correa, changes made to the legal system coincided with a steep reduction in the homicide rate. Those changes were assailed by HRW as an assault on judicial independence. HRW then applauded President Lenín Moreno's blatant assault on judicial independence (see chapter 10): "Ecuador Achieves Lowest Homicide Rate in 15 years," Telesur, January 10, 2016, https://www.telesurenglish.net/news/Ecuador-Achieves-Lowest-Homicide-Rate-in-15-Years-20160110-0011.html.
50. It also made a passing reference to North Korea and Burma but said more about Chávez's relations with Iran, Libya, Syria, and Cuba.
51. Simon Romero, "Leaders of Venezuela and Colombia, Ideological Opposites, Are Tightening Ties," *The New York Times*, October 19, 2007, https://www.nytimes.com/2007/10/19/world/americas/19latin.html.
52. Leonel Rosas Vera, "Venezuelan Foreign Minister: Uribe's intended lawsuit against Chávez in the ICC 'laughable,'" VenezuelAnalysis, March 5, 2008, https://venezuelanalysis.com/newsbrief/3237.
53. Johnny Crisp, "Santos attends funeral of Hugo Chávez," *Colombia Reports*, March 8, 2013, https://colombiareports.com/santos-attends-funeral-of-hugo-chavez/.
54. "Haiti—Diplomacy: The President Martelly welcomes the return of Hugo Chávez," *Haiti Libre*, February 20, 2013, https://www.haitilibre.com/en/news-7916-haiti-diplomacy-the-president-martelly-welcomes-the-return-of-hugo-chavez.html; "OAS Overturned Haitian Presidential Election in a 'Political Intervention,' New CEPR Paper Suggests," CEPR, October 17, 2011, https://cepr.net/press-

release/oas-overturned-haitian-presidential-election-in-a-qpolitical-interventionq-new-cepr-paper-suggests/.
55. Cuba deserves credit for that as well. A phone call from Castro to Chávez during the military coup in April may have prevented Chávez from losing all hope (see Bart Jones, 333).
56. Joe Emersberger, "Don't forget that Human Rights Watch, not only OAS Chief Luis Almagro, helped a US-backed military coup in Bolivia," *Znet*, June 22, 2020, https://zcomm.org/zblogs/dont-forget-that-human-rights-watch-not-only-oas-chief-luis-almagro-helped-a-us-backed-military-coup-in-bolivia/.
57. Ken Roth tweet: https://twitter.com/KenRoth/status/1033720158953656320; Vivanco tweet: https://twitter.com/JMVivancoHRW/status/1033520562084167681; Emersberger highlighted PoKempner's retweet: https://twitter.com/sarahmargon/status/1033514993860452353, https://twitter.com/rosendo_joe/status/1033777167262474245. Amnesty International's Erika Guevara-Rosa also used her Twitter account to spread praise for John McCain: https://twitter.com/rosendo_joe/status/1033787687231209481.
58. C.W. Nevius, et al., "McCain Criticized for Slur / He says he'll keep using term for ex-captors in Vietnam," February 18, 2000, https://www.sfgate.com/politics/article/McCain-Criticized-for-Slur-He-says-he-ll-keep-3304741.php. John Tirman, Executive Director, MIT Center for International Studies, noted in 2015 that Robert McNamara (the U.S. Secretary of Defense, 1961–8) estimated 2,358,000 dead while scholarly studies have estimated as many as 3.8 million: see https://www.huffpost.com/entry/the-real-cost-of-vietnam_b_7159976?1430224433=.
59. Bart Jansen, "'Risk-taker, daredevil': John McCain joked about his Navy flight record. He crashed three times," *USA Today*, August 28, 2018, https://www.usatoday.com/story/news/politics/2018/08/28/john-mccain-risky-history-navy-pilot/1119237002/.
60. Bob Dreyfuss, "John McCain's Vietnam," *The Nation*, December 15, 1999, https://www.thenation.com/article/mccains-vietnam/.
61. "John McCain: In Memoriam," HRW, August 26, 2018, https://www.hrw.org/news/2018/08/26/john-mccain-memoriam.
62. Steven V. Roberts, "Foreign Policy: Lot of Table Thumping Going On," *New York Times*, May 29, 1985, https://www.nytimes.com/1985/05/29/us/foreign-policy-lot-of-table-thumping-going-on.html; Joe Emersberger, "Distorting Past and Present: Reuters on Nicaragua's Armed Uprising," FAIR, August 23, 2018, https://fair.org/home/distorting-past-and-present-reuters-on-nicaraguas-armed-uprising/.
63. Youtube video: John McCain jokes about bombing Iran, https://www.youtube.com/watch?v=6UlIufDAvGA.

64. Rachael Boothroyd, "U.S. Expels Venezuelan Consul as 'Persona Non Grata,'" VenezuelAnalysis, January 10, 2012, https://venezuelanalysis.com/news/6737.
65. Max Blumenthal, "The Other Side of John McCain," Consortium News, August 27, 2018, https://consortiumnews.com/2018/08/27/the-other-side-of-john-mccain/.
66. Robert D. McFadden, "John McCain, War Hero, Senator, Presidential Contender, Dies at 81," *New York Times*, August 25, 2018, https://www.nytimes.com/2018/08/25/obituaries/john-mccain-dead.html.
67. Andrew Cohen, "John McCain's Spotty Record on Torture," *The Atlantic*, May 13, 2011, https://www.theatlantic.com/politics/archive/2011/05/john-mccains-spotty-record-on-torture/238842/; McCain also supported the death penalty but objected to botched executions: Burgess Everett, "McCain: Arizona execution 'torture,'" July 24, 2014, https://www.politico.com/story/2014/07/john-mccain-arizona-execution-109350.
68. "Saudi Arabia: King's Reform Agenda Unfulfilled," HRW, January 23, 2015, https://www.hrw.org/news/2015/01/23/saudi-arabia-kings-reform-agenda-unfulfilled.
69. See also Llana Novick, "Human Rights Watch's Ties to Saudi Billionaire Revealed," *Truthdig*, March 3, 2020, https://www.truthdig.com/articles/human-rights-watch-ties-to-saudi-billionaire-revealed/.
70. "Saudi man executed for 'witchcraft and sorcery,'" BBC, Jun 19, 2012, https://www.bbc.com/news/world-middle-east-18503550.
71. Joe Emersberger, "The Kings of Fake News: Over 60 years of the *New York Times* hyping 'reform' in Saudi Arabia," *Znet*, November 25, 2017, https://zcomm.org/zblogs/the-kings-of-fake-news-70-years-of-the-new-york-times-hyping-reform-in-saudi-arabia/.
72. Adam Johnson, "David Ignatius' 15 Years of Running Spin for Saudi Regime," FAIR, April 28, 2017, https://fair.org/home/david-ignatius-15-years-of-running-spin-for-saudi-regime/.
73. Christine Mai-Duc, "Saudi King Abdullah's legacy praised by U.S. leaders," *Los Angeles Times*, January 22, 2015, www.latimes.com/world/middleeast/la-fg-king-abdullah-death-reactions-20150122-story.html.
74. Yara Bayoumy, "Obama administration arms sales offers to Saudi top $115 billion: report," Reuters, September 7, 2016, https://www.reuters.com/article/us-usa-saudi-security/obama-administration-arms-sales-offers-to-saudi-top-115-billion-report-idUSKCN11D2JQ.
75. Mersiha Gadzo, "Canadians seek cancellation of major arms deal with Saudi Arabia," Al Jazeera, August 9, 2019, https://www.aljazeera.com/news/2019/08/canadians-seek-cancellation-major-arms-deal-saudi-arabia-190809191316431.html; Julian Borger, "US leads arms sales to Saudis, followed by UK, from 2014–2018," *The Guardian*, October

3, 2019, https://www.theguardian.com/world/2019/oct/03/us-leads-arms-sales-to-saudis-followed-by-uk-from-2014-2018.
76. Jim Rutenberg, "Reality Breaks Up a Saudi Prince Charming's Media Narrative," *New York Times*, October 14, 2018, https://www.nytimes.com/2018/10/14/business/media/reality-saudi-prince-media-narrative.html.
77. Marianne Levine, "Senate fails to override Trump's veto on Yemen," *Politico*, May 2, 2019, https://www.politico.com/story/2019/05/02/senate-trump-yemen-1298350.
78. "Saudi Arabia: Change Comes with Punishing Cost," HRW, November 4, 2019, https://www.hrw.org/news/2019/11/04/saudi-arabia-change-comes-punishing-cost.

13. Colombia's U.S.-Approved Horror Show Could Come to Venezuela

1. "Encuesta Nacional de condiciones de vida 2019-2020," ENCOVI, https://assets.website-files.com/5d14c6a5c4ad42a4e794d0f7/5f03 85bcac6fc144c367a679_Presentaci%C3%B3n%20ENCOVI%20 2019-Emigraci%C3%B3n_compressed.pdf.
2. Worth noting that as the U.S. and allies pile on pressure, the United Nations technical departments are not above playing politics with statistics. See https://zcomm.org/zblogs/the-un-is-not-above-playing-politics-with-its-mortality-statistics/.
3. The Colombian Civil War is usually considered to have begun in 1964 with the formation of the FARC, but conflict has been continuous in Colombia since the 1948 assassination of presidential candidate Jorge Eliecer Gaitan. On the death toll, see: "Colombian conflict has killed 220,000 in 55 years, commission finds," Associated Press, July 15, 2013, https://www.theguardian.com/world/2013/jul/25/colombia-conflict-death-toll-commission.
4. "UNHCR Mid-year trends 2016"; https://web.archive.org/web/20170316162515/http://www.unhcr.org/en-us/statistics/unhcrstats/58aa8f247/mid-year-trends-june-2016.html.
5. Joe Emersberger, "Media Rubbish about Venezuelans who have left to live abroad," Telesur, English, September 2, 2015, https://www.telesurenglish.net/opinion/Media-Rubbish-about-Venezuelans-Who-Have-Left-to-Live-Abroad-20150902-0008.html.
6. *New York Times* Editorial Board, "Venezuela's Crackdown on Opposition," *New York Times*, September 20, 2014, https://www.nytimes.com/2014/09/21/opinion/sunday/venezuelas-crackdown-on-opposition.html.
7. The story is told in Anthony Sampson, *The Seven Sisters: The great oil companies and the world they shaped* (Viking, 1975).

8. Hector Mondragon, "Plan Colombia: Gasolina al Fuego," *Nadir*, January 2001, https://www.nadir.org/nadir/initiativ/agp/free/colombia/mondrag2.htm.
9. "Ordenan detener a militares venezolanos por atentados," Reuters, November 19, 2003, https://www.prensa.com/impresa/mundo/Ordenan-detener-militares-venezolanos-atentados_0_1063393689.html.
10. As the face of the prosecution of the leaders of the April 2002 coup, Danilo Anderson was something of a "star" himself. Those eventually convicted in the assassination were among the participants in the 2002 coup. Toni Solo, "Danilo Anderson's Murder," *Znet*, November 29, 2004, https://venezuelanalysis.com/analysis/812; Greg Wilpert, "Venezuelan Legislator Says Anderson Murder Suspect Tried to Bribe Judge," VenezuelAnalysis, November 21, 2005, https://venezuelanalysis.com/news/1479.
11. "Venezuela: condenan a militar por ataques a embajadas," Associated Press, April 30, 2008, https://oklahoman.com/article/3236974/venezuela-condenan-a-militar-por-ataques-a-embajadas.
12. "Ex-General Sentenced for 2003 Embassy Bombings in Venezuela," Associated Press, April 30, 2008, https://www.theledger.com/article/LK/20080430/News/608091480/LL.
13. Rodriguez was also accused of hiring hit men to kill five people in February 2003, four of whom died, one of whom survived. According to the pro-Chávez site apporrea.org, the victims were soldiers who had participated in the April 2002 coup against Chávez and whom Rodriguez sought to silence before they co-operated with authorities. See Ciudad Caracas, "La sombra de los soldados persigue a 'El Cuervo,'" November 3, 2011, aporrea.org, https://www.aporrea.org/actualidad/n176628.html.
14. Justin Podur, "What is the Colombian Army doing attacking Venezuela?," *Znet*, April 3, 2003, https://podur.org/2003/04/03/what-is-the-colombian-army-doing-attacking-venezuela/.
15. Justin Podur, "Terrorist Plot Foiled!," *Znet*, May 10, 2004, https://venezuelanalysis.com/analysis/501.
16. Vheadline.com, quoted in Justin Podur, "Terrorist Plot Foiled!," *Znet*, May 10, 2004, https://venezuelanalysis.com/analysis/501.
17. The quote in this and the previous two paragraphs are from Justin Podur, "Terrorist Plot Foiled!"
18. Justin Podur, "Colombia's New Border Brigade and the Venezuelan Referendum," *Znet*, June 20, 2004, https://venezuelanalysis.com/analysis/553.
19. Justin Podur, "Colombia's war and Venezuela's foreign policy," *Znet*, January 29, 2008, https://podur.org/2008/01/24/colombias-war-and-venezuelas-foreign-policy/.

20. Justin Podur, "Colombia assassinates Raul Reyes of FARC," *Znet*, March 2, 2008, https://venezuelanalysis.com/analysis/3219.
21. "Venezuelan Military Deserters Abandoned by Colombian Government," Telesur English, March 16, 2019, https://www.telesurenglish.net/news/Venezuelan-Military-Deserters-Abandoned-by-Colombian-Government-20190316-0020.html.
22. Alan Macleod, "Pro-Coup Venezuelan Soldiers Now Locked Up in ICE Detention Center," *Mint Press News*, December 27, 2019, https://www.mintpressnews.com/pro-coup-venezuelan-soldiers-defected-to-us-locked-ice-prisons/263764/.
23. "Colombian conflict has killed 220,000 in 55 years, commission finds," Associated Press, July 15, 2013, https://www.theguardian.com/world/2013/jul/25/colombia-conflict-death-toll-commission.
24. "Parapolitics," *Colombia Reports*, May 22, 2019, https://colombiareports.com/parapolitics/.
25. Embassy Bogotá, "2009–2010 International Narcotics Control Strategy Report (INCSR) Part 1," Wikileaks Cable: 09BOGOTA3670_a, dated November 19, 2009, https://wikileaks.org/plusd/cables/09BOGOTA3670_a.html.
26. Embassy Bogotá, "Violence Against Indigenous Shows Upward Trend," Wikileaks Cable: 10BOGOTA349_a, dated February 26, 2010, https://wikileaks.org/plusd/cables/10BOGOTA349_a.html.
27. "Informe del Relator Especial sobre la situacion de los defensores de los derechos humanos," Naciones Unidas, Consejo de Derechos Humanos, December 26, 2019, https://www.colectivodeabogados.org/IMG/pdf/informe_michael_forst.pdf.
28. "Situation of human rights in Colombia: Report of the United Nations High Commissioner for Human Rights," United Nations Human Rights Council, February 26, 2020, https://reliefweb.int/sites/reliefweb.int/files/resources/A_HRC_43_3_Add.3_AdvanceUneditedVersion.pdf.
29. Adriaan Alsema, "Under Uribe, Colombia's military killed more civilians than guerrillas: study," *Colombia Reports*, April 8, 2018, https://colombiareports.com/under-uribe-colombias-military-killed-more-civilians-than-guerrillas-study/.
30. "Extrajudicial executions," *Colombia Reports*, June 14, 2019, https://colombiareports.com/false-positives/.
31. "Forced displacement," *Colombia Reports*, July 20, 2019, https://colombiareports.com/forced-displacement-statistics/.
32. Editorial Board, "Venezuela's Crackdown on Opposition," *New York Times*, September 20, 2014, http://www.nytimes.com/2014/09/21/opinion/sunday/venezuelas-crackdown-on-opposition.html.

33. Daniel Kovalik, "The U.S., Colombia & the Spread of the Death Squad State," *Counterpunch*, May 23, 2014, http://www.counterpunch.org/2014/05/23/the-u-s-colombia-the-spread-of-the-death-squad-state/.

Chronology: Six Coup Attempts

1. Ewan Robertson, "Where Is Venezuela's Political Violence Coming From? A Complete List of Fatalities from the Disturbances," VenezuelAnalysis, April 5, 2014, https://venezuelanalysis.com/analysis/10580.
2. "In Detail: The Deaths So Far," VenezuelAnalysis, July 11, 2017, https://venezuelanalysis.com/analysis/13081.

Index

Abrams, Elliott, 45–46
Afghanistan, 66–67, 218
Afiuni, María Lourdes, 165, 197–99
Alfaro, Daniel, 97
Almagro, Luis, 53, 146, 151
Alston, Philip, 209
Altamira Plaza "liberation" protests, 95–98, 106
amnesty, Chávez granting, 33, 106, 201
Amnesty International, 15–16, 87, 94, 209; aid from, 48; credibility of, 91–93; on economic sanctions, 49–50; Globovisión and, 122
amnesty law, 149–51
Anderson, Danilo, 106, 228
Anderson, Jon Lee, 170
Áñez, Jeanine, 22–23, 90, 156
anti-Semitism, 201
Argentina, 9
Aristide, Jean-Bertrand, 14, 18, 20, 208–16; overthrown, 90; violence blamed on, 210
Armed Revolutionary Forces of Colombia (FARC), 91, 217, 225, 229–32
al-Assad, Bashar, 161
Assange, Julian, 11–12, 93, 127, 146
audit, of voting machines, 111–14

al-Awlaki, Anwar, 126

Bachelet, Michelle: on economic sanctions, 56; statement by, 50–52
Bad News from Venezuela (MacLeod), 81, 184
Báez, María Victoria, 120
ballots, burned, 176
Ban Ki-moon, 209
Bartley, Kim, 78
Bastardo, Hender, 120
Beeton, Dan, 113–16
Bello, Marco, 169
Bellos, Alex, 82–83
Biden, Joe, 57, 90, 126
Bigwood, Jeremy, 87
Blitzer, Wolf, 46–47
Blumenthal, Max, 221
Bocaranda, Nelson, 119
Bolívar, Simón, 101, 147–48, 225
Bolivia: coup in, 22–23, 123; elections in, 48; managed float policy in, 124
Bolton, John, 16, 19, 21, 156–57; foreign policy and, 47–48; impact of, 42–43; *The Room Where It Happened* by, 57; tweets from, 45–46
Boothroyd-Rojas, Rachael, 150, 155

border wall, U.S.-Mexican, 41
Borges, Julio, 33, 98, 154
Bravo, Douglas, 65
Bravo, Isnardo, 164
bribery, 14
British Labour Party, 15
Brito, José, 54–55
Brownfield, William, 149
brutality, 14
Bush, George H. W., 20, 62–63
Bush, George W., 85, 96–97, 194

Cadena Capriles, 121
Cadiz, Mark, 133–36
Caldera, Rafael, 63
Calderón, Felipe, 116
Calderón Berti, Humberto, 55
Cameron, David, 32
Campbell, Duncan, 82
Canada, 17
capitalism, 185; poverty, inequality and, 81; power under, 10–11
capitalist democracy, 10, 13
Capriles, Henrique, 26, 93, 201; appeal by, 120; audit demanded by, 111–16; disqualification of, 33; López, L., arguing with, 125–26; murder by supporters of, 118; Obama supporting, 111; Primero Justicia Party founding by, 98; recall vote process pursued by, 153
Caracazo massacre, 62–64, 99, 139
Carmona Decree, 27, 73, 78, 80, 96, 205
Carmona Estanga, Pedro, 17, 76; deaths during uprisings against, 82–83, 93–94; IMF offering loans to, 88, 107; self-declaration of presidency, 73; supporters of, 96; U.S. backing, 94
Carroll, Rory, 16, 164, 183–205
Carter, Jimmy, 30, 112
Carter Center, 93–94, 115–16, 121–22
Carvajal, Leonardo, 87
Casey, Nicholas, 174
Castro, Fidel, 64

censorship, 92, 133, 135
Center for Economic and Policy Research (CEPR), 113–15, 141, 144
Chacín González, Rey David, 120
Chakrabarti, Shami, 15–16
Chamblain, Jodel, 211–12
Changing Venezuela by Taking Power (Wilpert), 67
Chávez Frías, Hugo, 9, 14–15, 22, 175; amnesty granted by, 33, 106, 201; blame for, 101; cancer fought by, 107–8; Chomsky denouncing, 197–99; Colombia and, 229–34; constitutional amendments proposed by, 194–95; crime rates rising under, 217; death of, 111, 124, 137, 184–85, 218–23; democratic reform from, 58; election of, 28; falsehoods against, 83–84; first coup attempt against, 73–74; HRW attacking legacy of, 218–19; inflation before and during, 187; kidnapped, 73; military coups attempted by, 62–64; mocked by opponents, 194; new constitution initiated by, 67–69; oil companies and, 196–97; as oppressive, 190; ousted, 27, 61, 91–92; Pérez, C. A., and, 66–67; professional class and, 203; racism used to attack, 195, 203–4; recruitment of, 64–65; remembering, 163; resignation of, 77–79, 85, 89, 95, 98–100; return to power, 80; second coup attempt against, 96–97; support for, 188; U.S. ambassador offending, 67; victories of, 94; votes for, 32
Chavismo, 21–22, 28, 31, 60, 137, 163, 228; *Caracazo* to, 62; criticism for, 144; democracy and, 69; as dominant political force, 58; glory years, 232; HRW attacking, 206–7; opposition defeated by, 124; overlooked foundations of, 65–66; professional class and, 185, 203–4; propaganda war on,

205; as ruinous, 100; support for, 35; turning against, 164–65; vilification of, 179
Chavistas, 49; exchange rate system credited by, 142; mobilization of, 77; murder of, 28, 82–83, 93–94; perspective of, 100; protesting, 76; victory for, 103
Chicago Tribune, 80
Chile, 53
cholera, 208–9
Chomsky, Noam, 197–99
Ciccariello-Maher, George, 49, 65–66
CITGO corporation (firm), 37
Citizens Power branch, 150–52, 155
Citizens United, 121
civil disobedience, 95–96
classism, 67, 171–72, 190–92
Clinton, Hillary, 122, 177
Coalition of the Willing, 17
cocaine, 56, 226
Cohen, Nick, 19
colectivos, 49, 66, 215
Colombia, 21, 36–37, 53, 225–34
Comandante (Carroll), 183–84, 198–204
Comisso Urdaneta, Daniel, 95
Committee to Protect Journalists (CPJ), 102, 136
Confederación de Trabajadores de Venezuela (CTV), 95–96
conspiracy, 11–12
Constituent Assembly (ANC), 173–79
Contra terrorists, 20, 45, 221
Corbyn, Jeremy, 15, 144
Corina Machado, María, 33
corruption, 33, 202; Afiuni imprisoned for, 165; economic problems blaming, 144–45; of Guaidó, 54–55
Council of Electoral Experts of Latin America (CEELA), 34
coup, 20; in Bolivia, 22–23, 123; Chávez attempting military, 62–64, 77–78; fifth attempt, 155, 162–73, 178–79; fourth attempt, 126; incitement of, 50; Maduro fear of, 148–49; media involvement in, 82; support for, 77; third attempt, 117, 122–23; U.S. denying involvement in, 85–88
coup, second attempt, 96–97, 106; economic policy impacted by, 110; as media-led, 102; poverty increase after, 104
court-packing law, 89–91, 204
COVID-19 pandemic, 12, 55, 107
Crick, Michael, 173
criminality, U.S., 48
Cuba, 21, 42, 61, 203–4
Cuban Revolution, 64, 227

Damming the Flood (Hallward), 214
Datanalisis, 26, 27–28, 31, 35, 111
Dawson, Thomas, 88
deaths: of Chávez, 111, 124, 137, 184–85, 218–23; of police, 213–16; of protesters, 23, 53, 74, 98, 119–20, 128, 164, 169–72; protest-related, 129, 160–63, 167–68; rate of violent, 210–11; during uprising against Carmona, 82–83, 93–94
democracy, 79, 106, 140, 220; capitalist, 10, 13; Chavismo and, 69; flaws in, 69; fraudulent, 62; human rights and, 177; invoking, 79; Maduro trampling, 156–57; meaning of, 10–11; military intervention benefitting, 80; undermining, 75, 77; in Venezuela, 27
democratic norms, 137–40
Democratic Party, 17
democratic reform: Chávez bringing, 58; as vilified, 69
Denmark, 17
devaluation-inflation spiral, 108, 124
dictatorships, 9–10, 14, 20, 53, 92
dignity, 203
Doctors without Borders, 209
domestic politics, 13
Dominican Republic, 20
double standard, 128

drug dealers, 66
drug trafficking, 54, 56
Duque, Ivan, 233
Dutka, Z. C., 195
D'vies, Donella, 165–66

economic crisis: policy adjustments to end, 29–30; popular support gained from, 159
economic depression, 16, 20
economic policies: protests against neoliberal, 53; second attempted coup impacting, 110
economic reforms, 52
economic sabotage, 19, 142–43
economic sanctions, 10, 18, 20; Amnesty International on, 49–50; Bachelet on, 56; CLAPs crippled by, 39–40; ending, 43; lies by omission regarding, 44; mortality due to, 39; as murderous, 36–37, 47; Obama imposing, 40, 160; oil production impacted by, 36–39; Rodriguez, Francisco, on, 36–39; by Trump, 30, 36–37, 143, 160, 173–74
economic strangulation, 9, 224
economic warfare, 21, 29–30, 51, 142–43
The Economist, 18
Ecuador, 11, 53, 123, 177–78, 232
education, 15, 59
El Salvador, 9
elections, 12; legitimacy of, 121; lessons from 2017 regional, 28–31
electoral fraud, in Honduras, 34
electoral system, technical aspects of Venezuelan, 112
Eliécer Gaitán, Jorge, 227
elite dominance, 12
Ellis, Edward, 164–66
empire, 13–14, 22, 57
employment, 11
enabling law, 74
Engler, Yves, 208–9
Escalona, Hermes, 165–66
European Union (EU), 132, 176–77
exchange rate system: Chavistas crediting, 142; Maduro refusal to change, 141–42; oil strike prompting implementation of floating, 107
exchange rates: black market compared to official, 107–8; currency used to stabilize, 108; inflation and black market, 109

Fairness and Accuracy in Reporting (FAIR), 80
Faith of My Fathers (McCain), 220
Falcón, Henri, 26, 76
Fernandez, Fernando M., 92
Fernandez, Gerardo, 120
Ferreres, Víctor, 102
Figuera, Orlando, 168–73
Financial Carpet Bombing, 18
Finnegan, William, 148–49
Fleischer, Ari, 85–86, 99
Foley, Conor, 194
food distribution, 49
Ford, Charles, 199
foreign currency bonds, 37
foreign exchange, 96
foreign policy: Bolton and, 47–48; independence from U.S., 207; think tank, 81
Forero, Juan, 99–100, 102–3
Foro Penal, 171
Fox, Michael, 191–92
Fox News, 21
France, 17
Franchini Oliveros, Enzo, 171–72
free press, 12
freedom, 79
freedom of association, 12
freedom of expression, 93
Freedom of Information Act, 87
El Frente Amplio Venezuela Libre (FAVL), 34

Gabbard, Tulsi, 19–20
al-Gaddafi, Muammar, 45, 218
Galeano, Eduardo, 225
García, Luis Eduardo, 120
Garner, Eric, 127
Gil Yepes, José Antonio, 27, 193

INDEX

Gini Coefficient, 186–88
Globovisión, 121–22, 147
Golinger, Eva, 87
Gott, Richard, 185
Granda, Rodrigo, 231
Grayzone News, 46
Great Unmasking, 77
gross domestic product (GDP), 60–61, 125, 141
Guaidó, Juan, 20, 35, 232; corruption of, 54–55; end to, 57; humanitarian aid allowed by, 43; interview with, 136; military uprising announced by, 54; protests called for by, 106; rallies led by, 43; self-declaration of presidency by, 24–25; Trump recognition of, 24, 40
Guardian, 16, 82–84, 183–86, 192–95; complaints to, 87–88; headlines by, 92
guarimbas, 33
Guatemala, 9
Guevara, Che, 64
Guevara, Keler, 119
Guevara Rosa, Erika, 48

Haiti, 9, 53; elected government in, 17–18; HRW and, 208–9; Institute for Justice and Democracy, 209; police force in, 213–14; president of, kidnapped, 18, 20; violence in, 217–18; violent deaths in, 210
Hallward, Peter, 214
Hamas, 138–39
Harper, Stephen, 119
Harris, Kamala, 127–28
Hart, Peter, 130
Hausmann, Ricardo, 99
health care, 36, 59; basic services, 119; universal, 15
Hernández, Johan, 120
homophobia, 122, 201
Honduras, 20, 34, 177
human rights, 15, 50, 140, 232; democracy and, 177; invoking, 79; Iraq War as violation of, 207–8; U.S. faults in regards to, 207; violations of, 48, 85
human rights organizations, 13
Human Rights Watch (HRW), 16, 22, 216–18, 221–23; Chávez legacy attacked by, 218–19; Chavismo attacked by, 206–7; determination of, 165; false statements by, 117; Haiti and, 208–15; judicial independence and, 90; press release by, 88–89; U.S. protected by, 91
humanitarian aid, 19–20; as fraudulent, 46; Guaidó allowing, 43; from UN, 52
hunger, as weapon, 48–49
Hussein, Saddam, 17
hypocrisy, Western, 176

ideological bias, 107
impeachment, of Trump, 126
imperialist policy, 13
imports, 10; hard currency needed for, 39; of medicines, 18–19, 39
income equality, 186–87
inequality: capitalism, poverty and, 81; decrease in, 108
infant mortality rate, 61
inflation, 108, 186–87; attempt to slow, 142–43; black market exchange rate and, 109; before and during Chávez years, 187; spike in, 124
Institute for Justice and Democracy, Haiti, 209
institutional lawlessness, 12
Insulza, José Miguel, 112
Integral Diagnostic Centers (CDIs), 119
Inter-American Development Bank, 99, 103
International Committee of the Red Cross, 43
international criminal court, 100
International Crisis Group (ICG): funding for, 117; reports by, 131–32
international justice, 48

International Monetary Fund (IMF), 9; forecasts for Venezuelan economy, 106–7; loans from, 88, 107, 200; loans rejected by, 55–56; programs by, 62
International Republican Institute, 81
international trade, 107
internet age: empowerment in, 222; media in, 84
intimidation, 112
invasions, U.S.: of Afghanistan, 66–67; of Iraq, 209, 218; of Panama, 20
Iran, 57, 60
Iraq, 210; disarmed, 17; U.S. invasion of, 209, 218
Iraq War, 42; based on lies, 47–48; human rights violation, 207–8
Israel, 139

Jimenez, Julio, 122
Johnston, Jake, 141
Jones, Bart, 63, 77, 97, 101
judicial independence, 172, 177–78; HRW and, 90; Maduro and, 155–56

Kaepernick, Colin, 127–28
Kelly, John, 234
Kerry, John, 133
Kessling, Amanda, 208
Khanna, Ro, 19, 47–48
Khashoggi, Jamal, 222–23
kidnapping, 17, 18, 20
Kim Jong-un, 161
Koerner, Lucas, 25, 33, 152, 162–63, 191–92
Krause, Clifford, 62
Kronick, Dorothy, 29–30
Kuwait, 62

Labrador Castiblanco, Juan Orlando, 130
Lameda, Guaicaipuro, 75
land reform, 28
Latortue, Gérard, 90, 208–16
Ledezma, Antonio, 33

León, Luis Vicente, 26–27, 103
León Natera, Douglas, 204–5
Lexis Nexis, 26, 59
liberal values, 12
lies by omission, 13, 35, 44
Lima Group, 18
living conditions, 59–60
Local Supply and Production Committees (CLAPs), 29, 49; economic sanctions crippling, 39–40; resources created by, 151
looters, 13
López, Carlos, 101
López, Leopoldo, 33, 55, 201; aborted coup lamented by, 122–23; Capriles arguing with, 125–26; jailed, 145; office held by, 95; Primero Justicia Party founding by, 98; as "Prisoner of Conscience," 87, 93; violent protests launched by, 125
López Obrador, Andrés Manuel, 116
López Rivera, Oscar, 126
Lucena, Tibisay, 111–12
Lula da Silva, 156
lynching, 168

Maccotta, Luigi, 196
Machado, María Corina, 87; punishment for, 145–46; violent protests launched by, 125; Weisbrot on, 136–37
MacLeod, Alan, 53, 81–84, 122, 133, 184–85, 191
Maddow, Rachael, 157
Maduro, Nicolás, 9, 14, 19, 40; aid acceptance by, 44; allegations mocked by, 53; allies of, 31, 176, 178; ANC called for by, 173–74; approach to crime, 216; attempt to oust, 126, 152–53; audit endorsement of, 114; blockade by, 44; bounty held on, 56; claim of abandonment of position, 154–55, 158; CLAPs set up by, 29; dictator label for, 46–47; election of, 24–26, 94, 111; exchange rate reform refused by, 141–42; fear of coup,

148–49; fund availability for, 52; insurrection against, 51; judicial independence and, 155–56; loans solicited by, 55–56; loyalty for, 137; observers requested by, 35; overthrowing, 20–21, 224; policy errors of, 59; under pressure, 133; profiteering opportunities under, 109–10; Ramos Allup undermining, 30; State of the Union by, 146–48; support for, 27–28, 160; sympathizers for, 118; test of strength for, 124–25; tirade against, 76; U.S. auditing election of, 117; victory of, 122–23, 137–38; vote tally for, 32
Main, Alex, 144
Mallett-Outtrim, Ryan, 155
Mandela, Nelson, 93
Manning, Chelsea, 11–12, 93, 127, 198
Mao Zedong, 226
Margon, Sarah, 220
market theory, 108
Marquez, Edgar, 162
Martelly, Michel, 219
Martin, Abby, 172–73
Martínez, Leopoldo, 87
Marx, Karl, 65
massacres, 23
May, Theresa, 31
McCain, John, 220–22
McCoy, Jennifer, 93–94
McQuaig, Linda, 50
measured provocation, 196
media, corporate, 128
media, private, 78; black out by, 79; influence of, 99–100; on *Pilin León*, 101
media, Western: censorship claims made by, 133; corporate, 53, 100; democratization of, 121; hostile, 75; impact of, 234; as insurrectionary, 76; in internet age, 84; military coup involvement by, 82; outlets, 13; private, 16; propaganda by, 136, 161; scrutiny of, 116

Media Insight Project, 193
Media Lens, 12
medical centers, Cuban staffed, 117–18, 126
medicines: importing, 18–19, 39; mortality from decline in, 39
Melimopoulos, Elizabeth, 174–75
meritocracy, protecting, 74–75
Mexico, 116
military attacks, 20
military invasion, 9
military uprising, Guaidó announcing, 54
MINUSTAH, 208–13
Miquilena, Luis, 75
Mitchell, Jason, 60
Mnuchin, Steven, 57
Molina, Carlos, 81
Mondragon, Hector, 228
Morales, Evo, 14, 22, 53, 90, 193; coup faced by, 123; overthrown, 109, 143, 156
Moreno, Lenín, 11, 90, 178
murder: by Capriles supporters, 118; of Chavistas, 28, 82–83, 93–94
mutiny, 75

El Nacional, 34, 55
National Assembly, 24–25, 29–30; disincorporation of members, 152–53; dissolved, 155; held in contempt, 150, 158
National Electoral Council (CNE), 73, 96; recall referendum process started by, 154; recount decision by, 111–12
national emergency, 10, 41
National Federation for the Defense of Human Rights in Venezuela (FENADDEH), 166
National Public Radio (NPR), 185–92
national security, 14
Navarrete, Pablo, 183, 191
Nelson, Brian, 217
Neuman, William, 128, 132–33
New Deal programs, 90
New York Times, 22, 46, 128;

absolving protesters, 160–61; Carter Center represented in, 93–94; corrections issued by, 131; democratic norms editorials compared, 137–40; evidence ignored by, 97; Forero reporting in, 102–3; half-apology from, 80; misleading reporting by, 132; as presumptuous, 68–69
Nicaragua, 9, 20, 41, 221
Niehous, William, 65
Nobel Peace Prize, 206
non-governmental organizations (NGOs), 48, 76, 94
North Atlantic Treaty Organization (NATO), 218–19
Norway, 17

Obama, Barack, 10, 30, 225; Awlaki assassination ordered by, 126; Capriles supported by, 111; economic sanctions imposed by, 40, 160; election results for, 31–32
O'Brian, Donnacha, 78
Ocasio-Cortes, Alexandria, 19, 90
Occupy Wall Street camps, 127
oil, 226; embargo on, 40; exporting, 60; exports, losses from, 39; in Venezuela, 21
oil industry: sabotage, 100–101; targeted, 96
oil lockout, 2002-2003, 33
oil prices: collapse in, 29–30, 59, 141, 160; projection of, 143; WTI, 141–42
oil production, 60; crippled, 102; economic sanctions impacting, 36–39; patterns in, 36–37
oil revenues, loss in, 36–37
oil strike, 61, 75, 201; costs of, 102–3; economy after, 106; exchange rate system implemented during, 107
oil tankers, violence on, 106
oligarchy, separation of, and state, 74
Omar, Ilhan, 19
Open Veins of Latin America (Galeano), 225

Oppenheimer, Henry, 179
opposition impunity, 106, 201
Organization of American States (OAS), 112; Democratic Charter, 41, 89–91; stance on protests, 132
Ortega, Carlos, 95; in hiding, 105; political asylum for, 105–6
Ortega, Daniel, 14, 197–98
Ortega Díaz, Luisa, 155, 161–68, 173
Oxfam, 209

Pacheco, Johnny, 120
Pact of Punto Fijo, 64–65
Panama, 20
Parampil, Anya, 52
Parra, Luis, 55
Patiño, Roberto, 170
PDVSA company (firm), 37, 74–75, 196–97; control of, 110; employees of, fired, 104; sabotage against, 96, 102
Peña, Alfredo, 75
Pence, Mike, 19, 46
Pérez, Carlos Andres, 62–63, 66–67, 99
Perez, Pablo, 34
Pérez Jiménez, Marcos, 64
PetroCaribe, 9
Pilger, John, 50, 201
Pilin León, 97, 100–101
Pinilla, Fernando, 42
Plan Colombia, 228
PoKempner, Dinah, 220
police: control of, 76; deaths of, 213–16; drug dealers and, 66; in Haiti, 213–14; killings by, 127; protests against, 127–28; in Venezuela, 215–18
political asylum, 11, 105–6
political campaigns, corporate funding for, 121
political polarization, 80
Pompeo, Mike, 19, 42, 44, 46, 56
Ponce Ordóñez, José Luis, 118
poverty, 58–59, 75, 100, 189; capitalism, inequality and, 81; coup attempts increasing rate of, 104; exploitation of, 81; rate of, during

coup, 84; reduction in, 108, 184, 192, 205
power: under capitalism, 10–11; Chávez return to, 80
power vacuum, 77
press freedom, 76, 79
Primero Justicia Party, 98
professional class, Chavismo and, 185, 203–4
propaganda, 13–14; bolstering, 93; Sanders and, 46; about targeted governments, 15–16; war, on Chavismo, 205; by Western media, 136, 161, 173
protesters: Chavistas as, 76; deaths of, 23, 53, 74, 98, 119–20, 128, 164, 169–72; *New York Times* absolving, 160–61; stigmatization of, 49; terror campaign against, 133; violence against, 46
protests: Altamira Plaza "liberation," 95–98; deaths related to, 129, 160–63, 167–68; Guaidó calling for, 106; López, L., and Machado launching violent, 125; against Maduro, 92; against neoliberal economic policies, 53; non-violent, 12, 85; peaceful, 140; against police violence, 127–28; against racism, 127–28; stigmatization of, 127; street, 122
Provea, 119
Prysner, Mike, 172–73
Puente Llaguno, 78
Puigdemont, Carles, 177
Putin, Vladimir, 86

racism, 67; Chávez attacked with, 195, 203–4; protests against, 127–28; of Ramos Allup, 148
rallies, Guaidó leading, 43
Ramirez, Carlos, 170
Ramirez Romero, Ignacio, 166
Ramos Allup, Henry, 152, 179; economic crisis made worse by, 157–58; Maduro undermined by, 30; popularity of, 148–49; rebuttal by, 146–48

Rangel, Henry, 120
Los Rastrojos, 54
Reagan, Ronald, 41, 221
rebellion, 19
recall referendum process, 153–54
recount, CNE decision on, 111–12
Red Points (*Puntos Rojos*), 33–34
regime change, 14
Reporters without Borders (RSF), 136
repression, EU-approved, 176–77
Reuters, 18–22; Bolton followed by, 42; damage control by, 169–70; Datanalisis described by, 26; false claims spread by, 130; headlines by, 44, 54–55; misleading reporting by, 132; Red Points depicted by, 33–34; reports by, 113, 124
The Revolution Will Not Be Televised (documentary), 78–79, 92, 200
Reyes, Raúl, 231–32
Reyes, Rosiris, 118
Reyes, Yonylexis, 118
Rico, Gerardo, 120
Rincón Romero, Lucas, 77
Roa, Ana Maria, 135
Rodriguez, Delcy, 179
Rodriguez, Felipe, 228
Rodriguez, Francisco, 26, 52–53; analysis by, 28–30; on economic sanctions, 36–39; projections by, 56; on UNASUR team, 144
Rodríguez Chacín, Ramón, 33, 93
Romero, Franklin Alberto Romero, 130
Romero, Sabino, 166
Romero Bracho, Angel Antonio, 166
The Room Where It Happened (Bolton), 57
Roosevelt, Franklin, 90
Rosnick, David, 112, 114–15
Roth, Ken, 90, 206–7, 220–21
Rousseff, Dilma, 156, 159
Rubio, Marco, 16, 19, 45–46, 52, 163
Russia, 86
Russian bots, 127

Sachs, Jeffrey, 18–19, 39

Salter, Lee, 84
Sanders, Bernie, 15–16, 19; Blitzer and, 46–47; coup opposed by, 22; propaganda war and, 46; silence of, 57
Santos, Juan Manuel, 219, 233
Saudi Arabia, 60, 184, 221–23
Schwirtz, Michael, 59
self-defense, 65, 140
self-determination, 156
Shifter, Michael, 103
The Silence and the Scorpion (Nelson), 217
Singham, Nate, 132
slaves, African, 226
social media platforms: as ad-dependent, 13; Trump banned from, 126
social programs, 204
socialism, 69
Solomon, Norman, 46
Soto, Pedro, 75
South Korea, 144–45
sovereignty, 156
Spain, 171, 176–77
Stalin, Joseph, 116
Stein, Jill, 122
stigmatization: of protesters, 49; of protests, 127
structural adjustment program, 62
super-predators, 13
Suprani, Rayma, 195

Televen, 121, 147
term shortening, 153
territorial integrity, 156
terror tactics, 9
terrorism, 229
Tierras Libres (film), 164
Tillerson, Rex, 42
Toothaker, Christopher, 115
Torino Capital (firm), 18, 26, 39, 40
Toro, Francisco, 154–55
Torres Núñez, Hernán Luis, 109
trade embargo, 52
transitional authorities, 67
Transitory Council of Citizens Participation and Social Control (CPCCS-T), 177–78
treason, 105
Treasury Department, U.S., 55
Trudeau, Justin, 32
Trujillo, Josmar, 127
Trump, Donald, 15–23; aid blocked by, 57; belligerence of, 29; collaboration with, 32; economic sanctions by, 30, 36–37, 143, 160, 173–74; election results for, 31; Guaidó presidency recognized by, 24, 40; impeachment of, 126; incitement of rioters by, 126; military option possibility from, 42–43; national emergency declared by, 41; as racist and cynical, 50; social media platforms banning, 126; State of the Union address by, 58; whining, 54
truth reversal, 14
tyranny, 92

UN Human Rights Council, 56, 206–7
UN Office of the High Commissioner for Human Rights (OHCHR), 170–71, 233
Union of South American Nations (UNASUR), 132; economic team for, 143–44; formation of, 123
unions: in Colombia, 227; greedy, 13
United Nations (UN), 34–35; donations for, 43; humanitarian aid from, 52
United Socialist Party of Venezuela (PSUV), 124–25, 145
United States (U.S.): ambassador from, offending Chávez, 67; Carmona backed by, 94; coup involvement denied by, 85–88; crimes against humanity, 55–57; criminality, 48; as empire, 14; funding from, 87; HRW protecting, 91; human rights faults of, 207; independence from foreign policy of, 207; invasions by, 20, 66–67, 209, 218; Maduro election

victory audited by, 117; Treasury Department, 55; victim status claimed by, 56; violence, 17
El Universal, 26–27, 119
urbanization, 65
Urdaneta, Yorman, 135
Uribe, Álvaro, 197–98, 218–19, 228–33
Urquiola, Adriana, 130

Vargas, Jimmy, 130
Vasquez Velasco, Efrain, 77
Vaz, Ricardo, 32
Venevisión, 121, 147
Venezuela Speaks (Fox), 191
Venezuelan Medical Federation (FMV), 204–5
Vietnam War, 220
Villegas Poljak, Ernesto, 93, 119
violence, 213; Aristide blamed for, 210; black-on-black, 13; in Colombia, 226; distribution of, 131; in Haiti, 217–18; inciting, 119, 126, 131; indiscriminate, 18; on oil tankers, 106; against protesters, 46; protests against police, 127–28; troops lost to acts of, 212; U.S., 17
Vivanco, José Miguel, 90–91, 178, 210–15, 220
Vold, Eirik, 78, 99–100, 104, 204
Voluntad Popular party, 24, 53
vote bullying, 26
vote-buying, 150
voters, 10, 13
voting bribery, 33–34
voting process, transparency of, 116

Wall Street Journal, 162–63
war crimes, 11
Warren, Elizabeth, 19
Washington Office on Latin America (WOLA), 36
Washington Post, 80–81, 87, 145
We Created Chávez (Ciccariello-Maher), 65–66
wealth: natural, 60; redistribution of, 190
weapons of mass destruction, 17
Weisbrot, Mark, 18–19, 39, 86–87, 108; analysis of audit done by, 114–15; articles published by, 186; on Machado, 136–37; oil price predictions by, 141; study released by, 112; on UNASUR team, 144
welfare queens, 13
Weltman, Dave, 84
West Texas Intermediate oil prices (WTI), 141–42
White, Michael, 126–27
Wikileaks, 11, 22, 149, 196
Wilpert, Gregory, 67–69, 73–74, 78, 90
Wilson, Scott, 81, 87
World Bank, 60
Wyss, Jim, 44–45, 191

Yarborough, William P., 226
Yukpa people, 166

Zayas, Alfred de, 50–51
Zelaya, Manuel, 14, 177, 199–200

ABOUT THE AUTHORS

JOE EMERSBERGER is an engineer, writer, and activist based in Canada. His writing, focused on the Western media's coverage of the Americas, can be found on *FAIR.org, CounterPunch.org, TheCanary.co, Telesur English,* and *ZComm.org.*

JUSTIN PODUR is Associate Professor on the Faculty of Environmental and Urban Change at York University. He is the author of *Haiti's New Dictatorship, Siegebreakers,* and *America's Wars on Democracy in Rwanda and the Democratic Republic of Congo.*